15.99

```
NFER LIBRARY
NATIONAL FOUNDATION FOR
EDUCATIONAL RESEARCH
IN ENGLAND & WALES
THE MERE, UPTON PARK
SLOUGH, BERKS. SL1 2DQ
```

DATE:	21.3.94
CLASS:	J5ENG
ACC. NO:	24013
AUTHOR:	NATIONAL COMMISSION ON EDUCATION

B 2 253253 6

Insights into Education and Training

PAPERS SELECTED BY THE
PAUL HAMLYN FOUNDATION
NATIONAL COMMISSION ON EDUCATION

HEINEMANN : LONDON

William Heinemann Ltd
an imprint of Reed Consumer Books Ltd
Michelin House, 81 Fulham Road, London SW3 6RB
and Auckland, Melbourne, Singapore and Toronto

First published 1994

Copyright © National Commission on Education

A CIP catalogue record for this book
is held by the British Library
ISBN 0 434 0013 25

Typeset by Falcon Graphic Art Ltd
Wallington, Surrey
Printed by Clays Ltd, St Ives plc

Contents

List of Authors   vii
Introduction   ix

I. Society today and tomorrow

1. The Transformation of Society – A. H. Halsey   3
2. Change, British Society and the Family – Michael Young   15
3. Values in Education – Cardinal Basil Hume   29
4. Conflict, Reconstruction and Education – Seamus Dunn   41
5. The Importance of Citizenship – Citizenship Foundation   59
6. Science and Technology – the Next 25 Years – David Phillips   65
7. A Businessman's View of Education and Training – Mike Heron   85
8. Changes in the Workplace – Peter D. Wickens   91
9. Graduate Recruitment in a Changing Employment Market – Trevor Thomas   105
10. The Role of Employers in Education Reform – William Richardson   119
11. Measuring the Value of Education – David Ulph   135

II. Learning and achievement

12. Is There Still an Untapped Pool of Ability? – Andrew McPherson   157
13. Thinking Differently about Education – Charles Handy   167
14. The Education of Children Under Five – Victoria Hurst   171
15. Educational and Social Benefits of Pre-School Education – Sue Taylor   179
16. Challenging the Effects of Urban Deprivation – Alan J. Ratcliffe   193
17. Mountstuart – a Community School – Betty Campbell   197
18. Commitment to Education in the Secondary School Years – Tim Brighouse   205
19. A Scottish Perspective on the Curriculum and Assessment – Cameron Harrison   215
20. Learning Support and Guidance for Pupils – Richard Staite   235

21.	Post-16 Curriculum and Qualifications: Confusion and Incoherence or Diversity and Choice? – Geoff Stanton	241
22.	In a Muddle on Training – John Cassels	257
23.	Continuing Education – Chris Duke	261
24.	Tracking the Experience of Young People – Josh Hillman	273

III. Policy, management and delivery

25.	Answers by the Department for Education to Questions posed by the National Commission on Education – Department for Education	297
26.	Pupils and Schools – Josh Hillman	323
27.	Multicultural Issues and Educational Success – Sue Taylor, Janice Robins and Robin Richardson	347
28.	Education in Northern Ireland – Josh Hillman	361
29.	Independent Schools – Josh Hillman	403
30.	Managing the Education System – Society of Education Officers	445
31.	The Quality and Training of Teachers – Eric Bolton	453
32.	Quality in Primary Teaching – Charles Desforges	463
33.	Teaching 9–11-Year-Olds – Robin Peverett	477
34.	The Preparation, Selection and Development of Headteachers – Josh Hillman	481
35.	Undergraduate Perceptions of Teaching as a Career – Josh Hillman	527
36.	Transatlantic Connections: Further Education in the United Kingdom and the United States – Geoffrey Melling	539
37.	The Interface Between Higher and Further Education – Michael Austin and Bernard R. MacManus	555
	Appendix A Statistics	563
	Appendix B The Commission's Vision and Goals	575

List of Authors

Michael Austin, Principal, Accrington and Rossendale College; Associate Commissioner, National Commission on Education

Professor Eric Bolton CB, Institute of Education, University of London; formerly Senior Chief Inspector of Schools

Professor Tim Brighouse, Chief Education Officer, Birmingham; formerly Professor of Education, University of Keele and Director of the University's Centre for Successful Schools

Betty Campbell, Headmistress, Mountstuart Primary School, Cardiff; Commissioner

Sir John Cassels, Director, National Commission on Education

Citizenship Foundation

Department for Education

Professor Charles Desforges, Deputy Vice-Chancellor, University of Exeter

Professor Chris Duke, Pro-Vice-Chancellor, and Chairman of the Department of Continuing Education, University of Warwick

Professor Seamus Dunn, Director of the Centre for the Study of Conflict, University of Ulster, Coleraine

Professor A. H. Halsey, Fellow of Nuffield College, Oxford; Associate Commissioner

Professor Charles Handy, Writer

Cameron Harrison, Chief Executive, Scottish Consultative Council on the Curriculum

Mike Heron, Chairman, The Post Office; former Director, Unilever

Josh Hillman, Research Officer, National Commission on Education

Cardinal Basil Hume, Archbishop of Westminster

Victoria Hurst, Lecturer in Early Childhood Education, Goldsmiths' College, University of London

Dr Bernard R. MacManus, Vice-Chancellor, Bournemouth University; Associate Commissioner

Professor Andrew McPherson, Co-Director, Centre for Educational Sociology, University of Edinburgh; Associate Commissioner

Geoffrey Melling, Director, The Staff College and Chairman, Association for Colleges

Robin Peverett, Director of Education, Incorporated Association of Preparatory Schools

Sir David Phillips, Chairman of the Advisory Board for the Research Councils and Acting Director General of the Research Councils

Alan J. Ratcliffe, Headmaster, Ley Hill Primary School, Birmingham

Robin Richardson, Director, The Runnymede Trust

William Richardson, Centre for Education and Industry, University of Warwick

Janice Robins, Secretary, National Commission on Education

Society of Education Officers

Richard Staite, Headteacher, Beeslack High School, Lothian; Commissioner

Geoff Stanton, Chief Officer, Further Education Unit

Sue Taylor, Research Officer, National Commission on Education

Trevor Thomas, former Deputy UK National Manager, Unilever plc; Associate Commissioner

Professor David Ulph, Head, Department of Economics, University College London; Associate Commissioner

Dr Peter D. Wickens, Director of Personnel and Information Systems, Nissan Motor Manufacturing (UK) Ltd; Commissioner

Michael Young (Lord Young of Dartington), Director, Institute of Community Studies

Introduction

Learning to Succeed, the report of the National Commission on Education published in November 1993, took a critical look at the state of education and training in the UK. We put forward a vision for the future and a set of goals (reproduced in Appendix B to this volume) designed to lead to a substantial improvement in individual learning opportunities and in national educational achievement. The Commission recognised that if progress was to be made towards achieving these goals, it would be essential to sustain a high level of public interest in and discussion about education and training. This volume of papers is planned as a contribution to that continuing debate.

During our investigation we gathered information and views from a diversity of sources to help in formulating our proposals. We received written and oral evidence, organised and took part in conferences and seminars, analysed research and statistical data and studied a wealth of literature. It would be impossible to produce a book which is fully representative of all the material which the Commission considered in drawing its conclusions. Our aim here is to bring to the attention of a wider audience a selection of the papers which have influenced our thinking, whether by suggesting directions we should follow, helping to confirm our standpoint, or causing us to question our approach.

Further material will be found in *Briefings*, a volume of research papers written for the Commission, and in *Universities in the Twenty-First Century*, a series of lectures on higher education organised jointly by the Commission and the Council for Industry and Higher Education and published with sponsorship from British Telecom. In addition, the National Foundation for Educational Research published in 1992 the report of a study which we commissioned on the subject of young people's attitudes towards school, entitled *'What **Do** Students Think About School?'*

As we investigated what will be required from our education and training system over the next 25 years, the connections between educational performance and society, the economy and technology were impressed upon us with increasing force. We therefore open this volume with a collection of papers on the theme of 'Society Today and Tomorrow' in which authors discuss the claims made on education by society, and also the way in which education is influenced by the very rapid social changes we are experiencing as we approach the millennium. Papers by Professor Halsey and Lord Young examine the implications for education resulting from a decline in family stability and the risk of a growing underclass in society. Cardinal Hume points to the lack of 'spiritual vitality' in contemporary culture and the contribution that educators can make to restoring it. Other papers concentrate on the impact of accelerating scientific and technological progress and the demands resulting from industry's need to compete in a global economy. Questions which are explicit or implicit throughout this part of the volume are: what is the purpose of education? What are the goals we are aiming to achieve? How do we reconcile personal, social and economic interests?

In Part II, 'Learning and achievement', we focus attention on the work of schools and colleges, the curriculum and qualifications, and factors affecting students' attainments. We begin with a research note by Professor Andrew McPherson, providing evidence of the existence of untapped educational potential in the population. This argument goes to the heart of the Commission's concern that we are wasting talent; that more could and should be done to enable everyone – children and adults alike – to succeed in learning and to reap the benefits of a good education.

McPherson's note is followed by papers pointing to ways of raising expectations and achievement − for example, pre-school provision which exploits the intellectual value of children's play; a school curriculum which offers incentives to keep on learning and which draws upon and enriches the life of the local community; a clearly defined structure for post-16 education and training for work; and learning opportunities which uncover and foster the widest possible range of abilities and kinds of intelligence. At the end of the book we provide a statistical appendix which includes background data on young people's participation and achievement in education and training.

The third part of the book, 'Policy, management and delivery', brings us to issues which concern policy makers and managers at national, local and institutional level. We begin with a paper by the Department for Education written in response to Commission questions and outlining the Department's position on a wide range of policy matters, from pre-school education to the alternatives to 'A' levels; from initial teacher training to the governance of schools. As further background to national policy, data on education expenditure appear in the statistical appendix.

From Government policy we turn to papers dealing with issues of parental choice, selection and diversity in schools. The authors raise important questions about how individual decisions affect equity: whether increasing diversity and parental choice in our education system demonstrate a healthy response to differing needs or a potential to increase inequality and social division. We include a report identifying aspects of policy and practice which may disadvantage ethnic minority pupils, emphasising the need for measures explicitly concerned with equity and social justice to be built into the new structures developing in education. A paper on Northern Ireland discusses the effects of selective secondary education and of a schooling system divided along religious lines. Another considers the performance of independent schools and their influence on the education system as a whole. To support this paper, a comparison of attainments in independent and maintained schools appears in the statistical appendix.

Throughout the Commission's consultations we were aware of the urgency of improving the standing and quality of the teaching profession. We include in Part III a number of papers concerned with the training, recruitment and continuing professional development of teachers, beginning with Professor Eric Bolton's analysis of the characteristics of good teachers and good teaching.

Finally, we look beyond schools to possibilities for the development of further and higher education. A paper by Geoffrey Melling considers what we can learn from the American system of community colleges. We follow this with a discussion of the value of working partnerships between FE colleges and higher education institutions.

Inclusion of a paper in this volume does not imply that the individual authors were associated with the Commission's work or that they are in agreement with the Commission's recommendations. Cardinal Hume's paper in Part I was not written specifically for the Commission but for an audience of Catholic secondary headteachers, and we are pleased to include it in this collection. Most of the remaining papers were prepared expressly for the Commission, as written evidence, as lectures or presentations at Commission conferences, or as background papers for discussions. In some cases the authors were members or Associates of the Commission or of its research staff. In publishing the papers we have not attempted to update them, preferring to present them substantially in the form in which they were originated. Given the pace of change in education, readers should bear in mind that some details of policy or provision may have altered and more recent statistical data may have been published.

Those who have read *Learning to Succeed* will recognise here some of the strands of thinking which influenced that report. And I hope that anyone who is keenly interested in the future development of education and training in this country will find this volume stimulating and thought-provoking.

Claus Moser.

Sir Claus Moser
Member of the National Commission on Education
Chairman of the Commission's Research Committee

I.

Society Today and Tomorrow

1. The Transformation of Society

Speech by Professor A.H. Halsey to a Seminar of the National Commission on Education, 'The Next 25 Years', Oxford, 3–5 April 1992.

Introduction

If I look back over the long period of my involvement in education, I ask myself the question: 'Has it been worth it? Was it a good idea to come into this particular kind of pedagogical profession?' When I ask myself that question I have a resoundingly comforting answer from memory, a memory about my Irish grandfather, who was a rather late (in the sense of relatively older-age) mature entrant to the British expeditionary force in 1914–17. He was very badly wounded in 1917 and brought back to St Thomas's Hospital and laid out with all the other people who had been survivors that morning, leaving the dead, of course, in Flanders. And it so happened that the Queen – that's the old Queen Mary – came round that very morning to look at the troops and happened to stop beside the bed of my old Irish grandad.

She looked at him in all his bandages, took a regal pace backwards and said: 'Oh my dear, poor man. What a terrible war. What a terrible, terrible war'. To which he replied: 'Yes ma'am, sure it's been a terrible war, but sure that's better than no war at all'.

And that's the way I tend to see what's happened to me in the last 20 years with respect to education.

Well, that's all I want to say about education as such, because I think that whatever the Commission remembers or forgets, it will not forget that the *least* important force in determining what is in the heads of people 25 years from now – what skills they have, what beliefs they have, what languages they speak and so on – the least important force is the education system. It is everything else in their experience which will determine these things. All the social relations they have, from the family, through the street, into the community and the workplace and so on: this is what really determines the level of culture by which they live. It is these social issues that I want to talk about.

How society functions

Production versus reproduction
Society is really two things at once. It's an apparatus for producing things and an apparatus for reproducing things: the first because the one thing that we firmly know about societies is that if they don't feed their members they don't survive, and the second because we also know that – with one important exception – people die eventually anyway. So there has to be production and there has to be reproduction.

What I take it we are doing in our particular time is to live through the *transformation* of both of these sides of our life together. At the same time – and this is the interesting bit – we live in a transformation of transformations. We don't really know what sort of movement of change we're going through. Everything is changing in relation to all of the other institutions that we experience.

Let's start with the productive side. My first – intended to be slightly acid – comment is that this Education Commission is rooted in a prejudice. It actually believes that production is of very great importance in whatever transformation it is that's going on now. I would want to persuade you, if we had time, that that is not the problem at all: that the trick of transforming society, viewed as a command over nature by human beings, is one that we licked a long time ago. We're getting more sophisticated about it. We used to apply very crude physics and chemistry to it and now we have rather more sophisticated physics and chemistry. But essentially that's not the problem. In other words we can take it for granted that over the next 25 years we shall see a continuation of the process of getting more and more for less and less effort out of our battle with nature.

Learning to live together
Now there may be all sorts of horrible things that may happen as by-products of that battle with nature, but I don't think that is of very great importance. What is important is how we acquire more control over that part of nature which is really ourselves. In other words, whether we can advance our capacity to live together with people, rather than our capacity to live together with things. And part of that must be learning better means than we have in the past to distribute those things in such a way as to keep the system as a whole in some sort of accord, in some kind of consensus.

This ought to be very much in our minds, living as we do – especially in the last decade or so – with a bombardment of messages telling us that the whole thing is made up of a lot of calculating egos; utility maximisers who know how to choose between this and that and the other and have a divine authority to interact, to measure and move together all of those utilitarian calculations which we call the market. The idea that somehow or other there should be introduced into it a *conscience collective* rather than a *conscience individuelle* surely ought to be part of the preoccupation of this particular Commission.

So I don't believe that we would be right in presupposing that we have an enormous production problem. Now that's going to cause a lot of difficulty because a lot of people sitting in this room will say that in that case, at least half of what we have been suggesting about how to reform the education system is beside the point and we should start all over again.

A new demographic balance

Declining populations
I've said that the second thing that one can talk about by way of transformation – and which is very much more interesting – is the transformation of society as a reproductive organisation.

Let me explain exactly what I mean. I mean that we've lived for over a thousand years in essentially a Christian civilisation dominated by the Roman Catholic Church, which has always been able to proceed on the assumption that, although most people most of the time disobeyed the decalogue and almost everything else that's written in the Bible, there was one thing they could be relied upon to do, which was 'to be fruitful and multiply'. But people no longer obey that law, and indeed, there is no version of rational choice theory available to us which would lead us reasonably to suppose, either in the next 25 years or beyond, that women will go back to a situation in which they were fruitful and multiplied.

For those who are not devotees of this demographic way of looking at the world, what you have to remember is that in order that we should have a steady state, meaning that the numbers in this civilisation should remain more or less the same, you have to have 2.1 births per woman in the course of her reproductive cycle. The 0.1 is to deal with infertilities and accidents of various kinds. Empirically 2.1 is the total period fertility rate at which you have a steady population. But if you look at the reproduction rate that we have, in this country it's 1.8, and in Sweden 1.8. And as you go down into Catholic Europe – through Germany and down into the South of Italy and to Spain – it gets smaller and smaller and you end up with 1.4s and 1.2s. By the middle or by the end of the 25-year period with which the Commission is concerned, and certainly by the middle of the 21st century, there will be a very serious problem of depopulation. There may of course be repopulation by migration, but among the natives in the southern part of old Catholic Europe there will be a problem of depopulation.

Already, there are two million fewer West Germans in Germany than there were 20 years ago. Our own country will start to go down fairly quickly in the 21st century if fertility continues at 1.8. Even Ireland – that marvellous exemplar of Malthusian theory in practice – has now gone below the 2.1 threshold. The last hold-out of a burgeoning population has now gone below 2.1.

A growing underclass
In a way that's all boring, but in another way it's not boring at all, because there are two great features of British and European society which are in effect extrapolations or deductions from that simple model that I've just sketched for you. One is that as a result of these kinds of developments there will be – if you take into account the peculiarities of the productive system by which we live – an increasingly numerous so-called underclass; an underclass of people who are firmly connected neither to the productive nor to the reproductive cycle of the society we are moving into.

New opportunities in the 'Third Age'
That's implication number one. Implication number two – and it's marvellous that this should be so cheerful by comparison with the gloom of the first one – is that we are creating a new world which Peter Laslett[1] called the Third Age and which Michael Young and Tom Schuller[2] want to call an 'ageless society'. Now they don't really mean an ageless society but they do certainly mean that it will be a society in which work and leisure and consumption will be much more loosely related to the life cycle of age than it ever has been in traditional society.

Young and Schuller don't like the Third Age notion because they quite correctly noticed that Laslett made the idea of the Third Age into a high status, highly privileged position for people to occupy for an increasing proportion of their life cycle, at the expense of a fourth age, which is the descent through decrepitude into death. Their idea is that you may increasingly hope to stay in the Third Age until a quiet death supervenes.

Think of this, all of this, in relation to what you learned at your mother's knee about the life cycle. We all know about Solomon Grundy who was born on Monday, christened on Tuesday and so on. That was the life of the average person in the past, with a very very tiny group of exceptions, mostly of lucky and privileged and wealthy people. The prospect before us now, resulting from this new demographic balance, is a new set of opportunities, not just for education but for living.

Let's just look at it in a bit more detail so that we can really savour its character. You first have to think of a country which has developed its productive organisation to such a level that it has the wherewithal to keep in good health and with lots of amenities people who are no longer obliged to be engaged in paid employment. That's the first criterion that you have to meet. Second, you have to think of a country in which this demographic balance has shifted to the point where at least 10% of the population are beyond the paid employment stage and into this golden autumn of their lives.

There's another way of putting it. If you like, the third criterion is to say: 'Think of a country in which at age 25 a man or a woman – and women of course get there before men – will have at least an even chance of living to age 70 when they're 25'. That introduces a sort of social psychology into the population which is totally different from the social psychology of ordinary working class people in the past, particularly that of working class men. I mean that such people can reasonably expect to have to prepare themselves for life way beyond work.

It is very difficult, even for people in this room, to see that; to imagine that as a kind of reasonable, calculated future, for which you should be making some provision. Of course it does depend on the first economic criterion. It also has to depend on the second criterion – that's the 10% one – which I would think of as the political one. By this I mean that when you get to this stage, you can rely on it that there are not only a lot of people like you, but that you are at least potentially a new political class which in a Parliamentary democracy can have an enormous clout in determining how the resources of the society will be distributed between all the age grades. And then, finally, there is the social psychological factor. It's a question of education, if you like. People need to learn the elements of demography; they need education about how to conduct their lives.

Education for a future society

Now put those two things together and think of them as a future society. On the one hand you have forces which suggest that we will have among us a growing minority of people who are outside both the productive and the reproductive system, where 'reproductive' is a reference to the kinds of loyalties, responsibilities, expectations that have come from a traditional family. In this way people are taught all sorts of manners and morals which in the new underclass can now be assumed to have disappeared. At the same time you also have increasing proportions of people who are, as it were, 'democratised aristocrats'. They no longer have to earn their living by the sweat of their brow. They have escaped the curse of Adam. They are able to enjoy themselves, to enjoy each other and in principle therefore contribute a great deal to society.

The interesting commonality between these two quite different classes is that they both need education. They are a challenge to our collective capacity to provide the appropriate education. In the case of the underclass it is desperately urgent. Unless people can find a way to enter the productive cycle and also (and I'll use a rather vague word because it would take a very long time to spell it out) to be part of that *rationality* which makes them use time, energy, allocation of resource in such a way as to produce a worthwhile life – a 'progress' rather than a 'processing' through the life cycle (and how else can they achieve that, other than through the sort of education that you need to become what we would call a citizen) – if that challenge isn't met, they are going to be a terrible threat, a terrible cost – a drain, in fact – all the time, on the society that breeds them. Meanwhile, at the other end you've got people who may or may not be able to optimise their status as what I have called democratised aristocrats.

Michael Young and Tom Schuller very correctly point out that if you look at people who are in our society now and could be classified as potential 'third agers', probably more of those people are negatively members of this new emancipated class than positively. They have negative freedom rather than positive freedom, though there are some examples – and they are very instructive – of people who have positive freedom.

Changes in families
Well now, if this is the situation that is looming up, then we are again reminded of the starting point that I insisted upon: that what will actually determine whether the challenge is met will not be the school organisation directly, but all the other educative and non-educative institutions of our society. Let me illustrate.

If you compare progress through the life cycle of children who have and children who have not been brought up by two active parents – you could say, brought up in the traditional family – then whatever the sillier radicals say, it is clear that the average performance of those people in the 'not' category is lower than that of people from traditional families. Remember, while we are saying this, that even last year 28% of our children were born outside what the Christians used to call wedlock. We're talking about a situation in which a third of all marriages are remarriages and so on. In fact, Grimm's fairy tales constitute the best elementary textbook on the sociology of the family that you could hope to find. What is it worse to have, a stepmother or a stepfather?

The point I'm making is that whatever this Commission says, if it doesn't refer to the importance of taking a positive view of what's happening to the family, it might as well not bother. What that means is that we have to be much more imaginative than we have ever been before about what to do in these circumstances. Of course you may say there's no imagination required. You simply get the whip out. Whip the women back into the kitchen and ban all American films and things like that; reinstate Polish bishops throughout the land and get it all back to where it was, or where you think it might have been, perhaps, in Victorian times.

A 'parenting' role for schools
But assuming that none of that is likely to work, the way to think about it is this: what possibilities are there for re-shaping the pedagogical professions, the teaching professions, as '21st century new parents'? In a way it's as old as the hills, isn't it? *In statu pupillari, in loco parentis*, were the descriptions of early teaching institutions. Our experience in our own lifetime is the complete rubbishing of all that. We have seen teaching being turned into a cognitive relation between older and younger people: somebody else is responsible for the character; we just take care of the brains; the easy bit, in other words. If we take the demographic description seriously, then we are challenged in the education system to find new ways of fulfilling those parental functions that we have been neglecting too much for too long.

If we ask ourselves how we are going to do that (and I thought that Michael Young had this right in the lecture on the family that he gave to the ESRC not long ago)[3] – aren't we right in seeing the emerging democratised aristocrats, the third agers, as the potential social force for putting back (I'll use Durkheim's terms) the *éducation morale* of the next generation? I know that there are very successful examples of women banding together to get rid of the latchkey child by forming clubs and societies in ordinary schools. I'm thinking of a particular project in which one of my daughters is involved in Lancaster. There, women come into school on an ancillary, independent basis; they are organised by the professionals; and they run curricula that would gladden Michael Young's heart because they satisfy both his criteria: they do something which the children love, and they do something which contributes to the *conscience collective* rather than just the *conscience individuelle*.

That is lovely. It's wonderful, and it can actually be made to work, with resources that are not all that hard to muster because of the social circumstances that I've been describing. It seems to me that this is very, very important as a general orientation that we ought to have over the next 25 years. I have in mind not so much the education service itself, but the creation of a new, high-status, highly-regarded set of professions who would have to have the position in society which would enable them to control their own working conditions. I would include in this a real say as to what shall happen about children's television viewing habits. And if that means that some illiberalities have to come into our society, in my view so much the better, as long as they are in the hands of an organised, professional body of teachers who say: 'We can't do this job properly unless we have control over things like that'.

Challenging the economic viewpoint

Education as a business
If you can accept that, let me just deal with the objection that I am sure we are going to hear from those who think that education is a business, the main task of which is to serve business. They have grown enormously both in their numbers and their confidence in the last 10 years. Let me say that from one point of view it looks as if demography is very much on their side. If you go back to the 1930s, the ratio of people who were in the labour force to those who were over 65 was about nine to one. It's now down to just over four to one, and the way things are going, it won't be all that far above two to one by the time the next 25 years are up. In other words, you're seeing an increasing burden – notice the word, 'burden' –

placed upon those who work to support those who are pariahs, dependent.

Now, you might ask: 'What about all that?' My reply is this: 'Never believe an economist'. That's a very, very important thing to remember, because in a way economics is really the substitution of a new religion for the old religion; a new religion which tries to establish order in the world by producing experts who can add up the joys and the sorrows of all of our experience. We have concepts like GDP and GDP per capita. We have a sort of international league table of competition for producing a better and better life. We even have a kind of alliance between medical people and economists to produce some sort of calculus about the amount of good life that we can deliver to ordinary people in modern societies: the expectation of life at birth, measures of morbidity and so on.

What I want to say about this is that I just don't believe it, for reasons which are to do with the process through which those calculations are made. I'm not an expert in this, but I do know that there are plenty of medical experts who would challenge the notion that people have a longer and better life now than 30 years ago. I don't deny that people live longer, but the experts can make out some sort of case for saying that it's survival in a less than perfectly healthy state. I'm not arguing about that. What I am arguing is this. When Alfred Marshall first gave his magisterial authority to the calculation of the national accounts, as a good Victorian he was what all the ladies present would expect him to be: someone who didn't have the faintest understanding of women. He was asked at that time: 'Shall we count as part of the national wealth, as part of the national product, the work that women do in the kitchen and in the household – the work of housewives?' And he said 'No'. He had a perfectly good reason, he thought, for saying no. All of that has been done away with: Chinese laundries, bakeries, all of the commercialisations of ordinary chores grow and grow and grow so that women's work, in that domestic sense, becomes a residual and smaller and smaller element in the total product of society.

Now think about reality. Just think about yourself, and ask: 'Does it matter whether I will, or won't be one of the 30% who don't have any relatives alive after I myself become 75?' (and you're going to become 75, you can be fairly sure of that). 'Does it matter whether I die in my own bed or am attended by persons in white coats in some impersonal institution; does it matter whether I do or don't have the sort of convivialities which my grandmother had?'

If you throw all those things into the pot as well, it's no longer at all certain that those league tables of GDP per capita are telling us what it's actually like to be alive.

Education for living

I do think that it's really vital for the Commission to accept this outlook on its own labours, because if it doesn't, then what the devil is education about anyway? It seems to me to be so important to recognise that education is what we used to think it was, at least what I thought it was, and was told it was, by the priest and the schoolmaster when I was a tiny boy. *It's a process of teaching you how to live.* Of course, you have to have education for a *livelihood* as well. But everything that we know about what we've done for the productive organisation of our society confirms that this is relatively unimportant by comparison with learning how to live. That, in summary, is my message to the Commission.

References

1 Laslett, P. (1989). *A Fresh Map of Life*. Macmillan.
2 Young, M. and Schuller, T. (1991). *Life After Work: the Arrival of the Ageless Society*. Harper Collins.
3 Young, M. (Lord Young of Dartington) (1990). *A Haven in a Heartless World. The Future of the Family. The First ESRC Annual Lecture*. Economic and Social Research Council.

2. Change, British Society and the Family

Speech by Lord Young to a Seminar of the National Commission on Education, 'The Next 25 Years', Oxford, 3–5 April 1992.

Family and school

A great deal of documented evidence shows how much children's families affect the way they fare in school. This is not just a matter of conventional wisdom. The inter-relationships are multiple. It would be extraordinary if this were not so. For the family is as much an educational institution as the school, and may well be the more crucial, shaping as it largely does the child's motivation to learn, the capacity to learn, and the willingness to accept the discipline that the collectivity of a school necessarily entails. The child who comes from a stable and supportive home which encourages effort and praises achievement has a 'head start' over the child whose home is towards the opposite extreme. You can see in almost any primary school in the inner city the relatively well-turned-out boy with brushed hair and bright face, sitting next to a boy with runny nose, dirty shirt and too-big trousers. You will know immediately whom the school, and whom life, is going to do well by, unless by some benign intervention the course of probability is altered.

Decline in family stability
This would have been true at any time in the last two centuries since industrialisation required families to share their educational role with schools. What is new is the decline – perhaps one should now say the rapid decline – in family stability. In recent decades there has in fact been a double decline in the family and in the school, with the result that

children have suffered neglect on a scale not known since an earlier period of the industrial revolution. The 1980s were the decade in which the nation neglected its children.

The battering which the family has taken over a longer period is so severe that some people, with some feminists to the fore, have even been saying that the family has ceased to exist. Mrs Thatcher said that there is no such thing as society; now, others are saying that there is no such thing as the family any more. If it exists at all, it takes so many forms — lone-parent families, step-parents, families with or without half-brothers and half-sisters, cohabitation families, children brought up by grandparents, gay families — that the word itself should be dropped as misleading, say some of the most trenchant critics of the institution, and some less loaded term substituted for it, like 'shared living arrangements', in which lodge not husbands and wives but genderless partners; arrangements in which people go in not for family planning but for non-family planning. A tiny bow in this direction has been made by the official statisticians, who now use the term 'births outside marriage' instead of 'illegitimate' births. But for my part I am going to stick with the old word.

Signs of change in the family
Now for some of the indices of change. First, divorce. Divorce rates in the UK have doubled in 20 years, the rate of increase being higher than in any other European Community country. The UK currently shares top place with Denmark, and we don't in the UK have the far-reaching Ministry of Welfare services that Denmark has to support families under strain. According to Dr Kiernan of the Family Policy Studies Centre, if current trends continue, one in four children born today can expect to experience their parents' divorce before they are 16.[1] If people marry again, the terminus may be the same. Second marriages have a higher chance of ending in divorce than first marriages.

Secondly, cohabitation or paperless marriage, as it has been called. Cohabitation before, between and after marriage has been increasing markedly. Among women marrying for the first time in 1987, 48% had cohabited before marriage compared with 7% at the beginning of the 1970s, and we are well behind Sweden where 90% of those marrying for the first time cohabit beforehand. There is also a new category in Holland called Living-Apart-Together cohabitation or LATs – weekend families – to puzzle the statisticians still further.[2]

Samuel Butler said that the question of whether to get married is just a question of whether to ruin your life one way or another. People are choosing to ruin it less often the marriage way. Serial and informal monogamy are becoming more the vogue. Births outside marriage have inevitably increased, to more than 25% of all births.

But the most important indicator is the number of children living with both their natural parents. In 1985 – the latest year for which the figure has been estimated – 80% of children under 16 were still living with both parents (78% with married parents, 2% with cohabiting ones). This was a reassuring figure. Much less so is the fact that the figure was declining steeply, and especially so for the proportion of children under five living with both parents.

Effects of family disruption

Now for some of the implications for education. There has been a build-up of evidence about the effects of family disruption. Some of the best of it comes from the longitudinal studies which have followed the samples of children born in 1946 (the Douglas study) and, later on, the 17,000 children born in 1958 (the National Child Development Study). The children in both studies have now grown up and are themselves having children so that some of the long-term effects of disruption in one generation can be assessed. When the 1946 sample was looked at from this angle[3] the children who experienced their parents' divorce before they reached 15 had lower levels of attainment at school as well as more emotional disturbance and more delinquency, and were themselves more prone to divorce or separation than those whose parents had remained married.

The 1958 sample has just been examined in the same way and the outcome is, if anything, more dire.[4] The people whose parents' marriages broke down are more likely to finish school at the minimum age and to leave home before they are 18; are much more likely to suffer from psychological problems; and the men are much more likely to be regular smokers. For children with a divorced parent and a stepfather or stepmother the differences from families with two natural parents are even more striking. Girls in step-families run twice the risk of being fruitful and multiplying outside marriage while teenagers, and we know from other evidence that they run more risk of sexual abuse too, not infrequently from stepfathers. Girls and boys in step-families are twice as likely to leave school at age 16.

It seems that children in families broken by divorce or separation suffer, in a sense, a fate worse than death. The death of a father or mother makes hardly any difference compared to the effect of losing a parent in another way. I am not, of course, saying that divorce and separation are the sole causes. They are also symptoms. Couples who stay together but only 'for the sake of the children' can provide just as harmful an early environment.

Ethnic minority families and education

High performance
I would like to mention some studies with a bearing on families, done while the Inner London Education Authority was still in existence, by Nuttall, Goldstein, Mortimore and others on the comparative educational performance of children from ethnic minorities. The O level results of 32,000 children in 140 inner London secondary schools showed that most minority children did better, often very much better, than white British children, though Caribbean children fared a

little worse than whites. Indians, Pakistanis and South-East Asians were at the top of the league; even Bangladeshis, many of whom had recently arrived in England, did a good deal better than whites. At age 11 Bangladeshis had very low scores but the added value they put on in their subsequent years at school was so striking that by the time they were 16 (especially if they were in single-sex schools) they had handsomely outpaced their white fellow pupils.[5]

The same sort of results have been produced again more recently. A colleague of mine at the Institute of Community Studies, Kate Gavron, is beginning to study Bangladeshi families and will be much interested in the fit with education, and the opposite – many parents are afraid that their children at school will be morally corrupted by Western values. The issue of whether Muslims are to have their own schools alongside Catholic, Church of England and Jewish schools is not going to go away.

Supportive families
As far as I know, the connection with minority family structure still has to be unravelled, but I expect that when it is, it will turn out that children from ethnic minorities do so well in good part because there is little of Grimm's fairy tales about them: they have families which stay together and which are very supportive of education. There are as yet hardly any lone-parent families amongst Bangladeshis in my own district of Tower Hamlets.

The same clue may account for Caribbean children being at the bottom of the league academically. There may again be a link with family structure. In Great Britain as a whole 42% of Caribbean families are lone-parent families, being among the poorest in the country, the worst housed, the most afflicted by unemployment, and with the fewest fathers around to act not only as fathers but as father-figures. Such families are not exactly havens in a heartless world: a heartless world, certainly, but without havens.

Insecure children

Accounts like these do no more than illustrate what to many people would be platitudes – that misery generates misery; that children who do not have the security which comes from feeling they are loved by their parents will grow up insecure, and without the capacity to love others, or to learn from them; that children who are made to suffer by their parents, and have no one else to turn to with time enough and attention enough to listen to them and to sympathise, can become determined to make society suffer in reprisal for what they have suffered, and all without necessarily being aware of the origins of their destructiveness. It would also, I think, be generally accepted that family disruption has reduced the educational chances of increasing numbers of children and posed increasingly difficult problems for schools.

Role of teachers

All this many teachers would no doubt agree with. Many would also go on to say that of course they need to be sensitive and sympathetic to the emotional problems of their children but, throwing up their hands, they would ask what more they can do about it. They cannot be *in loco parentis* when the real parents do so little. They will argue that teachers are not social workers, psychologists, lawyers, marriage-mediators, counsellors, or therapists. Schools cannot become therapeutic catch-alls for all the casualties of society. Teachers have their own job to do and they must get on with it.

I am sure that such teachers are right, up to a point; right at any rate that such problems go well beyond schools. I cannot, of course, go into these wider issues in any depth here. I merely want to say that I expect things to get a good deal worse before they get better. This is, at root, because the values which underpin the family when it is stable – duty, loyalty, love – have I think been in retreat for a long time now. In the family, seen as a small collective of a special kind, the emphasis is on cooperation rather than competition and on long-term commitment rather than choice. In the family, individuals are not valued so much for what they do – for their possessions or their success, their achievements or their accomplishments – as for what they are. As members of the family, they can have a commitment to other members which is more or less unlimited or, if limited, then less so than in most other relationships. At any rate in the ideal type of family, relationships are not based on a reciprocity of self-interest – 'I'll do this for you if you'll do that for me' – but on a bond which goes beyond self-interest and rational calculation. The mother does not enquire whether she will be repaid before she does the washing for a sick daughter, the daughter whether she can afford the time to nurse her mother through a long illness.

'Moral economy' versus market economy

Seen in this way, the family is at the heart of the moral economy. It teaches people the most precious ability of all, the ability to transcend self-interest and regard the interests of others as in some way their own: the kind of altruism which is at the heart of the collective conscience and which holds all societies together. When it is working well, the family is the seed-bed of the virtue from which all the civic virtues stem, just as, when things go wrong, it can be the fount of all the vices.

The moral economy is always in tension with the market economy. The market economy is bound to value people more for what they do than for what they are – for their efficiency, their productivity, their achievements – and to encourage people to compete against each other. The nepotism which is prized in the family is despised in the economy. The emphasis is on the choice which is beloved of economists and *Which?* magazine. Whatever it is they are doing, people are more aware of other places where they might choose to be, at other conferences, in other offices, with other men or other women, on other moonlit nights, and, particularly, in other beds.

Modern society is bedevilled by the profusion of choice which can play havoc with the tranquillity even of the ordinary relatively stable family, when all the members of it are hurrying down their own peculiar paths of individual fulfilment with hardly time to sit down together for a meal or just to be with each other. But the values of the market have become more dominant and, needless to say, I am not thinking just of the last 13 years.

Changes in the role of women

This has happened to the extent it has partly because more and more women have left behind the unpaid economy of the home and joined the paid economy of industry. The struggle for a rise in the all-round status of women has fired one of the great social movements of the century and, though there is still a long way to go before something like equality is achieved in the home as well as in the workplace, great progress has been made. But the drawback to my mind is that attention has focused so much on the relations between adult men and women. For every ten thousand words about the rights and interests of women in relation to men, there have been a hundred about the rights and interests of children.

I hope that in the next stage of this great debate, the goals of feminism will be modified and combined with what for the moment I will call 'childism'; and combined in such a way that the rights – and I hope the *duties* – of women *and* of men are related to the interests of children.

Responsibility of employers and government
This goes wider than the family. The needs of industry and the needs of the family can pull in opposite directions, but at least they will not do so if employers accept that they have a duty to support working mothers, and hence their children, much more comprehensively than they have usually done. Government policy on benefits is very much part of the picture too. In my opinion the case is very strong for a much higher child

benefit for mothers who stay at home. This would mean that they could make the decision to go out to work or not without so much of the current pressure to take the paid job rather than remain in the unpaid.

A leading role for schools

I have sketched some of the broader issues in order to show that I would agree with the teachers who say that if families are to regain some of their stability, all institutions in society are bound to be involved, not just schools. But I also hope there can be a measure of agreement that schools *are* very much implicated. My own view is that in their values, schools have been much too fully harnessed to the wage-economy; they have in other words put too much stress on *self*-fulfilment for the individual child, *self*-realisation, *self*-expression and on competition between children; and too little stress on cooperative fulfilment in the many activities in which the self can only be fulfilled when other selves are fulfilled at the same time.

Pressures on the education system
Such questions matter, because there must be a limit to how much family disruption an education system can stand before it collapses, bearing in mind that difficult children can take up so much of teacher time and stop other children from learning. No-one knows how much disruption a society can stand before it too breaks up.

One student of the family, Malcolm Wicks, has predicted that well before the end of the 25 years the Commission is concerned with:

> The combined force of single motherhood, children being born out of wedlock, divorce, remarriage and the rest, means that only about half of children in Britain will experience a 'conventional' childhood by the year 2000, that is, being born to parents who are married to one

another and living with those parents until the child is 16.[6]

At some point it could all become intolerable, with the strain on schools, on the social services, the police, the courts, the prisons, bed and breakfast accommodation, and the growth of cardboard cities for the homeless. We could reach breaking point. But before that happens a positive reaction may set in, and, as part of that reaction, schools could play a leading role.

A family policy for schools
It is very much my hope that the Commission will be able to consider what schools can do to support families — both those from which pupils come and those which, prospectively, pupils will create when they are adults, or, sadly, sometimes while they are still pupils. We also need to examine what can be done by schools to compensate as much as possible for the deficiencies of their pupils' families. If the family is doing less for children, as we know it is, the other main educational institution needs to do more for parenting, which means having more of the necessary resources. The first need is to work out what is feasible and, in the light of the kind of evidence I have presented, to develop a 'family policy' for schools and other educational institutions. This would aim to show how schools could cope better, and (amongst other things) the implications for teacher training.

It would surely not be part of a family policy that easy-to-teach children should be segregated in one set of schools and the children who have suffered from family disturbance in another set. I don't think very many people would be satisfied with a new kind of high-performing élite school occupied by the children of parents who have migrated from the Third World mixed with middle-class whites, and on the other hand, a new version of secondary moderns occupied by children from broken homes whose problems are mainly emotional. Nor will very many be satisfied with a division whereby in 25 years' time, supportive families will keep their children at home studying through a school-level equivalent of the Open University, and perhaps taking special courses in how best to support their children, while the rest attend schools where most of the teachers are trained in psychology and friendly neighbourhood police officers dressed in mufti form part of the staff.

In any proper coverage of what could be done, attention would need to be given to personal and social education, which has been rather sidelined by the national curriculum, both by the claims of the subjects that it contains and by the administrative work that goes with it. The same, unfortunately, applies to pastoral care more generally. In a period when, more than ever, children need attention from adults who can take an interest in their personal problems as distinct from their problems in keeping pace with the national curriculum, there have been cutbacks in pastoral care. Many secondary schools still have class teachers who double as tutors, form- or year-tutors or co-ordinators. But ministerial pressure on behalf of the national curriculum has not favoured the kind of work they do in their pastoral capacity. Any review would need to take account of what has happened and also of the good practice which still persists in some schools where the head recognises how much this kind of care matters for the teachability of children.

Support services for children and families

Preventative work
To conclude, I would like to return to the subject of disturbed children and to mention two particular topics – the support services around the school and after-school provision. I am thinking about the role that schools could have as *preventative* agencies, that is, in preventing emotional disturbance from interfering with learning. Education has lagged much behind the health service in preventative work generally. This is all

the more of a pity because teachers are so well placed to notice children who are in difficulties.

Education welfare officers
But what is the teacher to do? He or she has little time to spare, and the children's problems can be such that some special expertise is required to deal with them. Teachers need support but over many decades there has been a consistent failure to organise and resource that support so that, as well as reducing the size of classes to allow teachers more time with individual children, use is made of the skills of people outside the school. It was once envisaged that education welfare officers could have an extended training and an enlarged role in coping with difficult children. In the Plowden Committee nearly 30 years ago, we were rather optimistic about what could be achieved along these lines. We thought too that educational psychologists from the local education authority could do more as a second kind of back-up, and that generally there could be better liaison with fully-fledged social workers from the social services department and with the National Health Service.

I am sure action of this sort could have been taken, but it certainly has not been, and such welfare officers as there are have to devote more time than ever to their old capacity as attendance officers, checking on the records of truants, who are said in Birmingham and in my own borough of Tower Hamlets to number as much as 30% of the pupil population in the fifth year. Yet action to increase the number of welfare officers and to give them an enlarged role in preventing truancy rather than simply recording it is more necessary than ever. The cost could pay for itself many times over if the amount of juvenile delinquency were reduced as a consequence. I hope that the Commission will draw attention to the cost of *not* resourcing education. No doubt the Plowden Report[7] was too hopeful when it argued:

> Since all children spend several hours a day in school for

most of the year, and since it is relatively easy for parents to visit schools, there is much to be said for choosing the schools as a base for social work units responsible for helping families facing many kinds of difficulties.

Such proposals may no longer be realistic. But I am sure that the whole field would be worth looking at again. This time a review would also need to consider what could be done by a parent-child conciliation service, perhaps also based in schools. This might help to reduce the number of teenage children who are rejected by their parents.

After-school clubs
Now to my final point: after-school clubs, about which I have become rather obsessive, having recently set up a Foundation for After-School Activities to promote another aspect of pastoral care.

I can see no justification for primary schools closing at 3.30 in the afternoon and secondary schools at 4. These hours were settled in 1878 and have stuck like that for over a hundred years. They no longer make sense when more and more mothers are going out to work so that there is an increasing mismatch between mothers' working hours and school hours. The same goes for holidays and half-terms, which help to account for the fact that schools are only open for 30% of their capacity, that is, 30% of daylight hours. Sports fields, swimming pools, playgrounds, assembly halls, libraries and other facilities are liable to be closed when they are most needed.

The kind of club we will try to foster – with Bristol and Leeds our first two prospective model cities – will be staffed by teachers on second contracts and trained volunteers on expenses, including, especially, early retired people and people from the 'Third Age', but not excluding parents and much younger volunteers, and all paid for largely by charges on parents. Earlier this week I discussed with a Baptist pastor plans for a club for 5 to 8-year-olds at the inner city primary school where he is Chairman of the Board of Governors. The club would give very special emphasis to the needs of the many children in his school who are in distress, before they are past helping, and would be staffed largely by volunteers from his church.

Conclusion

This has been a rapid skim over a very large canvas. I hope however that I have managed to convey my own conviction that, unless there is countervailing action, the future of the family is going to make the future of education rather bleak. Global warming could be combined with an emotional chilling altogether too chilly to bear.

References

1 Kiernan, K. (December 1991). *Family Policy Bulletin*. Family Policy Studies Centre.
2 Kiernan, K. and Wicks, M. (1990). *Family Change and Future Policy*. Family Policy Studies Centre. See also: Dormor, D.J., *The Relationship Revolution*. One plus One, p. 3.
3 Maclean, M. and Wadsworth, M. (1988). *'Children's Life Chances and Parental Divorce.'* In: International Journal of Law and the Family, col. 2, pp. 155–166.
4 Kiernan, K. (December 1991), *op cit*.
5 Nuttall, D.L., Goldstein, H., Prosser, R. and Rasbash, J. (1989). *'Differential School Effectiveness.'* In: International Journal of Educational Research, 13, 769–776.
6 Wicks, M. (1990). In: Kiernan, K. and Wicks, M. (1990), *op cit*.
7 Central Advisory Council for Education (England) (CACE) (1967). *Children and Their Primary Schools*. (Plowden Report). HMSO.

3. Values in Education

Extracts from a Speech by Cardinal Basil Hume to Catholic Secondary Headteachers in the Archdiocese of Westminster at London Colney, 24 September 1991.

Introduction

I am very grateful to have this opportunity to be here and to speak to you today. I do so very willingly because of the vital importance of your role as headteachers not only in the Church but also in our society in Britain today. It is helpful, I believe, to reflect afresh on the aims of Catholic education, and to identify the priorities we must keep before us. I should also like to take this opportunity to consider some aspects of the changes which are taking place in state education at the present time.

Yours is not an easy task. There are two, related, reasons for this.

Change and uncertainty
The first is the climate of continuing change and uncertainty in the world of education. It is difficult to imagine a time when those involved in education were subject to such a tide of change and development. Within the last few years we have seen changes in the government of schools and the role of local education authorities, the introduction of teacher appraisal and new methods of examination and assessment. And all this and more against a background of tight financial constraints. Many of these developments have been positive and good, but the pace of change has brought severe pressures on teachers and administrators, with consequent bewilderment and loss of direction.

There is also, I detect, a lack of consensus about what the

priorities in education should be because there are deep differences of view as to what the real purpose of education is. I am not pointing here to a political controversy but to a much deeper spiritual and moral one about what is of real value in human life; what our deepest needs are, and how these can best be met.

The place of religion
The second reason why your task is hard is this: our contemporary culture has no place for religion other than as something of merely marginal interest. Many of the families from which your pupils come are lapsed. Either they do not practise their faith, or it is low among their priorities. What can you do in these circumstances? Remember that response to God should not be assessed only in terms of what we usually connect with Catholic practice. There is in every one of your pupils a space which only God can fill. I profoundly believe that each one of us is an *anima naturaliter religiosa*. When religious values are presented attractively they should find an echo within those to whom they are addressed.

I strongly urge you never to cease to strive to win for God the minds and hearts of the young under your care, nor to lose sight of the vision of what a Catholic school should be - a strong community in which teachers and pupils share a common philosophy of life, where the truths of our faith and the principles of Catholic morality are taught in a professional and competent manner. Our Catholic schools are distinctive and should be. But we also have much to contribute to the principles and practice of education in our society. After all, the Church was educating many centuries before the State made education one of its responsibilities.

Last month, just before the extraordinary collapse of communism in what was then the Soviet Union, I made a pilgrimage to the shrine of Our Lady at Czestochowa in Poland. I travelled with young people from this diocese and elsewhere in response to an invitation from the Holy Father. About a million and a half young people came together to celebrate, worship, learn and pray. Over 40,000 came from the Soviet Union. It was a remarkable experience of community. There was among the young an immediate acceptance of each other, a willingness to communicate and share. It was clear from the discussions we had and the response of so many that the fundamental values of the Kingdom speak powerfully to this generation and especially to those from countries where for decades those values were systematically denied and actively suppressed. Appeals to the personal values of life and love, and to the fundamental principles of truth, freedom and justice find an echo in their hearts and minds.

During that same pilgrimage to Poland I went for the second time to the concentration camp at Auschwitz, a place of such horror and tangible evil that it can stand as a lasting monument to man's inhumanity. The sheer hatred which condemned millions of Jews to annihilation plus the calculated cruelty which reduced humans to the status of guinea-pigs can still be felt in that place. It is in total contrast to the spirit of solidarity, trust and hope which was present at Czestochowa. But it is an urgent reminder to us that the civilisation of love is achieved only at great cost and with much conscious and sustained effort. Apathy and distorted values can quickly result in moral chaos.

Purpose of education

We tend in the West, and perhaps particularly in Britain, to believe that a value-free education is possible and indeed desirable. In our pragmatic and, we fondly imagine, common-sense way, we think more about how to do things than about the why and wherefore of our actions. Many in our society today consider education to be primarily a matter of equipping young people to earn a living in a world which is highly complex and constantly changing. They do not concern themselves over much with the assumptions which lie behind such an attitude. There is a great need in fact to devote time and energy to thinking about values in education and its ultimate purpose. We must begin by asking ourselves: what is education for?

We cannot answer that question without some understanding and agreement about the very nature of man and the individual worth of each person. As Catholics, rooted in the Judaeo-Christian tradition, we affirm that we are each made in the image and likeness of God and are created ultimately so that we might share the life and love of God for eternity. We are a unique whole, a physical reality which is also an immortal spirit. Education must help to develop to the full our spiritual and physical powers and prepare us not only for our earthly tasks but also for our eternal destiny.

Recovering 'spiritual vitality'

In 1933, as the Nazi threat was taking shape in Germany, Christopher Dawson wrote these words with, I believe, true prophetic insight:

> In fact, the great tragedy of modern civilisation is to be found in the failure of material progress to satisfy human needs. The modern world has more power than any previous age, but it has used its new power for destruction as much as for life; it has more wealth, yet we are in the throes of a vast economic crisis; it has more knowledge, and yet our knowledge seems powerless to help us. What our civilisation lacks is not power and wealth and knowledge, but spiritual vitality, and, unless it is possible to secure that, nothing can save us from the fate that overtook the civilisation of classical antiquity and so many other civilisations that were powerful and brilliant in their day.[1]

Christopher Dawson spoke even then of the need to recover 'spiritual vitality'. Nearly sixty years later that need is even more urgent. Education and schools can play a part in regenerating society. To achieve that aim, we must have regard to three inter-related objectives about which I have spoken publicly in the past. Our schools must promote in their pupils a personal spiritual life, a recognition and acceptance of objective moral norms and a vivid sense of social responsibility. May I say something on each of these?

Fostering a personal spiritual life
The first is the need to inculcate and foster a personal spiritual life in the young people in our schools. And by 'personal spiritual life' I mean the process whereby God touches both mind and heart and awakens in us an awareness of Him and a desire for union with Him. It is quite possible for someone to be brought up in the Christian faith, to be educated at church schools, to attend church regularly and never to feel close to God or to have a deeply religious experience. This is a tragic deprivation. For the spiritual life is not an other-worldly, rarely attainable luxury but an essential element in any fully human existence.

There has to be the expectation of finding God in all things. Our five senses are windows through which the glory of God enters into our inmost being. He is encountered in our every exploration into the worlds of science and nature, history, the arts and literature. This experience and knowledge has to be interpreted and integrated by a deep study of the Word of God which should form the heart of an imaginative and creative programme of religious education. Even more importantly it then has to be lived in community as the school seeks to realise in practice the fellowship and communion it professes in faith.

Schools have a special function to fulfil. Not only should a church school set out to teach the young the skills necessary to communicate and create community, but it should also help them to come to realise that God is the ultimate reality and the source of all human community. Teaching the young how to pray and not simply requiring them to pray at set times and on certain occasions is both profoundly educational and spiritually invigorating. It is also the most direct and positive way to help young people discover their inner selves and begin a lifelong process of growth.

Teaching objective moral norms
The second objective is to teach our pupils the importance of fundamental moral norms, to underline the objectivity of these norms and to make the all-important distinction between a rightly formed conscience and private judgement.

Today's secular world promotes the view that conscience has merely to do with acting as one sees fit. Individuals are thought to be free to pick and choose the precepts and commandments they observe. It is deeply unfashionable to assert the objectivity of moral values and the need to be guided by them. Indeed, such is the decay in our moral attitudes and common moral language that morality is often regarded today as entirely a matter of choice and opinion. Under no circumstances – on this view – can any system of moral values be imposed on others or even proposed seriously for their acceptance.

Yet morality is not only personal but also social in its concerns; it determines how we shall act in relation to others. In our schools we should harness the instinctive idealism of the young in order to serve the needs of the disadvantaged and marginalised. This is not first and foremost a work of charity – although undertaken in a spirit of compassion – but part of a necessary concern for justice. In our approach to morality we must reverse the contemporary fashion of privatising moral values, leaving public life and international relations to market forces and to self-interest. This is a false dichotomy. Unless society and States recognise the validity of objective moral norms and the legitimacy of legislation based on these norms, the door remains wide open to anarchy and the supremacy of the strong.

It is, of course, one thing to uphold moral values and to reach a coherent private and public morality and quite another to commend this to young people and help them to make these values their own. We have to start by demonstrating, at all times, the necessary link between a moral life and life that is worth living; one which is both fulfilling and genuinely human. The first disciples began to follow Jesus because they were attracted to him. Goodness is attractive and in fact deeply compelling. We must encourage that crucial inner movement from 'doing the right thing because I ought to' to 'doing the right thing because I want to and understand why'.

Teachers as role models
This whole process of moral education is made more credible and effective if it is promoted by educators who are themselves concerned and who are seen to be living that morality in daily life. The maxim: 'Don't do what I do, do what I say' was always suspect but today it is a recipe for failure. Today people of all ages demand a match between theory and practice, between principles and daily behaviour. As Pope Paul VI said, speaking to the Council of the Laity in 1974:

> Modern man listens more readily to witnesses than to teachers, and if he listens to teachers it is because they are witnesses.

The ideal, of course, is that the school itself should be a community where truth, justice, love and community are lived out in structures, relationships and activity.

Encouraging a sense of social responsibility
These considerations lead naturally into the third objective, which is to encourage a sense of social responsibility and a study of the Church's social teaching. In the past Catholics have been accused, perhaps with some justice, of stressing personal sinfulness and guilt and of over-emphasising the need for individual redemption. Today we need to proclaim more vigorously that the individual is in fact made for communion and community and that we are called to save the world and witness to the Kingdom.

Our commitment to the Kingdom and to its values and our concern for society are not passing, left-wing irrelevances. These are profoundly theological matters which have been carefully developed in successive social encyclicals, of which the latest was Pope John Paul's Centesimus Annus. I would commend their study to every Catholic school.

It is important to stress that religion and religious education are not flabby, self-centred, optional pursuits. They are part of the spiritual, intellectual and cultural heritage of the human race and should be made accessible to all.

Developing a coherent vision of education
In our schools we are committed to the pursuit of excellence at every level, academic, technical and physical, and to the integrating of them all into a coherent vision which benefits each individual in his or her total humanity. By so doing we are helping to stimulate that 'spiritual vitality' about which Christopher Dawson wrote. The passage I quoted earlier goes on:

> Now this question of spiritual vitality, whether in the case of the individual or society, is the very centre and essence of the religious problem. Religion is not philosophy or science or ethics, it is nothing more or less than a communion with the Divine Life whether it be regarded from within as the act of communion itself or externally as a system of beliefs and practices by which man brings his life into relation with the powers that rule the life of the universe.

That seems to me to sum up what I have been trying to say thus far about the fundamental spiritual values which should guide the educational process. It is reassuring to note that a similar spirit is evident in the opening section of the 1988 Education Reform Act. There it is officially declared that the curriculum should be a broadly-based and balanced one which:

- promotes the spiritual, moral, cultural, mental and physical development of pupils at the school and of society, and

- prepares each pupil for the opportunities, responsibilities and experiences of adult life.

These are indeed noble words and an inspiring concept, but we have surely a long way to go as a society if we are to do more than pay lip-service to this order of priorities which places the spiritual first.

Education – more than training for work

It is easy sometimes to get the impression that the main purpose of education is seen as being primarily to sustain our economic prosperity, to produce technicians and managers. These objectives are of course important, but there is a danger of too narrow a view of the purpose of education prevailing. I was struck when I read the following, written by a local authority Director of Education:

> In terms of national policy, it seems that education is no longer seen as having an intrinsic value in itself – as a process which enriches the lives of individuals and society. Schools are now being judged on the extent to which their 'products' meet the labour market needs of the day. Low level 'short-termism', political expediency and dogmatism have replaced educational philosophy and long-term strategic planning.

Even if this criticism appears to be too harsh, it contains nonetheless a salutary warning, which we involved in education should heed. I am not saying that it is undesirable to educate young people so that they may contribute to the nation's economy in their future career. That would be foolish. Again, fitting a young person for a future career must, of course, be a key objective of education. But there is more to education than training and preparation for a career or a job. And this must be recognised in the way in which education is funded and organised nationally.

Recall the objectives laid down in the 1988 Act: to prepare

'each pupil for the opportunities, responsibilities and experiences of adult life'. If we take this literally, it entails a far richer and fuller agenda than simply training for work. It includes nourishing and encouraging interest in the arts, in music, in sport, and in learning for its own sake. All these are part of adult experience, contributing greatly to the richness of the whole of life. Human lives will be more or less fulfilled to the extent that individual potential has been realised and drawn out by the education process. That, after all, is what education in its broadest sense means: a drawing out and development of a person's potential, gifts and creativity, and the realisation of personal wholeness and integrity. Of course the school is but a stage in this lifelong process, but it is a critical period in the life of each one of us.

The status of teachers in society

I have said on another occasion that a key test of any society's moral, spiritual and cultural health is the respect and reward it accords to the teachers and educators of the young. If as a society we think the young really matter, that they are worthy of respect, then we will show it by the priority we give to education. We will provide good facilities, promote the teaching profession as one of great value for our society, and ensure that teachers are properly rewarded and motivated.

I firmly believe that teaching is one of the noblest and greatest callings in life. And with the increasing public attention now being paid to educational issues, I hope that our society will progress towards according the teaching profession the status and position it deserves. If teachers are well trained and enthusiastic, as you all know better than I, what a world of difference it makes to pupils.

Key role of headteachers
The Church's work in education in this diocese is founded on a network of partnerships between parents, parishes, teachers, young people, local education authorities, headteachers and

governors, and the Diocesan Education Service. All have their roles in this common endeavour. In your role as headteachers, you all have highly responsible jobs, and I admire your dedication and professionalism. I would like to ask you never to underestimate or undervalue your contribution. The way you manage, the priorities you set, the expectations you instil, all these reverberate in a school and have side-effects which you may not have intended and of which you may not even be aware. I believe that the Church in this diocese is extremely fortunate in being so well served by men and women of your ability and commitment, and may I thank you and your colleagues for the work that you do.

Reference

1 Dawson, Christopher (1933). *Enquiries*. Sheed and Ward.

4. Conflict, Reconstruction and Education

Paper by Professor Seamus Dunn to a Seminar of the National Commission on Education, Queen's University, Belfast, March 1993.

Introduction

I want to begin by discussing a number of general issues about education because I believe that they have relevance for the particular circumstances of Northern Ireland at present, but also because they have growing relevance for the rest of the UK in the future. Education can be defined in a great many ways, but I am going to focus on two particular and opposing understandings because I believe the conflict between these two understandings is assuming increasing importance. I will use them first to make a short comparative analysis of a number of educational matters internationally, and I will then try to illustrate their salience here in Northern Ireland.

The first understanding perceives education as a way of preserving differences between groups, with reference to matters such as caste, class, religion, gender, intelligence, language spoken or nationality. For many of these groups, separate and distinctive schools are not just desirable but necessary if their particular form of difference is to survive and prosper.

The second, and contrasting, view of education is that it is a way of generating a sense of unity or common purpose or national coherence within a State or country, especially when the State is multinational in the wide sense of containing different national or ethnic or religious groups. This latter view can arise from a sense of patriotism in the wake of war, revolution and social disorder, or from a particular social or political ideology. The modern world can provide a great many examples of this reconstructionist view of education. A recent example comes from the African National Congress which has been describing how future South African schools and universities will 'function in the shaping of national goals'.

Much of the debate about this distinction is related to churches. The historically close relationship between religion and education ensures that strong pressure for separate schools has always come from religions and denominations. Their primary motivation of course rests not in a wish to preserve differences, but in the need and duty to educate the children of their own members about their special beliefs. But, whoever the separatists are, and whatever their motivation, the outcome is the same: separate schools for Catholics or Jews or Muslims or girls or whites or Irish speakers or the rich or the clever: it is perhaps cynical to notice that there is rarely much fuss about who controls schools for the not-so-clever.

There is, as I have said, an obvious contemporary relevance in this distinction. Until recently it was mainly discussed in relation to such obviously divided or plural societies as Northern Ireland, the US, Canada and India. The context in those cases prompted questions about the role and importance of education in relation to such matters as national unity, the ending of violence and the promotion of social equality. But the issue has assumed a wider relevance. Not long ago social theorists were arguing that cultural differences were disappearing in modern society, a process caused by mass migration, global industrial capitalism, modern communication systems, and so on; that the various ties and pulls of race, language, religion and ethnicity were slowly losing their vigour and intensity. Phrases like one world and the global village entered the vocabulary.

Even in retrospect that seems a reasonable contention, and yet all the recent evidence is that, on the contrary, all of these signals of modernity are tending to reinforce ethnic and cultural differences and that the modern world is becoming increasingly fragmented. Most countries now have their minorities and their recent immigrants. Older migrations have left widespread patterns of ethnic dispersion, notably and most visibly in Eastern Europe. The concept of the Diaspora, once used exclusively of the Jewish people, can now be applied to Muslims, Irish, Peruvians, Chinese, and many others. And, closer to home, we have all come to know of places like Brixton, Southall, Bristol, Moss Side, Handsworth – not to mention Belfast and (London)Derry.

Out of these worldwide ethnic stresses has emerged the current international debate about multicultural education and anti-racist education, a debate illustrating the continuing truth, dramatically made plain to Socrates, that education of the young is a political matter; it is to do with compromises over what it is important to know and what it is permitted to know. It presents particular choices about what is certain and what in question, what is significant and what unworthy of notice. It is for this reason that, down the centuries, popular education has been the source of almost continuous political and social conflict.

Of course anxiety about state education has a long history. John Stuart Mill reflected on the 'unspeakable importance of diversity of education', and, with words that have a strong contemporary resonance, said,

> A general State education is a mere contrivance for moulding people to be exactly like one another: and as the mould in which it casts them is that which pleases the predominant power in the government . . . in proportion as it is efficient and successful, it establishes a despotism over the mind.

And there is also the matter, dear to our hearts here, of the importance of local autonomy, whether with reference to culture, language, politics or religion. This is often castigated from the centre with words, intended as deprecating, such as 'provincial', 'regional' or 'parochial', although Irish poets from Yeats through Kavanagh to Heaney have argued against the simplicity of that exclusion.

Origins of multicultural education

With regard to multicultural education, much of the language and the bulk of the literature about this originated in the US where there has been a long history of attempts to understand and deal with the questions raised. Until the Second World War the dominant view among all the groups there, including liberals and black-support groups, was that all citizens of the US should and would become acculturated, and this would be closely followed by assimilation. The society would, in this way, become colour-blind, and indeed the only form of difference acceptable would be religious difference. The schools, it was thought, would make a large contribution to this process by promoting a curriculum that was about being American. Unfortunately it became apparent that both acculturation and assimilation might occur and even be embraced by minority groups – or at least some parts of them – without any accompanying decrease in the discrimination practised against them. Consequently the approach began to change as assimilation became perceived as an inadequate response.

There are difficult issues here which are not easily resolved. In all periods of history, some migratory groups have succeeded, at least in part, in holding on to their own culture, while others were assimilated more or less completely. The difference between the two cases defies simple explanation. The planters in Northern Ireland in the seventeenth century have remained unassimilated – steadfastly or stubbornly – depending upon your point of view. But there are examples of groups which, when circumstances make it possible, have become part of the native population, have learned the language and have become assimilated.

In modern times there has been a strong political and moral reaction against assimilation. In the thirties, the increased racialism worldwide stimulated by Nazi power was an important force in a movement towards the acknowledgement of pluralism. By the early sixties a stronger form of multicultural education began to emerge in the US and the State became much involved in effecting and financing change, beginning with the movement towards desegregation of schools and the great expansion of civil rights legislation in the late 1960s and early 1970s.

However, the impact of three decades of desegregation of schools has not had the dramatic effects that were anticipated, and in some parts of the US there is a voluntary movement back to segregation on the grounds that integration made the employment situation worse and had a detrimental effect on black culture. The hard economic climate of the seventies and the eighties helped to change the national mood towards more emphasis on achievement levels and employment patterns, and the election of Reagan in 1981 marked the virtual end of the State's support for attempts to use education to promote cultural variety and minority rights.

The economic arguments are very powerful, and have relevance for Northern Ireland, as much recent research by Cormack, Gallagher and Osborne bears out. Generally, if the first emphasis is put on the need for separated schools to maintain special-group identity – whether this is religious or ethnic or cultural – the figures seem to suggest that there is the danger of a consequent, negative impact on the economic welfare of that group as a whole. For example, the demand for and partial provision of separate schools with plural language facilities have not greatly improved the educational or employment figures for Hispanics in the US.

On the other hand, integrating pupils in an involuntary way, using legislation and techniques like bussing, has not had much impact on the educational or employment results for African Americans, where the figures suggest that a disproportionate number end up at the lowest and most unstable end of the occupational structure, and that their children appear to benefit least from the educational system. White flight and a fairly dramatic growth in the numbers of separated private schools – often run by churches – have combined with lack of long-term planning, no additional resources or long-term teacher retraining, to frustrate the good intentions of integrating state schools. The consequences in terms of conflict, crime and violence are well known and, at times, take on the high profile of recent events in Los Angeles. The message seems to be that structural change, by itself, is not enough. It is necessary to add that, when group membership is easily identified – because of physical characteristics like skin colour – prejudice is the most destructive and covert variable.

The modern situation in the US is therefore very confused. Hispanic groups argue for separated schools where the Spanish language can be given status; African Americans still – for the most part – want integrated schools because of their long experience and detestation of segregation. There is a segregationist movement among some Bible Christian groups who find the secular ethos and curricula of modern schools harmful to their beliefs, and similar Christian schools can now be found in Northern Ireland. A debate is going on among feminists about the figures which suggest higher achievement levels for women in single-sex schools.

All of these problems can be replicated to a greater or lesser extent in many other countries. In Britain there has been very little attempt by the State to create separated schools for new minorities, and the usually – though not always – unspoken assumption is one of assimilation.

For both financial and religious reasons some groups within the immigrant Muslim and West Indian populations have begun to demand separated education as a way of ensuring their cultural and religious survival. There are of course paradoxes in all this, and clear dangers. The dangers can be seen in the Northern Ireland experience of the effects of long-term cultural separation. If racial violence were to occur in Britain on any great scale the problem would undoubtedly acquire a higher profile. It is hard to argue, it seems to me, that separation adds anything to the process of understanding and destroying prejudice, and yet it is equally hard to justify insistence on a single system. However, the likelihood of inter-group conflict leading to violence and death is a variable that should be put on the scales when judgements are being made about the role of education and how it is structured.

The importance of religion can hardly be exaggerated, and the tension between cultural homogeneity and the dynamics of the world of migration and minorities is often closely related to religion. Increasingly attention is being directed to the Islamic faith. Where their numbers make it feasible Muslims are increasingly making demands for separate schools that reflect their religious views. Pluralism and multiculturalism have a different meaning in this aspiration, although there is the perhaps ironic twist that in some cases Muslims and Christians have joined forces against the common enemy of secularism. What is certain is that, in western countries where Muslims are in a minority, there will be more and more independent Muslim schools. This increasing presence presents us all with the dilemma that, although the historical values and principles of the Enlightenment are deeply rooted in our social, political and economic life, they are not universally accepted as invariant rules of civilisation.

Northern Ireland

The conflict in Northern Ireland during the past 24 years has led to a great deal of thinking about the role of education in a society where there is division which leads to overt violence. The violence arises out of disagreements about emotionally powerful ideas such as nationality, identity, culture and religion; and so the particular forms taken up by social structures and institutions such as education are inevitably influenced and shaped by these disagreements. The role of religion is of signal importance in all this, instinct as it is with resonances from and towards all the other variables, and so, in Northern Ireland, it cannot be isolated as something separate. The depth of feeling associated with religious, cultural and national issues is strong enough to cloud out others, such as those of class. So in Northern Ireland nationalism, religion and culture are trigger words rather than class or power, although I accept the sense in which they are obviously immanent and implicit.

The historical context can be dealt with briefly. When the violence began, in 1969, it was inevitable that social structures and institutions, and all policy decisions about them, began to be examined with great care. There was some, perhaps naive, optimism that such examination might provide information about the fundamental causes of the divide, and that such knowledge would lead to procedures and policies that would reduce the violence and the social segregation that both caused it and followed from it.

The educational system was an obvious subject of this appraisal, although many continue to make the argument that education is really about teaching children to read and write and add up, and that it should not be used for what is called social engineering; further that it is the home (or in some cases, the playground) rather than the school that matters. I hope it is clear from what I have been saying that education has always been used for social engineering. And, also, that most societies and groups within society appear to believe in the power of education as a medium for the making of their preferred type of citizen. Examples can be found in Tanzania, Cuba, Israel and recently in Britain, with the insistence on politically correct knowledge in subjects like history, literature and religion.

There were two separate and distinct school systems here, that were de facto Catholic and Protestant, although the Protestant system was de jure a state system. So, if we ignore a small number of exceptions, the existing system of schools is divided into two groups, that is, Controlled schools attended mainly by Protestants, and Maintained schools attended mainly by Catholics. Controlled schools have always received full state grants for both capital and recurrent expenditure, and are under the management of local authorities. Their Boards of Governors have a level of public representation high enough for them to be thought of as state schools; but the

Protestant churches also have a statutory right to membership of Boards of Governors, and so the Controlled schools have a legal connection with the Protestant churches which cannot be avoided. The great majority of Maintained schools are, in effect, managed by the Catholic Church at present through the recently established Catholic Council for Maintained Schools. The price the Catholic Church has paid for this is the need to find 15% of all approved capital expenditure, although a recent agreement makes available the option of full funding if accompanied by a change in the structure of school management. In addition, recent research by Cormack, Gallagher and Osborne has argued convincingly that there were other hidden funding differentials which further disadvantaged Maintained schools.

This system is not the result of casual or accidental processes. The educational separation mirrors almost exactly the cultural and political divisions that are at the root of the violence, and, as the work of Murray has made clear, it is this coincidence that is of interest. It means that, although the school separation is defined in terms of religion, it is also, in effect, a separation with regard to culture and national identity. So, although educational separation on the basis of religion is not unique to Northern Ireland, its conjunction with the more fundamental division in the society makes it crucial and profoundly enduring. Wright has argued that, had the conflict in Northern Ireland evolved around language – as it did in Czechoslovakia and Poland – then the disagreements about education might have centred on that signal of identity rather than on religion.

The churches, who have the power, have had little desire or motivation for change, and until recently no mechanism. The Catholic Church has not wavered from its position since the early nineteenth century, and maintains its support for separate schools without equivocation or apology. The Protestant churches have on occasion expressed support for experiments with integrated schools (see later), but there has been little evidence of this support on the ground, and they are in fact, at local level, powerfully constrained in what they do by history and public perception. They are also to some degree restricted by laws which have placed all Controlled schools in a particular relationship with the Protestant churches which they cannot avoid and have, to date, shown no wish to avoid.

I should add that it is also suspected that the range of forms of separation here (by religion, by ability, by social class and, until recently, by gender) might have something to do with the fact that this society is patriarchal, hierarchical, conservative and male-dominated.

Community relations and education

Whatever the substantive differences between the two school systems amount to – and there has been no research that has probed this question in any great detail: that is, that has got beyond the classroom door – it became widely believed that there was an insistent connection between the actual separation itself and the absence of an enabling community understanding and cohesion. Consequently there have been many experiments, projects and researches over the past 24 years trying to find ways of ameliorating the possible consequences of separation at school level. In the end two main programmes have been generated.

The first programme has responded to the apparent paradox that, while a great many people within the community wish to preserve divided school systems, many of these people have also expressed the view, in research surveys, that the separation is likely to be socially divisive. One logical way out of this paradox is to argue that, if children cannot be educated together, then everything possible should be done to make them and their separate worlds known to each other, and this should include as much contact as possible. The response has been to build compulsory themes relating to Education for Mutual Understanding (EMU) and Cultural Heritage into the curriculum, and to create enabling mechanisms for inter-school links and contacts that are structural, long-term and part of the normal pattern of school life. The ambition is that, in the future, no local pupil will be able to say, with Ulster poet Michael Longley, that he knew no Catholics as a boy in Belfast, and that, as a student at Trinity in Dublin, he did become friendly with two Catholics – an American and a Rhodesian.

The notions of EMU and Cultural Heritage have emerged out of a long series of curriculum initiatives and researches, and they rest to a considerable extent on two theories: first, the reconstruction theory, that is, that education can be used to reconstruct society; and, second, an elaborated version of the contact hypothesis – that is, that if two antagonistic groups are given the opportunity to work and play together within a programme that is constructed in a sophisticated way so that it is well-structured, controlled, educationally worthwhile in itself, unthreatening, long-term, and so on, then these groups will be less likely to offer each other violence. I should add that both of these theories are not universally accepted.

EMU and Cultural Heritage have therefore both a content dimension and a process dimension. The first emphasises plurality, mutual respect and tolerance of differences, as well as cultural matters, including both local and shared traditions and European and international traditions; the second focuses on the need to create relationships, which are complex and long-term, between pairs or groups of schools reflecting the two traditions, and which force them to rethink their social and community as well as their academic roles.

Although much of the initiative and energy in this area originated outside the educational authorities with voluntary bodies and research and development projects, the work is now being promoted and encouraged by the Department of Education for Northern Ireland which has provided special funds and resources, a guide for teachers, and has made the work a pair of compulsory themes in the new Northern Ireland common curriculum.

It is a little premature to have any clear knowledge about how successful these innovations are. Recent research by

Smith and Robinson has indicated that they are perceived by the education community in Northern Ireland as important but complex ideas, and that much remains to be done before they become well-defined in the understanding and practice of many teachers. Evaluation and development work continues in a variety of forms and the results of these will eventually help us to understand better the dynamics of what is an ambitious and perhaps unique programme. But it is of central importance that the momentum is not lost in the current more general changes.

Integrated schools

The second form of change is radical in that it has moved outside the system to establish new, planned, religiously integrated schools. These schools are being established by religiously mixed groups of parents, meeting together and deciding to do what has always been described as impossible and unwanted. As groups they represent no particular power-base in society, and are formally independent of the churches, and this seems to allow them to be acceptable to both sides. After some initial hesitation the Government now supports them to the extent of writing such support into the Education Reform Order, 1989. There are now 18 integrated schools with a total enrolment in 1992–93 of about 3,500. This of course is still very small, but, in so far as it is possible to predict, it appears that this programme will continue to grow and prosper.

There are three aims common to most of these planned integrated schools. These could be summarised as being to do with membership, ethos and management. With regard to membership, the intention is that each school should include children from both Protestant and Catholic backgrounds, and should be open to children from other religious backgrounds and to those with none. Ideally this means that the Catholic-Protestant split should be about half-and-half, and should certainly not fall outside a 60:40 split in either direction, and affirmative action is sometimes taken to ensure this. This balance in numbers also extends to all others associated with the school, including teaching staff, ancillary staff and management.

The second aim is about school ethos, and this is in some sense a consequence of the first, although it is fundamental in its own right. It argues that the ethos of the school should be pluralist, and should prepare children for life in a plural society. This means helping them to develop knowledge, understanding, respect and appreciation of the secular and religious culture of their own community, and of other community cultures. In particular it acknowledges the interpenetration which historically characterises religion, culture and politics in Northern Ireland where the conjunction of Catholic, Gaelic and Nationalist is usually opposed to Protestant, British and Unionist.

The new schools wish to celebrate both identities by allowing them to live and flourish side by side within the schools, with tolerance and respect. The connection between membership and ethos rests on the argument that it is only when there is a degree of parity in the numbers that curricular and cultural issues become significant and can be dealt with in an even-handed manner. For example, in a situation where the number of Catholics at a non-Catholic school is small, there is no obvious need to take seriously their position as a religious and cultural as well as a numerical minority, and to make adjustments to the curriculum, to the use of cultural symbols and to the school ethos. It is regretted by some that this connection between numbers and ethos was not acknowledged within the legislation.

The third major aim is to do with an emphasis on parental involvement and the view that parents should be involved in all aspects of the planning, management, and running of the schools. One school prospectus contains the words: 'Parents have the primary responsibility for the education and welfare of their children and this should involve them in the planning and content of the education of their children, structurally as well as in the curriculum'.

The role of parents is of course a topical matter and the experience of the integrated schools raises interesting questions. The situation is of course not typical. To begin with, the schools were created by parents, because they wished to have a school which suited their particular needs. But in order for their kind of school to emerge, they had to become involved in matters normally reserved for professional educators. So the relationship between parents and teachers could not be the same as in other schools, especially during the formative years.

This change in traditional roles can lead to difficulties and confusions and even to conflict. Teachers and principals can perceive their new roles as less autonomous and less professional. There are few complex models available of parental involvement in education, and very little experience, so the process is one of negotiation and trial and error, and the results display a degree of variation from school to school. In particular the role of the principal is a more socially complex one and may be changed and extended by realignments of powers and responsibilities. There is a little evidence that older models of the relationship are being re-established as the founding parents move on, but more research is needed on this.

Within Northern Ireland, and perhaps more generally, it is necessary to begin to develop theories about and systems of school management and decision-making which reflect ideas and developments of this kind. It is not enough to argue that parental involvement in a school always has advantages, when it is not clear exactly what this involvement amounts to – beyond formal structures – and what the detailed implications are.

The new integrated schools provide some interesting empirical evidence in this more general debate, and recent research by Morgan and Fraser indicates that there are different sets of expectations and experiences among and within the various constituencies, including parents, teachers and principals, and this variation leads to concerns about matters such as the nature of professionalism and the respective rights and appropriate levels of power of those involved. Among the questions raised are: how can parents be involved in discussions about (and implementation of) the curriculum? What administrative arrangements are helpful? (Many of the new schools have committee structures which include parent committees and teacher committees.) How does a Board of Governors maintain a sensitivity to the problems of a wider parent group? How can parents get a sense that their 'seemingly endless debates' have some point and that account is taken of them? How can the parents of new pupils entering the school each year be inducted into this new model of parental participation? Can the level of interest be maintained when the founding group ceases to have a direct involvement with the school?

At a more general level one of the side-effects is that parents begin to be established as a power group in the educational community as a whole. In the past their rights were much referred to but were mediated through the churches, and this helped to maintain the deeply embedded church influence and power in the educational system. It may be that parents can now begin to function on their own behalf when educational policy issues are being discussed.

There are other matters of a more general social nature that have been affected by the existence of these schools. Mixed marriages between Catholics and Protestants are a good example. Morgan and Fraser have described how people who become involved in such marriages, especially when one of the partners does not convert to the other's religion, often find that as a family they have moved out of both tribes and are caught in a social no-man's-land, since much of the social life of the province – from Scouts to Badminton clubs – is carried on under church auspices. For many of these the integrated schools provide a social as well as an educational context to which they can belong without ambiguity.

All of these changes raise general questions about education and so evaluation is an important matter which is not always given enough emphasis. To begin with, there is need for a continuing analysis of what is intended by the changes. The current language uses vague terms like community relations, and metaphors like attitudes. But it is not clear how these might be recognised or how changes might manifest themselves, at least in the short term. Meaningful evaluation can only be carried out if a great deal of thought is given both to more elaborate definitions of outcomes and to the means to be used to measure them. Forms of measurement should be at least as complex as the changes they are examining and must have a formative dimension.

There is also a basic question about the understanding or theory of education that is implicit in the total of these activities. The purpose and meaning of education is essentially contested in most societies, but in a society which is divided enough to resort to violence, the question can be examined in extreme surroundings.

In Northern Ireland, the particular historical and religious complexion of education may allow it to be characterised as unique, although the difference may increasingly be one of scale rather than of principle. The current responses within the system are examples of procedures which although designed for local circumstances may have wider significance. It should be emphasised that these changes are still at an early stage, but we have discovered that we must approach the task of schooling a divided society in a diverse and unobtrusive way, with an awareness of the hidden ambiguities and duplicities that characterise our life and speech, using, in the words of Seamus Heaney, 'echo-soundings, searches, probes, allurements'.

The wider world

In the wider world, old migration patterns have returned, as it were, to haunt us. Plural societies around the world, where minorities reflect earlier population movements, and where a degree of stability seemed to have been established, have quickly demonstrated the enduring power of ethnicity. Partly as a consequence, the number of independent States rises continually, and there is an increased level of political fragmentation and an almost atavistic resurgence in ethnic nationalism. This is particularly evident in Eastern Europe and tragically in the former Yugoslavia, but also in Great Britain, Canada, Spain, Sri Lanka, India and many other places.

Paradoxically this is paralleled by a counter-movement towards internationalism in such things as increasing economic homogeneity and worldwide communication systems. For example, multinational companies can integrate their production throughout the world in ways that are increasingly independent of governments, and the health of national economies is seen to be at the mercy of international speculators. A similar paradox exists in education, where there is evidence of the development of what might be called a global educational culture alongside a tendency towards exclusively national curricula.

The problems for education are practical and empirical in the end and there is unlikely to be one universal answer. But the dilemma I have been pointing to today is to devise a system that satisfies the two opposed aspirations towards separation and unity: such a system will have to allow for deeply-felt differences and yet aspire towards forms of social coherence if violence and conflict are to be avoided. The need to protect differences seems to be an entirely reasonable and acceptable aspiration, and there is no obvious logical reason why such a stance should be incompatible with social stability. And yet there is empirical evidence – especially here in Northern Ireland – that the peaceful co-existence of religiously and culturally distinct groups is difficult to manage and there does appear to be a correlation between such institutional separations as education, and the retention of bias and prejudice.

5. The Importance of Citizenship

Written Evidence to the National Commission on Education from the Citizenship Foundation, 28 February 1992.

Introduction

The Citizenship Foundation is an organisation devoted to increasing awareness amongst young people and the wider community of the rights and responsibilities of citizenship and of the importance of democratic participation in the development of a legal framework based on justice and respect for human rights.

The Foundation wishes the Commission to consider ways in which the importance of citizenship as a cross-curricular theme can be emphasised in its final report. We believe this theme is of cardinal importance and yet it is in danger of becoming marginalised. We set out here the reasons for this belief.

Why we need education for citizenship

- The increasingly complex nature of our society, the greater cultural diversity and the apparent loss of a value consensus, combined with the collapse of traditional support mechanisms such as extended families, mean that there has never been a greater need for schools to address the task of introducing young people to the rights and responsibilities of citizenship and the values on which concepts of law and justice rest.

- The ever increasing weight of legislation and use of the law to regulate many aspects of daily life has not been matched by corresponding efforts to acquaint citizens with the information they need to exercise their rights and duties with understanding and confidence.

- The apparent increase in political cynicism combined with a fall in voting activity amongst the youngest age group suggests that we may be witnessing the erosion of a general commitment to the democratic processes. The continuing accountability of governments to the people can only exist where there is an educated and informed citizenry capable of making reasoned and moral judgements concerning issues in the public domain.

- Evidence from the Royal Commission on Legal Services,[1] the Marre Committee on the Future of the Legal Profession[2] and organisations such as the National Consumer Council, all present a picture in which citizens do not claim their lawful rights because of ignorance that such rights exist, lack of knowledge concerning effective use of existing procedures, fear of 'the system' and lack of personal confidence and skills. Such a situation perpetuates injustice, increases alienation amongst those unable to use the established mechanisms and encourages citizens to take the law into their own hands.

- Erosion of public confidence in the police and the justice system is due in part to a failure to educate the public to distinguish between the legal system and those who operate it. What is needed is not a rejection of the rule of law but a strengthened commitment on the part of the whole community to ensure that policing and the administration of justice are conducted fairly and with equal regard to the rights of all citizens.

- Increasing levels of crime and anti-social behaviour are the result of many factors. However, there is evidence – presented for example in the Elton Report on discipline in schools – that schools can play a significant part in encouraging personal and social responsibility amongst pupils, through taught programmes incorporating citizenship education and through a heightened awareness of the role of the school's hidden curriculum.

These points underline the significance of the National Curriculum Council's guidelines on education for citizenship,[3] which recommend that schools should see citizenship as a necessary element of pupils' education at each key stage. There is, however, cause for concern that this theme will not receive the attention it deserves. There is a real danger that this could happen, for the following reasons:

- Citizenship is a 'non-statutory' theme and therefore seen as optional. In addition, for many teachers it is a hazy concept associated with outdated approaches to civic education.

- Components of citizenship are necessarily included in schools' personal and social education programmes. These lack the status of statutory programmes and are consequently devalued in the eyes of pupils, parents and even staff.

- Many of the components of citizenship education (including legal and political awareness and moral education) have not hitherto received widespread support. This means, in effect, that there is a deficit of experience in the school system at present and a commensurately greater need to provide teaching materials and training to overcome this lack.

- Education for citizenship is poorly supported financially from central government in comparison with the other cross-curricular themes, particularly economic awareness and health education which receive massive support from government. Whilst these are important in their own right, we do not subscribe to the view that education for citizenship is less vital to the future health of our society. We feel it is worth pointing out that within the current provision for education support and in-service training grants, there is no dedicated funding for this cross-curricular theme. Whilst there is funding available for the cross-curricular themes in general, there is nothing to prevent citizenship from being neglected in favour of the other themes.

Recommendations to improve citizenship education

1 We should like to see a fundamental review of the place of the humanities and social sciences within the curriculum. We believe it to be entirely unsatisfactory that significant elements of citizenship education should be relegated to second class status and left to the mercy of an individual school's curriculum policy.

2 We should like to see education ministers and the National Curriculum Council publicly stressing the importance of education for citizenship through curriculum documents and speeches.

3 We should also like to see steps taken to encourage LEAs and schools to improve their provision for citizenship through increased funding to support in-service training and development.

4 We should like to see the DES instigate grant schemes, similar to those of other government departments, to enable organisations like our own to carry out development work under contract. The present grants system, devolved almost entirely to local education authorities and schools, makes this virtually impossible.

5 We should like to see funding provision brought into line with other cross-curricular themes and dimensions such as economic awareness, health education and information technology.

Education for citizenship has been welcomed on all sides as vital to a healthy, open and democratic society. The Citizenship Foundation itself has received warm approval for its work from politicians on all sides, senior lawyers (including the last two Lord Chancellors), home secretaries and ministers for education. Yet there is as yet no evidence of a political will to bring the past neglect of this area to an end. We believe that our recommendations would ensure that citizenship is given the required prominence in schooling, and thus enable all young people to learn how they can make a full contribution to society.

References

1 *Report of the Royal Commission on Legal Services* (1979). HMSO.
2 Marre Committee (1988). *Report on the Future of the Legal Profession.* HMSO.
3 National Curriculum Council (1990). *Curriculum Guidance 8. Education for Citizenship.*

6. Science and Technology – the Next 25 Years

Speech by Sir David Phillips to a Seminar of the National Commission on Education, 'The Next 25 Years', Oxford, 3–5 April 1992.

Introduction

Thank you for your invitation to speak on prospects for science and technology over the next 25 years. I hope that I can live up to the confidence you place in me in setting me such a challenging topic. At the same time, it is pleasant to have an opportunity to look beyond the short-term concerns that seem at present to be making such clamorous demands on our attention, and to be among colleagues addressing long-term fundamentals.

Of course, I am no sort of spokesman on educational matters, but I hope that I can say from a personal standpoint that I very much welcome the work of the National Commission, and admire the boldness and breadth of its aims, spanning as they do the whole of education and training, and looking a long way forward into future needs and opportunities.

Having disclaimed any standing as a spokesman on education, I know, and you know, that the topic you have set me is vital to the concerns of the Commission; and that the concerns of the Commission are vital for the future of science and technology. It is no accident that the Commission should have had its initial impetus from discussions at the British Association for the Advancement of Science.

You ask me to look forward 25 years: to 'peer into my crystal ball', as the saying goes. It is an interesting saying, and indeed brings to mind the long association in the popular view between science and mystery, for example, the common confusion between astronomy and astrology. I am aware that there are those among the learned as well as among ordinary folk who would see attempts to forecast the future of science as not much better than the less reputable of these activities; but I think that the reality is not quite so bad as that.

Scientific opportunities

As you may know, I am the Chairman of the Advisory Board for the Research Councils, which advises the Secretary of State for Education and Science (more recently, the Chancellor of the Duchy of Lancaster) on the support for scientific research through the five Research Councils, the Royal Society and the Fellowship of Engineering – soon to be the Royal Academy of Engineering.

One of the exercises that the ABRC carries out annually, in order to inform its advice to the Secretary of State on the health of the Science Base (the universities and Research Council institutes), is to ask the Research Councils their 'predictions' about long-term prospects for research. With the wealth of work that the Board has to do to present coherent advice on the management and organisation of the Science Base, this annual session focusing on science, and in particular gazing into the future of research, is extremely refreshing. I am grateful to have this opportunity to share with you some of the prospects that have come out of these yearly exercises.

Defining technology
But interestingly, you asked me to discuss the next 25 years of science *and of technology*. In common usage we often elide these two terms. But, even when I look back over the many technical or policy-related documents on these subjects, I find that the precise definitions of the two terms are very rarely set out – and hence the exact implications of using one term, with or without the conjunction of the other, are not explored.

A 'back to basics' approach at this stage took me to my

dictionary, and to the definition of 'technology'. My dictionary first gives me a definition of technology as 'the theory and practice of applied science'; and second, as 'the totality of the means and knowledge used to provide objects necessary for human sustenance and comfort'.

The term 'applied research' with reference to technology is one familiar to those in the science policy arena. I will not trouble you by summarising the long – and possibly arid – debate on the differences between basic and applied research. For my purposes here, it is enough to stress that basic and strategic research are the principal business of the Science Base and this is also the main area of the ABRC's interest. The purpose of this basic and strategic activity is experimental or theoretical work to acquire new knowledge, but that is not to say that we are unmindful of application. Applied research indeed looks also to discover the 'novel', but its emphasis is on the 'practical'.

The second definition of technology expands on this practical emphasis, and is perhaps one of the most reassuring expositions of the term 'technology' – with its reference to 'human sustenance and comfort' – that I have come across. I discovered a more characteristic reference to technology recently, in a book on technological creativity and economic progress (*The Lever of Riches* by Joel Mokyr) which described it as the activity of the 'cold and calculating minds of research and development engineers in white lab coats worn over three-piece suits'.

The Lever of Riches emphasises not only the importance of technological creativity, but also its challenge, excitement, and intellectual vigour. To quote from that book, on how technology changes:

> Like science and art, it changes through human creativity, that rare and mysterious phenomenon in which a human being arrives at an insight or act that has never been accomplished before . . . It tends to be more mundane . . . Yet it does share with the arts and sciences its occasional dependence on inspiration, luck, serendipity, genius and

the unexplained drive of people to go somewhere where none has gone before.

Technical versus academic learning
That same text explores the particular phenomenon of 'technological creativity', and the dramatic effect it has had on Western development. A central debate in school education is the relationship, and relative importance, of technical and vocational education, as opposed – if opposition is the appropriate term here – to 'academic learning'. I think the tensions in this debate reach on upward in the education and research fields: up into a sort of 'gentlemen and players' attitude to scientists and technologists, which is perhaps characteristic of the UK, but less so of some of our industrial competitors, such as Germany and Japan. There is a danger in not recognising the vital importance of both these activities: a danger, in particular, when too many of the brightest are attracted into one rather than the other; a danger, to quote – and adapt – a statement made recently by Akio Morita, the Chairman of Sony Corporation, in the first UK Innovation Lecture, of putting too many eggs – or perhaps 'egos' – into the same basket.

Science, technology and society
One of the great myths in science policy, which the ABRC, amongst other organisations, has taken pains to debunk, is that scientists pluck great ideas from the air, which at some point are transmitted to technologists, and at some distant point become products which you or I, as consumers, will buy. That myth is wrong in two ways. First, it ignores the considerable feedback into science from technology. And second, it ignores the even greater feedback from society back into science and technology: in other words, the challenge posed to those who think and experiment – the scientists and technologists – from the demands and needs of people.

The sometime dependence of science on technology is surely not that surprising. That the need to solve a human problem is sometimes a more forceful motivation than the need to know, is a thesis which is immediately convincing. An early example of this dependence is the development of the steam engine, for it was the desire, even the need, to develop power technology that led ultimately to the construction of the steam engine, familiarly associated with the works of James Watt but incorporating the ideas of many others. As my text on technological creativity emphasises: 'The success of the steam engine preceded the establishment of a science that formalised the principles upon which it was based' (a science that became known as thermodynamics); or, more colloquially, 'science owes more to the steam engine than the steam engine owes to science'.

A more modern example of the dependence of science on technology is the discovery of high temperature superconductors, which have important implications for the efficient use of electricity. This breakthrough was actually made by people working for IBM, just 'messing about' in the laboratory looking for ceramics with useful properties. Previously, only metals and alloys were known to have these superconducting properties and then only when held at very low temperatures, which can be maintained only in complex apparatus by the use of liquid helium. These new materials found at IBM have such properties at much higher temperatures, which are readily produced by the use of liquid nitrogen. But, I emphasise, while this technological breakthrough was made five years ago, the science underpinning it is still not understood, and this presents a challenging agenda for research activity for the next decade.

Of course, we are all happy with the argument the other way round: that technology depends on science (although that is not necessarily always the case). Understanding the underlying scientific principles which allow the technology to work is essential to getting the most out of the initial discovery, and to making the most efficient use of resources through the technological process. As a result, we can often predict forward the future technological path, within the parameters of our understanding of the fundamental principles at any time, with a greater degree of certainty than is suggested for scientific discovery (peering into the crystal ball). For example, once an act of technological creativity had produced the transistor – invented by Shockley and others in 1948 in the Bell Telephones Laboratory – and other technologists had shown how it might be miniaturised, it was not beyond the bounds of human imagination – or Japanese imagination – to envisage how it might be used. The things that have actually sprung from it include: more powerful computers; control devices in all kinds of apparatus, domestic and scientific; communications devices; personal radios and tape recorders, such as the 'Walkman'; portable calculators; digital watches; and so on. The list is long and includes a host of devices that we take for granted in everyday life.

Unpredictability in science
The critical discoveries in science are also unpredictable, but the way in which they evolve is generally less predictable than the outcome of technological creativity unless, as often happens, they open up the way to technological advance. Looking at the macro-level, at the changes that have taken place in entire disciplines, we can see profound changes, for example, in both physics and biology. Until the turn of this century, scientists thought that the fundamental laws of physics had all been discovered, but the work of Planck and Einstein changed all that; and, as I shall describe later, work on DNA has had similar effects on the biological sciences. Such advances in scientific understanding often seem to come 'out of the blue' and are essentially unforeseen in their nature and consequence. But developments that are securely based upon solid foundations in science, and more particularly technology, are much more predictable. Consider, for example, the great national programmes in the USA during the period 1960 to 1980. At the beginning of the 1960s President Kennedy announced that the US would put a man on the moon by the end of the decade – and that is what happened. The space

programme was an almost entirely technological one and much of the science used in it had been known since the time of Newton. Contrast this, however, with President Nixon's programme to eliminate cancer during the 1970s. That programme was essentially a scientific one, and it failed in its aspirations because the necessary scientific understanding was not available.

Unpredictability is part of the intrinsic nature of scientific research. As Lord Flowers wrote:

> If what you expected was always the result of research, there would be no point in doing research, only in having expectations. Thus research is done in order to find out departures from expectation. Hence the unexpected is the whole point of scientific research.

But we must not forget that technological creativity also can be unpredictable. Montgolfier's development of the hot-air balloon is one example; a successful, and completely unexpected, solution to one of the oldest and most mystifying of human challenges — the ability to fly. Unexpected because it suddenly arose quite discontinuously from the path in which technologists at the time were trying to go — via mechanical, flying machines.

Potential of biological sciences

A theme that will run throughout my talk is the enormous and exciting potential of the biological sciences. I am sure many people's experience of biology at school gave them the impression that it was one of the most prosaic and mundane of the sciences, based almost entirely on observation and description. Watson and Crick, and others, changed all that. No-one envisaged in 1953 that the initial discovery of the structure of DNA — which appeared to have some relevance for genetics — would turn out to open up the whole area of molecular biology and genetic engineering. And there is still much more to be done, and will continue to be so for certainly as far as I can see into the future.

Understanding the genome

Much current work is focused on the understanding of the genome, with reference to humans and other animals, both large and small. The rapid pace of work will undoubtedly feed through into many other areas of science. The scientific possibilities do not come from the mere fact of sequencing genomes, amazing though that concept is in view of the complexity of the task. Knowledge of genome structure will form the springboard from which many new discoveries will be made. Of these, many will be unexpected – like the earlier discovery that individual genes have unexpectedly complex structures – but there can be no doubt that some of them will enable advances to be made in combating human disease. I shall speak in more detail later on about the specific example of recent work on cystic fibrosis.

The potential of this work is also being explored in relation to plants. Sequencing work with plant and micro-organism genomes has already opened up the possibility of genetic manipulation of these species to make new biotechnological products. You are no doubt aware of the recent debates about the ethical considerations relating to the release of genetically modified organisms. We have to take such concerns seriously, but we also have to be aware of the potential from this type of work – its potential, for example, for crop manipulation. Crops that yield new products and can resist the most extreme climates and worst pest infestations may be produced in the future. In terms of human society, this may transform the food and chemical industries and make the problems of famine and starvation a horrible feature of the past.

To give a full flavour of the spectrum of activity that may arise out of work on the genome, I must also mention research that is aimed at tailoring micro-organisms for pest control, waste disposal and other clean-up processes. Much of this, you will notice, is a prediction about the development of technologies that are now well rooted in science.

Advances in immunology and neurosciences
Very rapid advances in our understanding of immunology have also been made during this century, including Peter Medawar's work aimed at understanding the phenomenon of tissue rejection when it has been grafted into a foreign host. Many elements that make up the immune system have now been described in detail, and drugs have been developed which suppress the rejection of transplanted organs by the body's immune system. But there are problems with this approach. Current drugs strip the body of all its defences, and hence leave the individual, who is being treated for one illness, more susceptible to infection by pathogens such as bacteria or viruses. In addition, the invading organisms will have much more harmful effects because there is no natural defence to control them. In this sense, a person who has a transplanted organ can be regarded as similar to a person with AIDS, whose immune system is also destroyed. In the future, the current attention focused on the immunology of AIDS may well feed back to assist organ transplant recipients.

Another highly important growth area is the neurosciences, where exciting new possibilities for research and understanding have been opened up, not least by the introduction of new technologies – such as new forms of imaging that reveal the cellular structure of the nervous system in new detail – and the application of techniques drawn from molecular biology and immunology to studies of the molecules involved in the activities of nerve cells. Again the possibilities seem almost limitless. You may have heard, for example, of the discovery by St Mary's Hospital of a gene defect that is responsible for a form of Alzheimer's disease. There are many more such discoveries to come.

Understanding the environment
Much of the work that I have described in the context chiefly of human biology also has profound implications for our understanding of the natural world. Techniques drawn

from molecular genetics, for example, such as DNA fingerprinting, make possible the definition of family relationships in the plant and animal kingdoms and will certainly illuminate the processes involved in evolution and in speciation. This work is given current impetus by concerns about global environmental change and loss of species diversity.

On the same environmental front, the application of more and more advanced techniques, many of them based upon earth observation from space, will be used to monitor and predict changes in our environment. For example, research in the last year has shown that ozone levels worldwide, and not just over the poles, are decreasing significantly. This may well be due to the effects of CFC gases, which are in the course of being abandoned by international agreement, but it points also to the need for a better understanding of atmospheric chemistry – a surprisingly complex subject, especially for those brought up on a simple picture of oxygen, nitrogen, carbon dioxide and the rare gases.

Recent and planned earth observation missions can be expected to give further understanding of the atmospheric sciences and lead to the development of new techniques for extending atmospheric measurement from space to all levels of the atmosphere and its interaction with earth and ocean. Satellites will also provide:

- observations of soil moisture that may help us to predict floods or famine;

- observations of ocean biology, currents and sea-surface temperatures which are particularly important in understanding the interactions between the ocean and the atmosphere – and hence, will help us to predict how climate will change in response to increased concentrations of greenhouse gases;

- observations of the extent of sea-ice, deserts, tropical rain-forests, that will tell us how our environment is changing.

Science and the material world

If we turn now to the material world, another area with considerable potential is *nanotechnology* – engineering on an atomic scale. Eleven years ago the scanning tunnelling microscope was developed to produce images of surfaces showing the arrangement of individual atoms. Now, the tip of this microscope can be used to manipulate atoms. So far the technology has only been used to 'scrawl' miniature messages but the practical possibilities are enormous. It will certainly play a part in the continuing miniaturisation of electronic devices and probably in more radical advances that can only be envisaged hazily at the moment. They may include the creation of tiny sensors that could be put inside our bodies to monitor factors such as blood composition, or perhaps miniature robots that could be used to unblock arteries, or make delicate repairs to damage in the brain.

Over the next decade or so there will be important developments in *materials science*, arising from the ability to create and exploit 'designer materials' – materials tailored to precise needs. For example, new materials are in great demand for effective optical communications – and what we may be able to develop are speedy, extremely responsive devices, which vastly increase the information-carrying capacity of optical fibres. The result will be – if scientists are successful – much more rapid and efficient communication.

Particle physics and cosmology

What of the horizons in particle physics and cosmology? The diversity of the universe is believed to stem from a limited number of elementary particles, acting under the influence of four fundamental forces. This is known to physicists as the 'standard model'. By understanding the nature of matter on this very small scale, we can try to unravel the origin and structure of the universe. At the European Laboratory for Particle Physics – CERN in Geneva – the predictions and limitations of this standard model are being explored, one of the outstanding issues being the search for the explanation of the origin of mass.

Exploring space
Oddly enough, these studies of the very small relate directly to studies of the very large in the domain of astronomy, which has so fascinated humankind throughout history and continues to attract many young people to science. Here we touch the very origins of science, in studies of the sun, the moon, the stars and the planets, now extended to the galaxies, black holes and the Big Bang itself where, if current wisdom is to be believed, we encounter again the fundamental particles and forces of the standard model that is being investigated at CERN. At whatever expense, we can be sure of advances on these fronts over the next 25 years, though no one can tell what they will be.

Meanwhile, NASA celebrated last month the launch of the first spacecraft to leave the solar system – Pioneer 10, which was to fly to Jupiter and then explore interplanetary space. NASA expects to be able to track the spacecraft until the turn of the century. Already the project has been successful in sending back enormous amounts of data about Jupiter's magnetosphere and the extent of the sun's influence in space (the solar wind). Since the launch of Pioneer, the Voyager missions have captured the world's imagination by sending back impressively detailed images of the ring and cloud systems of Jupiter, Neptune and Uranus. In the next decade, the Cassini/Huygens mission to Saturn and its moon, Titan, will be launched, and NASA's Galileo probe will arrive at Jupiter in 1995. Both these missions should yield new insights into the composition and structure of the atmospheres of these bodies and may lead to new thinking on the origin of the earth's atmosphere. There is also George Bush's commitment to put a man on Mars. The prospects for space exploration are clearly awesome.

It is hard to give any practical applications which might flow from these opportunities in space physics and astro-physics. But they have a strong hold on the imagination, since they affect our view of the universe – and also of our place in it.

The place of the social sciences
The proliferation of information coming out of all the experiments I have described above poses another challenge to science in the future. The acquisition, processing, transmission, storage and interpretation of large volumes of data is a key challenge for the 1990s in all branches of science – including the social sciences.

I am one of those who see the social sciences as an essential part of the scientific scene. As I see it, one of the major challenges for the future is to integrate the approaches of the natural and the social sciences in efforts to solve problems of great difficulty and profound importance. Indeed, this Commission is engaged in such an activity.

Thus, the analysis of technological innovation is one of the key opportunities that will face social science researchers in the future. No doubt we all know that the UK has always been at the leading edge of scientific inquiry, but has failed to develop such successes commercially. Better understanding of the influences of social and economic factors on the introduction of new technologies – the interactive effects of market conditions, organisational skills and culture, and industrial competitiveness, for example – could enable us to turn around this record, and make fuller use of the scientific ideas I describe above.

Similarly, there is a need for work on the possibly major – and possibly unintended – social and economic *consequences* of new technologies, especially those affecting human communications and human relations. And there is also potential for further research, very relevant to our gathering here today, on the processes of human communication and learning. Drawing on models from information science and biology, we may be able to analyse further the circumstances which promote effective learning and the development of 'exceptional' skills. One area, which I shall pick up again later, is the interaction of learning and technology, where there is a promising avenue of inquiry into the use of technological aids in the learning process. Finally, more work will be needed on the social, legal and ethical implications of new technologies – for instance, the implications for people and society of new reproductive technologies.

Society, science and technology

People and technology
So much for my peer into the future of research. But my reference to the social sciences reminds me of my original argument, about the relationships between science, technology and society. Now I must turn to the interaction both of basic investigation, and technological creativity, with people – their 'sustenance and comfort'. Here I think that education has a very important part to play indeed.

Often, it is people's needs that spur on innovation. To give a rather playful example: bringing together the knowledge of how to miniaturise transistors, with observation of how people behave and the needs they may have, can lead to 'inventions' such as the 'Walkman'. Perhaps many of us here could live without that particular development, but its commercial value is obvious.

Responding to human need
More practical examples come from medicine. The pressure to relieve human suffering leads practitioners to try out alleviating methods – and, in turn, scientists explore just why certain lines of action are so successful. Observation of the use of herbal remedies, for instance, has led scientists to inquire into the composition and properties of plants – and this in turn has led to the development of drugs to treat major illnesses. The drug digitoxin, for instance, derives from inquiry into the use of foxgloves – digitalis – in common cures. Another good example of scientists being stimulated by the requirements of practice I take from Peter Medawar's autobiography. I men-

tioned earlier the exciting work in immunology that sprang from Medawar's research on skin grafts. Medawar's interest was aroused by an incident during the Second World War, when a colleague, as Medawar wrote:

> put it strongly to me that I should lay aside my intellectual pursuits and take a serious interest in real life. He insisted therefore that I should visit the patient [who was a young airman with 60% burns] and have some bright ideas as to how he might be treated.

A bridge between people and science
Science and technology, then, have a very close and intimate relationship, and a close relationship to human need. But one message I want to leave with you today is that technologies impinge more upon our individual lives than the sciences do – unless we are working daily at the laboratory bench in a university or college. Technology is the bridge between people and science: pressing the interests of the former into the development of the latter, but also taking the results of the latter (science) and making them into things and services which people can use. The example of the Montgolfier balloon is worth exploring, because it demonstrates very vividly the pivotal nature of technology. As well as spurring scientific investigation into the nature and properties of gases, Montgolfier's first flight had an enormous impact on society in accustoming people to the possibility of flight (even though the actual development of the technology of flight subsequently took a rather different route) and alerting them 'to the ability of human ingenuity and creativity to control the forces of nature'.

Science and the washing machine
I would suggest, however, that the majority of people are not aware of the scientific developments represented in a simple, everyday device such as a washing machine – even though they have continual contact with technology. The process of

washing clothing can be broken down into several very mundane and straightforward tasks, namely: heating water, immersing clothes in water, washing with soap, rinsing, wringing off the excess water.

These processes are all mimicked or replaced in the washing machine. The components of the machine draw on knowledge from many different areas of science:

- the centrifuge, motor, thermostat and pump are electro-mechanical and were originally devised from our understanding of physics;

- electronic control of water supply and temperature, cycle time etc. is much newer and has been made possible by research into electronics;

- the soap powders that we now use are newer still, and have moved from conventional stearates and detergents with optical brighteners added, to enzymic additives which dissolve the contaminants in a different way and are made by biotechnology.

It is easy to describe this machinery rather crudely, as I have, but the processes contributing to our ability to make such an object have taken a long time to develop. The more recent changes in electronic control and soap powders date from work mostly in this century: understanding of enzymes began in around 1900.

Tackling genetic disease
This examination of the technology involved in the washing machine suggests a second train of thought to me: the transition we have witnessed over the last two centuries from technology previously based on the physical sciences, to technologies of the future based on the biological sciences. It is in biology that the most exciting scientific developments are expected, thus fuelling further this transition into essentially biologically-based technology.

One obvious area where this new biologically-based technology is expanding, and will expand further in the future, is in medicine. Recent press attention has focused on new work related to the treatment of cystic fibrosis. One in 25 people are carriers of the cystic fibrosis gene and one in two thousand births are affected. The disease is a serious one for society: it kills people young, and it is characterised by symptoms such as mucus accumulation in the lungs.

The gene was cloned and sequenced in September 1989 by a group in Canada. You will all have read in the papers the other day that a baby has just been born free of the gene, and therefore of the disease, to parents who both carry the defective gene. This was made possible by testing for the absence of the gene in the fertilised egg before reinserting it into the mother.

Increased speed of innovation
And there is another important message from this example of cystic fibrosis. Less than two years after the gene was identified, there is an available technology based on it. In other words, the time lag between scientific discovery and technological exploitation is narrowing. New technologies and science are growing closer together, and hence allow 'squeezing' of the innovation cycle. This suggests that science and technology will grow even closer together in the future, and that we will have to cope with a world of rapid changes in products and processes — and products and processes of an increasingly sophisticated nature.

The challenge to education

I want to argue in conclusion that a very important challenge faces education in the future — arising in part from the likely developments in science and technology that I have charted. I imagine that many people have no idea of the scientific and technological work that has had to go into the construction of the washing machine. But this in no way impairs their ability to use such machinery – and to use it adequately and effectively. While it would obviously make our job in the ABRC easier if more people were aware of their dependence on science and technology, it is not a matter of major concern that some, or even many, are ignorant of how televisions, cars, or 'Walkmans', actually work.

But matters are rather different with the emerging biologically-based technologies. I have described one advance, on cystic fibrosis, but there are many more, not just in the medical sciences. For example, an environmental success has been the development of synthetic pyrethroids – pesticides which, unlike DDT and other organochlorines, are readily metabolised into harmless products in soil.

Need for better scientific understanding

As scientific advances in biology are translated into technology, we shall all become more aware of them and they will impinge on our lives more directly than the largely physics-based devices that we now take for granted. Most obviously in the medical field, we may be faced with decisions and choices – options made possible by biological research – that have profound effects on our health and welfare, or the health and welfare of our families. In these circumstances, we have to question whether we need – or rather our children will need – to have a better understanding of the underlying science, just because it will be very difficult to make informed choices without such understanding.

The need to understand biologically-based technology will become increasingly necessary to people, both as consumers, and as members of society. Public concern about the nature and pathway of scientific research grows. Ethical questions arise in relation to issues such as animal experimentation, embryo research, and genetic manipulation; and people need to be able to participate in debate on these issues in an informed way, so that they can weigh the likely benefits from the science against the moral dilemmas that arise.

Giving people the understanding and information they

need to be both intelligent consumers, and participators in social debate on science and technology, will present substantial problems for education. The body of scientific knowledge which it is necessary to appreciate is daunting. I was interested to read recently an interview with Luther Williams, who is head of the United States National Science Foundation's education directorate. He noted that in the last 15 years 'more has been discovered in biology than in the previous 200'. An alarming prospect for young people to grapple with, and a challenge for education – but a challenge that surely needs to be met.

I do not know how many of you will have read a recent article by Saul Bellow in the *Guardian* newspaper which caught my eye when I was preparing this lecture. It was ostensibly about Mozart, but Bellow gave a rather pessimistic account of how we have coped with the technological revolution. He said that we have reached the stage where:

> . . . man is unable to distinguish between a natural object and an artefact, a second nature object. We the 'educated' cannot even begin to explain the technologies of which we make daily use . . . Face to face with the technological miracles without which we could not live our lives, we are as backward as any savage, though education helps us to conceal this from ourselves and others . . . it would utterly paralyse us to ponder intricate circuits or minicomputers. These, however, are the miracles for which we have a very deep respect, and which perhaps dominate our understanding of what a miracle is. And we owe this to the scientific revolution.

I hope that our discussion here can contribute towards making the understanding of science and technology a more hopeful possibility in the future.

Technology to aid learning
How might advances in science and technology be able to help that learning process? The impact of new developments in communications technology on teaching methods is no doubt

a topic which the Commission has considered; I noted earlier that social scientists see roads for research in the future into the use of technological aids in learning. Luther Williams has also highlighted, in the interview I mentioned above, the work being conducted by the National Science Foundation to support computer networks of schools, so that, to quote Williams: 'a teacher in rural Nebraska will have access to all of the information that is available'; he also highlights new ideas to explore whether computer-based communications networks could be used to disseminate curriculum material.

Such new techniques will allow freer access to almost unimaginable amounts of information. I described earlier the new work in nanotechnology – with the scanning tunnelling microscope – to trace out and image surface details with atomic resolution. Those working in the field envisage the possibility of storing the entire contents of the US Library of Congress on a silicon disc only 30 centimetres across. And of producing computers with the power of our modern, most powerful supercomputers, but small enough to slip into one's pocket. Cheaper and more powerful technologies will aid in data storage, access and communication.

There is a clear danger that over-dependence on such technologies will tend to weaken our grasp on reality: it would not do, as the New English Bible puts it, 'to see only puzzling reflections in a mirror' – or on a screen, for that matter. But happily, it may also be possible for schools, given the increasing availability of technologies at low cost, to get access to some of the sophisticated equipment – even the scanning tunnelling microscope – which is now available only in research laboratories.

Encouraging enthusiasm for science
Finally, a question that needs to be addressed in this forum is how all these new possibilities can be used in an imaginative way to encourage the enthusiasm of the young for exploration and discovery and hence lead them into science, but more importantly, into scientific understanding of the world they live in.

7. A Businessman's View of Education and Training

Extracts from a Speech by Mike Heron to a Seminar of the National Commission on Education, 'The Next 25 Years', Oxford, 3–5 April 1992.

Introduction

Can I first of all say that these are my personal views; they come purely from my own observations of what we need, primarily in the UK, but they also apply to the rest of the world, including Europe. I am pleased to be able to join you because there is no doubt that in business we would put education among the top three of our strategic needs. If you were talking about long-term goals, I am sure it would be right at the top of the list. So it is important to the business world and I think they recognise that.

But to me education is more important than that: it is a social need that all civilisations will require. I happen to be of the view (and I know I differ from a lot of other people), that the real problem in the future is going to be expanding the world of work to cover everybody throughout their working lives. I think the chances of that happening are practically nil, and that presents the developed world with real problems. There is no doubt whatsoever in my mind that right at the heart of the solution is the education of individuals to be able to face a long life with only a relatively short period of formal work in it.

Changes in industry

Let me start by talking a little about the nature of industry itself, because there is no doubt that the world out there is changing at an unprecedented rate. You have talked about this today: the application of electronics; the application of IT;

the accessibility of data; the automation of equipment – these things are moving so fast that the world is changing with a rapidity which we just cannot keep up with. For instance, if someone were to say: 'name a major change that has happened in business or in our society in the last 10 years', I don't think many people would put down the fax machine. Yet if you think about the fax machine, it has totally revolutionised our lives and we haven't even noticed it. I asked the other day: why do we have to work so hard? One of the reasons is that when you write a letter you get the reply back within five minutes. In the business world it used to be the case that you would wait a week. So the whole process of decision making has speeded up. That is just a small example, but it is one that most people recognise.

Another factor is that more than ever before, economic success depends on the brainpower, the abilities and the creativity of our *total* workforce. It is not muscles we are paying for any more; it is not blind obedience; it is the application of expertise at all levels. The resulting increase in productivity has reduced the number of people in industry. To give you an example: in Unilever in 1978 in the UK, we employed 90,000 people. Today we employ 30,000. You can account for some of that by the disposal of businesses, but on the other hand, we have acquired some. Out of the difference of 60,000, there will certainly be something like 35,000 people who have just moved out of the business. We produce more volume now, with more profit, with 35,000 fewer people. So you can imagine that the contribution of those people who are left is very significant. If you walk from time to time round modern factories, what will surprise you is the lack of people.

So my first message is the speed of change, and the second is that we are now looking at a workforce that is much smaller, but one in which people are employed for the totality of their ability, not just for their muscles. Any thought that we should be educating people to take jobs that are not taxing is wrong: manufacturing industry is no longer a dumping ground for the unskilled. Because change is occurring so fast, workers require a number of characteristics that were not necessary before. There is no doubt that people need to be more broadly skilled and able than before, because they will have to make changes during their career and they will have to put their hands to different skills at the same time. 'Multiple skilling' will be an aspect of change. Transferable skills are now more important than ever.

The last element of industrial change which I want to comment on is competition. Whether we like it or not, the UK is in a highly competitive world: much more competitive than it has ever been. The single European market is going to impose major pressures on the UK. It will be important to encourage major businesses to site their factories or their research and development units here in the UK. The *location* of functions is going to have an important impact on the community and the education it requires. That will become more and more an issue in the single European market. For instance, as the UK regional director of Unilever, I am always trying to draw either research or factories or test markets here to the UK. The key element here is the skill of the employees.

Qualities in the workforce

Given that background, what does industry need from the workforce – from *all* the workforce? The first all-important requirement is the core skills of literacy and numeracy. You can develop one in 3,000 Einsteins, but I tell you that the basic characteristic you want is people who can count, who are comfortable in the use of numbers and have a feel for them. A feel for figures is of vital importance. Of course, the need for literacy skills goes without saying.

The second requirement is the understanding of ideas. Now this sounds simple but it is not as simple as we think. The ability to think conceptually and be able to understand quickly the message that is coming across is becoming more and more important.

The third requirement is economic awareness. I think that

in this area we are probably weaker than most European countries and the Government is aiming to put that right. But it needs working on continuously, particularly at teacher level, because at the end of the day an awareness of the economic realities is vital.

The fourth requirement – and this applies to all employees – is the ability and the desire to learn continuously. We have talked a lot about that today, but I want to emphasise that amongst the workforce itself it must become a daily occurrence that people should want to understand and to learn.

The last requirement is initiative and self-discipline. The factories of today and of the future are very unlikely to have supervisory layers within them. It is much more likely that employees will share the same information and the same data. I am now talking about teamwork, and to do that people will have to be more self-disciplined, more able to see what needs to be done and then to go and do it.

Implications for education

What implications does all this have for our education system?

The first is that we cannot afford to waste our early years at primary school. If we need to get the basic bricks in place in our school years, on which we can then build in terms of vocational training and learning, we do not have a lot of time. Therefore, I would say that we have got to use those primary school years a lot better than we do. For example, it strikes me as incredible that children do not generally learn foreign languages at primary school. At Unilever we send people all around the world, as you would imagine, and it takes the children about six weeks to play in the streets or in the playground with the foreign children. Within six weeks they are actually communicating with each other. They may not have a big vocabulary, but the fact is that they cope.

The second implication is this. Education must be broad-based, at least until the age of 18. It seems to me almost criminal that at 14 we start specialising in order to prepare for

GCSE and then A levels. Now, when I meet my colleagues from Europe this simply is not so. Their education is broad-based, certainly up to the age of 18 and indeed beyond. If we really take seriously the need to be able to communicate, to be scientifically literate, and to be a part of the learning society, we just cannot afford to specialise too early.

The third point is that students must be encouraged to stay on beyond the age of 16. I really do believe that industry itself is culpable: we employ 16-year-olds; we do not pay for A levels; we do not recognise NVQs.

I have already mentioned my fourth point: the implications for business of literacy and numeracy. To me they are a *sine qua non* for everybody.

The fifth point is the production of world-class specialists, and behind them, more scientifically literate generalists.

The sixth is that students leaving school must be familiar with computers and able to understand and apply data. Industry has a part to play in making the necessary resources available.

The last implication is perhaps the one I really feel most strongly about. People tend to put training and education together. I think the key is that education should be about developing those things that children have within them, to form the base on which they can then train and learn for the rest of their lives. That is the continuum.

Aiming high

I would like to end by saying that I do not think that we are as bad in the UK as we sometimes imagine. A lot of intelligent thought goes into the debate about education: take for example the work of the National Commission, that of industry itself, the Confederation of British Industry, the Council for Industry and Higher Education, Business in the Community. There are many bodies that are keen to take part in this debate and to help. Our good students are among the best in the world, and indeed, when the Japanese come here and apply their techniques, our productivity is at least as good as that in Japan. So there is nothing in my book that says that we are worse than anybody else. It could in fact be argued that conceptually and creatively we are sometimes better. The problem is that we have accepted standards that are too low, and my fear is that we will accept standards which are too low for the future. What I would say to the Commission is this: remember that there are some very able competitors out there, and they are getting better. We must aim very high indeed.

8. Changes in the Workplace

Extracts from 'Preparing for Work Today and Tomorrow: A Paper for the National Commission on Education' by Dr. Peter D. Wickens, 1992.

The pressures for change

While it is wrong to say that anything is permanent, we have in the last 15 years or so experienced fundamental 'macro' changes in Western industrial society which permeate all we do and are certain to have long-term effects on the way organisations are managed. These changes have significant implications for the type of people the world of work needs. In turn this must impact on the education that is required if those in full-time education today are to be fitted for the world of work in the 21st century. The pressures for change are numerous, but I will limit myself to just three: the growth of international competition; technology; and the shift from the collective to the individual.

International competition
For most manufactured products there is now virtually a global market and, as important, global manufacturers. Transnational companies are able to operate in those countries which best suit them and this ensures that all are exposed to the latest production technologies, materials – and costs. All companies in all economies are exposed to the standards established by the most successful. There are now few captive markets, few people who are prepared to wait, few companies which can say: 'This is what we produce or provide – that is all you can have'. We have for the most part changed *from a producer-led to a customer-led marketplace.*

International trade used to be in the basics – food, raw

materials and primary products. Now there cannot be a product or service that is not traded. International travel for the mass market barely existed until the late 1950s and then was initially restricted to Europe. Now the growth sector is 'long haul' travel.

In the last 20 years the whole basis of international competition has changed. Indeed, both internationally and domestically the determinants of competitive advantage have metamorphosed. Without great exaggeration one can say that until the 1960s producers demanded more and more volume, being able to sell everything they produced. As manufacturing capacity developed throughout the world and competition intensified, price often became the determining factor. This in turn impacted on costs and led to the transfer of production to low-cost countries (80% of Canon's cameras will be produced in countries other than Japan in 1992). The 1970s was the era of quality, particularly as high-quality but low-priced Japanese products started to enter Western markets in significant numbers. During the 1980s production capacity exceeded demand and manufacturers offered an ever widening range of products. The basis of competitive advantage has become complex. *Today's marketplace demands that manufacturers compete on price and quality and product range.*

A major technological factor contributing to − or even causing − the growth of international marketing is the development of telecommunications. Fibre optic cables, first laid across the Atlantic and Pacific in the late 1980s, combined with satellite communication systems, are facilitating a single, worldwide telecommunications network. In the financial sector there are no longer separate markets for Europe, America and the Far East. Electronic transfer of funds, whether from your supermarket to your bank or across the world, facilitates international trade. Britain, not only because it has the language of international communications, but also because in its time-zone it is able to communicate with Japan in the early morning and with the United States in the afternoon, is particularly well placed to take advantage of this new technological capability to communicate instantly in any medium: voice, data, text or image.

The miniaturisation of products is a factor which assists the growth of the global economy, whether we are speaking of the Japanese-led miniaturisation of consumer electronics (a classic example of manufacturers responding to specific marketplace requirements, led by the small Japanese house) or of aeroplanes which are able to carry increasingly large payloads in relation to the materials and fuel used in that transportation.

Technology
The impact of technological developments in the last 25 years or so has been immense and diverse.

Dr Bruce Merrifield, when the US Government's Assistant Secretary for Productivity, Technology and Innovation, said:

> Life cycles have collapsed. What fuelled the world economy in the past were production processes that had a 10 to 12 years' life or more. These are now down to three or five years, or even less in consumer electronics, and rarely more than five to 10 in other areas. What this means is quite simple – whoever is generating new technology will conquer the marketplace.[1]

Rapid product innovation made possible by the ability to use technology for rapid product development results in highly competitive companies being able continuously to leapfrog each other.

There is the favourite story of the camera. The Brownie camera was in production for 12 years to 1964 with only minor changes. In the first seven years of the Canon Autofocus camera there were five model changes, each more technologically advanced than the previous one. Go to a camera shop today and try to find a product identical to that which you purchased six months ago. You will fail.

Technology, by eliminating mountains of paperwork and putting more power at the fingertip, allows companies to offer a better service to the customer and at the same time to eliminate vast numbers of people: supervisors, managers and departments whose previous task it was to process that paperwork. Computers, when first introduced, created highly specialised centralised departments with specialist staff and expensive mainframes. Now computing power can be distributed throughout an organisation. Those people who were initially afraid of a computer terminal now welcome it as what it is: a tool which helps them do the job better.

Shift from the collective to the individual
The exercise of individuality by individuals manifests itself in many ways: the lack of respect for established authority; the view that you have to earn respect rather than automatically receive it; the fact that many people now expect work to fit in with their lives rather than life with their work; the extension of home ownership and other personal investments. These are all fundamental changes which affect all aspects of the employment relationship and question not only the employer-employee relationship but also that between trade union and member. A job for life now rarely exists. Commitment (if it exists at all) is to the profession rather than to the company.

While we still criticise our education system there is no doubt that compared to the first half of the century there has been a significant improvement in the level of education of the majority of our young people. One impact of this is that the individual now has the opportunity to develop through his or her own efforts.

Structural changes

In addition to changes in the type of work and worker required we are experiencing a number of structural changes in our economy. Among these are the growth in the small firms sector; the changing age structure of the workforce; and the increasing proportion of women in employment.

Small and medium sized enterprises (SMEs)
Small firms continue to grow in importance. The number of businesses registered for VAT in the UK increased by 50,000 in 1990 (235,000 registrations and 185,000 deregistrations). The importance of small firms to the economy was highlighted by an article in *Employment Gazette* in November 1991, which showed that in 1987–89 firms employing fewer than 10 people created over half a million jobs – almost as many as the larger firms, despite their having only a quarter of total employment. 'It is those firms employing fewer than 10 people which are the major engines of job growth.' However, this sector is also the most volatile. Dun and Bradstreet reported in March 1992 that company collapses were running at 160 a day, most of which were SMEs.

Employment in small firms is the norm in Britain. Over 13 million people work in small and medium sized enterprises. A study by Michael Daly and Andrew McCann (reported in the February 1992 issue of *Employment Gazette*) shows that there were 2,025,000 businesses with only one or two employees. Forty-eight per cent of employment is in companies with fewer than 100 employees. In Britain there are only 2000 businesses employing more than 500 people. In total employment terms, those 0.1% of businesses with over 1000 employees actually employ 34% of the working population. However, the critical point is that of the 2,988,000 businesses in Britain, 2,970,000 employ fewer than 100 people. These figures are important for many reasons, but for the purpose of the Commission's work the key points are that:

- small businesses are less likely to undertake systematised training;

- the smaller they are, the more flexible the staff will have to be;

- small firms are less likely to use technology.

As the SMEs develop over time, it becomes necessary for them to move from skill-specific to more broad-based training, but attempts at systematic training often fail through lack of in-house expertise. Another problem occurs when, to put it simply, the job that has to be done outgrows the capability of the original people. The original entrepreneur may in fact be the problem. As Daly and McCann put it:

> In setting up the business they learnt from doing. That knowledge can be difficult to pass on. They could also be unwilling to do so as it might equip their employees to become competitors.

Another important factor noted by Daly and McCann is that SMEs will often underestimate the amount of training they already do. Much continuing development is taken for granted:

> SMEs' training systems might not fit with theoretical best practice but may be appropriate to their circumstances. Human resource development in SMEs can appear informal and uneven, but the study found examples of definite commitment to developing people.

It is important to understand the factors that affect the approach to training in SMEs. Some of the key factors are:

- short-run performance and the need to remedy problems

- new technology

- customer influence, particularly for enhanced quality

- prescribed quality and performance standards

- growth stimulates training but can also make it more difficult to fit in

- management's attitude

- workforce expectations

- difficulty of release for training.

Age structure of the working population
A few years ago the 'demographic time bomb' was the most fashionable topic of business conversation. Superficially, it seems that, because of the recession, the topic has rapidly disappeared as an area of concern. When companies are oversubscribed at a ratio of 20:1 whenever they advertise and unemployment is approaching three million, what cause is there to worry?

The obvious answer is that the recession will not last forever and the facts of the reducing birth rate will not change this. However, this paper is not the place to rehearse the previous arguments. Instead I would wish to concentrate on one aspect of the subject which impacts on the type of people who will be employed: this is that *in the next two decades we will experience an ageing workforce*.

In 1982/83 the total number of school leavers was 911,000. Since that time it has continued to decline and is expected to reach its lowest point in 1993/94 (613,000). The figure is then expected to rise to 701,000 in 2000/2002.

The declining number of school leavers available for employment is further reduced by the very considerable increase in the numbers entering full-time further education. In 1982/83, of the 911,000 school leavers, 253,000 entered full-time further education, leaving 658,000 available to enter the labour market. By 1993/94 it is projected that 226,000 of the 613,000 school leavers will enter full-time further education, leaving 387,000 available for work. By the turn of the century the figures will be: 701,000 leavers; 267,000 entrants to full-time further education; and 434,000 available to enter the labour market. Thus, direct entry into paid employment at age 16+ is no longer the norm.

The average age of the population of working age will

increase markedly, with the number of young adults falling by nearly 20% over the rest of this century. The ageing workforce is important for a number of reasons. Older workers cost more both in pay and benefits. Paul Johnson of the London School of Economics estimates that ageing in the British economy is likely to increase labour costs by 2.5% to 3% by the end of the century. Perhaps more important though is the view of many current managers who believe that age is a significant determinant of individual productivity, dynamism, flexibility, skill and ability to learn – the older the population the lower the performance level in each of these areas. While age is also believed to bring experience, wisdom, common sense and so on, managers who take the former view will be very concerned about the ageing workforce.

Another important factor resulting from the demographic change is the impact on promotion opportunities. Not only have organisations moved to flatter hierarchies resulting in fewer promotion opportunities, but because the post-war 'baby boomers' are now in mid-career, there are far more of them competing for fewer jobs. In retrospect the career path which was open to people born in the period 1935–1945 may come to be regarded as a golden age, in which a comparatively small number of people were available to be promoted into the multitude of jobs created by the multi-layered bureaucratic organisation which, as we have seen, peaked in the 1960s and 1970s. Charles Handy has identified the problem thus:

> The assumption . . . that if you are older you are probably wiser, you are probably more senior and you are probably richer, and the curve of your life earnings goes up until you retire, in which case it drops, has got to be broken.[2]

The key issue arising from this is: how do you continue to motivate people in flat hierarchies when perceived promotion opportunities disappear? Part of the answer lies in the concept of continuous development.

Women in employment

In 1971 women comprised around 36% of the workforce. Currently the 11.7 million women at work account for 43% of the workforce and by 2001 this is expected to rise a percentage point or two.

Forty-three per cent of female employees worked part-time in 1990 (compared with 5% of males). In real terms this has meant a rise from 3.4 million in 1979 to 4.8 million in 1990. The vast majority of these (72%) worked part-time because they did not want a full-time job.

Women employees are much more likely to work in the service sector than in other industries – perhaps because most part-time jobs are in that sector. No less than 81% were in the three sectors which include hotels, catering, financial services, nursing and education. The figure for men in these sectors is 53%. Thirty per cent of women are in clerical work, compared with only 5% of men. Twenty-eight per cent of women are in managerial and professional work, compared with 35% of men. However, this hides the fact that women are not 'at the top'. As women now form nearly half the workforce, but only a small percentage are in top jobs, a huge amount of talent is being wasted. Many women must be working below their true potential and it is not because they lack ability. It is a combination of preconceived roles, employment and working patterns designed for men, and the inevitable career breaks. But what is important for this paper is that the 1990s could well be the decade when women really force their way through, demanding the same opportunities as men and expecting employers to respond by changing their attitudes and practices and providing the same development opportunities for them as for male employees.

It is not only in the upper echelons that the presence of women will be increasingly felt. The Institute of Employment Research (IER) at Warwick University forecasts a substantial expansion of employment opportunities for women in almost all of the major occupational groups during the 1990s. By the year 2000 the number of women in the civilian labour force is expected to grow by 700,000 to 12.9 million. Most growth is expected in the following occupational categories: managers and administrators, professional, associate professional and clerical and secretarial, but the IER expects a disproportionate share of these jobs to be part-time.

A summary of changes affecting people at work

Organisations are people
The pressures for change which I described earlier are having a major impact on people in organisations, on the demands made upon them, on their roles and on the skills and qualities required. Perhaps most fundamental is the recognition that organisations are really little more than the people in them. Without a properly selected, well trained and highly motivated workforce, the survival, let alone the success of any organisation, is in doubt. The major change factors and their results are:

Producer-led to customer-led organisations (or supplier/client)

- Recognition that the purpose is to provide a service or product *for* the customer.

- Competition based on the totality of price, quality, choice, response time and pace of innovation.

- Greater awareness of what the competition is doing.

- Deeper understanding of marketplace requirements.

- Working *with* customers to ensure their specific needs are understood.

- Product customisation at a late stage in the development process.

- Working in partnership with the supply chain in supportive, long-term relationships.

Development of 'new' technology

- Flexible manufacturing systems which allow rapid change and economic, small batch production.

- Simultaneous engineering which enables rapid product development.

- Integration of technologies.

- High level of control of systems and processes allowing 'right first time' quality.

- Distributed and networked information technology facilitating supply chain integration.

- Rapid information flow deep into the organisation and out to the geographical perimeter, facilitating devolved decision making.

- Major changes in the skill structure, including multi-skilling and both more complex and more simple tasks.

- Requirement for computer literate, multi-functional staff able to accept role changes.

Structural change

- Recognition of the need for a clear definition of business strategy and vision.

- Restructuring of multi-layered organisations into flatter, simpler structures.

- Reductions in headcount with dramatic improvements in unit labour costs.

- Decentralisation and subsequent devolution of decision making.

- Restriction of organisations to their core business, with large parts of indirect activities being contracted out to a growing SME service sector.

- Recognition that it is the task of the remaining indirect functions to provide a *service* to the direct functions of the business, not to control them.

- Breakdown of internal functional barriers leading to the establishment of multi-functional groups, both on a long-term and functional basis.

- Concentration on the core workforce, with greater use of contract, temporary and part-time staff.

- Elimination of demarcations between functions, with a subsequent growth in multi-skilling.

- A changing role for trade unions, which are becoming committed to the success and growth of the organisation.

Attitudinal change

- Recognition that all individuals are able to contribute to the success of the organisation.

- Acceptance of the need to improve continuously the product or service, and that it is the people in the organisation using their brains as well as their hands who are best able to do this.

- The role of management is changing to one of leading and motivating the workforce. In particular, at first line supervisor level the role is changing from 'progress chaser' to 'team leader'.

- Flexibility is replacing restriction (both in trade union and management practices and structures).

- Teamworking is replacing non-involvement.

- Commitment to quality of product/service is becoming 'organic' rather than an 'add on'.

- Recognition that sustaining high quality over the long term demands both the commitment of the workforce and control of the production process.

- The continuous development of all staff and the need for lifelong learning are becoming recognised as key ingredients for success.

- Both individuals and trade unions recognise that personal long-term security and growth depend on the success of the enterprise.

- Arbitrary differences in the treatment of different categories of employees are being eliminated.

- Reward is being related to results, with individual contributions being recognised.

- Technology will not replace people. On the contrary the 'people' contribution is being increasingly valued and the concept now is the integration of people and technology.

All of these trends apply to both the manufacturing and service sectors, public and private. It is clear that a restructuring between the manufacturing and service sector has taken place, the main impact being in the new demands which this change will make on the workforce.

From the information available to us, it seems likely that such trends will:

- create an increasing number of part-time jobs mainly filled by women;

- demand a much higher calibre managerial/professional group in the retailing/leisure sectors;

- require people capable of handling increasingly sophisticated technology, particularly in the retail sector;

- bring about totally new professions, such as logistics management and environmental technologists;

- accelerate the development of SMEs, the vast majority of which operate in the service sector;

- increase the number of people providing 'low level' (but necessarily high-quality) personal services.

The challenge now facing the Commission is to develop proposals which would ensure that young people receive education and training of high quality, enabling them to play a full part in this rapidly changing world of work. We are fast approaching the time in which the somewhat élitist term 'knowledge worker' will have to be generalised. In the successful organisation of the year 2000, *every* worker will be a knowledge worker.

References

1 *Times*, 16 February 1987.
2 House of Commons Select Committee on Employment (January 1989). *Inquiry into the Employment Patterns of the Over 50s*. HMSO.

9. Graduate Recruitment in a Changing Employment Market

Paper presented to the National Commission on Education by Trevor Thomas, July 1992.

Introduction

The graduate employment market has changed radically in the past 40 years, and particularly so in the last decade. Changes have come about not only because of the increasing number and range of graduates, but also because of increased demand from employers. The nature of demand has also been progressively modified to reflect the changing structure of British business and industry.

By the year 2000, there will be a further significant increase in the number of graduates; and on the demand side, British business will have gone through a cathartic decade of change. Its need for graduates will change — in terms of the attributes looked for as well as the overall numbers required. In looking forward to the next century, it is difficult not to be overly affected by the current recession. However, it is assumed that unlike the 1930s, when the depression dragged on for an extended period, there will be economic recovery, both in the UK and worldwide, and that there will be a steady economic growth through most of the period.

The employment market for graduates is dynamic. Rarely will supply and demand be in equilibrium, not least because of the lead-time for the production of a graduate. This paper explores the trends in the graduate employment market and the impact of changes in the world of business upon employers and their recruitment policies.

Trends in the graduate employment market

The changing industrial structure
Table 1 shows the total numbers in employment for the economy as a whole, and the percentages represented by the principal sectors in 1954 and 1991, and the projected figures for the year 2000.

Table 1: Employment by sector, United Kingdom.

Thousands and percentages

	1954	1991	2000
Total Number in Employment	23,570	25,671	26,121
Primary and Utility	10.7	3.8	2.9
Manufacturing	34.6	19.7	16.9
Construction	6.1	6.4	6.2
Distribution and Transport	24.8	27.2	26.8
Business and Miscellaneous Services	9.0	22.1	25.3
Non-marketed Services	14.8	20.7	22.0
Whole Economy	100.0	100.0	100.0

Source: Review of the Economy and Employment, Institute for Employment Research, 1993.

The figures indicate the considerable structural change in employment, in particular, the decline in the *primary and utility* sector, which includes agriculture and mining, and in *manufacturing*; and the substantial growth in *business and commerce*.

Graduate employment in the 1980s
Developments in the graduate employment market in the 1980s should be seen against the background of the changing industrial structure. As Table 2 shows, the number of first degree graduates increased by 31.6% between 1979 and 1989, with the most rapid expansion coming from the former polytechnics.

Table 2: First degree graduates, 1979, 1989, Great Britain.

Thousands and percentage change

	1979	1989	*Percentage change*
University Sector	64.3	69.9	+ 8.7
Polytechnics and Colleges Sector	31.5	56.2	+ 78.4
Total	95.8	126.1	+ 31.6

Source: Department for Education: Statistical Bulletin 10/91.

In the same period, the recruitment of graduates grew by 25%, but with very different patterns in the different employment sectors, as Table 3 shows.

Table 3: Graduate recruitment by sector, 1979-1989, United Kingdom.

Sector	*Percentage change*
Banking, Insurance and Finance	+ 137
Law Training	+ 106
Other Commerce (inc. retailing and management consultancy)	+ 98
Accountancy	+ 48
All Sectors	**+ 25**
Education	+ 19
Manufacturing	+ 17
Public Sector	+ 14
Teacher Training	− 49

Source: IMS Graduate Review 1991.

Graduate unemployment surged rapidly in the recession of the early 1980s from 5½% in 1979 to 13% in 1981. Thereafter, it fell consistently through the decade to just over 5% in 1989. However, about 4% of graduates were in short-term work, often regarded as a form of graduate underemployment. With the current recession graduate unemployment has risen again, as Table 4 shows.

Table 4: First destinations of graduates, 1990, United Kingdom.

Percentages

	Universities	Polytechnics
Unemployed	6.4	10.7
Short-term UK Employment	3.7	7.9

Source: AGCAS 1992 Survey.

Employment trends in the 1990s
Table 1 projected an increase of about 2% in total UK employment between 1991 and the year 2000. Within the total, occupational change will be dependent, in part, on sectoral change, but studies carried out by the Institute of Manpower Studies and the Institute for Employment Research project that the fastest growing job categories, each expanding by over 20%, will be: scientists and engineers; other professions; managers and entrepreneurs; and technicians/associate professionals. Increasingly, vacancies in the first three categories are filled by graduates. More are also entering the fourth.

The business environment in the 1990s

The environment in which British business operates is becoming rapidly and inexorably more exacting. Larger businesses both in manufacturing and the services sector are the first to be affected, but smaller and medium-sized companies (SMEs) will, progressively, begin to feel the change. The organisational structure, style and capability of businesses will be profoundly affected by a number of factors, including:

- *Competition* – to survive and prosper, businesses now have to match international standards of performance. For many companies, with the completion of the Single European Market, the standard will be European. For a growing number, the standard will be global – and performance will have to be benchmarked against the world's best. The UK has been a low-productivity, low-pay economy. In many sectors, however, it now has to compete not only against the high-productivity countries, but also against the high-productivity/low-pay economies such as those in the Pacific Basin. A number of UK companies are world class in performance; most are not.

- *Quality* – this represents an aspect of competition, but does not give a competitive edge. It is, however, a necessary condition for entering the race. For the future, the quality commitment – 'right first time' for all customers – will have to be comprehensive and pervasive.

- *The microchip* – this has been transforming manufacturing, and will continue to do so.

- *Information technology* – the rapid digestion, analysis and transfer of information will profoundly affect organisation and procedures. For example, the concept of supply chain management – optimising operating and inventory costs in the whole chain from the consumer right back to the suppliers of raw materials – is only practicable with the emerging IT capability. It cuts right across the traditional organisational models.

- *Innovation* – speed to market will be a source of competitive edge; the first to the market is likely to get a significant and enduring advantage. The Japanese are securing dramatic reductions in the lead-time to launch new products. At the same time, rates of obsolescence are increasing and product life-cycles shortening.

By the turn of the century, successful businesses are likely to exhibit the following characteristics, many of which are already evident in larger organisations today:

- *International perspectives* – businesses will probably be multinational in their organisation and staffing. For many this may mean a European focus, with a network of offices and plants across Europe to serve enlarged markets. In the UK market, there will be competition from European or global companies. Products and services will be developed for European or international markets.

- *A workforce which is leaner, more flexible, and highly skilled* – to deliver quality and innovation to international standards will require a business to draw on the capability and commitment of all of its employees, as well as its specialist staff. Employees will have to be skilled and ready to update their skills continuously. The business will have to be an 'Investor In People' and to be committed to 'Lifetime Learning' objectives for its employees.

- *Flatter management structures* – traditional management hierarchies will be of little significance. Organisations will have been de-layered, with tranches of management levels eliminated. Groups will be self-managing rather than controlled by management. Ad hoc project teams will form and reform, drawing from a range of departments and activities as appropriate. They will be task-oriented and job levels will not be of consequence.

- *A hi-tech environment* – there will be significant investment in hi-tech plant and equipment.

The implications for graduate recruitment policy and practice

Points of entry
Changes in the business environment and in the characteristics of organisations will impact upon graduate recruitment policies and practice. At the same time, as the higher education system diversifies, graduates will be recruited from different points of entry, and for different career tracks. Employers will categorise entrants in the following broad groups:

- management trainees – the high-fliers recruited for their future career potential

- 'direct entrants' – appointed to specific jobs on the basis of their vocational degrees

- post-graduates – appointed for research and development work

- mature graduates.

Initial training will vary for each of the groups, but, thereafter, individuals are likely to be promoted on merit – irrespective of their entry point, and whether they are graduates or not. The new ladders provided by National Vocational Qualifications (NVQs) will open opportunities for many who have hitherto been denied them.

A profile of attributes
When recruiting – and particularly during the process of identifying potential high-fliers – employers tend now to define a profile of attributes which they seek. Typically it will include the following:

- academic achievement: demonstrated application and high standards of performance

- analytical skills

- communication skills: listening, speaking, writing

- group skills

- commitment and capacity for hard work

- ability to set attainable goals

- maturity, tenacity, independence, organisation

- decisiveness

- imagination and creativity.

These attributes will continue to be important into the next century, with the ability to work in a team – group skills – becoming increasingly so. Looking to the future, however, most employers will also be explicitly seeking:

- numeracy and confidence in handling quantitative data
- confidence in using information technology
- literacy in science and technology
- competence in a foreign language. (Language competence on its own is unlikely to bring special recognition; larger companies can show that where there is reasonable aptitude, necessary languages can be learned.)
- a readiness to be mobile, nationally and internationally.

The aggregation of these attributes relates closely to the 'core skills' which employers are concerned to see incorporated and assessed in the national curriculum, and in study at further and higher level. The full implementation of the national curriculum by 1996 should give greater assurance that the university entrants of the future will have the necessary knowledge, skills and understanding upon which to build.

Training graduate entrants

High-fliers

In the UK, the typical graduation age of twenty-one or twenty-two is two or three years younger than on the continent, where graduates joining business have also usually had a longer period in higher education and have undertaken appropriate vocational studies. Except where specific disciplines are required, as in the sciences, major UK employers have tended to be indifferent to the academic subject studied and to offer the necessary foundation business training after recruitment. As Sir Bob Reid said: 'the wonders of classics and the mysteries of physics are as good a preparation for management as the discipline of economics or the increasingly popular pursuit of business studies'. There seems to be no disposition on the part of UK employers to move towards the continental model.

Practice in training high-fliers is likely to take one of two forms depending on the size of the organisation. First, the bigger employers will continue to organise the training of their graduates in-house, drawing in teachers from higher education and elsewhere as necessary. They will look for fast, efficient conversion. Increasingly, they will work with business schools to secure accreditation of their internal training programmes in programmes leading to a diploma or master's degree in business administration (DBA, MBA); to provide reassurance about the efficiency of the learning; and to foster the personal plans of individuals. Other businesses, where the benefits of scale are not available, will look to higher education institutions to provide the training and then recruit first degree graduates in business studies and related disciplines and also those with MBAs.

Direct entrants
Companies will continue to recruit graduates with the relevant vocational degrees directly into jobs: e.g. engineers, market researchers, senior accountants, actuaries. Their numbers will increase as companies upgrade the skills of their workforce. These recruits will tend to be offered help to complete their professional training, and be given general business training. Although companies will have recruited direct entrants primarily for their present competences rather than for their future potential, they will promote those whose performance is meritorious.

Research and development
Recruitment here will continue to be primarily at the postgraduate level, and mainly from those with doctorates. The inflow will need to be enriched by limited recruitment, from

higher education, of post-doctoral researchers who are world class in their fields. The competition for these scarce resources will be international.

Employers will provide a business orientation for such recruits – for example, by continuing to support Collaborative Awards in Science and Engineering (CASE), and by providing the foundation business training offered to the high-fliers and direct entrants. Increasingly, they will look for the attributes that they seek in high-fliers and particularly for the ability to work in teams, as multi-disciplinary project groups become the order of the day.

The management potential that is within this group has often been neglected in the past, but is now being addressed positively by some companies. They have adopted such measures as foundation business training; mentoring arrangements; secondments to the operational business; records of achievement and personal development plans; and scientific ladders which correspond to line-management promotional ladders. However, the supply chain for this stream has alarming weaknesses.

Mature graduates
Mature graduates can be considered in two categories: those who graduate whilst in the employment of the business; and those from outside the business. The development of NVQs, the growth in accreditation of prior learning, and the commitment of businesses to develop all their employees – as Investors In People do – will, in due course, result in some employees moving on to higher education, probably on part-time courses and using distance learning. They are likely to be encouraged by being allowed time off; by sabbatical leave arrangements; and by financial rewards. There will be strong mutual commitment, and those securing their degrees will be challenged by increased responsibilities. Their number will increase steadily as this channel of opportunity develops.

Mature graduates from outside the organisation will be in competition with young graduates for 'direct entry' vacancies, as they are likely to have taken vocational degrees. Businesses will continue to be reluctant to accept mature entrants as high-fliers, but once into employment would expect to offer them the same foundation training and development opportunities.

The outlook for graduate employment

General projections on supply suggest that the number of graduates seeking employment will increase by over 60% in the present decade. Of those recruited, nearly 50% will be women. Many businesses already recruit nearly as many men as women but few, so far, have been able to demonstrate that women can penetrate the glass ceiling to the senior echelons of management. Issues of policy and psychological factors are at the root of this situation, but they are capable of resolution in the 1990s. Graduates from the ethnic minorities will be more prominent among recruits in the future and, it is to be hoped, the new century will see them proportionately represented in graduate intakes.

It is difficult to project the level of demand from employers, but there are a number of indicators suggesting that it will increase significantly:

- the bigger companies will recruit more, although against a tightening profile of attributes;

- small companies have not generally been direct recruiters, but hire 'first bounce' graduates who have had their induction and early training in big companies. The employment of graduates in this sector increased in the 1980s and that trend should return after the recession of the early 1990s;

- IMS/IER surveys project a 20% increase in the number of scientists and engineers;

- new sectors, such as the leisure industry, are increasingly interested in recruiting graduates;

- more professional institutes are likely to follow the lawyers and accountants and specify graduate entry;

- initiatives such as the Management Charter Initiative are raising awareness of the inadequacy of the education and training of British managers.

But there is also likely to have to be some moderation of expectations. For example, the Civil Service Executive grades, which traditionally recruited an A level intake, draw in an increasing number of graduates. The experience of other countries, where businesses have more graduates, suggests that, over time, the graduates steadily displace the non-graduates in the higher levels of management, but also that the floor is lower and that many graduates start from supervisory levels.

The IMS Graduate Review of 1991 concluded that by the end of the century 'there may well be considerable oversupply of new graduates'. This underestimates the latent demand for graduates. The profound changes that will occur in British business and the whole community, driven by economic imperatives, will open up many employment opportunities for graduates that are difficult to specify today.

Employer concerns

Employers share a number of serious concerns about the appropriateness of the preparation which the educational system currently provides for graduates seeking to enter the world of work. These are concerns which need addressing now, and which will only intensify as the changes in the business environment accelerate over the coming decade. Foremost among their concerns are:

- *Science and technology* – the whole supply chain is weak. A high proportion of secondary school teachers are not ideally qualified to teach their subject. The ACOST report *Science and Technology Education and Employment* (1991) stated: 'Too many pupils are being turned away from science by poor teaching, inadequate preparation and ineffective and irrelevant practical work'. Good teachers inspire their students. Fewer students are enrolling for A levels in Chemistry, Physics and Maths. The application/acceptance ratio for Mathematical Sciences, Engineering and Technology and Physical Sciences places at universities and polytechnics is very low as compared with Social Sciences and Business and Administration. The enrolment of graduates from these disciplines on to post-graduate teacher training courses is insufficient and inferior in quality.

- *Foreign language teaching* – there is again a shortage of qualified teachers, which will result in future graduates having inadequate foundation training.

- *Parity of esteem* – employers regard A levels as too narrow and specialised. Similarly they want vocational qualifications (General National Vocational Qualifications, now renamed vocational A levels) to be recognised on a par with A levels and accepted as such for university entrance. They will judge undergraduates by their performance at university and elsewhere and become less concerned about the route into higher education.

- *Core skills* – employers want the disciplined minds that graduates bring. But they also want the core skills described earlier. Schools are coming to terms with them slowly (but the TVEI programme, which emphasised core skills, is likely to close); they are integral to the GNVQ; they find expression in the 'Enterprise in Higher Education' initiative. But, for many academics, the recognition is token and not secure. Our future graduates will benefit from a more wholehearted commitment to core skills throughout their years of education.

- *Careers guidance* – the UK compares badly with other countries in careers guidance and the advice given in school and at further education level. In higher education the careers services are under funding pressures. By the year 2000, there will be a very different employment market and, in anticipation of that, future graduates deserve sustained, high-quality careers advice.

Conclusion

In 1987, the Council for Industry and Higher Education's Report *Towards a Partnership* stated:

> The UK's prosperity, vitality and international standing depend on its becoming a more highly educated nation which recognises brainpower and applied ingenuity as its distinctive assets . . . We need a different kind of higher education system to provide for larger numbers, recruit them from a much wider segment of the population . . . (It should be) rebalanced towards mathematics, science and technology . . . and offer (students) a diversity of learning methods and opportunities, often work related, at different stages of their lives.

Employers would subscribe even more strongly to that statement today.

10. The Role of Employers in Education Reform

Paper by William Richardson for the National Commission on Education, 1993.

Introduction

Employer involvement in education reform is an increasing international trend. The recent acceleration of this trend is due to the economic and social pressures which have been exerted upon schooling in most of the advanced industrial countries (AICs) since the mid-1970s. The structural reasons for the realignment between the national education systems of AICs and the economies and labour markets they serve are complex and continue to form the subject of detailed research. Nevertheless, most analysts are agreed upon several key elements in this process and their consequences for education provision (see Box 1 overleaf).

Whilst most AICs have an established tradition of employer relationships with universities and polytechnics,[2] employer involvement in other sectors of national education systems is diverse. Such relations have, in particular, been strongly influenced by the varied organisation of secondary schooling, post-compulsory education and vocational training in different countries. Education-business partnerships, for example, have emerged in countries such as the United States where the national education system is based upon a 'schooling' model (involving late vocational choice by pupils[3]) and in Great Britain where a combination of economic problems and government pressure has encouraged employer involvement in schools.[4] Common to such initiatives is a growing awareness among all partners – government, employers and teachers – that the adequate preparation of pupils for adult working life is a major challenge. The remainder of this paper examines how this challenge has shaped aspects of British education reform, particularly that of employer involvement in schools.

Box 1: Realignment between the economies, labour markets and education systems in AICs: causes and consequences[1]

Causes of the realignment between the education systems, economies and labour markets of AICs:

- the beginnings of a major shift in patterns of work organisation (the 'crisis of Fordism') due to the internationalisation of world markets and the increasing pace of technological innovation;
- a consequent acceleration in demand for jobs requiring high levels of skill;
- the reinforcement of labour market segmentation between high skill, high wage and low skill, low wage jobs in most western economies;
- a reduction of investment in education by the governments of weaker western economies due to deep recessions following the oil crises of 1973 and 1980.

Consequences of this realignment for education provision in AICs include some or all of the following:

- a need to redesign curricula to reflect changes in workplace technology and skills demand;
- a major disruption in the transition from school to work caused by unprecedented levels of youth unemployment;
- a change in political climate from that of expansion in capital education expenditure, based upon a faith in 'human capital' models of education and training investment, to that of funding decisions driven by considerations of efficiency and cost-saving.

Britain: a decade of education-employer initiatives

Although the history of British education since the late 1860s is littered with appeals for greater collaboration between education and industry,[5] this need was given little policy attention in the 30 years following the Second World War. Not until the mid-1970s did a set of political circumstances – an unpopular industrial policy, the need for public expenditure cuts and the personal interest of a new Prime Minister –

create a climate in which the Labour administration of the period revived government interest in the education-industry issue.

The result, to the irritation (but not to the disadvantage) of the Department of Education and Science (DES), was the mounting by James Callaghan's Downing Street Policy Unit of a substantial public relations exercise, ironically labelled the 'Great Debate', concerning the future role and purpose of school-based education. Taking as its main theme the failure of schools to recognise the 'needs of industry', this shift in post-war education policy also stressed the need for a core curriculum and the curbing of extreme forms of 'progressive' teaching.

Less heralded at the time, but more significant in the longer term, were two considerations – one economic and one political – which have remained central aspects of government thinking. These are a belief that, for the foreseeable future, Britain is no longer able to afford an education system funded primarily upon principles of equality, capital expansion and study for its own sake, and an increasing concern to limit teachers' autonomy and curb the influence of teacher unions.[6]

Consequently, since 1976 one of the main ways in which educational 'opinion formers' and successive governments have sought to reorientate teaching is through increased employer involvement in schooling. Until 1979, the Labour government encouraged a social partnership model for developments such as the involvement of local education authorities (LEAs), trades unions and employers in school reform in England and Wales under the guidance of the Schools Council;[7] Conservative administrations, since 1983 in particular, have either systematically excluded social partners or reorganised their relation to central government, through instruments such as contract compliance of LEAs to the Manpower Services Commission (MSC) for Technical and Vocational Education Initiative (TVEI) funding. Over this latter period, the pace and frequency of reform initiatives promoting education-employer relations have been unremitting (see Box 2).

Box 2: Major education reform initiatives involving employers, 1984-93

Year	Initiative	Sponsor	Objective	Policy Mechanism
1983–98	Technical and Vocational Education Initiative (TVEI)	Dept. Employment	To enhance technical and vocational education for 14-18 year olds	Contracts with all LEAs for curriculum development
1983–	Youth Training Scheme	Dept. Employment	To provide foundation training for school leavers (increased from one- to two-year programme in 1986; relaunched as 'Youth Training' in 1990)	Training providers (employers or private training companies) recover costs from government; trainees receive an allowance
1986	Industry Year (Industry Matters 1987-89)	RSA	To change 'anti-industrial' attitudes in education	Exhortation, local committees
1986	Industrial School Governors*	DES	To secure greater employer involvement in school management	Education Act No. 2
1986	National Council for Vocational Qualifications (NCVQ)+	Dept. Employment/DES	To create a comprehensive framework of vocational qualifications	Industry 'lead bodies' create sectoral qualifications
1988–	Compact Programme	Dept. Employment	To increase motivation of low achieving pupils	Contracts with 62 local agencies; employers make formal commitment to pupils achieving personal goals〈
1988–	Enterprise in Higher Education Programme	Dept. Employment	To broaden undergraduate curricula	56 contracts with universities for curriculum and staff development
1989	National curriculum*	DES	To reflect the working world in the teaching of the school curriculum	Education Reform Act: Technology (statutory subject); Economic and Industrial Understanding (non-statutory theme)
1988	City Technology College Initiative#	DES and companies	To provide alternative technology-oriented schools	Joint funding of non-LEA schools (15 established by 1992-93)

Box 2: Major education reform initiatives involving employers, 1984-93 (continued)

Year	Initiative	Sponsor	Objective	Policy Mechanism
1989–91	Enterprise and Education Initiative	DTI	To change 'anti-industrial' attitudes in education	144 advisers promote pupil work experience, teacher placements in industry, employer issues in teacher training
1990	Training and Enterprise Councils (TECs)⟩	Dept. Employment	To secure high-skill labour force	Funding to 105 local agencies for employment programmes; some discretionary funding
1991–	Training credits	Dept. Employment	To stimulate demand among young people for training (re-titled 'Youth Credits' in 1993)	'Credit' issued to young people to 'buy' training: phased introduction through TECs; national coverage by 1996
1991	National Education and Training Targets	HM Govt./ CBI/TUC	To boost NVQ take-up	Exhortation to employers and funded agencies
1991–	Education Business Partnership Programme	Dept. Employment	To co-ordinate previous education-employer activities	Funding through TECs to 103 local agencies
1992	General National Vocational Qualifications[+]	NCVQ	To provide higher status vocational qualifications for the 14–19 age group	NCVQ oversees course design in vocational areas (e.g.: care, retailing, etc.)
1992	Technology Schools Initiative*	DFE	To stimulate technology teaching with a strong vocational emphasis	LEAs and GM schools bid for funding; 118 schools in receipt of 1993/4 funds

⟨ *Funding now administered through TECs/LECs*
* *England and Wales only*
+ *England, Wales and Northern Ireland only. The Scottish Vocational Education Council is responsible for parallel arrangements in Scotland*
⟩ *Local Enterprise Companies in Scotland*
\# *England only*

Education-employer initiatives: participants' motivations

During the 17 years since the Labour Government made its decisive intervention, the level of employer involvement in British schools has grown considerably. Despite this, the specific motivations for involvement of participants from the two sectors remains an under-researched question.

Business
Within the business community, concern about the quality of labour supply – in either the short or longer term – has been the most common criticism of education from employers in both the small and large firm sectors. Furthermore, the vast majority of firms have looked to government or employer interest groups to set a specific agenda for resolving this problem. Individually, however, they have tended only to turn from their general concern about educational 'standards' to active involvement with schools in response to direct approaches from educators or to satisfy their own recruitment needs.

This is particularly true of small firms where work schedules are tight and business survival is the central priority. Moreover, policy makers have a particular interest in promoting education and training in this sector – 97% of all business enterprises employ fewer than 20 people, yet between them, they account for 35% of all employment outside government.[8] However, the competitive pressures prevailing in an unregulated labour market are a major barrier to small firms' closer involvement in current education and training reform in Britain, whether in supporting schools or through participating in the work-based assessment of employees for National Vocational Qualifications (NVQs). Because of such constraints, agencies responsible for fostering education-business links report that personal motivation is a powerful stimulant in this sector where, for example, staff in small firms are the parents of school-age children or are already involved in education as school or college governors.

Box 3: Variables which shape the involvement of large companies with schools

- Personal intervention of chief executive or key board member
- Internal organisation of responsibility for education
  - personnel, or
  - corporate/community affairs
- Career profile of lead education manager
- Geographic distribution of the company's sites
  - concentrated at large plants, or
  - dispersed through many communities
- Stage of company life cycle
- Organisation of education activities within different sectors, e.g.:
  - existence of an independent lead body
  - one company which leads for the sector
  - companies which lead their suppliers and customers
  - open competition between companies
- Nature of company's core business
  - environmental impact
  - schools/pupils form an important market for a company's goods or services
- Manpower needs/recruitment patterns

Amongst large firms, many organisations are reviewing the co-ordination of their links with education and training providers as the momentum behind business-education partnerships grows. However, research evidence indicates that, as yet, very few major British firms have reached a point at which they are either confident that skills investment is at a level in their sector which protects them from the 'poaching' problem, or view systematic investment in education as a key to competitive advantage in markets demanding high value goods and services. If such strategic motivation is to be developed, it would seem that direct co-operation between employers rather than the exhortation of education-business partnership agencies will be the likely cause. Meanwhile, large firms commit resources to education primarily for narrower, functional reasons – either to support community relations/public affairs programmes or as part of human resource policy, including recruitment (see Box 3).[9] Furthermore, some large firms have concluded that a reactive response to requests from schools and colleges suits both the nature of their business strategy and the *laissez faire* labour market conditions which prevail in Britain.

Education
The educational rationale for partnership with business is equally complex. Economically, the recessionary pressures to which the British system has been prone since the mid-1970s have redirected some educators towards the business community for alternative sources of support – in kind, or through direct finance. Of specific concern has been the availability to schools, via traditional funding channels, of a sufficient quantity of the technological equipment used in the modern workplace.

This trend has been reinforced by pedagogic considerations. Although at first a small minority, a growing number of educators in Britain (and elsewhere) have come to believe that much of the curriculum now appropriate to the school systems of the AICs can only be provided by giving pupils access to the technology, training techniques and professional qualities of adults in the wider community beyond the school. The development of this argument and its pedagogic implications can be traced through 15 years of publications by the School Curriculum Industry Partnership (SCIP) – an organisation created as part of the Schools Council's response to the Labour Government's curriculum challenge of 1976. By 1992, DFE figures indicated that 92% of secondary schools and 56% of primary schools had links with business; in the same year, the OECD reported that the use of business as a major vehicle to modernise pedagogy was a phenomenon mirrored across a wide range of AICs.[10]

Clearly, considerable efforts have been made by schools and businesses to address the complaints of government in the mid-1970s that the two sectors had grown isolated from each other. At the same time, however, there have been significant contradictions in government policy which have had the effect of amplifying ambiguities inherent in the school-business relationship. This is apparent, for example, in debates surrounding the reform of curricula, assessment and qualifications, and these issues are discussed in greater detail in the next section.

Employer involvement in British education reform: unresolved tensions

Perhaps inevitably, given both the political history of education in Britain since the war and the superficiality of understanding about the motivations for business and schools working with each other, an assessment of the impact of this education reform strategy reveals a number of unresolved and fundamental tensions – and consequent policy problems.

(a) *The claim that English education is 'anti-industrial' may have some foundation, but has acted as a smoke screen obscuring policy failure.*

It is probable that a sizeable (and in recent years, largely silent) body of teachers remains indifferent to appeals that educational provision should more closely mirror labour market requirements, although little research has been undertaken into such teacher attitudes. Nevertheless, the accusation that English education reflects anti-industrial attitudes – made most influentially by the historian Martin Wiener,[11] espoused by the RSA during 'Industry Year'[12] and overtly embraced by Lord Young at the DTI during 1987–89[13] – has laid disproportionate blame for Britain's economic decline upon teachers. An alternative explanation of the contribution of education to economic decline lies in the structural weakness of government policy making both in its short-term expediency and in its institutional divisions (see NCE Briefing No. 5).[1] In 1987 for example, the unveiling of the national curriculum by the DES had the effect of forcing into reverse much of the work overseen by the MSC through TVEI.[14]

(b) *Curriculum reform, especially TVEI, is being driven at the school level by concerns for equity as well as efficiency.*

The Government's £1.3bn investment in TVEI since 1984 has not been directed solely towards pupils' acquisition of technical and vocational skills. Central to much of the teacher momentum behind TVEI has been the development of consensual teaching styles and learning methods for 14–18 year olds which stress pupil achievement and which challenge the traditional ascendancy of academic examinations such as A levels. Whilst this blurring of TVEI's original aims (a work preparation complement to YTS) might have been unwelcome news at the Treasury (see below), it is of interest that those business people who have been involved in TVEI have largely come to support teachers' operational objectives for the scheme and the implications of these for pupil assessment.[14] Very many more employers, however, remain unaware of such issues and are content to use traditional examinations as recruitment filters.

(c) *The effect of policy for 14–16 examination and curriculum reform is to expose continuing uncertainty about employers' priorities for education reform and effective pupil work preparation.*

The announcement in July 1991 of the Conservative Government's intention to reduce the amount of assessed coursework leading to the award of GCSEs has been greeted with widespread dismay in the education sector and by many employers involved in education-business partnerships. This confrontation is symptomatic of a wider tension, which may be expressed as the search for an accommodation between two rival outlooks: the concerns of educators and those employers and Employment Department officials who favour curriculum 'enrichment' and 'breadth' through initiatives such as TVEI (based, ironically, on mainstream DES/HMI thinking since the late 1970s),[15] and the beliefs of an unlikely alliance – Conservative ministers, their education advisers and labour market analysts at the National Institute for Economic and

Social Research – that both school curriculum design and pupil assessment should more demonstrably serve the specific 'needs of industry'. The most recent clash between these two perspectives has centred upon revisions to technology teaching in the national curriculum;[16] more generally, this tension feeds on the disparate views of politicians, teachers and employers as to the relation between assessment techniques and educational 'standards' (see NCE Briefing No. 10).[17]

(d) *Employers' practices conflict with their aspirations for education reform.*

British and American studies indicate that there is considerable disagreement among employers about how education should better satisfy the 'needs of industry'. In Britain, despite two decades of public criticism of the education system, analysis of what employers say they want from it reveals a picture of incoherence, reinforced by a lack of informed knowledge and, in the case of the Institute of Directors, a direct hostility towards teachers.[18] Notwithstanding, since 1988 the CBI has published a number of influential reports on education and training which indicate the direction that its leading figures believe reforms in this area should take.[19] Inevitably, however, the significant impact of the CBI upon policy formation is limited in the practical sphere by the strong factors which depress employers' investment in skills (see NCE Briefing No. 5) and which make the task of changing the practices of its own members considerably more difficult than that of influencing a politically friendly government.

(e) *Education-employer initiatives have been designed to serve a dysfunctionally wide range of policy goals.*

The initiatives listed in Box 2 serve a range of education, employment and social policy goals; some programmes – such as compacts and youth credits – are simultaneously concerned with all three policy strands.[20] Moreover, the volume and frequency of separate initiatives over a decade or more is testimony to the nexus of policy problems thrown up by the economic trends summarised in Box 1. From the point of view of education policy, the pace and range of initiatives emerging from a series of government departments and private organisations has had a number of deleterious policy effects:

- teachers have experienced 'innovation fatigue';

- evaluation method and design in business-education partnership initiatives have typically reinforced an almost exclusive emphasis upon programme management at the expense of a critical assessment of pupil benefits;[21]

- the evaluation process itself has been called into question by the pre-emptive way in which pilot schemes such as training credits have been pronounced 'successful' by ministers and extended nationally before either the pilot or its evaluation has been completed;[22]

- the low quality of many Youth Training programmes has suggested to large numbers of participating companies and young people that, for policy makers, educational concerns have taken second place to those of (un)employment policy;

- contradictions have arisen between the initiatives of separate government departments. The Department for Education, for example, is encouraging businesses to sponsor individual schools[23] whilst the Employment Department is urging them to work through the business-education partnerships of Training and Enterprise Councils.

The way forward

The tensions described in the previous section illustrate the complex dynamic that exists between employers, educators and government and some of the policy problems which result.

Undoubtedly, research and evaluation which generates results of significance for long-term policy making in this field is difficult to design and costly to undertake; without it, however, policy objectives will remain blurred. For instance, as early as 1987 Treasury officials had concluded that the local application of TVEI funding was spinning out of control. None of the many research studies of the initiative could demonstrate that TVEI students were advantaged in the labour market, and local evaluation was primarily of a developmental, promotional kind designed by LEAs to meet the MSC's funding criteria rather than allay the fears of the Chief Secretary to the Treasury that TVEI's contribution to employment policy was merely a 'gesture of faith'.[24]

This episode well illustrates the internal tensions of 1980s policies. By 1993, however, there are signs that policy is moving beyond the reactive, multi-purpose mode of the last 15 years and that the foundations of a strategic school-to-work education policy are emerging in England, Wales and Northern Ireland.[25] The main features of this new policy landscape are:

- the emergence of General National Vocational Qualifications (GNVQs) as a nationally recognised vocational learning route for young people from the age of 14/16;

- an acceptance that a national curriculum (in England and Wales) based upon a 'liberal', all-subject model to the age of 16 is too ambitious and that vocational education should be more widely available in school years 10 and 11 (ages 14–16);

- a continuing involvement of employers in schooling, designed to broaden the general curriculum, encourage staying on at the age of 16, and develop individual pupils' skills;

- the gradual acceptance that 'core skills' should form an integral component of the curriculum for all pupils over the age of 14.

This new agenda has already begun to influence employer involvement in education but its ramifications are, as yet, far from clear. In particular, a much greater understanding is required about the match of these educational developments to changes in the workplace utilisation of skills. Emerging policies for the consolidation of separate vocational and academic study routes for 14/16–19 year olds could, for example, have the consequence of reinforcing labour market demand for students destined for polarised, low skill and high skill occupations.[26]

In the meantime, however, the benefits of education-employer initiatives continue to appeal strongly to all parties in Britain in that they serve a number of specific interests:

- government secures, through employers, increased control over defining the purposes of, and funding conditions for, education;

- employers secure, through direct intervention in education, public relations benefits or the supply of specific skills;

- schools and colleges secure additional resources and new learning environments; and

- individual teachers and employees value the opportunity to trade expertise.

This balance of interests at home, coupled with the economic pressures which are driving education reform across western countries, seems likely to ensure that education-employer initiatives will remain a central plank of policy in Britain for the foreseeable future.

Notes and references

1 Finegold, D. (1992). *Breaking Out of the Low-Skill Equilibrium*. NCE Briefing No. 5; Finegold, D. (1992). *The Low-Skill Equilibrium: An Institutional Analysis of Britain's Education and Training Failure*. Unpublished D Phil. thesis, University of Oxford; McNabb, R. and Ryan, P. (1990). *Segmented*

Labour Markets. In: Sapsford, D. and Tzannotos, Z. (eds.), *Current Issues in Labour Economics.* Macmillan; Fiddy, R. (1985). *Youth, Unemployment and Training: A Collection of National Perspectives.* Falmer Press.
2 OECD (1984). *Industry and University – New Forms of Co-operation and Communication.* OECD. For Britain, see Sanderson, M. (1972). *The Universities and British Industry 1850–1970.* Routledge and Kegan Paul.
3 OECD (1985). *New Policies for the Young.* OECD. Japan, with its near universal participation in schooling to the age of 18, is a conspicuous exception to this trend.
4 For an analysis of the circumstances which have led to widespread education and training policy exchange between the USA and Britain, see Finegold, D., McFarland, L. and Richardson, W. (eds.), *Something Borrowed, Something Blue?* Oxford Studies in Comparative Education, Vols. 2(2), 1992 and 3(1) 1993 (Triangle Journals).
5 The best short survey is Reeder, D. (1979). *A Recurring Debate; Education and Industry.* In: Bernbaum, G. (ed.), *Schooling in Decline.* Macmillan.
6 Donoughue, B. (1987). *Prime Minister: the Conduct of Policy under Harold Wilson and James Callaghan.* Jonathan Cape; and Beck, J. (1983). *Accountability, Industry and Education.* In: Ahier, J. and Flude, M. (eds.), *Contemporary Education Policy.* Croom Helm.
7 See Plaskow, M. (ed., 1985). *Life and Death of the Schools Council.* Falmer Press.
8 Employment Department (1993). *Skills and Training in Small Firms.* Skills and Enterprise Briefing, No. 4/93.
9 Source: Finegold, D. and Richardson, W. (1991). *Making Education Our Business.* Centre for Education and Industry, University of Warwick.
10 DFE (1993). *Survey of School/Business Links.* Statistical Bulletin 10/93; OECD (1992). *Schools and Business: a New Partnership.* OECD.
11 Wiener, M. (1981). *English Culture and the Decline of the Industrial Spirit.* Cambridge University Press.
12 Chandler, G. (1988). *Changing the Culture.* In RSA Journal, Vol. 138.
13 Department of Trade and Industry (1988). *DTI – the Department for Enterprise.* Cm 278, HMSO; Hennessy, P. (1990). *Whitehall.* Fontana Press.
14 Finegold, D. (1993). *The Importance of the Institution: the Case of the Technical and Vocational Education Initiative.* In: Wellington, J. (ed.). *The Work-Related Curriculum: Challenging the Vocational Imperative.* Kogan Page.
15 The definitive statement of this tradition – in the form of an 'essay' – is DES (1977). *Curriculum 11–16.* The 'Red Book', DES; the current version – in the corporate language of its time and shorn of philosophical content – is National Curriculum Council (1990). *The Whole Curriculum.* NCC.
16 See: DFE (1992). *Technology for Ages 5 to 16.* DFE; and Bierhoff, H. and Prais, S. (1993). *Britain's Industrial Skills and the School-Teaching of Practical Subjects.* NIESR.
17 Foxman, D., Gorman, T. and Brooks, G. (1992). *Standards in Literacy and Numeracy.* NCE Briefing No. 10.
18 MacGuire, K. (1989). *Business Involvement in Education in the 1990s.* Journal of Education Policy, 4(5), pp. 107–117; Keep, E. *What Do Employers Want from Education? A Question More Easily Asked Than Answered.* University of Warwick [unpublished mimeo]; Wellington, J. (1993). *Fit for Work?*

Recruitment Processes and the 'Needs of Industry'. In: Wellington, J., *op cit*; Morgan, P. (1990). *Address to the IOD Annual Convention*. IOD, mimeo.

19 CBI: *Building a Stronger Partnership Between Business and Education* (1988); *Towards a Skills Revolution – Task Force Report* (1989); *Routes for Success – Careership: a Strategy for All 16–19 Year Old Learning* (1993).

20 See Richardson, W. (1993). *Employers as an Instrument of School Reform? Education-Business 'Compacts' in Britain and America.* In: *Something Borrowed, Something Blue?* Oxford Studies in Comparative Education, Vol. 3(1) (Triangle Journals).

21 See for example: Employment Department: *The Compact Development Handbook* (1989); *The Partnership Handbook* and *Partnerships in Education: A Toolkit for Evaluation* (1991). Institute of Manpower Studies (1993). *Progress in Partnership: Baseline Study*. Employment Department. In the United States, dissatisfaction with a similar chain of events has led employers to move from support for 'partnerships' with schools to campaign for more fundamental 'school restructuring'; see Richardson, W. (1994, forthcoming): *School-Business Partnerships*. In: *The International Encyclopedia of Education*. Pergamon Press.

22 Unwin, L. (1993, forthcoming). Training Credits: the Pilot Doomed to Succeed. In: Richardson, W. and others (eds.). *The Reform of Post-16 Education and Training in England and Wales*. Longman.

23 DES (1986). *City Technology Colleges: a New Choice of School*. DES; and (1992) *Choice and Diversity*. Cm 2021, HMSO.

24 Dale, R. and others (1990). *The TVEI Story: Policy, Practice and Preparation for the Workforce*. Open University Press. See also note 14.

25 Strategy in Scotland is being played out in response to the recommendations of the Howie Report (1992). *Upper Secondary Education in Scotland: Report of the Consultative Committee to Review Curriculum and Examinations in the Fifth and Sixth Years of Secondary Education in Scotland*. HMSO.

26 See Richardson, W. (1993). *The Changing Nature of Work: Responses for Education*. In: Wellington, J., *op cit*.

11. Measuring the Value of Education

Presentation by Professor David Ulph to the National Commission on Education, October 1992.

Introduction

The Commission's final report will contain recommendations for changes that should be made to our education system. Some changes will simply involve using existing resources in what we believe are better ways; some will be recommendations to reduce the amount of effort and resources we devote to some activities; but it seems likely that many recommendations will involve increases in resources. Unless we believe that we are making such a complete hash of our education system that we could bring about all the improvements we wish with no additional resources, it seems inevitable that taken together, the recommendations will involve a net overall increase in educational resources. So the question arises as to how we might justify this: how might we convince a sceptical government that the value of the additional benefits from the improvements is at least as great as the additional resource costs? Putting a cost on the changes is, in principle, fairly straightforward. But how do we value them?

I will start by setting out what I think can and cannot be usefully said about this question. I then want to suggest that this is not the most useful question to be considering and that there may be more fruitful ways of thinking about educational reform. Finally, I will indicate what I think are some important but relatively neglected issues in thinking about education over the next 25 years.

The rate of return to individuals

Human capital theory and rates of return
The area of economics which bears most directly on this issue is what is called *human capital theory*. This was initially developed to explain why occupations involving greater or longer amounts of education and training (such as lawyers or doctors) were paid more than those involving less (such as shopkeepers or factory workers). At its simplest, the idea is that, faced with a choice of alternative occupations, an individual capable of pursuing either will be willing to take the higher-training job only if it pays an additional income, which is sufficient to compensate for:

- any additional direct costs in terms of tuition fees;
- maintenance that might be required to gain the extra education;
- the income that could have been earned during the additional period of study, in an alternative job requiring less training over this additional period of education.

An alternative way of thinking about this is that the rate of return to an individual of additional education is the rate of interest which makes the value of the extra income from the education equal to the additional costs in terms of both direct costs plus foregone income.

If there were a sufficiently rich menu of clearly defined alternatives open to an individual, he or she would acquire education up to the point where the rate of return equalled the rate of interest he or she could earn on other assets. However, because education tends to come in lumpy amounts (secondary education, 3-year undergraduate degree, 1-year Master's etc.), and because there is a great deal of risk and uncertainty about the future income prospects (it is hard to know now how much an accountant will be paid in 30 years' time), the rate of return people obtain from education may differ from the rate of interest. Rates of return on education are what economists have in mind when talking about the value of education, and what they have spent a great deal of effort in trying to calculate.

There is no doubt that such an account of education is excessively crude. Researchers are well aware of this and the versions of the theory which are actually used are very sophisticated. This will be taken up later. Nevertheless, despite its simplicity, this viewpoint gives some very useful insights.

Variations in the rate of return
There is no such thing as *the* rate of return on education. Rates of return will vary with the type of education being discussed. So they will vary with the level or stage of education we are considering, whether secondary education, undergraduate degree or postgraduate degree. They are also likely to vary by type of education: for example, it could depend on the particular subjects studied at either school or FE institute. The enormous disparity in demand by students to study science and engineering compared to economics or business studies illustrates how rates of return might vary by type of subject. They are also likely to vary greatly across individuals, for a variety of reasons (such as ability or background), so that some will gain more from particular additions to their education than others. Moreover these last two dimensions in which rates of return vary interact, so that one individual can get a higher rate of return from studying science than languages, while for another the ranking is reversed. Finally, rates of return will also vary across time. Since one of the costs of education is foregone income, in times of recession when employment prospects are lower, rates of return will increase. So, for example, demand for MSc courses in economics has successively doubled in each of the last two years.

As an illustration of these points, consider Table 1, giving some of the most recent UK estimates of rates of return from different levels of post-compulsory education to young people from different family backgrounds.

Table 1: Expected private real rates of return (per cent) by father's socio-economic group.

	Professional/ employer/ manager	Intermediate/ junior non-manual	Skilled/ semi-skilled manual	Unskilled manual	Overall sample
Males:					
A Levels	10.41	−0.25	5.78	−0.90	6.04
Higher Education	4.00	7.95	6.10	25.10	7.08
Females:					
A Levels	4.85	15.32	10.59	13.49	9.80
Higher Education	6.28	5.15	5.33	8.42	5.84

Source: Bennett, R. et al (1992). *Learning Should Pay*. LSE.

These estimates reveal quite striking differences. Thus a boy coming from an unskilled manual background staying on to get A levels would not, on past experience, improve his earning prospects sufficiently to offset the earnings foregone by leaving school before getting A levels. However, if he could get to university, a dramatic improvement in prospects may be provided. For boys coming from a professional background, getting A levels is important for the kinds of jobs into which they would typically go, those which pay good salaries. Consequently for these people the additional improvement in earnings from getting a university education is not so great, so their rate of return from university education is lower than for the previous group. For girls this pattern is reversed. Those from professional backgrounds have a higher return from university education than from A levels, while those from other backgrounds gain more from A levels than from university education.

So when economists talk about measuring *the* rate of return from a particular type of education they are either talking about the rate of return to a specific type of person at a particular time or some kind of average across some sample of individuals over some period of time.

Obsolescence of human capital
The earning ability that individuals acquire through the combination of their own talents and the education and

training they receive can be viewed as their *human capital*. Although in the simplest version of the theory it is assumed that this capital is acquired either before or during the early stages of an individual's working life, it is important to recognise that, like all capital, it is subject to both decay (loss of physical and mental agility) and, more importantly, obsolescence as new types of skills and knowledge become required and older ones are made redundant. This implies that, not only may an individual have to go through many periods of education and training, but also, the anticipation of the potential future obsolescence of particular skills will be a factor taken into account in determining what types of education to acquire.

A wider concept of value
In the view outlined above, the value of education is reflected in the additional earnings required to compensate for the direct and indirect (foregone income) costs of education. Of course no one believes anything so simple-minded, and economists are aware that the value of education to an individual is more wide-ranging. Amongst the additional factors that have to be recognised are that:

(1) Individuals receiving more education may not necessarily get jobs which pay a great deal more whilst in employment – but it may give access to jobs with greater employment security.

(2) Individuals receiving more education may get access to jobs which are more attractive in many ways which are not reflected in the salary. So, for example, the rate of return from a PhD as calculated in the simple-minded fashion above can turn out to be negative. But this just reflects the fact that most people doing PhDs end up in academia, which was never the way to make a fortune but certainly used to offer a relatively comfortable income coupled with attractive job features, such as considerable opportunity to pursue one's own research interests.

(3) Education may confer benefits which are entirely unrelated to employment. It may enhance the ability to enjoy literature, art, scientific discovery, travel or food. We can all no doubt think of endless such ways in which education may benefit people.

Two important points now arise. First, the feature of the benefits referred to in (2) and (3) is that they are non-pecuniary: they are not measured in monetary terms, and would never be reflected in conventional pecuniary measures of economic well-being such as GNP. This does not mean that economists are either unaware of them or that they ignore them. Nor does their existence mean that rates of return measures of education are necessarily wrong. So, for example, if the ratio of non-pecuniary to pecuniary benefits from education was the same for all types or amounts of education, and if the direct costs of education were trivial compared to the indirect foregone costs (both pecuniary and non-pecuniary), then a conventional rate of return calculation based on purely pecuniary factors would give almost precisely the true rate of return that included both pecuniary and non-pecuniary benefits. Of course neither of the above assumptions is likely to be correct. If tuition and other direct costs of education are non-trivial, then ignoring the non-pecuniary benefits of education will mean that the conventional pecuniary calculations will certainly underestimate the true rate of return. Likewise if the ratio of non-pecuniary to pecuniary benefits were to increase with the level of education.

Secondly, a distinction is sometimes drawn between education as a consumption good and education as an investment good. It is also sometimes thought that the purely employment-related benefits such as earnings and those factors included in (1) and (2) above are what is included in the investment aspects of education, whilst the consumption good aspects of education incorporate the sort of benefits referred to in (3). However, this is a mistake. Investment involves using current resources for *future* benefits even if they are non-pecuniary, and even if they accrue almost immediately (such as the pleasures of being able to swim or read which start as soon as the skill is acquired). So all the benefits of education discussed so far are investment benefits. Consumption benefits of education are any benefits which arise *directly* from the process of education. Obvious ones are enjoyments such as participating in club activities, acting in plays, and playing in orchestras or sports teams. Of course these 'benefits' can be negative.

Clearly much of the attention focuses on the investment benefits of education, but it is important not to ignore the consumption benefits. There are also important questions about the link between investment and consumption benefits of education, for example, the classification of play in primary education.

Who is the individual?

At this point it might be worth briefly mentioning another question: to whom do the private benefits of education accrue? It might seem obvious that it is the person being educated, but that is far from clear. In dealing with schooling and also higher education (HE), it is clear that the parents of the person being educated also have an important interest in the amount and type of education being received. In particular, for very young children we know that the work decisions of the family, in particular the wife, depend critically on whether or not the child is attending nursery school. To a greater or lesser extent, parents also have a say in educational decisions. How much of a say depends in part on how the educational system is organised and financed: for example, parents may have more of a say if they are paying fees directly. There is no correct answer to the question of who the consumer really is. We have to recognise that there are many people with an interest. As the government passes more of the educational decision back to 'the individual' it is going to have to be clearer who that individual is.

Limitations to the theory

We have seen that the *human capital* approach to education sees people as choosing the amount of education to acquire by trading off potential future benefits (both pecuniary and non-pecuniary) against the costs of education, both direct (tuition fees) and indirect (foregone earnings). The theory cannot attach any absolute measure to the value of education, but can try to help us calculate the rate of return which measures the return these benefits yield on the costs. At its simplest level the theory can appear quite crude, but it can be made quite sophisticated, and while the measures we actually obtain are obviously based on limited considerations, it is not obvious that they are systematically biased.

However, there are some obvious limitations of the theory. It depends on there being some *choice*, so it is of limited use when trying to value education of people who have limited choice. Those below compulsory school age have little choice about the quantity of education they receive, but, depending on how the education system is organised, may have some choice over quality, such as what subjects they can study. It also depends on individuals making quite sophisticated decisions under conditions of considerable uncertainty – who knows what the real incomes of various occupations are likely to be in 30 years' time? That is not in itself a problem, because we just have to think of individuals making some estimate of the future based on the information available to them. But it does mean that how well the education system works will depend in part on how well people make these forecasts as well as on what resources and opportunities for education are made available.

As the theory stands there is no necessary implication that education in any sense produces these additional earnings (or other benefits) that the individual receives. Rather these benefits have to be present to persuade the individual to acquire the education. Thus the theory just deals with the *supply side* of educated people. To complete the picture we would have to turn to the *demand side* and say why employers were willing to pay higher earnings to people with more education. At its simplest we could think of education as a process which simply gives individuals certain skills which employers value, and the higher earnings attached to greater education is just a reflection of the value to future employers of these extra skills. An alternative view is that education doesn't change or augment people's skills, it just acts as a screening process for identifying those skills and labelling them for the purposes of future employers. These views are not mutually exclusive, and the extent to which education plays either of these roles will vary across individuals and types of education. Moreover it is not correct to say that the 'skill augmentation' view of education necessarily makes education more valuable than the 'screening' view. Both aspects are valuable to both individuals and society.

The social rate of return

A theoretical background
This brings me to the distinction between the private or individual rate of return of education and the social rate of return. Let us imagine a world without externalities (that is, no way in which the acquisition of education by individuals conferred direct benefits on others). If, in such a world, wages correctly reflected the value of jobs, and capital or insurance markets worked well, the social value of the education acquired by all the individuals in a society would just be the sum of the individual values.

In such an idealised world in which markets worked perfectly there would be no reason why, on efficiency grounds, governments should intervene in the provision of education and shouldn't just let individuals make their own decisions, co-ordinated through the market. Of course, no-one seriously believes this, and, for the reasons discussed below, the private returns perceived by individuals could well differ from the social return, thus justifying some form of government intervention.

Nevertheless this idealised view is useful for clarifying a number of issues. First, the fact that some of the benefits of education are non-pecuniary does not affect arguments about the distinction between private and social rates of return.

Secondly, it is sometimes thought that the fact that education may increase an individual's productivity, and so make him better able to produce goods and services which other people value, constitutes an externality which justifies public provision. Thus it is sometimes argued that if we had more engineers and scientists, a better educated workforce and better trained managers, British industry would be more productive and so there would be more goods and services for everyone to consume, and that this justifies spending more on education. But if this additional education really is beneficial, it should be reflected in the additional wages for acquiring skills and so should lead people to choose to get more education. Thus, in principle, all these additional benefits should get fully reflected in private calculations, and there is no real externality involved. The importance of this point is that just finding a link between education and GNP does not necessarily imply that there is some extra benefit from education which is being incorrectly taken account of in individual calculations.

Thirdly, it is often reported that the private rate of return to education is higher than the social rate of return. But this arises because the calculation of the private rate of return incorporates the fact that, in most Western economies, tuition costs are very heavily subsidised, whereas, of course, society still has to incur these. However, this subsidy is often a reflection of other social benefits from education not taken account of by individuals, and so is an attempt by governments to bring the social and private calculus into line with one another. What we need to investigate are the more fundamental features of education which could give rise to a divergence between private and social returns.

Finally, the important implication of the idealised view is that it shifts thinking away from the question of the value of education and how this compares with the cost, to the question of whether the social return might differ from the private returns (whatever those might be) and what kind of policy implications any such deviation might have. This is important because the former question is pretty hard to answer, while we might be able to say a bit more about the latter. Let me now turn to this.

Education policy implications for government

I want to start by running pretty quickly through a number of fairly standard arguments about government intervention in the provision of education. I do not want to spend a lot of time on them because they are probably fairly well agreed upon, and their implications are broadly accepted. I will then turn to a discussion of some potentially more controversial but interesting issues.

Externalities

One reason why private and social returns might differ is the presence of externalities: we may all benefit from living in a better educated society. So, for example, it is sometimes argued that a better educated society may make better political choices, and so lead to the pursuit of improved government policy from which we all benefit. Alternatively, education may make society more socially cohesive by giving people a better understanding of their own and others' history and culture. Finally, it is sometimes argued that education promotes cultural continuity, since, by teaching people about their culture, it keeps it alive, and so makes it available for future generations.

If we set aside specific public information campaigns on particular topics (such as AIDS), then while it is hard to deny the potential for general education to provide such benefits, it seems clear that the link between education and all these alleged benefits is at best problematic. It is equally hard to be convinced that beyond a certain point there is a great connection at either the individual or social level between the amount of education received and the quality of public decisions and behaviour. These advantages would seem to depend more on the content of what is taught, or how it is taught. So while there may be a case for government prescribing what should be in the curriculum, these arguments do not in themselves lead to a strong case for government provision of education. It is also clear that there is a great deal of sensitivity about how far education should get involved in inculcating particular moral views.

Market failures
It is useful to distinguish between general education and specific training. General education is the imparting of skills that can be widely used in many contexts, while specific training is the imparting of skills that can be used in only a very specific context or employment. The distinction is really one of degree rather than kind: there is very little knowledge other than, for example, the layout of a particular workplace that will not be of some relevance in another context. Moreover, the distinction is not the same as that between academic and vocational education, though academic education is more likely to be general while specific training is fairly inevitably vocational. There are clearly important connections between education and training: the greater or better the general education a person has, the easier it might be to give specific training. I will take this point up again below.

However, the distinction is important because on the whole employers have very little incentive to provide a general education to their workforce – they incur the costs but may find it hard to recover the benefits. This suggests that it is really up to individuals who directly benefit from a general education to acquire it themselves. But then there are various reasons why, left to market forces and their own decisions, they may not acquire the 'right' amount; for example, the failure of capital markets to provide the right kind of insurance or loan arrangements in the face of very incomplete information about the benefits of education.

There are other potential capital market failures. Since education is an investment decision, the rate of interest is crucial in determining decisions about how much to acquire. It is often argued that, for various reasons, individuals are too short-term in their decisions, and discount the future too heavily, thus undervaluing education. Moreover, if a combination of tax and other policies encourages individuals to believe they can earn a high rate of return by, say, investing in property, this will discourage them from investing in education.

As an illustration of these points, consider again the evidence in Table 1. If these estimates of rates of return to education are correct, then it suggests that boys from professional backgrounds are facing no difficulties in getting access to HE and are investing in it up to the point where the real rate of return is around the real long-run rate of interest. However, the figure for boys from unskilled manual backgrounds suggests that they are facing problems getting access to university education, since their rate of return is way above the real long-run rate of interest. So even if one does not believe that rate of return calculations measure the true value of education, these figures show how the calculations can be used to inform discussion about market failures.

Finally, the recent discussion has been in terms of market failures which relate primarily to efficiency considerations in resource allocation. There are also important equity considerations to be taken on board. These can often conflict with efficiency, and quite a few of the shifts in education policy have, at their heart, an attempt to change the balance between these conflicting aims.

Applications to education

Schooling
The above considerations taken together are generally acknowledged to provide a case for government provision of primary and secondary schooling, not necessarily in the sense

that schools must be in the public sector, but that at least the government should meet the costs of an individual acquiring a basic primary and secondary education.

Having acknowledged this, there are many detailed issues over the nature of primary and secondary education that need to be taken into account: how broad or narrow the curriculum should be; how much individual choice there should be and the potential role of a national curriculum. As far as I am aware there are no comprehensive studies of rates of return to different types of secondary education that could provide us with much guidance on these questions.

Higher education
What is less clear-cut is what these arguments have to say about the provision of post-secondary education, in particular, higher education. For the same kinds of reasons as for general education, it is clear that fundamental research is not likely to be an activity that is well provided by the private market, and there is broad acceptance that governments should fund this. An important aspect of undertaking research is producing the next generation of researchers, so there is a case for government funding of research degrees. There is clearly also a gain to disseminating new knowledge quickly, though, in the absence of market failures, it is far from clear that these gains are not generally private, and captured through private returns. However, given the complementary nature of teaching and research, it seems that the best teachers of new material might be the researchers. So we arrive at a concept of universities whose role is the creation and dissemination of fundamental research, some of whose funding comes from the government for the research or research training role, and the rest of whose activities are largely involved in providing teaching whose returns are largely private.

In terms of the issues involved, the rest of the HE system then falls into essentially this teaching role of the universities. As we saw when the Government tried to get private banks to administer a student loan scheme, there are still problems associated with capital market failures that will limit the ability of private institutions or individuals to fully realise the private gains, but what we get then are arguments to do with how governments can correct these failures, which leads us to the debate over what form of finance system is appropriate. Issues of first principle do not get you much further here, and the discussion has to get down to the technical details of the merits of various procedures (for example, student loans or student grants recouped through a graduate tax) for correcting market failures.

There are also many important issues to do with the role of the kind of quasi-markets in HE that the Government has created and how well they can ensure the quality and variety of HE that might be required. These issues are not confined to HE and arise at the primary and secondary levels as well. However, discussing those would take us beyond the scope of this paper.

Applications to training

Acquisition of training

There are two ways in which individuals might acquire training. The first is by having their employer provide it directly. The cost of this could then be recouped by the firm by paying wages that were lower than was fully reflected in the productivity of the workers. If training genuinely increased productivity by more than the cost of the training, then the firm could afford to pay workers a wage higher than they could have got without training. So if individuals were faced with a choice between two jobs, one of which offered training and one which didn't, they would choose the job with training. However, these need not be the only options on offer, particularly if we recognise that almost all training will involve imparting skills that will be of use to other employers. Thus if a firm came along that offered wages to trained workers that fully reflected their higher productivity, workers would have an incentive to join the firm that offered training, quit after receiving it, and join a firm paying even higher wages. Unless the firm that offers training can fully recoup the training costs during the period of training, the potential poaching of trained workers will lead to a failure of training provision by employers. This leaves the alternative that employees directly pay the fees for training. There are then interesting questions as to who provides it, whether it is still employers, or whether it is specialist firms or institutions that specialise in providing training.

Training policy issues for government
An important policy issue, then, is how these tuition fees are treated for tax purposes. If they are not deductible against income tax then the fact that the rewards from training are taxed could lead to a reluctance of individuals to get trained. However, that is not in itself a reason for making the costs tax-deductible, because income tax reduces the return to all areas of labour supply, and it is not clear why training should be specifically exempt. One argument could be that the training decision is much more sensitive to taxes than other aspects of labour supply. We don't have much evidence on this.

So training gives rise to important policy issues for government. The rapid speed of change suggests that successful economies are going to need a high degree of mobility of workers between occupations. But this gives rise to potential problems if the mobility is between employers. Thought has to be given to how to reconcile these.

The link between education provision and training
In the idealised view in which prices work wonders, any benefits that acquiring an education will give rise to when subsequently taking up specific training should get reflected in the appropriate prices. So the fact that acquiring a certain amount or type of education may enhance an individual's subsequent capacity to benefit from training does not give rise to an externality, any more than the fact that taking certain

kinds of food and drink in combination mutually reinforces their enjoyment. We take it that this all gets internalised, in more ways than one. However, if there are market failures that give rise to state provision of education free of charge, then some of these signals are missing, and so the amount and type of education being provided does have external effects which should be taken account of when designing education provision. This is clearly a key policy issue. This does not mean that education should be tailored to the needs of training, far less it should duplicate the kind of work that training should cover. On the other hand it does imply that secondary education should not be designed solely with the interests of HE in mind.

Some further issues

What I have given is a fairly standard treatment of some of the key reasons why private and social returns may differ, and their policy implications. I will finish with a less frequently discussed set of issues which have recently surfaced.

The importance of innovation

An important set of market failures are those arising from imperfect competition – the ability of firms to get excessive profits by charging prices above costs. To be able to do this firms need to operate in markets in which they face little competition. With the general breaking down of barriers to trade, this lack of competition can only really arise if firms have a technical superiority which gives them access to some product or technology to which their rivals have no access. Of course any such superiority will be quickly dissipated as rivals imitate or succeed in their own technological developments. Thus the ability to earn rents from the world market can only fundamentally arise if firms continually innovate ahead of their rivals. The profits from this give rise to greater GNP. There are many factors that contribute to this ability to dominate world markets through continual innovation, but access to a highly trained workforce is almost certainly one of them (though, as indicated above, the ability to retain that workforce is another). As governments become more limited in their ability to use trade restrictions to protect their industries and give them competitive advantage, attention will focus on the more fundamental determinants of market success, and hence on how governments might give their firms access to more highly trained labour. Thus education and training will become an issue of strategic economic competition.

It might seem that this is an argument for more generous educational subsidies, though we know very little about what particular types of skills we need to promote to generate educational advantage. This would certainly be true if labour were internationally immobile. However, great care is required here, for if labour is highly mobile internationally, then an educational subsidy is positively harmful since it simply provides rival firms with a cheap source of trained manpower. Just how mobile labour is internationally is hard to determine, so it is not clear just what is the correct policy. Nevertheless, whatever the precise policy conclusion, the link between the educational policies of a country and its ability to gain technological advantage is likely to become an area of intense policy interest.

International mobility
If we are looking ahead over the next 25 years or so, it seems fairly safe to assume that one of the major trends will be the increasing international mobility of production and of workers. The implications of this for how we think about education, particularly at the post-secondary level, are potentially profound. For example, we need to think about whether, if we give grants to 'UK' students, they should be required to study at UK universities. If students get grants and then go and work abroad, we may not be able to recoup the cost of the grant through a graduate tax. This could shift the balance of the argument in favour of student loans. If there is to be

harmonisation of EC taxes, should there also be harmonisation of their schemes for provision of HE? When individuals can go and work abroad, what is the obligation of the UK government to provide them with some kind of subsidised education? Put differently, whose gains from education are we adding up when trying to arrive at the social return from education? Should we be encouraging international competition amongst universities and other HE institutions for the market in trainable youth, and if so, how will these institutions continue to operate and be funded?

These are perhaps somewhat rarefied concerns that only operate for a very small percentage of people passing through education. But they signal a more profound shift away from the view that education is training 'our' young people to work in 'our' economy, and its implications need to be taken on board.

Conclusions

There is no question that education provides great benefits to both individuals and society, in ways that go far beyond simply equipping them with skills that will be useful in earning a living, important though that is. However, the mere fact that it provides such benefits does not automatically lead to conclusions that it has to be provided by government. Rather than trying to determine just how valuable education is, we may often get a better guide to policy by asking if there are reasons to think that the value placed on it by individuals is an incorrect reflection of its true value to society. I think that in the area of further education and training this is a particularly fruitful approach.

Finally, it is important to stress that I have been talking about the provision of education solely in terms of the question of who finances education, and solely in terms of how many resources go into education. I haven't said anything about how resource allocation decisions are to be taken, whether through state schools or universities or some other form of more or less independent private schools or universities. That is, I have focused on arguments about the quantity of resources going into education rather than about the efficiency with which those resources are used. It is important to stress that not only is the way in which resource allocation is to take place an equally important (and increasingly topical) dimension of the issue of where one draws the boundary of state responsibility for education, but that it is almost logically independent of where one draws the boundary on the financial issue.

However, just as in the case of funding, there are many bad arguments used in this debate, but it would take another paper to go through these.

II

Learning and Achievement

12. Is There Still An Untapped Pool of Ability?

Note by Professor Andrew McPherson to the Research Committee of the National Commission on Education, December 1992.

The question

I was asked by the Research Committee whether there were evidence that there is still an untapped 'pool of ability'. This note is an attempt to respond to that question using some of the key research findings principally from the United Kingdom (UK).

The Robbins Report operationalised the question in terms of the differing achievements of pupils/students who had the same prior ability, but who differed in terms of social characteristics (social class, sex, area, country or school type).[1] A more general formulation could ask whether pupils/students with the same attainment at time 1 diverged in attainment at time 2, for whatever reason. An even more general formulation would be whether the spread of attainments increases as people get older, again for whatever reason. Here the focus is on whether or not people progress at the same rate, irrespective of whether they had the same ability or attainment at time 1. The claim would be that divergence in rates of progress indicates untapped ability. Robbins was primarily concerned with the 'ability' to benefit from higher education and complete a degree. This note does not concern itself either with the greater diversity of abilities that such a definition might now imply, nor with the 'tapping' of ability for purposes other than those of education as we currently know it.

Types of evidence

Several sorts of evidence are relevant:

- longitudinal studies of individuals in the UK, all having some measure of prior ability or attainment – of these, the nationally representative studies are less up-to-date than local studies;

- studies of outcomes for adult or pupil populations across time, measuring final outcome and social characteristics, but not initial ability/attainment;

- international comparisons of final achievement levels of comparable social groups;

- action research and evaluation studies.

The evidence from the first type of study is probably strongest, but the three other types all add to the argument.

Longitudinal studies of individuals in the UK
The following types of longitudinal studies are available:

- National birth cohorts:
  1936 Scotland (Maxwell 1969;[2] Hope 1984[3])
  1946 Britain: (Douglas 1964;[4] Douglas, Ross and Simpson 1968[5])
  1958 Britain: National Child Development Study (NCDS) (Davie, Butler and Goldstein 1972[6])
  1970 Britain: Child Health and Education Study (CHES) (Butler, Golding and Howlett 1986[7]).

All have 'prior' ability/attainment measures, but only Douglas and NCDS are fully publicly reported, and even they are dated. CHES publications at present cover progress only to 5 years of age, though further analysis is currently under way at the Social Statistics Research Unit of City University.

- National year group/cohorts:

Is There Still An Untapped Pool of Ability? 159

Northern Ireland: Northern Ireland Council for Educational Research – at 11 years[8]
England and Wales: Youth Cohort Study (YCS) – at 16 years[9]
Scotland: Scottish Young People's Survey (SYPS) – at final compulsory year (approximately age 16).[10]

The YCS and SYPS studies have no measures of prior ability, and their first measures of prior attainment are at 16 years. But they are up to date.

- Local authority year-group cohorts:
Inner London Education Authority (ILEA) (various);[11]
Other English (various);[12]
Scotland: Fife.[13]

All these studies have test data at 11 or 12 years, plus gender and age. Some ILEA data also have ethnic group. Only Fife has data on socio-economic status as well as prior attainment/ability.

- Examples of other cohort studies:
Fifteen Thousand Hours: a study of 12 inner-London comprehensive schools[14]
School Matters: a study of 50 inner-London primary schools[15]
The School Effect: a study of 20 multi-racial, urban comprehensive schools.[16]

Studies of outcomes for adult or pupil populations across time:
The Oxford Mobility study[17]
The Nuffield/SCPR Election Studies[18]
Scottish cohorts from 1948 to the present.[19,20]

International studies reported by:
The International Educational Achievement (IEA) programme;
The Organisation for Economic Co-operation and Development (OECD).[21]

Action research and evaluation studies:
For example, studies of schemes to promote access to higher education.

The arguments

Taking the four main types of study in reverse order, we can work through the types of arguments they support:

Action research and evaluation studies

- Unpublished figures for Scotland demonstrate that students admitted to higher education by *non*-traditional means (and often from non-traditional backgrounds) have high success rates.

- Mature students do well.[22]

- Quality pre-school provision boosts attainment (see for example Osborn and Milbank, 1987).[23]

International studies

- Other countries do better, but there is no reason to think that UK ability is lower.

- Scotland 'graduates' a higher proportion of its population than England and Wales.

Studies of outcomes for adult or pupil populations across time
Social-class relativities in educational outcomes have been fairly constant this century both in England and Wales[24,25] and in Scotland.[26,27] This is circumstantial evidence for the persistence of untapped ability, but it is not conclusive because attainment in later cohorts is also higher. The persistence of social-class relativities could, therefore, be consistent with a model in which each social class was today at, or much closer than previously to, some notional ceiling of attainment.

However, such a model does not seem convincing. We know from national cohort studies that such relativities were evidence of untapped ability in earlier cohorts (see next section). (The Oxford Mobility study[28] reaches similar conclusions by modelling educational attainment using ability data from other studies.)

We also know from contemporary cohort studies that social class affects outcomes for pupils of similar ability or prior attainment. Thus the evidence that social-class relativities among today's young people are of the same order as in earlier cohorts can still be read as evidence of untapped ability. We can say this even though our most up-to-date nationally representative studies (the Youth Cohort Study and the Scottish Young People's Survey) lack measures of prior attainment/ability before 16 years.

Longitudinal studies of individuals in the UK
The older national studies are reasonably well known. The more recent non-national studies furnish a consistent picture of cumulative and sustained social and school effects on progress for pupils of similar prior attainment/ability. Typically, social factors associated with disadvantage depress average attainment at school.

Piecing some of this evidence together, we find the following:

Primary

- School and social-class effects on progress between 8 years and 12 years in Fife in the late 1970s;[29]

- School and social-class effects on progress in reading and writing.[30,31]

Secondary

- School and social-class effects on progress in secondary school between the first year and 16 years of age in Scotland[32,33] and between the second year and 16 years of age in England and Wales;[34]

- School effects on progress between 11 and 16 years in various LEAs in England and Wales;[35,36]

- School and social-class effects on progress after 16 years both in England and Wales[37] and in Scotland.[38,39]

The issues

Threats to validity
One threat to the validity of this interpretation of the evidence is underspecification of the variables, and especially of prior ability/attainment. Variations in progress between social groups at a fixed level of prior ability/attainment could arise solely from unmeasured ability/prior attainment that is correlated both with the social groups and with the outcome measure. Where does the onus of proof lie?

Underspecification is closely related to the problem of 'counterfactuals': namely, we can never be certain that an individual, given a change in circumstance (such as social class), would behave according to the new circumstances rather than the old. Nor can we be certain that a change in one circumstance would not alter other relevant circumstances, but in unanticipated ways.

Cumulative effects
I do not know of a published study that measures the cumulative effect of school membership or social group from the first year of primary school to the end of secondary education (but Sammons, Nuttall and Cuttance planned such a study).

Social-group effects on prior attainment/ability
Most studies show cumulative social-group effects on attainment and all studies show correlations between social class and the earliest measures of ability or attainment. Any estimate of the size of an 'untapped pool' is likely therefore to be an underestimate.

Education's own boost to attainment
Other things being equal, better-educated parents have higher-attaining offspring. This relationship has remained stable as the proportions of better-educated parents have themselves risen over a decade or so.[40,41] Education can itself boost the capabilities of a population.

Conclusion

Putting the four types of argument together, I reach the same sorts of conclusions that Robbins reached 30 years ago, namely that:

- Pool of ability calculations are 'extremely artificial',[42] and

- There is untapped educational potential among pupils that can be exploited for the foreseeable future.

However, the language of 'pool of ability' could be counter-productive. It might be preferable to adopt a more general formulation focusing attention on *realising all abilities to the full*.

References

1 Committee on Higher Education (1963). The Robbins Report. HMSO, Appendix 1. Cmnd 2154-1.
2 Maxwell, J. (1969). *Sixteen Years On*. University of London Press.
3 Hope, K. (1984). *As Others See Us: Schooling and Social Mobility in Scotland and the United States*. Cambridge University Press.
4 Douglas, J.W.B. (1964). *The Home and the School*. MacGibbon and Kee.
5 Douglas, Ross and Simpson (1968). *All Our Future*. Peter Davies.
6 Davie, R., Butler, N.R. and Goldstein, H. (1972). *From Birth to Seven: A Report of the National Child Development Study*. Longman.
7 Butler, N.R., Golding, J. and Howlett, B. (1986). *From Birth to Five: A Study of the Health and Behaviour of Britain's 5 year olds*. Pergamon Press.
8 Daly, P. (1991). 'How Large are Secondary School Effects in Northern Ireland?' School Effectiveness and School Improvement, 2(4) pp. 305–323.
9 Employment Department/Manpower Services Commission (various dates), England and Wales Youth Cohort Study. Reports 1–22.
10 Raffe, D. (ed.) (1988). *Education and the Youth Labour Market*. Falmer.
11 Nuttall, D.L., Goldstein, H., Prosser, R. and Rasbash, J. (1989). '*Differential*

School Effectiveness'. International Journal of Educational Research 13, pp. 769–776.
12. Gray, J., Jesson, D. and Sime, N. (1990). *'Estimating Differences in the Examination Performances of Secondary Schools in Six LEAs: A Multi-Level Approach to School Effectiveness'*. Oxford Review of Education, 16(2), pp. 137–158.
13. Willms, J.D. (1992). *Monitoring School Performance*. Falmer.
14. Rutter, M. and others (1979). *Fifteen Thousand Hours*. Open Books.
15. Mortimore, P. and others (1988). *School Matters: The Junior Years*. Open Books.
16. Smith and Tomlinson (1989). *The School Effect. A Study of Multi-Racial Comprehensives*. Policy Studies Institute.
17. Halsey, A.H., Heath, A.F. and Ridge, J.M. (1980). *Origins and Destinations: Family, Class and Education in Modern Britain*. Clarendon Press.
18. Heath, A.F. and Clifford, P. (1990). *'Class Inequalities in Education in the Twentieth Century'*. Journal of the Royal Statistical Society, A, 153(1) pp. 1–16.
19. Gray, J., McPherson, A.F. and Raffe, D. (1983). *Reconstructions of Secondary Education: Theory, Myth and Practice Since the War*. Routledge.
20. Paterson, L.J. (1992). *'Social Origins of Under-Achievement Among School Leavers.'* In: Maguiness, H. (ed.). Educational Opportunity: The Challenge of Under-Achievement and Social Deprivation. Paisley College Local Government Centre, pp. 4–16.
21. For example: Foxman, D. (1992). *Learning Mathematics & Science. The Second International Assessment of Educational Progress in England*. NFER; OECD (1992). *Education at a Glance*.
22. Smithers, A. and Griffin, A. (1986). *The Progress of Mature Students*. Joint Matriculation Board.
23. Osborn, A. F. and Milbank, J.E. (1987). *The Effects of Early Education: A Report from the Child Health and Education Study*. Clarendon Press.
24. Halsey, A.H., Heath, A.F. and Ridge, J.M. (1980), *op cit*.
25. Heath, A.F. and Clifford, P. (1990), *op cit*.
26. Gray, J. and others (1983), *op cit*, chapter 12.
27. Paterson, L.J. (1992), *op cit*.
28. Halsey, A.H., Heath, A.F. and Ridge, J.M. (1980), *op cit*, chapters 4 and 8.
29. Bondi, E. (1991). *'Attainment at Primary Schools: An Analysis of Variations Between Schools.'* British Educational Research Journal, 17(3), pp. 203–217.
30. Mortimore, P. and others (1988), *op cit*, chapters 7 and 9.
31. Sammons, P., Nuttall, D. and Cuttance, P. (in press). *'Differential School Effectiveness.'* British Educational Research Journal.
32. Willms, J.D. (1992), *op cit*.
33. Paterson, L.J. (1992), *op cit*.
34. Smith and Tomlinson (1989), *op cit*, chapter 17.
35. Gray, J. and others (1990), *op cit*.
36. Nuttall, D. and others (1990), *op cit*.
37. Jesson, D. and Gray, J. (1990). *'Access, Entry and Potential Demand for Higher Education Amongst 18–19-year-olds in England and Wales'*. Research and Development, 60. Training Agency.
38. Paterson, L.J. (1991). *'Socio-Economic Status and Educational Attainment: A*

Multi-Dimensional and Multi-Level Study'. Evaluation and Research in Education, 5(3), pp. 97–121.
39 Paterson, L.J. (1992), *op cit*.
40 Burnhill, P., Garner, C. and McPherson, A.F. (1990). *'Parental Education, Social Class and Entry to Higher Education.'* Journal of the Royal Statistical Society, A, 153(2), pp. 233–248.
41 Jesson, D. and Gray, J. (1990), *op cit*.
42 Committee on Higher Education (1963), *op cit*. Appendix 1, Part III, paragraph 27.

13. Thinking Differently About Education

Extracts from a Speech by Professor Charles Handy to a Symposium organised by the America-European Community Association Trust in conjunction with the National Commission on Education, 'Education: Direction of Future Policies' (Leeds Castle, Kent, 19–21 March 1993).[1]

Workers not products

We have got to stop thinking of our students as products. I once did a study of schools as organisations. I said that the perfect model for the school was a factory; the only trouble was that the students were not the workers, but the products – raw material going through various processes, stamped, inspected for quality, with only certified goods going out. What we failed to do was to recycle the rejects.

What an exciting thing it is to see schools where the students are actually treated as the workers, not the products; where they work in groups, solving problems and looking to the 'managers' for resources, help and some instruction.

Higher education for all?

We have talked about higher education for 30%, perhaps for 40% of our people; why not 100%? I would love to see society say to every young person at age eighteen: here is a bond, a guarantee that we will pay your fees up to a certain amount per year for, say, two years, at any recognised institution at any time in your life. And I would like another bond which says: we will guarantee you two years' work at a relatively basic wage in a variety of institutions which we as brokers will find. You can cash that in too at any time. But we will not give you any welfare unless you have cashed in those two bonds, because society will invest in you whoever you are, but you must do something in return.

Learning abroad

I would also like every child in Europe at the age of thirteen to spend at least one semester in a school in another country. It wouldn't cost anything except the travel. This should not just be for a few privileged children but for everybody. If you want to understand that your nation is part of something bigger, you have to live abroad and do it early.

Multiple intelligences

I want us to understand that everybody is intelligent; it is just that they are intelligent in different ways. Howard Gardner lists seven 'multiple intelligences'. I would list around ten: factual, linguistic, analytical, spatial, practical, musical, physical, intuitive, inter-personal; the list goes on. The point is that some of us are lucky enough to have four or five intelligences; I believe that everybody has at least one, and the primary job of education is to find out what that one is, and to foster it, because then at least you will feel that you have capabilities and have something to contribute. We send half of our children out of school feeling that they are basically stupid.

The cycle of discovery

You will know about the cycle of discovery: it starts with curiosity and is followed by ideas, trial, review and reflection. Karl Popper said that conjecture and refutation are the basis for learning and discovery. The implicit and secret message I got at school was that all the problems of the world had already been solved; that somebody somewhere knew the answer – if not the teacher, then the writer of the textbook. When I left school, every time I met a problem, I would look for the expert. It never occurred to me that *nobody* knew the answer to a lot of these problems. But in those days the world was an organised system – we just didn't know the details; now there is space in the system, and schools, universities and businesses are beginning to realise this. We can kill curiosity so easily and give people no space to test out their ideas, no room to reflect or review, no feedback.

Action learning

We have a lot to learn from the place where most education in this country happens and where a great deal of money is spent: inside the work organisation. When I started teaching managers 20 years ago, we tried to teach the way I had been taught. We put them in classrooms, I lectured, they wrote it down, I tested – had they remembered? But managers are difficult students; they didn't tolerate this for very long. They said: you are giving us interesting information, but it doesn't in any way relate to the questions we come in with; you don't give us a chance to try out these ideas, we have no chance to see whether they work or not. Follow us into our organisations, we will tell you the questions, you help us to find some solutions, we will test them out, you can help us to review them. Action learning, in effect.

Standards which all can reach

Why are we the only country in the world except Russia that makes every child take the same examination at age sixteen? If everybody took their driving test on their seventeenth birthday, we would probably have half as many good drivers and the others not allowed to drive at all – safer roads, maybe, but a lot of frustrated people. What I want to see are 'standards' which, like music tests, you take when you know that you can pass. No age bonding, but lots of standards – and it should be the responsibility of the school to make sure that everybody reaches those standards, rather than making it the responsibility of the child to beat everybody else.

A totally different kind of education

In ten years' time, everybody will have a telephone so small, so cheap, that they will carry it in their breast-pocket. The telephone will belong to the person, not the place. In 20 years' time they will have their own computer, television and fax modem; they won't need to go to school half the time; you won't need to use the teacher to convey the information. What are children doing when they are not in school? They are playing with technology, working in groups, being entrepreneurial in the streets. The role of the teacher is going to be to manage the learning of a whole lot of independent individuals who have to be connected in other ways into society, to meet other adults, to have other role models; all of which implies a totally different mind-set. It will need a totally different kind of education.

The National Commission is looking 20 years ahead; don't pitch your sights on tomorrow, because it won't happen tomorrow. Be humble. The same set of buildings may be there, but many different things will go on in them. Also be brave. Have the courage to create things that you won't live to see; don't underestimate the power of ideas. Then maybe we shall undo some of the harm I think we have done. For many people, we have taken away their god, work, and we need to replace it with something else.

Note

[1] Reported in: *Symposium, Leeds Castle, Kent, 19–21 March 1993. 'Education: Direction of Future Policies'*. The America-European Community Association Trust in conjunction with the National Commission on Education.

14. The Education of Children under Five

Written Evidence to the National Commission on Education by Victoria Hurst, 28 June 1992.

Introduction

This submission seeks to explain the crucial role that nursery education can play in the lives of individuals, in the whole education system, and in the fostering of creative and adaptive responses by individuals and communities to the challenges of life in the coming years. This belief originated in my experience in secondary and adult remedial education, and has been confirmed by my experience as a parent governor of nursery and primary schools and most recently as a nursery teacher and lecturer in early childhood education.

I write now as a lecturer in early childhood education at Goldsmiths' College, University of London, but my experience as a teacher began in the 1960s when I had overall responsibility for the history curriculum of a small inner London grammar school (George Green's School, E14), and also undertook voluntary work with adult illiterates under the Cambridge House Literacy Scheme. During this stage of my professional career I became concerned about the variation in educational outcomes among children and adults of apparently similar ability and experience. I gradually came to believe that investment in quality in early education would have a beneficial effect on all children, but most particularly on those who might otherwise be alienated from education by early influences or difficulties.

Disaffected pupils
A significant number of the pupils I taught were disaffected in two crucial ways. They, and their parents, did not feel that they had anything to gain from being educated, but rather

that their natural interests and concerns lay outside school, and that release from the classroom was the best that could be hoped for. These were often lively and forward-looking children who could have been expected to do well academically in different social surroundings. Equally worrying were pupils who, although they had been selected for grammar school, were markedly less good than their peers at handling abstract concepts and arguments. In much the same way, I saw my adult pupils unable to relate the operation of reading and writing systems to their own needs and purposes. Some fundamental understanding seemed to be lacking in both children and adults. Remedial work was slow, because it required the building of links between the learner's personal concerns and understandings, and the capacity for the use of symbols and abstract discourse which they needed to acquire.

As a result of this experience with secondary and adult learners, and of my subsequent work in nursery education, I have now come to see the quality of early education as crucial for the success of the efforts of teachers, pupils and parents throughout the maintained sector of education. This insight prompted my decision to train for infant education and then to convert to nursery teaching. I do not see nursery education as a vaccination against educational failure, but as a high-quality input at a crucial time in children's lives.

Attitudes and understandings in young children

Importance of early experience
I believe that there are key processes in effective education in the years before five which can exercise a positive influence on the formation of attitudes to education in children and in parents, and can lay down the foundations for mathematical thinking, literacy, scientific exploration and hypothesis and all the other essential disciplines of knowledge and understanding of the world and our place in it.

Parental attitudes
Attitudes in children are formed very largely by their experiences in the early years of life. The nursery curriculum places a high value on children as active and autonomous learners, which in turn contributes to their and their parents' awareness of their potential as learners. Family and community attitudes to education are the most influential, but school can play a part as well, particularly if – as in good quality nursery education – parents are seen to be the partners of trained staff in the education of children. The respect for parents shown by staff, and the sharing of insights into the beginnings of the educational process, can much improve parents' attitudes to themselves as well as their appreciation of their children's educational potential. This is one of the key factors highlighted by the long-term American research into effective education of young children, undertaken as a part of the Headstart programme.[1] Indeed, a British researcher[2] has found that a nursery programme that involved parents had a beneficial effect on the non-attending younger siblings of the children in the programme, as well as on the older children who took part.

Value of play in intellectual development
Understanding of the world and of how we look at it is built up through active exploration, experimentation and play in the early years. The recent search for improvements in the education system has sometimes taken the form of an attempt to 'improve' the education of young children by excluding play from their curriculum. This is due to a confusion of two meanings of play – play as not-work, and play as a mental and emotional activity, as in 'playing with an idea', which is often the source of new understandings in adults.

The difficulty that adults sometimes have in catching the intellectual quality of children's play has led to all play being characterised as a relief from work. It is only fair to the critics, however, to say that play in nurseries has not always been of high intellectual value and that much remains to be done to improve the standard of play opportunities provided in schools. When adults see play as the force for mental challenge and extension that it can be, children gain experience of mental mastery and manipulation of their expanding knowledge of the world. We do not yet know enough about how play in early childhood encourages adaptability and creativity, but it is likely that the freedom to invent, develop, combine or alter solutions to problems in play gives experience in mental agility and the imaginative resolution of difficulties.

Instead of fearing play, we should be looking critically at the quality of play provision offered to children by teachers, and asking how effectively teachers are observing and assessing children's thinking as it is demonstrated in play. The capacity of teachers and nursery nurses to learn from children's play determines how skilful they are at providing a curriculum that builds on and extends children's creativity and imagination.

Provision of nursery education

Within the education system as a whole, nursery education has a positive influence on the work of teachers at later stages. The national curriculum is founded on children's early educational experiences and the assessment of 7-year-olds is already showing that different pre-school experiences affect their later achievement. Current research discussed above indicates that this is likely to be a long-term effect, and that admitting children under the age of five into infant reception classes may cause problems. Early exposure to formal learning is not likely to foster independence of thought, creativity or adaptability.

Unfortunately, there is so little maintained nursery education available that local authorities are now trying to spread its benefits even more thinly. Children need at least five terms to develop their full learning potential in nursery schools and classes, and the majority of parents would like a full-time place for their children. Instead, it is increasingly common for children to have two terms at most, and even this may be offered part-time and for fewer than five days a week.

The thoughtful and wide-ranging reports of the House of Commons Education, Science and the Arts Committee[3,4] have pointed to the contribution that education can make to the development of under-fives. The Committee's call for a steady expansion of nursery education, and for the provision of high-quality training for sufficient numbers of nursery teachers and nursery nurses, indicates a recognition that it is the quality of provision that must be seen as the key ingredient, whatever the setting. It is vital to maintain this principle at a time when the already wide range of forms of provision is undergoing rapid change in response to the increasing participation of women in the labour market.

European comparisons
At present we stand very low in the European table of provision of education before the statutory age of schooling. To our 24% in nursery schools and classes, Belgium, France and Italy can all show approximately 90%, while Spain and Portugal are committing significant proportions of their budgets in the attempt to meet this need; Spain has already reached a level of provision of 66%, and Portugal is making rapid progress. High percentages quoted for under-fives participating in education in this country are artificially inflated by adding on the 80% of children in this age-group who have been admitted prematurely to infant reception classes.

However, we have much to appreciate in the quality of the small amount of provision that we do have, and in the quality of our education and training of practitioners for nursery education. Comparisons show that we are ahead of most other countries in our courses, although we are so far behind in our levels of provision.[5]

Professor Margaret Clark's review of research in the field of education for the under-fives[6] has pointed to one outstanding feature of the present situation. During the period of her investigations the position changed from that of the 1970s, when proposals were made to expand nursery education, to a situation in which nursery education came under pressure without ever having had the opportunity to provide what has for so long been recognised as the appropriate educational experience for the nation's under-fives.

Continuity of learning
Some vital issues, according to Professor Clark, are still under-researched — the continuity of educational experience from age 3 to 7 or 8, for instance. Due to pressure of time and money, only studies of the transition from pre-school experience to school were undertaken during the period she reviewed; Gill Barrett[7] focused on one continuum, that from home to school. We now need evidence on the kind of continuity which is challenging but not stressful; on the different levels of literacy and maths awareness in young children; and, in contrast to the 1970s approach, longer-term studies to ensure that early fluent readers receive adequate recognition.[8]

It is most important that research on young children should be undertaken with academic rigour, and that teachers should be counselled in how to use research findings in an informed way.

Monitoring progress from nursery to infant education requires continuity; observations need to be sharply targeted and assessments focused, as in Hughes' work on numeracy in very young children.[9] The value of different kinds of play must be examined, as must children's dependence and independence in class. Teachers need training in a high level of organisation to monitor this.

Training for nursery education

The Select Committee report[10] has indicated that it sees good practice as occurring in both nursery classes and nursery schools, but recent work[11] has given warning that there may be greater difficulty in reaching high standards in nursery classes in infant schools, perhaps due to the lack of nursery colleagues' support. Whatever may ultimately be decided about this, there is no doubt at all about the crucial role of nursery schools both as centres of excellence and as the trainers of the teachers and nursery nurses of the future. Nursery schools need support if they are to continue to play this essential role; we must include them in planning for the future of services for the under-fives. Research at Goldsmiths' College into how workplace nurseries may be monitored is beginning to show how much staff appreciate the input of a trained nursery teacher.[12]

Professor Clark's research review points to the necessity of providing sufficient numbers of nursery-trained teachers and nursery nurses to staff educational establishments for under-fives, and of ensuring that there are sufficient numbers of nursery-trained and experienced staff to train the teachers and nursery nurses needed now and in the future. At present the extreme shortage of nursery teachers has a most unfortunate effect on the capacity to train the next generation. There is also an acute shortage of people with nursery experience for other key posts, in particular in the advisory field.

Conclusion

If we need adaptable, innovative and creative people, we must reform our education system in the direction of the processes which foster these qualities. Nursery education has a part to play in these reforms. The key ingredient is educational quality. It is time to recognise the contribution that nursery education can make to the responsible development of provision for under-fives. Our present patchy, limited, unplanned, unco-ordinated, non-statutory and under-funded arrangements for nursery education contrast significantly with what is taken for granted in Europe. At a time when schools must take account of the requirements of the national curriculum, it is particularly important to give children under five a fairer start to their education.

References

1. Schweinhart, L.J. and Weikart, D.P. (1980). *Young Children Grow Up: the Effects of the Perry Preschool Program on Youths through Age Fifteen*. High-Scope Foundation. Monograph No. 15.
2. Athey, C. (1990). *Extending Thought in Young Children*. Paul Chapman.
3. House of Commons Education, Science and Arts Committee (1986). *Achievement in Primary Schools*. HMSO.
4. House of Commons Education, Science and Arts Committee (1989). *Educational Provision for the Under Fives*. HMSO.
5. Pascal, C., Bertram, A. and Heaslip, P. (1991). *Comparative Directory of Early Years Training for Teachers*. ATEE/Worcester College of Higher Education.
6. Clark, M. (1988). *Children under Five: Educational Research and Evidence*. Gordon and Breach.
7. Barrett, G. (1986). *Starting School: an Evaluation of the Experience*. Assistant Masters and Mistresses Association (AMMA).
8. Clark, M. (1988), *op cit*, Chapter 5.
9. Hughes, M. (1986). *Children and Number*. Blackwell.
10. House of Commons Education, Science and Arts Committee (1989), *op cit*.
11. Osborn, A. and Milbank, J. (1987). *The Effects of Early Education*. Clarendon Press.
12. Hurst, V. (research in progress).

15. Educational and Social Benefits of Pre-School Education

Note by Sue Taylor for the National Commission on Education, March 1992.

Introduction

This paper provides a brief outline of key points arising from research and other evidence on pre-school provision, as background for a discussion on the following question:

> How strong is the case on educational and/or social grounds for making nursery school provision available for all children between 3 and 5 years of age?

Research evidence and informed opinion point to educational and social benefits to be gained from pre-school education. Although the research evidence falls short of providing simple and conclusive proof of a long-term impact, strong arguments are advanced for more and better pre-school education, both on social and educational grounds. In addition, two recent studies have analysed the potential economic gains that would result from expanding pre-school provision.

A recent report by Kiernan and Wicks (1990) on future family policies points to the danger of deciding child care policy in isolation from employment policies and from other aspects of family policy. Key points from this report are summarised on pages 186–7.

Some of the main benefits of pre-school provision highlighted by teachers and by those who advocate expansion can be summarised as follows:

Pre-school education can

- have positive effects on children's cognitive development
- improve their aspirations and self-esteem
- benefit those from disadvantaged backgrounds
- give children 'learning orientation', establish attitudes and behaviour patterns which support future educational and social development
- cater for the child's immediate needs, taking social pressures into account
- reduce child poverty
- improve pay and career opportunities for women
- provide gains for the Exchequer in the form of 'flowback' from tax paid by women in employment, and savings in benefits.

Educational and social benefits of pre-school provision

It may be argued that, in order to present a convincing case for funding an expansion of pre-school provision, one would need to demonstrate long-term beneficial effects on children's education. In a climate in which low political value has been attached to the quality of young children's learning experiences, and plans for pre-school education have been hindered by financial constraints, the advocates of expansion have been under pressure to produce unequivocal evidence that pre-school education is an essential part of the public education and welfare system.

So what does the evidence tell us? Reviews of the research are cautious in their interpretations: there is no simple and conclusive proof that pre-school programmes will have lasting effects. This is partly due to the difficulty of generalising from studies undertaken in specific contexts, and partly because the research has not been designed with the purpose of considering the long-term impact in depth. Studies have tended to look at pre-school provision in isolation from other aspects of education. Thus, the absence of massive permanent effects might result from lack of continuity, or from a conflict of aims between the different stages of education.

Having acknowledged the need for a degree of caution, it is possible to state that 'there are strong positive indications about the long-term benefits to be derived from well-planned pre-school provision' (Woodhead, 1987). Research evidence from the UK and the USA is summarised on pages 187–190, based on a report by Margaret M. Clark to the DES, published in 1988. Clark found that some studies showed gains over a limited period, and some indicated longer-term gains.

The only large-scale study undertaken in the UK (Osborn and others, 1984 and 1987) claimed to offer 'conclusive evidence that pre-school education provided by ordinary nursery schools and playgroups in Britain can have a positive effect upon the cognitive development of the children who attend them'. Clark supports this general statement, whilst expressing certain reservations about the detail of the research.

Research evidence from the USA includes the High/Scope programme, which has received publicity in this country, notably the claim that every dollar spent on the programme represents a saving to taxpayers of six dollars in expenditure on special education, crime and welfare. Children who attended the High/Scope programme were followed through to age 19. They were found to have better success in high school and in finding jobs, and were less likely to have been in trouble with the law, than children from a control group who did not attend the programme. Two important messages to be drawn from this work are:

- that pre-school education can raise children's competence sufficiently in the short term to enable them to make a more positive start in schooling;

- that raising parental aspirations is a significant element in improving children's chances in school.

Sylva (1990) feels that the American research justifies the optimism about the potential of pre-school programmes: they can be the trigger for 'self-confidence, school commitment, learning orientation and higher career aspirations'. In attempting to draw conclusions from the High/Scope experience for the UK, however, one would need to bear in mind the fact that the programme catered for severely disadvantaged, mainly black communities, and that low ratios of children to adults, and weekly home-visits were key features.

In addition to work cited elsewhere in this paper, the National Children's Bureau Early Childhood Unit in its evidence to the National Commission, as well as Professor Peter Mortimore, have drawn attention to the work of Athey (1990), who found that significant cognitive gains were made by children from disadvantaged backgrounds in a highly structured pre-school 'enrichment' programme. Mortimore states that this approach demonstrates the possibility of narrowing the gap between the performance of children from disadvantaged and advantaged backgrounds.

The NCB Early Childhood Unit's evidence also indicates that recent research from Leeds University (in press) will show that children who had the benefit of nursery education performed significantly better than others in assessment tasks at the end of Key Stage 1.

The Education, Science and Arts Committee (ESAC), which reported on provision for the under fives in 1989, took evidence from academic experts and practitioners regarding the educational and social value of pre-school programmes. It did not find the research evidence on long-term benefits conclusive, but was sufficiently persuaded by the overall case to recommend a major expansion in nursery education. ESAC took the view that the case for under fives education should not be put solely in terms of long-term effects. The characteristics of urban life, modern family patterns, and pressures on parents, all of which affect the child's experience, should be taken into account. Pre-school education 'is not merely a preparation for something else, but caters for the child's needs at that time and may be justified in those terms'.

Following the ESAC report, the Rumbold Committee inquired into the quality of provision for 3- and 4-year-olds. The Committee's report includes the following statement:

> Attitudes and behaviour patterns established during the first years of life are central to future educational and social development. Particular attention has thus to be given in these early years to the process by which a child acquires the disposition to learn and necessary competencies for learning.

Economic benefits of pre-school provision

Cohen and Fraser (1991) argue that an expansion of public child care could contribute to a significant reduction in child poverty. They present data showing the correlation between child poverty and mothers not working. Survey material indicates that a high proportion of non-working mothers would like to take up employment, education or training if suitable child care were available.

Employment rates for women are rising, however, and more women with a child under 5 are taking up paid employment (approximately 37% in 1988 compared with 29% in 1985). Employment rates among lone mothers are lower.

Table 1 overleaf shows employment participation rates of mothers of children under 5 in the EC in 1988. Only the Netherlands has a lower percentage of mothers working full-time. The UK has the second highest percentage of mothers in part-time employment.

Table 1: Employment participation rates of mothers of children aged 0-4 in the European Community, 1988.

Percentages

	F.R. Germany	France	Italy	Netherlands	Belgium	Luxembourg	UK
Full-time	15.63	37.51	34.95	4.17	36.98	27.09	11.26
Part-time	18.08	14.23	4.91	24.77	15.83	9.20	25.27
Total in Employment	33.70	51.74	39.86	28.94	52.81	36.29	36.53

	Ireland	Denmark	Greece	Portugal	Spain	Euro 12 (average)
Full-time	19.04	45.86	33.01	54.49	23.98	24.79
Part-time	6.03	28.89	6.49	6.18	4.20	15.13
Total in Employment	25.07	74.75	39.50	60.67	28.18	39.92

Source: Unpublished Eurostat Labour Force Data prepared for the European Childcare Network. In: Cohen, B. (1990).

Table 2 shows employment participation rates of lone mothers of children under 5 in the EC. The rate of full-time employment among lone mothers with a child under 5 in the UK is the lowest in the EC.

Cohen and Fraser, and more recently Holtermann (1992) have analysed the costs and benefits of expanded child care programmes. Holtermann's conclusions are reprinted at the end of this paper. The findings of these studies suggest that expanded provision would be economically beneficial in providing 'flowback' to the Exchequer in the form of tax paid by women working, and by reduced benefit payments. There would be potential for new income creation (with tax flowbacks) from extra jobs in child care. Women's pay and career opportunities would also be enhanced: their loss of earnings from time spent caring for children would be reduced, and they would have access to higher incomes as a result of increased work experience.

Table 2: Employment participation rates of lone mothers with a child aged 0-4, European Community, 1988.

Percentages

	F.R. Germany	France	Italy	Netherlands	Belgium	Luxembourg	UK
Full-time	25.94	44.85	52.90	7.37	32.09	72.56	6.34
Part-time	15.26	8.39	4.72	10.51	10.04	2.38	11.72
Total in Employment	41.20	53.24	57.62	17.88	42.13	74.94	18.06

	Ireland	Denmark	Greece	Portugal	Spain	Euro 12 (average)
Full-time	13.13	38.86	41.03	55.96	43.89	25.85
Part-time	3.85	30.67	5.98	9.23	5.86	10.98
Total in Employment	16.98	69.53	47.01	65.19	49.75	36.83

Source: Unpublished Eurostat Labour Force Data prepared for the European Childcare Network. In: Cohen, B. (1990).

Other significant issues

In formulating proposals on pre-school education, the Commission will need to address a number of other significant issues, including:

- The nature and quality of the curriculum appropriate to the needs of 3- and 4-year-olds. It is important to note that concern has been expressed about the inappropriateness of some primary school settings to the needs of this age group, and the pressures which may result from the national curriculum and assessment at 7. A narrow '3Rs-based' curriculum can be counter-productive and cause children to 'switch off' from school learning.

- The combination of care and education required to meet the needs of children and working parents.

- The training of teachers for the early years.

- The extent to which pre-school provision should be targeted towards those parents and children in greatest need.

- Ways of encouraging parental involvement, since this has been recognised as crucial to the success of early education.

It may be useful to conclude with the report by Kiernan and Wicks (1990), which widens the context for discussing pre-school provision, by suggesting that we should look at child-rearing practices in relation to employment policies and other areas of family policy (including for example financial support). These authors are concerned with child care generally, rather than with the specific question of pre-school education.

Kiernan and Wicks predict that the modern British family will increasingly be headed by two workers rather than one, and that women's economic activity rates will continue to increase, as a result both of their own work aspirations and the demand for women to fill new jobs. In future, women's employment patterns will be far less different from men's than in the past. Policy makers are urged to look at the dangers as well as the opportunities inherent in this situation.

The continuing trend towards diversity in family patterns suggests that by the 21st century, perhaps only 50% of children will experience a 'conventional' family life-cycle, with parents married at the time the children were born and continuing married until they are grown up. Many children will experience family breakdown and/or economic insecurity. These are the 'forces for insecurity' that policy makers need to bear in mind.

Kiernan and Wicks suggest that we need an honest debate about the impact of the dual worker family on the welfare of the child. They pose the following questions: what is the role of parents in relation to child-rearing? What are the implications for fathers? What employment policies are required (part-time work, parental leave, flexible hours) to accommodate the competing pressures affecting parents in terms of work and child-rearing? Most importantly: how does one place the welfare of the child at the centre of the child care debate?

References

1. Clark, M.M. (1988). *Children under Five: Educational Research and Evidence. Final Report to the Department of Education and Science, United Kingdom.* Chapter 16 (Long-term effects of pre-school education: issues and evidence).
2. Cohen, B. and Fraser, N. (1991). *Childcare in a Modern Welfare System. Towards a New National Policy.* Institute for Public Policy Research.
3. Cohen, B. (1990). *Caring for Children. The 1990 Report. Report for the European Commission's Childcare Network on Childcare Services and Policies in the United Kingdom.* Family Policy Studies Centre.
4. Education, Science and Arts Committee (1989). *Educational Provision for the Under Fives.* Volume 1.
5. Holtermann, S. (1992). *Investing in Young Children: Costing an Education and Day Care Service (Summary Report).* National Children's Bureau.
6. Kiernan, K. and Wicks, M. (1990). *Family Change and Future Policy.* Family Policy Studies Centre.
7. Mortimore, P. (1991). *Bucking the Trends: Promoting Successful Urban Education.* Times Educational Supplement/Greenwich Annual Lecture.
8. National Children's Bureau Early Childhood Unit (1992). *Draft Submission to the National Commission on Education.*
9. Pugh, G. (1990). *Developing a Policy for Early Childhood Education: Challenges and Constraints.* Early Child Development and Care, Vol. 58, 3–13.
10. Rumbold Committee (1990). *Starting with Quality.* The Report of the Committee of Inquiry into the Quality of the Educational Experience Offered to 3- and 4-year olds. Chaired by Mrs Angela Rumbold. HMSO.
11. Sylva, K. (1990). *Evaluating Early Education Programmes.* Early Child Development and Care, Vol. 58, 97–107.
12. Utting, D. (1991). *What the US Teaches Today.* Guardian, 26 November.
13. Woodhead, M. (1987). *Some Lessons from Research into Pre-School Effectiveness.* Concern, Summer edition.

Studies Reviewed by Clark

1. Evidence from the UK

At the time of Clark's report, there had been only one large-scale study of the long-term effects of pre-school education, namely that of Osborn and others, reported in 1984 and 1987. This research was based on information from the Child Health and Education Study, which used a national sample of 13,000 children, but was not originally planned to study pre-school education and its effects. The researchers examined the relationship between the children's pre-school experiences and attainment as measured at five and ten years of age. Although she expresses certain reservations about the research, Clark concludes that the evidence supports the general statement (by Osborn and Milbank, 1987) that it is the first study to provide 'conclusive evidence that pre-school education provided by ordinary nursery schools and playgroups in Britain can have a positive effect upon the cognitive development of the children who attend them'.

Other research in the UK looked at short-term effects, for example:

Clark and Cheyne (1979). Children who had attended a new nursery school in an area of multiple deprivation were assessed shortly after entry to (primary) reception class. Psychometric tests showed differences in favour of the nursery children; these were greatest in tests involving copying and drawing, and in tests administered closest to entry to primary school. Children who had two years' pre-schooling performed better than those who had only one year.

Donachy (1979). This experimental study was designed to assess the effects of a programme involving the parents of pre-school children. The timescale was limited (intelligence and language tests before and after a four-month parent programme). Significant differences were found for the children attending nursery school whose parents had not been involved in the programme; more differences were found where parents were also involved.

Turner (1977). Here the focus was on playgroups for disadvantaged children. The methodology included assessments of the effects of attendance on the children's language and cognitive development. Significant differences were observed between attenders and non-attenders on measures of listening vocabulary and general reasoning ability. (It is not clear at what stage the children were tested.)

Jowett and Sylva (1986) studied 'working class' children who had attended either a playgroup or a nursery class. The children were observed and tested in their first term in reception class and again six months later. It would appear that the researchers compared the nursery class children with the playgroup children, but without any other control group. They found a number of differences between the two groups; some of these persisted six months after entry to school and in some the gap narrowed. Nursery class attendance was shown to have a significant effect on purposeful and creative play, and this was still noticeable (though to a lesser degree) six months later. Differences between the two groups were also apparent in more school-related activities, and these increased over the six-month period for the nursery class children. Social participation was comparable between the two groups. Differences in the amount of language apparent on entry to school had disappeared by the time of the second observation, though the nursery children were more likely to engage in connected conversation.

2. Evidence from the USA

Clark looks at two major sources of evidence from the USA: Bronfenbrenner (*Is early education effective?* 1974) and the Consortium of Longitudinal Studies (*As the twig is bent: lasting effects of pre-school programmes.* 1983).

Bronfenbrenner is tentative, warning for example of the need to replicate results and stressing the narrowness of certain forms of assessment when judging the whole development of the child. He claims that without family involvement, pre-school intervention is unlikely to be successful, and the few effects are unlikely to last. In the case of disadvantaged families, he recommends long-term intervention up to age 12 'on a wide front'.

The **Consortium of Legal Studies** reported on a range of research including widely differing types of programmes and curricular approaches. It concluded that early intervention with low income families can have measured effects throughout childhood and into adolescence. Children who had participated in pre-school programmes were more likely to succeed in school, showed better self-esteem, had more realistic vocational expectations and were prouder of their achievements.

The **High/Scope** programme (one of those represented in the Consortium) aims to encourage and support children in initiating their own activities. An article on the programme (Schweinhart, Weikart and Larner, 1986) claims that in a long-term comparison, participants were superior to those who had taken part in a more instruction-based programme. It is argued that the effectiveness of pre-school programmes should not be judged solely on intellectual and academic measures. Social competence should be taken into account.

Two writers have considered the relevance of American experience to Britain. *Woodhead* (1985) stressed the need to bear in mind factors such as the populations of the US programmes (severely disadvantaged and mainly black), the resources available, adult-child ratios, parental involvement and the influence of subsequent school procedures. He argues for a more complex model which recognises the possibility that short-term cognitive and motivational gains may have long-term influences on educational motivation and achievement. *Cheyne* (1987) reviewed evidence from the States on short- and long-term effects of pre-school education, and pointed out that any effects which last for even three or four years represent a major influence, but these tend to be discounted. As Clark suggests, instructional programmes need maintenance if their effects are to survive, but the research tends to overlook what happens in the intervening school years.

Investing in Young Children: Costing an Education and Day Care Service (Summary Report). National Children's Bureau.

Conclusions

- It would cost about £550 million extra (an increase of about 25% on present expenditure) to improve the quality of existing services to an acceptable level.

- To satisfy parental demand, the number of day care places needs to increase by a factor of about four, and education for the under fives needs to double. The greatest needs are for an expansion of schemes for out-of-school and holiday care, and for nurseries offering a combination of care and education.

- These new services will cost about £6 billion a year, in addition to the £2 billion spent at present. About £450 million of the increase will be for state education for the under fives (including £100m capital expenditure).

- The state will continue to bear the whole cost of state nursery education and will increase its financial support to playgroups, so that parents are not deterred from using pre-school educational services by their cost.

It is suggested that the costs of day care are shared so that parents pay on average a third of the cost, with their individual contributions related to their incomes, and that the state is responsible for the rest. The state's contribution will be substantially reduced by the flowback to the exchequer of extra tax and reduced benefit payments, and in time, if the full expansion programme is maintained, will be eliminated. Employers might be required to make a contribution to getting the expansion of services underway by the use of a temporary levy on employers not already giving assistance for childcare.

Everyone gains:

- Children gain better day care and early education and many are lifted out of poverty.

- Parents gain from the knowledge that their children are being well cared for and given a good start in education. They gain from greater opportunities in the workplace and a higher real income.

- Early years workers gain from working in adequately funded services.

- Employers gain from an enlarged pool of experienced workers.

- The national economy gains in the long run by the skills of better educated children and in the short run by the addition to net national output of parents who can enter paid employment.

- The government gains from a reduction in the dependence of families on state benefits and an enlargement of the tax base.

And no one loses.

16. Challenging the Effects of Urban Deprivation

Written Evidence to the National Commission on Education from Alan J. Ratcliffe, Headmaster, Ley Hill Primary School, Birmingham, 24 March 1992.

Introduction

Ley Hill Primary School was opened in the middle years of the 1950s to cater for children from an overspill estate of mainly flats and maisonettes developed by the city council.

In my time as head during the last fourteen years I have seen a significant change both in family life and attitudes. The vast majority of our families experience long-term unemployment and frequently move from estate to estate. The constant movement brings its own problems and creates for some children a restlessness which can pervade the school. We try very hard to redress the balance, and have succeeded in creating an effective school ethos which promotes interest, motivates children, provides stability and encourages social responsibility.

Effects of deprivation

The nature of deprivation on our estate embraces the social, intellectual and cultural components of all-round development. It is a fact that many of our children are tired, deprived of sleep for many reasons; many experience no routine or settled existence at home; concentration is difficult; listening skills have hardly been developed before arrival in nursery at three; and, perhaps most significantly, the standard of language on entry to school is very poor. Add to this almost non-existent social skills, and it is clear that we have inadequate foundations on which to build.

Many of our children have very young, inexperienced parents, who do not themselves have the support of a wider family and have become isolated. Many children have a single parent or live in families where the adult figures change from time to time. Attitudes to education vary but at worst there is no expectation from the parents for their children and little initiation of dialogue with the school.

A positive approach

Our approach is very positive and starts from the early stages of learning.

We have developed a pre-school programme which provides two years' involvement of parents in a toddler and playgroup *prior* to the child's admission to nursery. Our parent support programme has provided parents with opportunities to work on their own parenting skills, to review household management, to consider their response to children's behaviour and to work with health visitors on issues relating to birth control and general health care.

We have also devised part of our community education programme with the intention of bringing home and school closer together. In recent years we have felt that the gap between the expectations of home and school has widened. In tackling this particular problem we have had to develop strategies to break down barriers of apathy and negative reactions to authority. We feel that a combination of our 'open door' policy, frequent home visits, regular contact in school and the demonstration of the genuine desire to help has addressed the problem with a reasonable degree of success.

We make it widely known to parents that we expect their children to feel happy, relaxed and safe in the school community. My staff work systematically as a team to improve attitudes towards discipline and behaviour and to develop self-esteem, whilst creating a school society which demonstrates care and concern for all its members. Parents are frequently consulted and brought in for advice and help at an early stage if it is thought that a problem needs immediate attention. Together we look to promote co-operation and collaboration, which may involve the help of other agencies.

Tackling basic skills
Without question the national curriculum has imposed excessive demands on us. Though we have approached its introduction in as positive a way as possible, we are very conscious that many of our children have learning difficulties (45% of the school population fits into the Warnock definition of special needs), which in themselves need time for solutions to be found. The national curriculum does make the assumption that children have basic literacy and numeracy skills. At Ley Hill we cannot make that assumption.

Ninety per cent of our children leave us for secondary school with a measured reading age no more than one year below their chronological age. Considering the paucity of their language at the beginning of their educational careers, I would argue that this one example alone is an indicator of effective schooling.

Understanding the community
In considering the effectiveness of education it is important to have a deep understanding of individual and community attitudes. Many of our children lack application, have emotional and psychological problems and learn very slowly. The pace at which they acquire knowledge and skills quite obviously affects our programming for the delivery of the national curriculum. Underpinning all other considerations is our belief that correct attitudes and responsibility for caring should be fostered through *all* learning opportunities. This belief is so important that it is built into the school's mission statement.

17. Mountstuart – a Community School

Presentation to the National Commission on Education, 30 April 1992, by Betty Campbell, Head of Mountstuart Primary School.

Introduction

Mountstuart School is in the area of Butetown, Cardiff, once known as Tigerbay, and once a lively thriving sea port in the days when coal was referred to as 'black diamonds'. Butetown owed its prosperity to the Bute family, who built and developed the Docks of Cardiff between 1839 and 1882. After the Second World War, the Docks started to decline, and in the last 20 years iron foundries like Guest Keen and Nettlefolds have closed, along with the Rover Works and other industrial concerns. In the 1950s many of the old houses in the area were demolished and replaced by council houses, but despite being a council estate the area has remained culturally unique.

Within yards of each other, there are buildings which remind one of the multi-ethnic population who first came to Cardiff over 150 years ago as seamen, and the men who ruled their lives, i.e. the ship owners and coal merchants, the Reardon Smith and Cory families among them. The Mountstuart Exchange stands as a witness to all the coal transactions which went on at that time.

Mosques, and churches – Catholic, Anglican, and Greek Orthodox – and chapels were all built for special reasons. The local Catholic church was built to serve the needs of the Irish immigrants and the Spaniards who fled from Spain's Civil War. The Mosques served the hundreds of Moslem seamen who settled in the area, and a Methodist chapel built in 1892 served the many Africans who came to Cardiff. The recently re-erected Norwegian church, now a museum, is the place where Roald Dahl was baptised.

Thus, this small area is a tremendous historical, environmental and cultural resource for Mountstuart School.

Mountstuart Primary School

Mountstuart Primary School, built in 1973, is situated in a designated social priority multi-racial area of Cardiff. An extension and refurbishment of the school was due to take place four years ago, but was postponed. Cardiff Bay Development Corporation (C.B.D.C.) had promised to build a new school which would open in September 1991. Because of delays outside the school's control, it has been necessary to add three extra portable classrooms to the school as well as *outside* toilets. The school is now known as 'Tent City'. Last month C.B.D.C. finally decided to carry out their pledge and Section 12 notices have now been posted in the area stating that a two-form entry school should be ready to admit pupils in September 1993.[1]

When I became Head in 1973, only two children in top infants had a reading age of seven years; everyone else was five years or below. Yet in 1985 four pupils successfully gained entrance to Howells Independent School for Girls.

A community school
The school sees itself as a community school and uses the curriculum to reinforce its own sense of community, as well as a means whereby it can contribute to the community of which it is so clearly a part. The aims of the school are:

- to use the local environmental resources to develop the school's multicultural curriculum, and to make the children proud of the rich heritage of the place where they live;

- to acknowledge the contribution of different cultures to world development;

- to encourage the children to think of others, including the sick and elderly, and to devise ways of fund-raising for projects here and overseas to link with social needs.

In 1990 Mountstuart School received a Schools Curriculum Award in recognition of its approach to community involvement in the curriculum.

A multicultural curriculum

The school has been trying to develop a multicultural curriculum for many years, and has used the local environment and the normal school curriculum to do this. Originally the headteacher was responsible for all aspects of multicultural work, but now that philosophy has become a permanent feature of Mountstuart School, and all staff are quite capable of following and implementing multicultural guidelines. Recently the school has produced a multicultural booklet suitable for use by other teachers; a booklet offering comprehensive guidance to anyone wishing to undertake a project on the Caribbean; and a collection of class multicultural assemblies dating from 1973. These will prove extremely useful to new members of staff.

The school draws strength from its environment by using as resources the many different ethnic groups, the changes in the industrial scene, the rise of Cardiff as a 'media' city and the history of Cardiff Docks. In return, members of the community are invited in to share the resources of the school.

The community and school assemblies

We also involve the community in our class assemblies each Friday morning by inviting anyone to share this time with us. This initiative began about ten years ago, and has now become an integral part of school life. If I had to identify the 'jewel in the crown' of Mountstuart, I would say it was the endurance of Friday morning assemblies. They are generally multicultural and involve art work, language and religious education, etc. The children themselves conduct the assembly and each class participates in turn. By attending assemblies, parents have an opportunity to discuss the religious education offered at the school. Originally it was parents only who formed the audience, and often their attendance declined as the children moved from the infant to the junior department. Now it is other members of the community who come to participate in the assemblies. It is extremely rewarding to see Moslem and Rastafarian fathers attend these assemblies, and to see each cultural group showing tolerance and understanding towards the children's different beliefs.

Whenever possible the school produces special assemblies for visitors which portray the children's own culture and that of the visitors. Recently students and lecturers from Sweden took part in an assembly about Albert Nobel, Martin Luther King and Mother Theresa. Three weeks ago a group of black educators from South Africa joined in an assembly concerning Nelson Mandela. Titles for these assemblies ranged from 'Men of Peace' (Martin Luther King, Gandhi) to 'Smile, Jamaica', and from 'St Francis of Assisi' to 'The Arab World'. Assemblies are generally linked with the topic of the moment and nearly always involve reference to the local community.

Community insights through education competitions

Another way in which the curriculum is enriched is by the school participating in any education competitions run nationally or locally. When the subject is applicable to the school, we enter the annual *Western Mail* and *Echo* St David's Day Competition. In 1985 we were runners-up in the competition entitled 'My Christian Heritage'. This project involved many areas of the curriculum and the environment, and has proved to be a valuable teaching aid for everyone. Through research and photography, we demonstrated a link between the Benedictine Monks, St Mary's Parish Church in Butetown, and the Church of Africa. We noted that one local curate became Bishop of Rhodesia and another visiting African priest became the first Bishop of Ghana. Father Trevor Huddleston of South Africa was a visitor to our area in the Sixties. The information contained in this project has now become a firm part of the syllabi for environmental studies and religious education.

The second *Western Mail* topic (1989) was 'Industry, Past, Present and Future', and our environmental project was so interesting and stimulating that we were awarded first prize of £500. Before we entered this competition we had already been involved in school/industry links and both Siriol (Welsh SuperTed Creators) and the school had been awarded certificates for working together. The school had also been involved in creating mini-industries to raise money for charitable events. Thus, this project gave us a desire to look even more closely at the industrial changes taking place in our area.

We selected as our main issue the decline of the coal and shipping industry and the emergence of the media industry and computer businesses. Through the project we recognised that all the work in the area was managed by indigenous white people, and that only the Black Film and Video Team represented the multi-racial community.

Help given to the community by the school

The school was instrumental in introducing a Karate club into the area. Twelve years ago a local man approached the school to ask if he could train the children in Karate. Two hundred pounds was raised and suits were bought for the pupils. For about two years the children met at the school, but when the class expanded it had to meet in the local Community Centre. It is still going strong now, meeting twice a week. The group has produced several British champions and its instructor, Mr Von Johnson, refuses to accept any fee. This is another way in which the school has contributed to the community. Children from all over the area attend, but the majority are still from Mountstuart.

On Monday afternoons English classes, run voluntarily by a part-time member of staff, are held in the school for Moslem parents from several different countries. Our nursery, which opens on fund-raising Bingo nights and parents' evenings, is supervised by parents and members of staff.

Local dancing classes are held every Tuesday evening, and during holidays the school was used by children for steel pan sessions. Local bands practise over weekends.

School is an annual focus for Hallowe'en and Bonfire Night Celebrations, raising much-needed money for the school fund and entertaining the community.

Visitors to the school

The school's philosophy on multicultural education in the community has interested many people from all over the world and our visitors' book bears witness to this, with some visitors returning more than once. For example, we have had an enduring contact with visitors from the Soviet Union since 1982. We now write to several schools in Voroshilovgrad, now Lugansk, and have had our art work exhibited there. As headteacher I correspond with a lecturer from the Training College in Lugansk and have addressed many of the students on my visits there.

Each year when the cultural group from Lugansk arrives, a visit to Mountstuart is on the agenda. The school entertains them with dance and song (a universal language), from the Caribbean, Wales, Asia and the Ukraine. Our Ukrainian dances have so impressed the Soviet visitors that this year they will be presenting the school with genuine Ukrainian costumes.

The visits of these wonderful people have been recorded on video for us by the local Black Film and Video Team. It was a rare sight to see Black Rastafarians and the people from the Ukraine conversing with each other – or at least, trying to! We have learned a lot from them and they in turn have gained by their contact with the school. Our next task is to arrange an exchange of our top juniors with School No. 36 in Lugansk.

A new contact has recently been made with Nantes, a city twinned with Cardiff; a group of 25 children will soon be travelling to France on an exchange visit to take part in a European Schools Festival.

Mountstuart's role in Wales

The community-based, multicultural emphasis within the curriculum has generated media interest, which in turn has provided opportunities for pupils to become involved in television productions, including BBC's *'The New World'* and two Welsh St David's Day programmes: *'Wales? Wales!'* (BBC), and *'The Dragon with Two Tongues'*.

The BBC is currently producing a series of programmes on *Citizenship for Schools* to be shown in the UK. Mountstuart School was chosen to be part of the first programme, which will be broadcast in English and in Welsh.

We give prominence to the Welsh language and culture at the school. St David's Day celebrations have been held regularly since 1973, and perhaps the most memorable one was when Neil and Glenys Kinnock celebrated with us. The Curriculum Council for Wales has made use of material from Mountstuart in its book, and I was appointed to the Council's sub-committee. The Cardiff Bay Development Corporation has also used material from Mountstuart School to compile a teachers' pack on Cardiff Bay, which is now selling for £30.

The Heritage Project

This is one of the most ambitious projects undertaken by the school. It is designed to kindle an interest in the children's environment and their cultural background. The multicultural nature of the local area means that there is a wealth of history for the children to investigate and explore. The use of information technology will enable exploration at a far deeper level than would otherwise be possible and will make information easily accessible to others interested in the area. We hope that parents and the local community will become actively involved in the project.

Conclusion

I foresee a very exciting future for Mountstuart School: our community is rapidly changing and we can look forward to entering new school premises in September 1993. With more space and facilities we hope to become even more strongly linked with our community and to produce papers that will help *other* schools to develop a curriculum for *all* their children.

I would like to end with comments made by some of the many and varied visitors to Mountstuart:

> 'Excellent visit; given insight into community police relations with schools.' (M.A. Alhassan, A.S.P. Ghana Police, *West Africa*.)

> 'Thank you very much for your introduction about the education in your school.' (Y.Xu, F. Qin, *China*.)

> 'Thank you for a wonderful St David's Day Concert. Cymru am byth.' (*Glenys Kinnock*.)

> 'To Mrs Campbell and Staff. You are making a commendable contribution to the enhancement and well-being of the multi-racial communities, which stands to benefit not only this country, but many other countries, especially those of the Third World.' (Christopher M'Lango, *Zambia*.)

Note

1 The building of the new school began at long last in September 1993 and is planned for completion in time for the start of the new school year in September 1994.

18. Commitment to Education in the Secondary School Years

Paper for the National Commission on Education by Professor Tim Brighouse, based on presentations to a Seminar of the Commission held at Manchester Polytechnic, 7 July 1992, and to a Seminar held at Wadham College, Oxford, September 1991.

Introduction

I understand that the Commission has a particular concern about the secondary school years, which I will summarise as follows:

> Young people in this country seem to emerge from primary school with enthusiasm for learning. Then it appears that something happens during the teenage years which makes them less likely to carry on with education than their counterparts in other countries. But the change cannot just 'happen' at 16. Young people do not *suddenly* decide not to continue in full-time education. So what has occurred earlier in their schooling to discourage them?

Let us start with some background.

First, there *is* a significantly lower staying-on rate in this country in the years after compulsory education than in almost every other developed country; moreover, the difference becomes even more marked one year *after* the end of compulsory schooling.

Secondly (and obviously) this lower staying-on rate is not uniform across the country or even within regions of the country. For example, the staying-on rate in the town of Leek in North Staffordshire is 65%; eight miles away, however, in two of the six towns which make up Stoke-on-Trent, it is 25%. The Leek staying-on rate is not very different from that of some of the most salubrious parts of the South-East – South Oxfordshire for example – yet socio-economically Leek has more of the characteristics of Stoke. But it appears to be three times more successful than Stoke in persuading youngsters to show at least the first signs of taking education seriously when the compulsory years are over.

Thirdly – and based on my second point – I make a plea that whatever solutions we find to the problem we apply them *discretely and particularly*. I believe that one of the unfortunate characteristics of education policy-making over the last 10 years is that we treat the whole system as if it were everywhere the same. Media and politicians alike go to it with a zest and with an enviable certainty of purpose which arises from a sometimes tenuous appreciation of some of the real problems of schools. Whatever else the Commission does, I hope it manages to stress the need for discrimination in the application of solutions.

Cultural influences

Ignoring for a moment my own advice to concentrate on the particular, what can we say in general terms about the experiences of 13–16-year-olds and the implications for education?

Commercialism
We surround our young – as do the Americans, Canadians and Australians – with a commercial culture which preys on their consumerism not merely for records and music, but for designer marked clothing and shoes, sport and leisure wear, electronic goods, videos and computer games. For young people and their families, finance by credit has become a way of life. There is nothing new about the availability of drink and tobacco, but there is about the drug culture which stalks the perimeter of urban high schools.

Families and education
Home life too has changed. The family is more loosely connected. Many 13–16-year-olds will not be living with both their natural parents; many will have gone through or be

experiencing the trauma of family break-up. And for a single parent in socio-economically deprived circumstances, life must often be daunting, even well-nigh insupportable.

We should not forget the differential impact of traditions within families. For example, there is evidence that mothers' levels of education affect a child's progress and a school's success from as early as the pre-school and infant years.[1] There is, too, a correlation between a child's likelihood of staying on post-16 and into higher education, and the parent's own real experience of education. In short, if your parents stayed on it is more likely that you will. Thus, the much-maligned 1960s, when we saw such a dramatic expansion of participation in higher education, are today bequeathing a fruitful legacy. In 20 years' time we may well witness another surge as yet another generation wants for its young what it enjoyed itself.

Religious differences
Tradition can, however, leave a more depressing legacy. Nowhere is this more apparent than in the Shankill and Falls Roads in Belfast, where there are, respectively, Protestant and Catholic working-class communities. In recent years in the former, no Protestants have continued into higher education, whereas many in the Catholic community have done so. Why? Is it, as the Irish would jokingly tell you, because the Catholic mother wants at least one of her sons to become a priest and you need 'the education' for that? Or is it because if you are a Catholic in that strife-torn land, you need education in order to 'get on' in any sphere?

Employment traditions
What singles out the Protestants' unwillingness to stay on? Is it the family tradition which enabled a parent to get you a job in the linen mills or at the Harland and Wolff shipyard? Here, then, we have a different set of cultural influences. There can be little doubt that the early industrialisation of the country, with its heavy dependence on unskilled and semi-skilled

(especially male) labour, has handed on from generation to generation a belief that: 'Never mind, lad' – and it usually was 'lad' – 'school will soon be over, so it doesn't really matter what you do there. Your dad's had a word with the foreman and there'll be a place for you in the works'.

Which towns, or more precisely which bits of towns, come to your minds as a result of such a phrase? For me it is Cowley in East Oxford; it is most of Stoke-on-Trent; it is estates in Coventry, Liverpool, Sunderland and Middlesbrough. No-one wanted to stay on at school in those places. Schools were actually child-minding; everyone knew that. Teachers said, and still do say: 'What more can you expect of them?' If your parent went to college or night-school you were more likely to stay on; if he or she went to the car works, that's where you would go too. Sadly, the number of jobs in the car works at Cowley has declined in the last 15 years from something like 30,000 to under 4,000. Happily, you may say, the Nissan works have opened in Sunderland and will do so shortly in Derby. But it is not yet clear what impact these developments will have on young people's educational prospects; it will be interesting to observe how staying-on rates in the three areas are affected.

Peer group pressures
The first Briefing for the National Commission on Education[2] highlighted another cultural influence: that of peer group pressure within schools. In my own work I have found that in the least favourable circumstances, peer group pressure is opposed to achievement, so that, for example, third, fourth or fifth formers in Stoke-on-Trent and Oxford respectively use the words 'chuffer' or 'groff' as terms of abuse to signal their mockery of achievement. In those towns and elsewhere 13–16-year-olds learn to find their achievement outside school or to hide it if it becomes evident within school.

I have drawn attention to several influences on young people's attitudes to education:

- Commercial culture

- Home life

- Parents' experience of education

- Religion

- Employment traditions

- Peer group pressures.

All these play their part. But we must now turn our attention to schooling.

Young people's experience of schooling

Earlier maturity
First, we have to bear in mind that youngsters have changed. They now mature more rapidly physically:

> During the last hundred years there has been a very striking tendency for the time of adolescence, as typified by menarche or the growth spurt, to become earlier.[3]

In 1850 the average age for girls to begin menstruation was 17; in 1950 it was 13½; now it is 12. In addition to sexual development starting sooner, young boys and girls are now taller and heavier. But whereas it used to be the case that children would grow into adulthood alongside adults in an adult, not a childlike community, and would find themselves as 16-year-olds working on farms or in factories or mines alongside men and women, they are now sitting in rows at desks, listening to lesson bells in the same establishment and subject to the same rules and customs as those applied to 11-year-olds. As one writer has suggested:

> Where society does not permit the adolescent to assume a social role comparable with his physical and intellectual development, but keeps him dependent . . . adult

maturity is come by with more difficulty.[4]

A 'dip' in motivation
From research at Keele University,[5] to which I will refer in more detail in a moment, it is clear that in the third year of secondary schooling there is a significant dip in youngsters' satisfaction with school, in their motivation towards their studies and in their attitudes to teachers. There is also other evidence to suggest that many mark time or go backwards in their academic achievements between 14 and 16.[6] And there is a significant proportion of pupils in the 13–16 age range for whom the existing diet of schooling simply does not seem to work.

In our research at Keele we have investigated the habits and views of 11–16-year-olds, concentrating in particular on their satisfaction with schooling, their commitment to school work and their attitudes to teachers. We have surveyed nearly 4,000 pupils in 20 schools in Hampshire, Cheshire, Staffordshire and Shropshire. All were in 11–18 or 11–16 schools. Our instrument was a series of questions randomly arranged and derived from work in the United States and elsewhere. Our sample – of between 20% and 25% – was taken in the Spring term in the middle of a week, and ideally from a strictly random sample drawn from each of the year groups, or occasionally a mixed ability tutor group intended to be representative of each of the year groups. In future we shall insist on random samples from year groups, since the 'tutor effect' is enormous.

What do we learn from our survey?

On average, the results indicate a steady falling-away in commitment to work, attitudes towards teachers and general satisfaction, from year 7 to year 11. There is, increasingly, a 10% gap between the picture for girls (higher commitment, more positive attitudes) and that for boys (lower commitment, less positive attitudes), which mirrors the growing discrepancy between girls and boys in examination performance at 16-plus. (If comprehensive education has achieved one thing, it is a better deal for girls.) Nevertheless, we have also learned how individual schools can differ from the average. Evidence of such differences enables perceptive leadership to see which particular aspects of school culture, home culture, organisational arrangements and so on, it needs to address. The lessons learned reinforce my earlier points: we do not need universal panaceas, merely particular treatments. Other messages also emerge. For example, we learn of children's unchanging habits in the number of hours spent watching television. In addition, it has been interesting to note the number of nights out, the hours spent on homework and so on. All these messages reinforce the need to establish high expectations and more serious habits among pupils.

Some of the apparent decline in motivation may be due to the assessment arrangements for the national curriculum, with a long two-year developmental gap between levels. Another factor is the presence of an examination at 16+ which coincides with the end of the compulsory period of schooling and which, for an increasing number of pupils, marks a change from school either to work or to a post-16 college. This acts as a 'watershed'; a stage when we lose too many from the education system. Indeed, we actually encourage youngsters to leave education by giving them 'leaving certificates' at 16+ awards evenings.

Action to improve motivation and commitment

There are certain things that we cannot expect to change. Taking risks, trying things out, being rebellious – these are all normal features of adolescence and young adulthood. Some societal phenomena which influence youngsters' attitudes – such as consumerism – are beyond the immediate influence of those working in education. Nevertheless, there are measures which in my view could succeed in improving motivation and commitment towards education in the secondary school years.

I propose the following:

- A fundamental change in the organisation of the curriculum and schooling from age 13/14. Many schools have already experimented with modular courses. One of the virtues of this approach is that it allows youngsters to follow their particular interests whilst still achieving breadth and balance over a period, helped by appropriate personal guidance. It is worth noting that for many pupils, the only thing that has kept them in 'the system' has been the ability to pursue their burning interest, even if this has resulted for a time in a rather unbalanced experience of the curriculum.

- A change in the focus of public examinations, from age 16, to age 14. The national curriculum could be compressed in order to end at 14, and the GCSE brought forward. A certain minimum score would normally be achieved at 14 (though it could be achieved later); from 14 onwards, youngsters would make a fresh start, following individual paths through education, work experience, training and community service. Students would work in interest-led, mixed-age classes, rather than being organised according to age groups. Schooling or training would culminate in an Advanced Certificate or Diploma for Education and Training achieved at the age of 19 or 20.

- 'Education-extra' courses as a natural 'top-up' to normal schooling for those who want them. These extra studies for the purpose of compensation, reinforcement, extension or enrichment could be offered by schools – or better still by groups of schools – after school hours.

- Work without training for those aged under 21 would become illegal.

The need to raise expectations

I would like to conclude with another observation which emerges from our work. It is to do with the decline in happiness with schooling, the view which pupils think teachers have of them, *the unchanging expectations which they have of themselves*. They are far too convinced that they are 'average'. I cannot resist quoting a poem given to me by Michael Buscemi, a colleague in America, where they perceive themselves as having a similar problem:

The Average Child

*I don't cause teachers trouble
My grades have been OK.
I listen in my classes
And I'm in school every day
My parents think I'm average
My teachers think so too
I wish I didn't know that
'Cause there's lots I'd like to do
I'd like to build a rocket
I've a book that shows you how
Or start a stamp collection
Well, no use in trying now
'Cause since I found I'm average
I'm just smart enough you see
To know there's nothing special
That I should expect of me
I'm part of that majority
That hump part of the bell
Who spends his life unnoticed
In an average kind of hell.*

First presented at 1979 National PTA Convention
by Michael Buscemi, Quest International.

The Americans have tackled this by working to raise pupils' self-esteem and confidence. That is certainly an important first step, but it must be accompanied by *a determination to raise youngsters' expectations of what they will actually achieve*. I am convinced that until we overcome that 'averageness' we will not make genuine progress in solving our national problems. Criterion-referencing, not norm-referencing; keeping people 'journeying hopefully' for a longer period; viewing ability in a discriminating and multi-faceted way; all these will contribute towards a solution. So will the 'adoption' of schools by universities and colleges, to encourage in pupils from the earliest possible stage an expectation of higher education. But let's not attempt that simultaneously across the whole country. Let's first tackle the problem where the need is greatest. And our research evidence shows this to be among pupils in urban areas, from manual backgrounds.

Finally, I would like to mention that at the Centre for Successful Schools at Keele, we are now offering a national service to schools, helping them to examine their own performance in relation to some of the most important features of successful schooling: pupils' commitment to their work; their attitudes towards teachers; the extent to which individual pupils are able to establish a worthwhile relationship with at least one adult in school; and their overall satisfaction with schooling.

References

1 Tizard, B. and Blatchford, P. (1988). *Young Children at School in the Inner City*. Erlbaum.
2 McPherson, A. (1992). *Measuring Added Value in Schools*. National Commission on Education Briefing No. 1.
3 Tanner, J.M. (1978). *Growth at Adolescence*. Blackwell Scientific Books, p. 145.
4 *Ibid*, p. 148.
5 University of Keele Centre for Successful Schools (research in progress).
6 See especially the findings of the Assessment of Performance Unit (APU).

19. A Scottish Perspective on the Curriculum and Assessment

Extracts from a paper prepared by Cameron Harrison on behalf of the Scottish Consultative Council on the Curriculum, as background to a presentation to the National Commission on Education in May 1992.

Introduction

A broad interpretation of the curriculum
Education is more than what goes on in school. It is based on relationships between the school and the home, and between the school and the wider community. The curriculum consists of all the planned experiences which the school offers the child – the programmes, the learning processes and the human relationships involved.

A characteristic feature of Scottish schools is their concern with the individual child as a developing member of society. The curriculum should provide each pupil with opportunities to acquire a range of skills and values to allow full participation in that society.

Importance of school ethos
The ethos of the individual school has a significant effect on the curriculum. The physical environment of the school and the classrooms; the organisation for learning within classrooms; the relationships among pupils and adults in the school; the informal counselling that takes place between teachers and pupils; the quality of partnership between home and school all combine to have a powerful influence on what children learn, and how effectively they learn. Another important influence is what is sometimes described as 'the informal curriculum', including activities of a social, recreational or sporting nature.

There are also powerful influences on children outwith the school. While schools may have no control over these factors, they do have a responsibility to be aware of, and to take account of, external influences in reviewing and planning the curriculum for their pupils.

The task of education

The task of education is two-fold: it must satisfy both the needs of the individual and the requirements of society. Implicit in that is the importance of carrying forward the development of knowledge, understanding, skills and values. The curriculum must therefore recognise and make provision for all three of these claims:

Needs of the pupil as an individual
Pupils vary in aptitudes, abilities and achievements as well as differing in how they learn. The design of the curriculum in schools should reflect these differences, but this should not be taken to imply an expectation on schools to provide an individualised curriculum for each child. Rather, the emphasis for schools should be to find ways of organising learning that take account of the range of differing needs within any group of pupils, recognising the psychological, physical, cultural, and social differences that exist within the school community.

Requirements of society
The dynamic nature of society demands a constant re-evaluation of the aims and practices of education. Schools must consider how appropriate the curriculum is to equip children for all aspects of our rapidly changing world, for future stages of education, and for the eventual demands of adult life in the 1990s and into the 21st century.

Development of knowledge, understanding, skills and values
In responding to the needs of individual pupils and the requirements of society, teachers must ensure that knowledge, understanding, skills and values are built up progres-

sively so that children can make sense of the world and be able to cope with the increasingly complex requirements of living now and in the future.

Aims of schooling

Schooling, through the provision of a broad range of progressively demanding experiences, should help each child to acquire and develop all of the following:

- positive attitudes to learning and personal fulfilment through the achievement of worthwhile objectives;

- knowledge, skills and understanding in literacy and communication, numeracy and mathematical thinking;

- understanding and appreciation of themselves, the changing world and its people;

- respect for religious, social and moral values in a multicultural society;

- the capacity for independent thought through, for example, enquiry, problem solving, information handling and reasoning;

- the capacity to make creative and practical use of a variety of media to express feelings and ideas.

Essential features of the curriculum

In attempting to give practical expression to the claims on the curriculum and the aims of education described above, schools must pay special attention to the following essential features which have relevance for every pupil at every stage of primary and secondary education and should permeate every area of the curriculum:

- knowledge and understanding

- key skills and elements
- personal and social development.

Knowledge and understanding
No matter what the context for learning, there will be a body of related knowledge which is fundamental to achieving understanding. The acquisition and presentation of such knowledge needs to be structured carefully if pupils are to assimilate and recall it and understand its relationships with other learning experiences.

Key skills and elements
In the process of learning and in the context of daily life, all children and adults require a range of skills. Few, if any, of these skills can be identified solely with separate areas of the curriculum; they are not discrete elements but are developed in all learning situations. They include for example the use of language and numeracy; reasoning and problem solving; and the use of information technology.

Personal and social development
The school provides a major opportunity for personal and social development through practical experience, personal involvement and the exercise of responsibility. Key aspects of personal and social development encompass, for example, an understanding of: healthy living and physical fitness; rules and responsibilities; and the concepts of equal opportunities, tolerance and self-esteem.

Key skills and personal and social development form a vital component of the curriculum. We return to them later in this paper.

Scotland's unique curricular framework

Consensus not legislation
Scotland does not have a statutory national curriculum. Government ministers in Scotland have stated a preference for

the existing system based on consensus rather than legislation. Within this consensus all education authorities and most independent schools have agreed to work within the curriculum guidelines prepared by the Scottish Consultative Council on the Curriculum (SCCC). With regard to assessment, they operate under arrangements for secondary schools prepared by the Scottish Examination Board (SEB) and by the Scottish Vocational Education Council (SCOTVEC) (together with SCCC and Her Majesty's Inspectorate), and under arrangements for primary schools prepared by the Scottish Office Education Department (SOED). Nationally standardised tests for pupils in the fourth and seventh years of the primary school are devised by the SEB.

All schools work within a national curricular framework prepared by the SCCC for the primary and secondary stages. The frameworks for the 12–14 and post-16 stages are shown as examples in Figures 1 and 2 on pages 230–233. Each school (or group of schools) works out programmes of study and selects courses suited to the needs of the school and its community to form the local curricular provision. For older pupils there are increasing opportunities to select courses suitable to interest, aptitude, ability, special educational needs or exceptional circumstances.

Primary schools
In primary schools the curriculum is built around five 'areas'. These are:

Language
Mathematics
Environmental studies
Expressive arts
Religious and moral education.

Secondary schools
In secondary schools the curriculum is built around eight 'modes'. These are:

Language and communication

Mathematical studies and applications
Scientific studies and applications
Social and environmental studies
Technological activities and applications
Creative and aesthetic activities
Physical education
Religious and moral education.

In describing the secondary curriculum in Scotland, the term 'mode' has been adopted to categorise 'distinctive ways of knowing'.[1] Modes are perceived as categories of curricular activity through which stated educational aims can be achieved. They are used as a means of achieving balance and breadth, and they assist in the operation of choice within the negotiated curriculum of individual pupils.

Within its curriculum guidelines SCCC does not suggest any departure from a management structure for secondary schools based on subject departments; however, the Council is aware that, rather than teaching exclusively in subject terms, teachers increasingly contribute to wider aspects of the curriculum. The greater flexibility of such an approach enables curriculum planning, both in schools and nationally, to be conceived in terms of modes and courses which are related to an overall curriculum rationale and to the needs of pupils.

Key skills and elements

Set alongside the modes and courses approach to curriculum planning is the belief that a number of key process skills and elements of personal and social development are essential to every pupil's development. A student's basic educational entitlement is considered to encompass:

- *Personal and social development* which includes health; rules, rights and responsibilities; the concepts of equal opportunities, understanding and tolerance; care of the environment; critical appreciation of the media; preparation for everyday living and future employment.

- *Basic skills and process skills* which include communicative language and numeracy; accessing and processing information; learning to learn; reasoning; problem solving; designing and practical applications.

Key process skills and elements of personal and social development underpin both the curricular areas (age 5–14) and the curricular modes (age 12–18). These aspects of learning are a measure of the extent to which the curriculum in the Scottish system has moved away from considerations related purely to subjects. The effect of this shift on classroom methodologies has been marked and positive.

In implementing this approach, a three-part strategy is being encouraged:

Permeation
By this we mean that all of the key skills and elements are the responsibility of every teacher of every subject at every stage. They are part of the climate in which learning takes place. They permeate the whole curriculum.

An effective permeation strategy requires that attention should focus on teaching methods and on the nature of pupils' learning experiences as well as on overt course content. Most often and most successfully, the acquisition of process skills and key elements of personal and social development is achieved through discursive, enquiry and activity approaches as well as by expository teaching. Careful selection of course materials and contexts should provide pupils with planned opportunities to develop, practise and apply the skills and attitudes which it is intended to promote. This approach is exemplified in all Standard Grade courses for 14–16-year-olds and in the supporting course materials now available to schools.

Curriculum inserts/enhancement
Aspects of the basic entitlement are built into all courses wherever relevant. For example, all the new Standard Grade courses for 14–16-year-olds are structured and assessed on the

basis of identified elements, often three in number; while one of these elements is concerned with knowledge and understanding, the other two relate to relevant process/practical skills and to investigatory/problem-solving approaches.

Special courses
Additional special courses (often of short duration) are available in most schools, e.g. Systematic Approaches to Problem Solving; Organisation of Practical Skills; Enterprise Activity; Word Processing; Life and Work; Health and Consumers. The implementation of this part of the strategy has been greatly assisted by the development within Scotland of a large number of nationally-certificated short courses and modules.

Breadth and balance

Breadth and balance are significant factors in the provision of a basic curriculum. The introduction of modes as a basic curricular construct assists in the provision of breadth and balance. Courses within all modes provide rich contexts for the meaningful development of language, numerical, personal and social skills. These modes represent the core of the curriculum for all pupils aged 12–16. They articulate well with the five established areas of the primary curriculum and they assist coherence between each secondary stage.

Structure of the curriculum
In Scotland, basic education for all pupils aged 5–16 includes systematic and active learning within the curricular structure shown on page 223.

Flexibility and choice

Flexibility and choice are especially important in the secondary stages to maintain motivation and to cater for the emerging needs, interests and aspirations of pupils. At all stages a flexibility factor of at least 20% of curriculum time is

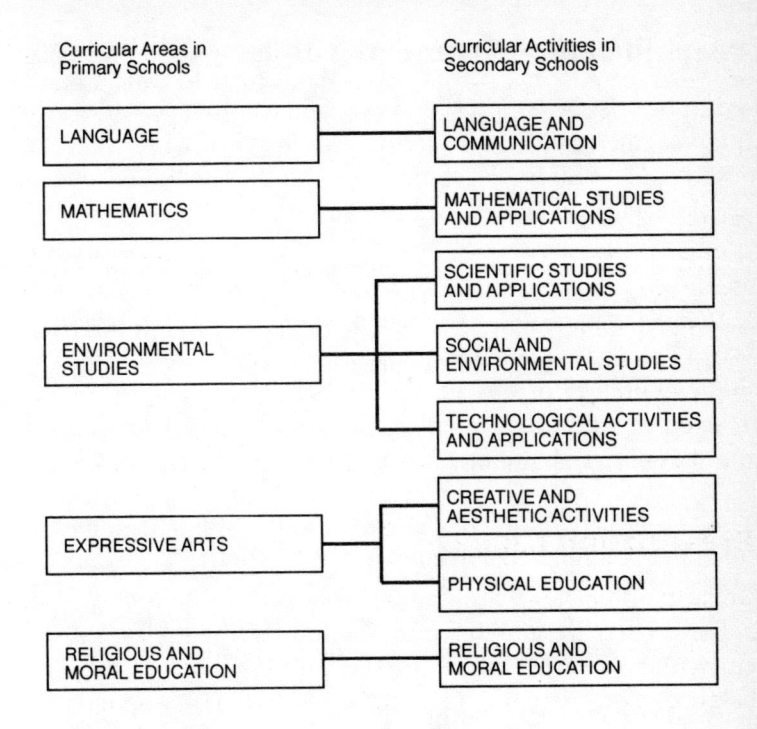

Curricular Areas in Primary Schools	Curricular Activities in Secondary Schools
LANGUAGE	LANGUAGE AND COMMUNICATION
MATHEMATICS	MATHEMATICAL STUDIES AND APPLICATIONS
ENVIRONMENTAL STUDIES	SCIENTIFIC STUDIES AND APPLICATIONS
	SOCIAL AND ENVIRONMENTAL STUDIES
	TECHNOLOGICAL ACTIVITIES AND APPLICATIONS
EXPRESSIVE ARTS	CREATIVE AND AESTHETIC ACTIVITIES
	PHYSICAL EDUCATION
RELIGIOUS AND MORAL EDUCATION	RELIGIOUS AND MORAL EDUCATION

provided to enable schools to adapt their local curricular provision to suit the needs of the school and its community. Increasingly through the secondary stages, the national curricular framework of modes and courses assists in the provision of pupil choice through a system of core studies and options.

The principles of core studies and options are illustrated in the guidelines for the 12–14 curriculum shown in Figure 1 on pages 230–231. A notional minimum allocation of time required for each mode constitutes the core, but often a choice of subject courses, multi-disciplinary or short courses is permitted within that core. A flexibility factor of 20% or 30% allows for further pupil choice within or outwith the core. By indicating which courses we believe contribute to each of the modes, we believe that we ensure breadth and balance.

Teaching and learning methods

Schools must be concerned about *how* children learn, as well as *what* children learn. Therefore, the ways in which teachers teach and organise learning opportunities for children are crucial factors in achieving a proper curricular balance.

Styles of teaching
Teachers usually adopt the following approaches in the classroom to a greater or lesser degree:

- *expository*: characterised by the imparting of information, explanations and instructions to whole classes or groups;

- *discursive*: stressing oral work in groups with initiation of ideas by children and guidance by teachers;

- *enquiry*: involving the creation of opportunities for choice, individual planning, and investigation;

- *activity*: emphasising the use of creative and practical approaches across the whole curriculum.

By selecting one or more of these styles of teaching for individuals, groups or a class it is possible for teachers to help children to attain planned objectives. A flexible, but carefully structured, approach to learning and teaching not only confirms the importance of an active role for children in learning, but also the need for careful judgement by the teacher in selecting the appropriate methods.

Importance of differentiation
It is important that the curriculum is differentiated in terms of the pace and the approaches to teaching used to meet the needs of the individual pupil. This requires a professional assessment of children's existing knowledge, understanding and skills; an appreciation of their previous experience and

development; and an awareness of the resources available to the teacher.

Careful judgement will determine the appropriate level of work, task or expectation. All pupils, including those with special educational needs, should be progressively challenged by the activities provided by teachers so that the qualities of initiative, independence and creativity necessary for life in a modern society can be developed. If it is to develop coherently, a differentiated curriculum also requires the maintenance of a systematic record of pupil progress.

Pupils working together
Whereas differentiation stresses the need for the task or level of work to relate to individual needs and abilities, co-operative learning emphasises the social value and practical utility of pupils working together. Opportunities exist in all curricular areas for pupils to work together, to support each other, to experience helping as well as being helped, and to appreciate the effectiveness of teamwork. Differentiation and co-operative learning bring differing but complementary advantages. They must be balanced carefully in determining the patterns of organisation across the curriculum.

Cross-curricular links
Teachers should also strive to take advantage of the opportunities available to them to emphasise the links that exist across the curriculum. This is an important principle and one which arises in the primary school from the teacher's overview of all the learning experiences of a class of pupils as well as of each child's view of the world as an integrated whole. It is through these links that primary pupils will encounter the variety of ways of understanding the world and will be 'given some awareness of the processes of problem solving and handling experience which inform the thinking of those who seek to explore and explain the world as scientists, historians, mathematicians, etc'.[2] Similarly, in the secondary school attention

needs to be given to the relationships between the different parts of the curriculum.

Assessment and certification

The arrangements for assessment and certification differ for 5–14 and 14–16-year-olds:

(a) *For ages 5–14*, a new, more rigorous, assessment system is being phased in. For each of the five curricular areas (language, mathematics, environmental studies, expressive arts, religious and moral education) we are identifying sets of attainment outcomes and attainment targets related to five very broadly defined levels of attainment.

In mathematics, for example, there are four attainment outcomes: problem solving; information handling; number, money and measurement; and shape, position and movement. An attainment target related to 'information handling' might be to interpret a graph or a pie chart.

All assessment at age 5–14 is classroom- and school-based, except that national standardised tests will be administered at ages 9 and 12 in language and mathematics. Progress will be recorded by teachers for discussion with parents for transfer purposes.

(b) *For ages 14–16*, new assessment and certification arrangements are now operating. Certification at age 16 is for all pupils, right across the ability range.

All Standard Grade courses (two-year subject or multi-disciplinary courses) are graded Foundation, General and Credit with seven overlapping levels. The assessment system is a 'quasi-criterion-referenced' one, using grade-related criteria (GRC). These are positive descriptions of performance against which a candidate's achievement is measured. Direct comparisons are not made between one candidate and another. Achievement in each course is reported on a profile based on identified elements for each course. There are GRC for each course element.

Short courses and modules (40 hours, free-standing or clustered) are criterion-referenced (award, repeat, fail).

Strategies for national curriculum development

Consultation and co-operation
All major curriculum development guidelines are devised by working groups with representation from a wide range of interests. Nevertheless, a general principle for all working groups is that they should have practising teachers in a majority. Other bodies represented include colleges of education (teacher training institutions), education authority advisers, HM Inspectors and, in some cases, universities.

Central support groups (CSGs) are established by SCCC for all new courses to advise on the preparation of staff development, starter and exemplar course materials. Each CSG is composed of practising teachers with a college of education representative and an HMI, and is usually chaired by an education authority adviser or headteacher. CSGs identify the range of support materials required for implementation of the new course and co-ordinate their preparation. Support materials may be written by the CSG members but most have been prepared by local writing groups of teachers set up by education authorities.

We have set up around 40 central support groups involving in the region of 300 teachers and others; in addition to this, perhaps twice as many teachers have been involved in local support groups, producing specific packages of materials. Personally, we believe that this involvement has of itself made a major contribution to staff development within our system.

To date SCCC has produced and distributed around 1000 different packages of support materials across the whole range of new courses. We have found in a recent evaluation exercise that while teachers have complained about the deluge of paper which is arriving on their desks and about the quality of particular parts of particular packages, the overall assessment is that this support has been critical to the success of the new courses. From our point of view as a national curriculum organisation, we would have to say that these arrangements have led to an unprecedented degree of sustained and close co-operation between SCCC and practitioners in schools and colleges. This has been a refreshing experience for us. We like to hope that it has given practitioners a clear sense of the SCCC's basic aim, which is to provide well-grounded support for teachers in the classroom.

Training for curriculum delivery
At national and local level a cascade approach is used for training purposes.

For the 14–18 curriculum, each central support group is responsible for planning a national in-service course; such national courses often focus on using and refining the emerging staff development materials. The finalised materials are then disseminated for use in local training at regional or school level.

At local level, staff development proceeds by a variety of approaches and not necessarily solely through a cascade approach. We have, for example, a great deal of school-based staff development; our system provides for a number of day closures of schools to permit staff development. In addition, our teachers' contract includes a specified number of hours for what is called 'planned activity time'; these planned activities are often of a staff and curriculum development nature.

Curriculum audit
At school level the strategy of 'curriculum audit' is increasingly being employed by headteachers for monitoring purposes. This development has been stimulated by the need to track individual pupil opportunity and progress in key process skills and in elements of personal and social development, as well as in the activities and experiences required within each curricular mode. The flexibility inherent within the new

system is also encouraging more imaginative use by headteachers of alternative curricular pathways.

Conclusion

Over many years, consultation and discussion have produced a large measure of agreement on the kind of curriculum that all pupils in Scotland should experience: the result is the unique national curricular framework for primary and secondary schools outlined in this paper.

References

1. Scottish Education Department/Scottish Consultative Council on the Curriculum (1977). *The Structure of the Curriculum in the Third and Fourth Years of the Scottish Secondary School.* (The Munn Report.)
2. Scottish Consultative Council on the Curriculum (1987). *Curriculum Design for the Secondary Stages.*

Figure 1: Curricular framework for S1/S2. SCCC Guidelines for schools.

MODE	LANGUAGE AND COMMUNICATION	MATHEMATICAL STUDIES AND APPLICATIONS	SCIENTIFIC STUDIES AND APPLICATIONS	SOCIAL AND ENVIRONMENTAL STUDIES
Short Description	Reading, writing, speaking and listening skills; linguistic resourcefulness; study of literature and the media; study of a second language	Numerical skills; mathematical understanding; problem-solving; practical and everyday applications	Scientific observation and experiment; problem identification and solving; practical applications	Knowledge, understanding and investigation of aspects of the community, society and the environment past and present; economic awareness

KEY SKILLS AND ELEMENTS	
a. Process Skills	COMMUNICATING AND LEARNING SKILLS: language and numeracy - accessing and processing information - learning strategies TECHNOLOGICAL AND CREATIVE THINKING: reasoning and problem-solving - designing - practical applications ◄——— permeating all modes, courses and activities ———►
b. Elements of Personal and Social Development	HEALTH; RULES, RIGHTS AND RESPONSIBILITIES EQUAL OPPORTUNITIES, UNDERSTANDING AND TOLERANCE CARE OF THE ENVIRONMENT; CRITICAL APPRECIATION OF THE MEDIA GUIDANCE RELATED TO EVERYDAY LIVING AND FUTURE EMPLOYMENT

NOTIONAL MINIMUM % TIME OVER THE TWO YEAR PERIOD	Minimum 20%	Minimum 10%	Minimum 10%	Minimum 10%
CORE 80%	20% FLEXIBILITY FACTOR			

CORE				
Courses making major contributions to the Mode	ENGLISH MODERN FOREIGN LANGUAGE	MATHEMATICS	SCIENCE	SOCIAL SUBJECTS

ENRICHMENT				
Examples of additional courses/ activities	Additional Languages Classical Studies Media Studies Scottish/Celtic Studies	Computer Applications Money Management	Electronics Energy Studies Safety	Classical Studies Economic Awareness European Awareness International and Multicultural Studies Media Studies Scottish/Celtic Studies

Figure 1 (Cont'd): Curricular framework for S1/S2. SCCC Guidelines for schools.

MODE	TECHNOLOGICAL ACTIVITIES AND APPLICATIONS	CREATIVE AND AESTHETIC ACTIVITIES	PHYSICAL EDUCATION	RELIGIOUS AND MORAL EDUCATION
Short Description	Development of technological and practical skills; designing, making and using artefacts; practical problem-solving and applications	Aesthetic appreciation; design; expressive, practical and creative activities	Physical activities; health and well-being; movement; leisure skills and interests	Study of religion; religious awareness: moral development; human conduct; related personal and social issues
KEY SKILLS AND ELEMENTS a. Process Skills b. Elements of Personal and Social Development	\multicolumn{4}{c}{COMMUNICATING AND LEARNING SKILLS: language and numeracy - accessing and processing information - learning strategies TECHNOLOGICAL AND CREATIVE THINKING: reasoning and problem-solving - designing - practical applications ◄——— permeating all modes, courses and activities ———► HEALTH; RULES, RIGHTS AND RESPONSIBILITIES EQUAL OPPORTUNITIES, UNDERSTANDING AND TOLERANCE CARE OF THE ENVIRONMENT; CRITICAL APPRECIATION OF THE MEDIA GUIDANCE RELATED TO EVERYDAY LIVING AND FUTURE EMPLOYMENT}			
NOTIONAL MINIMUM % TIME OVER THE TWO YEAR PERIOD CORE 80%	Minimum 10%	Minimum 10%	Minimum 5%	Minimum 5%
	\multicolumn{4}{c}{20% FLEXIBILITY FACTOR}			
CORE Courses making major contributions to the Mode	TECHNICAL EDUCATION HOME ECONOMICS	ART, MUSIC AND DRAMA	PHYSICAL EDUCATION	RELIGIOUS AND MORAL EDUCATION
ENRICHMENT Examples of additional courses/ activities	Computer Applications Electronics Enterprise Activities Keyboarding Skills	Design Leisure Activities Media Studies	Health Studies Physical Education Recreation	Related Personal and Social Issues

Figure 2: Curricular framework for S5/S6. SCCC Guidelines for schools.

Broadly through these MODES	LANGUAGE AND COMMUNICATION	MATHEMATICAL STUDIES AND APPLICATIONS	SCIENTIFIC STUDIES AND APPLICATIONS	SOCIAL AND ENVIRONMENTAL EDUCATION
and from KEY SKILLS AND ELEMENTS	COMMUNICATING AND LEARNING SKILLS: language and numeracy - accessing and processing information - learning strategies TECHNOLOGICAL AND CREATIVE THINKING: reasoning and problem-solving - designing - practical applications			
there derive certain features	←——— permeating all modes, courses and activities ———→ HEALTH; RULES, RIGHTS AND RESPONSIBILITIES EQUAL OPPORTUNITIES, UNDERSTANDING AND TOLERANCE CARE OF THE ENVIRONMENT; CRITICAL APPRECIATION OF THE MEDIA GUIDANCE RELATED TO EVERYDAY LIVING AND FUTURE EMPLOYMENT			
which are integral to a well-balanced individual curriculum at S5/S6	Development and application in all formal and informal contexts, in and out of school, of: SKILLS OF COMMUNICATION, NUMERACY AND LEARNING TECHNOLOGICAL, CREATIVE AND CRITICAL THINKING PERSONAL, MORAL AND SOCIAL DEVELOPMENT			
Development of KNOWLEDGE and UNDER-STANDING and application of essential features will take place in the context of COURSES AND ACTIVITIES of an increasingly vocational and specialised nature	AT NATIONAL LEVEL the choice derives from: (i) Scottish Certificate of Education Courses (ii) Certificate of Sixth-Year Studies Courses (iii) SCE Short Courses (iv) National Certificate Modules. AT LOCAL LEVEL the choice may be enhanced through work experience, community involvement or other special programmes arranged by the authority and school with FE colleges and local employers and other local bodies. INDIVIDUAL CURRICULA should be negotiated at school level to ensure coherence, breadth and balance on the basis of these principles.			

Figure 2 (Cont'd): Curricular framework for S5/S6. SCCC Guidelines for schools.

Broadly through these MODES	TECHNOLOGICAL ACTIVITIES AND APPLICATIONS	CREATIVE AND AESTHETIC ACTIVITIES	PHYSICAL EDUCATION	RELIGIOUS AND MORAL EDUCATION
and from KEY SKILLS AND ELEMENTS there derive certain features which are integral to a well-balanced individual curriculum at S5/S6	COMMUNICATING AND LEARNING SKILLS: language and numeracy - accessing and processing information - learning strategies TECHNOLOGICAL AND CREATIVE THINKING: reasoning and problem-solving - designing - practical applications ⬅ permeating all modes, courses and activities ➡ HEALTH; RULES, RIGHTS AND RESPONSIBILITIES EQUAL OPPORTUNITIES, UNDERSTANDING AND TOLERANCE CARE OF THE ENVIRONMENT; CRITICAL APPRECIATION OF THE MEDIA GUIDANCE RELATED TO EVERYDAY LIVING AND FUTURE EMPLOYMENT Development and application in all formal and informal contexts, in and out of school, of: SKILLS OF COMMUNICATION, NUMERACY AND LEARNING TECHNOLOGICAL, CREATIVE AND CRITICAL THINKING PERSONAL, MORAL AND SOCIAL DEVELOPMENT			
Development of KNOWLEDGE and UNDER-STANDING and application of essential features will take place in the context of COURSES AND ACTIVITIES of an increasingly vocational and specialised nature	AT NATIONAL LEVEL the choice derives from: (i) Scottish Certificate of Education Courses (ii) Certificate of Sixth-Year Studies Courses (iii) SCE Short Courses (iv) National Certificate Modules. AT LOCAL LEVEL the choice may be enhanced through work experience, community involvement or other special programmes arranged by the authority and school with FE colleges and local employers and other local bodies. INDIVIDUAL CURRICULA should be negotiated at school level to ensure coherence, breadth and balance on the basis of these principles.			

20. Learning Support and Guidance for Pupils

Paper for the National Commission on Education by Richard Staite, Headteacher, Beeslack High School, Lothian, 1993.

Introduction

Our aim in this paper is to describe briefly how we organise learning support and guidance for pupils at Beeslack High School and the philosophy which underpins our practice.

Principles of learning support

We wish to stress that learning support is the antithesis of a system in which students requiring extra help with learning are separated from mainstream classes and sent to a specialist 'remedial' teacher who administers the 'cure', thus seemingly absolving the class teacher of responsibility.

Instead, we adopt a *whole-school* approach to learning support, reinforced by a written statement of school policy which is known, understood and operated by all staff. It is made clear that all teachers deliver learning support for all students. This approach demands *integrated and consistent methods*, involving consultation and co-operative teaching, largely in mainstream classes, but supported by workshops to deal with particular problems. A good indicator of the success of the programme is the willingness of students to *refer themselves* for learning support.

The way in which learning support is structured gives powerful signals about the school's commitment to young people. Therefore, to emphasise the very positive view we take of learning support, the term 'learning needs' rather than 'learning difficulties' is used. The emphasis is on *differentiated* learning in mainstream classes.

Learning support in practice

These principles presuppose that the classroom atmosphere and the methodology of the *mainstream curriculum* are appropriate, otherwise what is offered will be simply 'well-supported failure'.

Specialist learning support staff are employed to provide a range of help, for example:

- reviewing/writing/redesigning curriculum units in collaboration with subject specialists;

- working on agreed learning tasks with particular classes or with particular children;

- providing evidence of a particular teaching approach (such as discussion skills or the use of a text);

- making available to a department a specific skill possessed by the learning support specialist(s);

- assisting a department in devising assessment profiles.

Teachers may refer students for learning support, or indeed students may refer themselves. *Small group workshops* form part of the learning programme. They last for about twenty or forty minutes and are used for a variety of purposes. The most common problems dealt with in workshops would be spelling, handwriting and reading, although mathematics and specific areas of work from other subjects would also feature. The *transfer of skills from workshop to mainstream classroom* is the key, and it is therefore essential that students' work is monitored, through clearly specified arrangements, in subject classrooms. In short, the learning which takes place in workshops must be reviewed in the light of classwork and monitored by class teachers.

We place considerable emphasis on *regular staff development* to draw the attention of all teachers to their responsibility for students' learning.

A staffing structure for learning support

Our staffing strategy for learning support is consistent with the underlying principle of delivery across the curriculum, and with the need to maintain a high level of awareness about learning support among all staff: in other words, learning support staff are not placed in a separate 'learning support department'.

The learning support programme involves a combination of *blocks of time* (when a range of departments are visited on a rota basis by a learning support specialist), and *continuous contact* between learning support staff and particular departments (e.g. mathematics) in the course of the session. *Planning and review cycles* are required within these blocks of time, to allow for genuine consultation between teachers (e.g. to review progress in co-operative work). This is done partly through formal questionnaires, and partly through informal discussion.

The cross-curricular approach cannot be sustained by learning support specialists alone. They require the immediate support of an *extended team of staff*, namely:

- *Guidance staff* working in classrooms (other than their own subject), with particular pupils in their year.

- *Subject teachers within department(s)*: some additional time is allocated to departmental staff to allow co-operative teaching between departmental colleagues.

- *Subject teachers* working directly with the learning support specialist. Each session, staff wishing to work directly in learning support are given time in addition to their subject commitment in order to achieve this.

- *Senior teachers* have a cross-curricular/methodology remit and work to agreed programmes in consultation with an assistant head and the learning support specialist. Their remits are: language; numeracy; health education; open learning; and technology.

These different kinds of strategies require:

- a staffing policy which recognises this extended team approach, rather than a (separate) remedial 'department';

- co-ordination by the learning support specialist and a member of the senior management team.

Principles of guidance

The primary responsibility of guidance staff is to provide *pastoral continuity*: to care for the welfare of all students in their cohort and to monitor progress; in particular, the progress of those with special needs and those who are underachieving. Their central concern is *students' personal and social development*. Thus, the guidance system has a major role to play in the emotional health of the school and gives important signals as to the values and the caring nature of the institution.

As with learning support, we adopt a *consistent, whole-school, collective approach*, with all members of staff, both teaching and non-teaching, sharing knowledge and understanding relating to guidance work, and delivering guidance according to the school's agreed policy.

Communication on guidance matters has to be effective, timely and appropriate. This applies in all contexts: internal/external to the system; formal/informal; written/oral. The guidance office is responsible for the feed-in/feed-out of information and is integral to the running (and therefore the management) of the school.

An important measure of the success of the guidance system is the extent to which students refer themselves for guidance, and their willingness to be engaged in informal contact with teachers.

Guidance in practice

In practice, guidance is an onerous task, requiring the combined skills of managing the whole cohort and providing sensitive counselling for individual youngsters. First and foremost it has a *preventative function*, requiring the ability to spot patterns rather than being forced to react to crises. Truancy, for example, is often due to a cluster of factors – social, emotional, psychological, curricular. Good guidance must identify problems immediately and initiate prompt action.

To achieve this, *good links* between guidance staff and class teachers, parents and other agencies are vital. Identifying, recording and communicating are key functions of the guidance system. Guidance is an important vehicle for the school's internal/external communications. In addition to routine contacts with parents, guidance staff will make early contact with them in the event of any problem. In return, they will normally be the first point of contact for parents, for whom the guidance teacher becomes a well-known and approachable person.

Guidance is also important to the system of *standards and discipline* in the school – not, we would stress, in the sense of the direct delivery of punishments, but in conveying the values which pupils will assimilate.

A staffing structure for guidance

The school has a number of *promoted posts* (posts of responsibility), based on the pupil roll, with specific responsibility for pastoral, curricular and careers guidance. These posts are allocated additional non-teaching time so that guidance staff are available and approachable on a regular basis. All other teaching staff are involved in *'first line guidance'* and are seen as an extension of the guidance team, meeting with students in daily registration, issuing information, supporting personal development work and offering support to their groups.

Guidance staff and first line group tutors move on through the school with their cohorts, in order to provide pastoral continuity.

All *subject teachers* must understand (with assistance from a staff development programme):

- their role in relation to the guidance system;

- their direct involvement in the personal and social development of young people, essentially through the methodology adopted in the teaching of subjects.

Conclusions

How the curriculum is taught, learned and experienced is at the heart of effective schooling. This has vital implications for the way in which we organise and carry out learning support and guidance for *all* pupils, across the whole range of ability. In other words, for learning to be managed effectively, schools need to have in place: reliable mechanisms for diagnosing individual pupils' needs; guidance staff; specialist subject or cross-curricular support for teachers; and a management structure which allows all teachers to contribute to learning support and guidance. This paper illustrates how we endeavour to achieve these aims at Beeslack.

21. Post-16 Curriculum and Qualifications: Confusion and Incoherence or Diversity and Choice?

Paper by Geoff Stanton for the National Commission on Education, 1993.

Introduction

Some commentators look at the range of qualifications taken by people after the end of compulsory schooling, and the diverse routes to these qualifications, and see a situation which is so confused, and so difficult to explain, as to discourage both participation and progression. This view can lead to arguments for the creation of a 'Key Stage 5' of the national curriculum, to apply from 16 onwards. Others welcome the range and the diverse routes as reflecting the complexity of adult life and occupations, and the divergent interests of individuals who are volunteer learners. Those who take this view fear that provision which was too monolithic would damage participation and achievement by failing to recognise all kinds of excellence and personal circumstances. Most people would now accept that there is a balance to be struck: that what is wanted is not uniformity but a unified system. What this means and how to achieve it is less clear.

The current situation and where we have come from

It is difficult to provide a straightforward account of the current situation, either in words or numbers. Twenty years ago things appeared much simpler, at least as far as 16–19-year-olds were concerned. The school-leaving age had just been raised from 15 to 16. Young people who passed five or more O levels, and who were motivated and could afford to do so, stayed on in schools and took A levels (14%). Some stayed on to repeat their O levels (4%). The vast majority went out to work. Only 4% went on to study vocational courses full-time in colleges. It was estimated that of the 74% who left full-time education, about half received little in the way of further education or systematic training. Of those that did, many attended college on day or block release, and most were male (in the ratio of 4:1).

Since 1973, the following have occurred:

- the range of ability among those remaining in full-time education after 16 has become much wider;

- many new kinds of vocational and pre-vocational programmes have been developed;

- in particular, the numbers taking one-year courses post-16 have multiplied;

- youth unemployment has grown by an order of magnitude, and a series of schemes and methods of finance have been introduced in response.

Where we have reached

By the 1991–92 academic year, 67% of 16-year-olds in the UK were staying on in full-time education after 16. That was an increase of over 20 percentage points since 1980. If part-time students are included, the figure for those now participating at age 16 goes up to 76%. In the UK context, the inclusion of part-time figures is important. Most part-time students are participating in Youth Training (YT), and as such are intended to be full-time learners, even if not based in schools or colleges. Via YT, they have access to modes of provision which some will find different and attractive. They also work towards National Vocational Qualifications, and receive a training allowance. This latter fact may mean that some would have attended full-time at school or college had an equivalent maintenance grant been available. On the other hand, some full-time students who fail in that mode might have achieved more in an employment-based scheme.

In general, however, full-time participation has been increasing at the expense of part-time in the last few years. Suggested reasons for this are:

- the recession reducing the number of YT places;

- a more appropriate and wider range of provision post-16;

- the positive effect of GCSE pre-16.

The relative importance of these or other factors is unclear.

Part-time students are more likely to be male, more likely to be following vocational programmes, and more likely to be working towards City & Guilds or RSA qualifications (as opposed to BTEC). By 17+ 49% are participating full-time, and a further 14% part-time. There has therefore been some transfer from full- to part-time at this point, but also a significant drop-out or failure to continue. These figures are also some 20% up on those for 1980.

At 16, the majority of full-time students are at schools or sixth form colleges (41.9% of the age group), with 25.2% at an FE (or tertiary) college. By 17, 28% are at school (down 14.9%), whilst 20.7% are at an FE college (down 5.5%). From April 1st 1993, sixth form colleges and FE colleges in England and Wales joined to form one sector, funded through Funding Councils. The new Colleges Sector will have just over half of the full-time students at 17+.

The qualifications being sought
1. *Full-time students.* Currently, about 35% of those staying on are working towards A levels, with those repeating GCSE forming the next largest group (11.6%), closely followed by BTEC at 9%. Eleven per cent are on other, mostly vocational,

provision. The GCSE numbers have stayed fairly constant over the past decade, whilst those on BTEC courses have shown a fourfold increase.

2. *Part-time students.* Apart from adults on non-examinable courses (30%), the largest single group of part-time students are studying for City & Guilds qualifications (20%). BTEC and RSA numbers are approximately equal at 8% each. Slightly more are working towards GCSE, and slightly fewer towards A level.

How well are they doing?
Traditionally, this question has been answered in terms of qualifications gained. More recently, there has been much interest in 'value added', meaning some measure of progress made or 'distance travelled' between school leaving results and qualifications obtained at 17 or 18.

GCSE. Thirty-seven per cent of 16-year-old school leavers get five or more GCSEs at grade A–C, compared with 25% 10 years ago (GCSE grades D/E are set at a level which the average 16-year-old is expected to reach). However, the national average conceals marked regional and local differences, and even more striking differences between subjects. In 1990, 90% of pupils entered for GCSE English, and 45% achieved grades A–C. The figures for physics were 32% and 16% respectively. As we have seen, over 11% of students re-take GCSEs at 16+. However, a sample study by the Audit Commission and HMI showed that in 10 institutions out of 18, the average student's increase in the number of subjects with at least a grade C result was less than two subjects. However, the level of customer demand for GCSEs post-16 has remained stubbornly high, despite the development of effective vocationally-oriented alternatives over the past decade. In September 1992, the national curriculum core subjects of English, maths and science were introduced for 14-year-olds. Therefore, the GCSE examinations in 1994 will, for the first time, be based on national curriculum attainment targets. Each subject has a number of such targets, for each of which there will be statements of attainment at ten levels. It will be 1997 before the GCSE tests the attainment targets for all national curriculum subjects.

A levels. The minimum usable level of achievement at A level is generally held to be two passes at grade E or above (though even this has little credibility for some purposes). Nearly 35% of the age group take A level compared with 26% a decade ago, but only 22% of the cohort get two passes. In other words, one third of those taking the course leave with no usable results. The Audit Commission found a strong correlation between GCSE scores and A level scores, and most schools and colleges require five or more A–C grades at GCSE as a prerequisite for A levels. However, the Audit Commission also found that institutions could make a significant difference. The best 10% of schools and colleges add an estimated six or more UCCA points (equivalent to two grades in three subjects) compared to the worst 10%, even when GCSE attainment at entry has been taken into account. There is little correlation between this and kind of institution, group size or cost per head. The Audit Commission argues persuasively that value added evaluation provides much more relevant data for decision makers and managers, and also shows that value added ranking of institutions gives quite a different picture from league tables based only on final outcomes.

Vocational programmes. The Audit Commission found little correlation between GCSE scores at 16 and subsequent performance in some vocational qualifications. This means that GCSE scores cannot be used as a baseline for measuring value added in these cases (nor, incidentally, can GCSE results be used as a legitimate means of selection). Some vocational qualifications obviously measure *different* abilities, rather than just higher level ones. Statistics on attainment within vocational programmes are more difficult to analyse in any case, because awarding bodies have traditionally used different assessment regimes. They also do not report percentage pass rates, and the DFE does not have statistics on each body's results.

Current problems and action being taken

Despite considerable improvement in the staying-on rate at 16+, there is a continuing need to:

- increase the number of people studying full-time at 16 (particularly in some localities) and reduce the number who leave at 17;

- reduce the failure rate, and increase the average amount of progress made, on all routes;

- broaden the range of achievement of individuals, as well as the level.

Evidence for the first point has been shown in the last section. The report *Unfinished Business*, produced in January 1993 by the Audit Commission and OFSTED, provided evidence for the second point. However, the situation is not straightforward, since:

- some apparent drop-outs may have transferred to other provision or gained employment with training;

- a certain failure rate *should* exist, if schools and colleges have an appropriately flexible admissions policy.

This last point may be contentious, but the fact is that many applicants whose previous record is unpromising prove themselves able to succeed when given a second chance. For others, their previous record does prove to be a reliable indicator. The problem is to know which is which.

The need for learners to have a broader and better balanced programme post-16 is less susceptible to hard proof, but it is certainly the case that by international standards 16–19-year-olds in England and Wales specialise more and earlier than their counterparts in the rest of Europe or North America. The need for a range of common learning outcomes was stated in the CBI report *Towards a Skills Revolution*, and the promotion of autonomy, flexibility and breadth is one of the national training targets. The Government is addressing the first two of these problems by:

- supporting national education and training targets
- creating three major and parallel routes post-16
- increasing the supply of student places in FE
- promoting motivation towards (and 'ownership' of) training opportunities through training credits for those who leave school at 16 or 17.

The National Education and Training Targets for foundation learning (full-time students) are:

- Immediate moves to ensure that by 1997 at least 80% of all young people attain National Vocational Qualification/Scottish Vocational Qualification (NVQ/SVQ) Level 2 or its academic equivalent in their foundation education and training.

- All young people who can benefit should be given an entitlement to structured training, work experience or education leading to NVQ/SVQ Level 3 or its academic equivalent.

- by the year 2000, at least half of the age group should attain NVQ/SVQ Level 3 or its academic equivalent as a basis for further progression.

- All education and training provision should be structured and designed to develop self-reliance, flexibility and broad competence as well as specific skills.

The *three major routes* are:

- A/AS levels

- General National Vocational Qualifications

- National Vocational Qualifications.

However, as we have seen, GCSEs also remain a popular option post-16. These routes are policed by two 'Accrediting Bodies':

- The School Curriculum and Assessment Authority (SCAA) for GCSE and A and AS levels;

- The National Council for Vocational Qualifications (NCVQ) for NVQs and GNVQs.

Although there are a number of examining bodies who offer A and AS levels, SCAA is developing criteria which all syllabuses and examination procedures have to meet. SCAA also approves the examinations put forward by the GCSE Boards for 16-year-olds. NVQs are intended to attest to the fact that an individual can undertake an occupational role to workplace standards. They are offered by a wide range of awarding bodies, with City & Guilds, BTEC and RSA being the largest. Before NCVQ will accredit a qualification, it requires evidence that the qualification embodies standards defined by the relevant 'Industry Lead Body'. There are currently almost 200 such bodies (though there are plans to create a smaller number of overarching 'Occupational Standards Councils').

NVQs exist at five levels, numbered 1–5, determined by the requirements and structure of the occupation concerned, and therefore ranging from operative level, through craft and technician levels to those with senior management or professional status. The occupational competence required by NVQs means that aspects of them may need to be learned and assessed in a place of work. This may make them inaccessible to people who are not employed, and they may also be too narrowly focused for people whose precise future occupation may be uncertain.

General NVQs are being developed to enable schools and colleges to prepare full-time students for a vocationally relevant qualification, which also has parity of esteem with A levels, and which will provide an alternative route to university. In the first place, they are being offered by CGLI, BTEC and RSA, and these bodies will eventually adapt their existing qualifications to meet either GNVQ or NVQ criteria. GNVQs also embody Core Skills Units. Both NVQs and GNVQs define qualifications in outcomes to be achieved, and attempt not to constrain the means adopted, or time taken, to reach these outcomes.

In short, although there will continue to be occupationally specific qualifications involving a large number of interested parties and awarding bodies, the plan is that each will be labelled as an NVQ at Levels 1, 2, 3, 4 or 5. Similarly, all General National Vocational Qualifications, whichever the awarding body, will be labelled a GNVQ at the same levels, just as the generic label 'A level' already takes precedence over the name of the awarding bodies concerned. In the summer of 1993, the Government announced that GNVQs at Level III were to be named 'Advanced' Vocational Qualifications, with Level II becoming 'Intermediate' and Level I 'Foundation'.

Increasing the volume of provision
The Government believes that schools and colleges can become more responsive and efficient if they become independent of local authority control. All FE and sixth form colleges became incorporated institutions, funded via central councils, from April 1st 1993. A funding council to provide for schools who opt out of local authority control was set up in the autumn of 1993. The colleges have been asked to increase student places by 8% in each of the next three years, in which case funding will be increased by 5% in each year. The funding arrangements are likely to be developed further in order to encourage and reward both efficiency and effectiveness.

Unresolved issues

Financial support
For some, participation in full-time education post-16 is hindered by lack of financial support, rather than insufficient places or inappropriate programmes. Over the next few years, it is planned that all those who leave full-time education should qualify for a 'training credit', which will provide both course fees and a small training allowance. However, in a time of recession, Training Enterprise Councils and local industry may not be able to provide either sufficient places to meet demand, or a wide enough range of opportunities to meet the legitimate interests and motivations of potential learners. The same problems are faced by TECs attempting to provide the training places which are presently guaranteed to unemployed school leavers. A local FE college might be in a better position to offer the right range, but the use of training credits to support college places would produce an anomalous situation as far as full-time students were concerned. Unlike university students, full-time FE students have no entitlement to maintenance grants or student loans. Local authorities can offer discretionary awards, but policy on these varies from place to place, and is everywhere becoming less generous.

Guidance
Unacceptably high drop-out and failure rates may be caused by a lack of accurate and impartial advice. However, independent institutions, competing with each other for students, may be tempted not to fund or offer such guidance. On the other hand, a free-standing guidance service may find it difficult to establish the kind of liaison with providers which both keeps its information up to date, and provides feedback on quality issues to them. A recent White Paper from the Department of Employment makes proposals about the future of the Careers Service. The recent document from the Funding Council, *Funding Learning*, correctly identifies the fact that

guidance is required during the course of a programme, as well as on entry and at exit.

The need to bring more coherence to the funding of post-16 provision, and of post-16 learners, is widely recognised. There is also much talk of the need to ensure accurate and impartial guidance. The plethora of post-16 qualifications is, as we have seen, to be rationalised into three major categories. However, there is a remaining problem which is not only highly important in its own right, but is also likely to undermine moves towards more effective funding and guidance.

The need for a common framework post-16
When the three major post-16 'routes' are established we will – unless something is done in the near future – find that they are all drawn on separate maps, and that each of these maps differs from that upon which the national curriculum (and therefore future GCSE) is laid out. The maps use different scales, and each has its own benchmarks against which to measure length of journey and level reached. None of the routes has a measurement for breadth. Even the conventions used in order to describe standard features (such as core content) vary. Student 'travellers' need to progress from one route to another: GCSE to A level or GNVQ 3; GNVQ 2 to A level; GCSEs or GNVQ 2 to NVQ 3; GNVQ 3 or A levels to higher education or employment. Some, even after receiving guidance, will wish to change routes before reaching the destination, and they and their teachers will wish to plan the most efficient path from one route to another. Those giving guidance need to be able to explain the differences and similarities between routes and destinations. Offering three different maps does not allow this. Nor does it help those who wish to combine qualifications from different categories. This is an increasingly common phenomenon. Those analysing the results of institutions, whether as customers or funders, cannot identify strengths, weaknesses or cost-effectiveness. The irony is that recent developments in all qualifications could be on the verge of offering us a technical solution.

There has been much recent interest in, and work on, the idea of defining qualifications in terms of the outcomes to be achieved (that is, what candidates have to demonstrate they know, understand and can do). Unfortunately, each system of qualifications has chosen to describe outcomes according to different conventions. What would be necessary in order to clear all this up? All qualifications are composed of groups of outcomes which I shall call 'Units of Assessment'. Some qualifications are explicit about this (NVQs, for example). Other qualifications are less 'transparent' in this respect, but an A level in physics, for example, can be analysed into units relating to electromagnetism, mechanics, fluids, and so on. It may also contain some units of assessment which require these other units to be used in combination. In practice, all these units are clearly reflected in the way in which examinations are structured and marked.

When (as a learner) deciding between qualifications, or (as a recruiter) selecting someone on the basis of their qualifications, or (as a teacher) helping someone progress or transfer between qualifications, what is needed is a description of *what* has been (or has to be) achieved, the *level* of that achievement, and *how much* has been achieved. In other words:

- *What* is in the units concerned

- The *level* of the units

- The *size* and number of the units.

We can be reasonably precise about the 'what'. The optimum degree of precision is debatable. NVQs and A levels occupy different ends of a spectrum in this respect. We also have to agree a common approach to describing the outcomes concerned. There is an important debate to be had about the rationale for selecting given outcomes for each qualification. For NVQs, this is (explicitly) the requirement of a specific occupational role. For A levels it is (implicitly) the traditions of scholarship in the academic subject concerned. The national curriculum and GNVQs mix these in different proportions, together with a few outcomes derived from the requirements of adult life and citizenship more generally. Being clear about the outcomes at least enables the debate to take place about the proportion to be taken from various sources, as we have seen from the controversy which has surrounded the definition of subjects through the national curriculum. It is noticeable, however, that the specification for vocational qualifications has been examined much less rigorously (if at all) by those outside the specialism concerned.

Agreeing the 'conventions' by which the outcomes of a unit are to be described, and the procedures by which to allocate levels and decide volume, would allow us to draw up a single map upon which all these units, and the qualifications of which they are a part, could be located. Analysing qualifications into units of assessment need not affect the nature or timing of assessment, nor does it require modular delivery — though it can allow this. Therefore, nothing will be changed by the mapping process itself. Many things might be revealed, however, including where vocational and academic qualifications overlap. It could also reveal where two different A level subjects overlap — something which may indicate that some combinations give an even narrower programme than already feared. It will be recalled that one of the National Education and Training Targets is that autonomy, flexibility and breadth should be promoted. This mapping process would allow various qualifications, or combinations of them, to be checked against this requirement. Those, such as GNVQs, which already include core skills, go some way to providing for flexibility and autonomy. It is predictable, however, that no existing post-16 qualifications will guarantee appropriate breadth — however defined.

Breadth
There are alternative definitions of this term, of which three will be identified here:

1 For some, the most important aspect of 'breadth' is whether learners continue to have some involvement with the Humanities, the Social Sciences and the Sciences during their further education.

2 The national curriculum identifies a number of cross-curricular themes, most of which seem even more relevant after 16. These are: Environmental Education; Careers Education; Health Education; Economic and Industrial Understanding; Citizenship.

3 Another important balance to be kept is that between theoretical studies, applied studies, and practical activities. The 'applied' category occupies the middle ground between the other two, being a test of whether someone can act upon what they know, and/or whether they understand the principles underlying what they can do.

Even bearing in mind the importance of not overloading the post-16 curriculum, and the even greater imperative of not including material which would alienate volunteer learners, it would still be possible to enhance existing programmes – once they were clearly mapped. In general, a sensible approach would be to identify the extent to which existing subject-based qualifications, or grouped vocational qualifications, already addressed the cross-curricular themes mentioned under category 2 above, and then to look for opportunities to include the missing elements. In vocational provision this would nearly always be possible within an integrated programme. In the case of some A level combinations, it might be necessary to offer one of the cross-curricular 'themes' as an additional unit – a complementary or general study. This is already a common approach for those studying A levels full-time from 16 to 19 – and something which most concerned would wish to see preserved and protected, despite pressures for cost-effectiveness. Separate provision of some of the cross-curricular themes would enable core skills to be developed in all students, even where their A level subject could not easily absorb the skill without 'distortion'. It would also provide a forum within which students on different kinds of programmes could meet in order to work together on common tasks and issues.

Conclusions

Describing all qualifications in terms of outcomes:

- will help to preserve public confidence in them, even when the education service succeeds in enabling more people to achieve these qualifications;

- will enable teachers and curriculum designers to provide a variety of flexible learning programmes (depending on the needs and backgrounds of the learners) without detracting from the stable national standards which need to be embodied in the qualifications.

If, once all qualifications were expressed in terms of groups of outcomes, these could be located in the same framework or map, it would then become possible to:

- provide more effective and understandable guidance;

- establish greater parity of esteem between different routes;

- encourage credit accumulation;

- allow credit transfer;

- avoid duplication or voids when moving from one programme to another;

- calculate added value more systematically;

- enhance all programmes by checking them for breadth and the inclusion of some important common outcomes.

It would also be possible to maintain the quality of qualifications, in terms of their fitness for purpose as far as 'gatekeepers' are concerned, by varying in an evolutionary manner over time either the nature of specific units within a qualification, or the range of permissible combinations of units.

The development of separate criteria for measuring the quality of the learning programme, in terms of its fitness for purpose as far as learners are concerned, would enable us to strike the crucial balance described at the beginning of this paper between the need for variety and flexibility, and the need for coherence and unification. The quality of learning programmes could be monitored via the development of 'learning agreements', as part of entitlements under consumer charters. The standards embodied within qualifications, and their necessary development over time, would be controlled by either SCAA or NCVQ. Meanwhile, teachers would be freed to respond creatively to the needs of their clients with regard to the methods by which they helped them to reach these clearly defined outcomes.

22. In a Muddle on Training

Article by Sir John Cassels, first published in the *Financial Times*, 4 June 1993.

Education and training for 16- to 18-year-olds is in a mess. Everybody is agreed – the Confederation of British Industry, the Trades Union Congress and Government included – that all young people should continue formal learning until at least 18, but that remains a remote target.

A recently published Briefing for the National Commission on Education by Mr David Raffe[1] shows that in 1990 only 37% of 16- to 18-year-olds in the United Kingdom were in full-time education. Of the remaining 63%, only 15% were in Youth Training and the rest – almost half – were in an 'others' category, with only a minority receiving any part-time education.

We lag badly behind other countries in the Organisation for Economic Co-operation and Development. Mr Raffe says that the UK had the lowest full-time participation rate among 16- to 18-year-olds in 1986: its rate was then 33%, half the average for the other 12 OECD countries. If part-time provision is included, our rate at 64% was much closer to the average for the other 12 of 75%; but given the uncertain quality of our part-time provision, we can take little comfort from that.

Muddle-headedness
Our poor performance is sometimes held to show that we have a cultural block that prevents us doing better, or that employers, who are supposed to be responsible for training, are incurably short-sighted. In fact our real ailment seems to

be muddle-headedness. We do not make it easy for people to behave sensibly. Clear our heads a bit, and things could improve.

Four areas need attention:

- **Responsibility**. There is a conflict between the interests of employers, which are bound to be fairly short-term, and the needs of young people, which stretch more than 40 years ahead. It is reasonable to expect employers to provide training related to the job; but further education is also needed, and should be provided by colleges or other providers at public expense – as in full-time education.

- **Costs**. Making it clear that it is not the employers' responsibility to provide further education makes it easier to return to the financial basis of all successful apprentice systems: that the net cost to an employer of each apprentice is broadly neutral. The cost of pay plus the cost of training is balanced by the value of the apprentice's output. If you achieve that, there need be no limit to employers' willingness to provide training places.

- **Incentives**. Why should young people be prepared to train for qualifications if employers do not show that they value them? Pay structures must be overhauled, first to reduce the pay of trainees in recognition of the costs that employers incur in training them, of their absence one day a week or more at college and of their comparatively low output, and second to increase the pay of employees who have acquired relevant qualifications.

- **Traineeships**. Experience shows that there need to be formal 'traineeships' signed by employer and trainee (and perhaps a parent); they must be seen to lead to recognised qualifications, now made possible by the NVQs introduced by the National Council for Vocational Qualifications; and there must be proper inspection to establish and maintain standards.

Get these things right and the upshot should be traineeships of good quality for all 16- and 17-year-olds entering the labour market. Young people will get a lasting benefit; employers should be delighted, so too should the trade unions. And the government should be pleased because youth unemployment will dwindle – a result achieved at much less expense to the taxpayer than the current arrangements, which do not work.

A couple of snags
But there are a couple of snags. One is that employers often attract 16- and 17-year-olds into jobs with no training but quite high pay. That is one reason why the UK's staying-on rate in full-time education is so low. We probably need legislation obliging any employer who wants to employ a 16- or 17-year-old in a regular full-time job to provide him or her with a traineeship.

The other snag is that the pay of most young people in work is based on the presumption that they are fully productive workers – not surprisingly, since that has been the reality in most cases – and not trainees. For a trainee, the example of German apprentices suggests that starting at 30% of the adult rate would be about right. But it would not be easy for any individual employer to move to that level of pay on his own initiative. Either there needs to be a concerted movement by leading employers or, if that proves impossible to arrange, legislation needs to step in here too, providing for a statutory body to determine the wages of young people in traineeships.

Negotiating these snags may seem tricky, even formidable, but the stakes are high. Do nothing and we are set for continuing failure, whereas the prize for success is immensely valuable.

Reference

1   Raffe, D. (May 1992). *Participation of 16–18 Year Olds in Education and Training*. NCE Briefing No. 3. National Commission on Education.

23. Continuing Education

Paper by Professor Chris Duke for the National Commission on Education, 1993.

Nature, scope and terminology

Of all educational categories and propositions, continuing education (CE) is presently among the most fluid, problematic, and challenging. Looking back a third of the way through the 21st century it may well appear to have been the most significant, and self-evidently necessary, aspect of the educational transformation of the late 1990s.

The meaning of continuing education
There are different interpretations of the term 'continuing education'. Its meaning and synonyms are changing. The now commonly accepted broad meaning is all education which takes place after completion of initial full-time education (whether at 16, 18, 21 or an older age). It is thus sometimes referred to as 'post-experience' education with the implication that school education is pre- or even non-experience education.

CE is sometimes treated as synonymous with 'adult education', the broad term still favoured by international bodies such as OECD and UNESCO. In Britain, adult education tends to connote voluntary, traditionally non-award-bearing, liberal or recreation education for personal development. Until recently, CE was confined in Britain, by contrast, to the various kinds of updating or 'diversifying' education and training to do with employment. These areas of work are now most commonly referred to as 'continuing vocational education' (CVE). From 1982 to 1993, there was a Government programme to promote CVE known as 'PICKUP' (professional, industrial and commercial updating). The term PICKUP is still sometimes used as a synonym for CVE. Other closely related terms include continuing professional development (CPD) and human resource development (HRD). Training is often added on to education, producing acronyms like CVET.

Recurrent education for the lifelong learner
CE is an ideal and vision as well as an administrative category. An alternative broader term which does not get confused with categories of educational provision is 'recurrent education'. This essentially continental European concept stresses alternation between education and other kinds of activity throughout life, as distinct from finite front-end-loaded education taken and completed before launching into the world of full adulthood. The idea of the educated man or woman contradicts the idea of recurrent education, and even the notion of a degree (Bachelor, Master etc.) begins to feel ill-fitted. Recurrent education looks rather to the educable person or, more commonly, to the lifelong learner in a learning society.

Changes of focus and scope
The focus for CE thus moves from education and teaching in school and college to learning, often to self-directed learning, in many ways and places in a society characterised by continuous change. It shifts, too, from almost exclusive preoccupation with the individual pupil's or student's educational attainment against a set national curriculum to the continuous adaptation (relearning, unlearning etc.) of all the members of a constantly changing society for which, at all levels, learning becomes a condition of survival. This insight is shared whether the threat is seen as competition from other advanced economies; as loss of ecological equilibrium for survival globally; or as the breakdown of social order internationally and at home.

The scope of CE is thus large, diffuse and difficult to grasp, since individuals' learning occurs throughout life and in many settings – workplace, community, family – as well as at school and college; and also since each of these settings and institutions is itself subject to change and needs to learn. CE turns our attention to the learning organisation as well as the learning society, rather than focusing only on the learning individual. It also perhaps constitutes a threat to the very idea of education as a system of professional teachers and administrators concentrated in schools and colleges and following an instructional curriculum.

Adult learning and education

We tend to equate education with what is formally taught in schools and in further education (FE) and higher education (HE). We tend to think of education as principally preparing young people for their roles in society. CE challenges this in two important senses, apart from the obvious one to do with student age. First, whether the term is education and/or training, it recognises that much of this deliberate planned and provided activity takes place outside formal educational institutions, especially through employment and at the workplace, but also through distance, self-directed, computer-assisted and other new educational forms. Sometimes these latter are classified generically as open education, whether work-based or away from employment and college in one's own place and time. It has been estimated that more is spent on education and training outside than within the formal (school, FE and HE) system, in Britain as in the United States.

Secondly, it has become the practice among CE professionals to talk and write increasingly about adult learning rather than education. Thus the trade journal of the National Institute of Adult Continuing Education (NIACE), *Adult Education*, gave way to the more modern magazine format *Adults Learning* in 1989. For more than 20 years now, the Canadian adult education researcher, Tough, and others following him in many different countries, have exposed the scale and diversity of self-directed learning among adults. On even the most conservative criteria for what constitutes deliberate learning this far exceeds in scale the volume of effort which goes into CE.

Added to the relatively modern recognition that learning is not an activity confined to the young, this recognition of the scale and variety of adults' learning and of the cost and variety of adults' education and training amounts to a revolutionary reappraisal of the place and importance of both CE and continuing learning throughout society. The latent implications for thinking about schooling and the school curriculum are large. They have yet to be grasped. In particular a CE perspective, informed by enhanced awareness of adults' often self-directed learning potential and activity in a changing society, invites us to think afresh about the different functions of school education: as between the conservation and transmission of knowledge, skills and values on the one hand, and equipping new members of society to become self-transforming, self-directed, lifelong learners on the other. The question is as much about learning processes and what is often called the hidden curriculum as about the prescribed content of the school curriculum.

Factors contributing to the need for a new perspective

The changes affecting society are diverse, mutually interactive, and well rehearsed. They include the following.

Obsolescence of knowledge and skills
Technological advances mean that especially in the applied sciences, knowledge rapidly becomes out of date. The current half-life of the knowledge of an engineer is variously put at seven, five or nowadays even fewer years. Mandatory CE is being canvassed or introduced in many occupations. There is concern about how to renovate initial professional education

fast enough, jettisoning old curriculum elements to make way for new, perhaps interdisciplinary, areas of necessary knowledge, attitudes and skills.

Less obviously, obsolescence is a problem in the social sciences and even in the humanities. Management methods and theories are vulnerable to rapidly changing cycles of insight, interpretation and fashion, as well as to new circumstances confronting managers. New circumstances require new content, insight and techniques in management, business and administration. EC membership, for example, affects law and welfare practice in many areas and ways, as well as increasing the desirability or necessity to speak several languages. From the most simple levels of knowledge updating in new techniques and new legislation, to far deeper requirements to take on board new attitudes and values, obsolescence raises the profile of CE and sharpens questions about the curriculum (in all senses) of initial education.

Demography
Ours is a dramatically ageing society. More and more people may expect as many years of often active life after retirement as they experience in employment. The situation and contribution of retired people is becoming a major policy consideration from many points of view. Retirement for many occurs, voluntarily or through enforced unemployment, at a much younger age than the current statutory 60 years for women and 65 for men. Concurrently with the changing demographic balance (falling birth rates and increasing longevity) we have seen a growing awareness, through the literature on learning and ageing, that potential for learning changes in character but does not significantly fall off until very late old age. Changing demography and new understandings of learning and ageing processes thus tilt the balance towards investing in adults', including older adults', learning rather than concentrating such effort almost exclusively on the young.

Economic, employment and equity considerations
Low birth rate has meant small cohorts of young people entering the labour market. In industry and for economic planning it has increased the necessity to think of retraining the present workforce rather than just recruiting and replacing from below. Paradoxically, sustained recession and persisting high unemployment currently mean that many young people entering the labour market and those made redundant have extreme difficulty finding employment.

There appears to be a bipolar trend towards a highly trained and regularly updated workforce for whom continuing vocational education is normal and even mandatory, and a growing unemployable and socially excluded underclass, for whom special remedial, basic or restorative CE will be necessary. Here economic, equity and educational questions become entangled but again raise the profile of CE.

CE, especially in the adult education tradition, has always had a preoccupation with equity issues. It has provided routes whereby early school leavers, underachievers, may gain access to education, either as its own end or as a means back into formal education. Adult basic education, return-to-learn and access courses provide steps and ladders into formal study for qualifications: either onto programmes followed by full-time younger students or into specially tailored programmes which may be full- or part-time. Access courses, mainly offered by FE colleges, have become a significant means of widening second chance access to higher education. The Open University is exclusively dedicated to adult part-time provision as a second-chance CE institution.

Economic considerations and equity considerations are often contrasted ideologically, but human resource development is one window through which inequality in an individual or social class sense can be seen as compatible with concern for waste of the key national asset of human resources. Nevertheless, those who succeed in initial education are the most natural clients of CE. Voluntary CE classically attracts the already well educated. Remedial, compensatory education of adults is an inefficient substitute for initial educational success. It is likely to be much harder for the individual to achieve in this way; and there are limits to how far CE can actually function as a different, counterpoising, system over against the dominant school system. If initial education is essentially reproductive, it is unlikely that CE alone can redress the balance by empowering the excluded.

Political and civic considerations
Education for citizenship, or political education, is part of the adult education tradition as well as featuring in the school curriculum. In post-war Germany and Japan, adult education was seen as a means of rebuilding civil society and underpinning stable democracy. There is less conviction that CE in Britain is to do with such matters. Non-vocational education of adults tends to be more about individual self-development and leisure-time intellectual and other recreation pursuits than about civic or political participation. Similarly, the Speaker's Commission on Citizenship paid attention to citizenship education in the formal school curriculum but largely ignored the education of adults, and at present the consumer-led curriculum of CE largely omits those subjects which might be expected to provide the core curriculum of citizenship.

In summary, there have been attempts to consider CE rather as a further (post-experience) category of instructional provision. The term 'quaternary' has come and gone from favour. It is inappropriate, since CE is that which follows any break from full-time schooling, and may be pitched at the level of adult basic education for those for whom schooling was unsuccessful, or those entering this society from a different society, culture and language, as well as adding, for example, management skills to graduate engineers' qualifications on-the-job and retraining those whose skills have become obsolete.

Resources for CE

Especially for policy makers allocating scarce resources across competing needs, this scenario may seem frustratingly unhelpful. The natural tendency is to attempt to weigh the needs of education against those of health, defence, social security, etc. and to emerge with a budget allocation for the sector as a whole, and for its competing sub-sectors. These may be primary versus secondary, FE versus HE, general versus occupation-specific (or versus special needs, disadvantaged regions or ethnic groups and so forth), science and technology versus other fields, specific skills versus general or generic competences and so on, at different levels.

Then there are questions about modes of payment (to providers or to students); and about degrees and forms of planning, control and accountability. The much broader church of CE, with its plethora of voluntary, public and private sector providers, is harder to relate to. Simple transparent devices to pay for the education determined as public policy, and to ensure quality with economy, point towards standard payments, preferably via the customer. But this may be the employer or the economy rather than the individual student.

As the frame widens beyond education to learning (and indeed to learning to learn) simplicity and transparency recede further. This may partly explain the current inclination to pay for the gaining of competences via National Vocational Qualifications rather than for the teaching itself. It probably suggests some further movement towards payment by results. This will be unattractive to the education system, and further open up access to the 'education dollar' for employers, private training agencies and others who can achieve government-determined attainment targets.

At a superficially simpler level, the economics of CE appears easier to address. Return on an individual's educational investment (whoever foots the bill) looks better the earlier qualifications are taken and the longer earning power throughout working life is enhanced. This underlies calculations to do with students or their parents paying for FE and HE.

On the other hand this may confuse qualifications with performance, and it may mask problems of obsolescence. Thus a qualification may come to have a limited life and lapse if it is not renewed. More seriously, this approach restricts what can be included in the financial calculation, for example, lost earnings during adult full-time study as well as the shorter earning period of a person qualifying later in life. It also excludes other costs incurred by society through later lost earnings, and costs to other budgets such as health and social welfare, since lack of education may hinder full economic and social participation.

Adequate study of resourcing for CE requires a much more complete consideration of the different stakeholders, and of dispersed hidden as well as obvious opportunity costs, than the current economics of education allow.

Organisation and policy issues

Within the CE profession a debate rumbles on, which is more about organisation and management than about teaching and learning: the mainstreaming versus separation (or marginality) debate. Such controversy poses questions about the extent to which CE is a different form of activity apart from and perhaps contrasted with formal, initial education or schooling.

Ideologically the extent of the difference may be broadened by approaching CE as an empowering, liberating or transforming education, whereas initial education is seen as socialisation, induction into society and its roles, even as domestication. Alternatively the differences may be set out by emphasising CE compensation and a second chance, as via access courses, for those initially disadvantaged; those for whom it is said the school system failed, rather than they failing it.

Tension is increased when it is realised that there are now more adults (or CE clients) in FE and HE than there are young post-school students; and when it is remembered that getting access to regular education (the mainstream) was what much socially purposive CE was about. Adults have thus entered, and become, the mainstream; yet marginality is felt, and often still preferred, for the greater professional autonomy it may allow.

These general considerations currently manifest themselves in the following policy considerations:

- the organisation and funding of CE – separate or earmarked, versus mainstream;

- making more continuing professional education mandatory – loss of right to practise without periodic updating;

- the certification or accreditation of courses as a condition of funding, the extension of formal award-bearing recognition to CE undertaken at the workplace, validation or recognition of employment-based learning through accreditation of prior experiential learning and credit accumulation and transfer systems;

- quality assurance and assessment of CE with its great diversity of clienteles, modes of delivery etc. and its strong tradition of learner-centredness which militates against predetermined curricula.

More generally still, CE poses questions to the still dominant initial or school system:

- about recognising and normalising the full range of places and ways in which adults learn;

- about sectoral and segmentary thinking and planning as against integrative, trans-institutional and trans-sectoral planning and support of learning opportunities and resources;

- about the failures experienced in the education system and experience of the young, which produce the many casualties for later-life remedial effort;

- about the extent to which it is still helpful to make educational arrangements for a lifelong learning society in the institution-centred, profession-based, and segmentary way with which we are familiar.

The very concept of an *education system* is brought into question.

Further reading

1 McGivney, V. (1990). *Education's for Other People: Access to Education for Non-Participant Adults*. NIACE.
2 NIACE (1990). *Learning through Adult Life: A Policy Discussion Paper on CE*. NIACE.
3 NIACE (1993). *The Learning Imperative*. NIACE.
4 Sargant, N. (1991). *Learning and 'Leisure': A Study of Adult Participation in Learning and its Policy Implications*. NIACE.

24. Tracking the Experience of Young People

Report by Josh Hillman on the National Commission on Education Research Committee Seminar on the Youth Cohort Study and the Scottish Young People's Survey, October 1992.

Background

The Research Committee's seminar which discussed the findings of the two longitudinal studies of young people was an important influence on the Commission. Peter Mortimore, in the chair, described the two central goals of the meeting as:

1. To make the Research Committee and the National Commission more aware of the value of the work of the Youth Cohort Study (YCS) and the Scottish Young People's Survey (SYPS).

2. To explore how the evidence can best be drawn upon for the Commission's final recommendations.

Trends in characteristics and outcomes – Andrew McPherson

SYPS: structure and background information
Three different areas were covered under the heading 'trends in social demography':

1. Changing characteristics of the school population.

2. Changing outcomes in the school population.

3. The relationship between 1 and 2.

The SYPS samples 10% of the school population of Scotland

and has been going for 20 years. Almost all of the research and statistics reported about the three areas listed above were compiled in Scotland but most apply to England, Wales and Northern Ireland. It was pointed out that there has been little serious research on ethnicity in Scotland, so very little of the evidence that was presented took this subject into account.

Demographic characteristics and outcomes
Figure 1 on page 290 shows trends in the demography of 18-year-olds in Great Britain by social class, with the dip in classes III–V. This is borne out by the SYPS, with an increase in the number of those surveyed having fathers in Registrar General (RG) social classes I and II, from around 20% to 30%. This is explained by changes in occupational structure and a falling fertility rate amongst classes III–V. It should be mentioned that some young people are not classified by any class category, since they only qualify for a classification if their father is in employment. There has also been a rise in the proportion of pupils living with one parent, from 10% in 1981 to 15% in 1991.

Between the years 1971 and 1990, girls have continually performed better than boys in England in examinations at the end of compulsory education, but only recently so for A levels. The differential in achievement between girls and boys is larger in Scotland than in the rest of Great Britain. In both cases the gender gap is widening.

There has been a very substantial increase in the proportion of pupils staying on. This is partly due to the fact that their parents were more likely to have stayed on, due to changes in fertility rates and general education expansion. It is likely that this will continue, with post-ROSLA pupils becoming parents. Figure 2 on page 290 shows the rise in the proportion of school leavers who have at least one parent who stayed on.

There have been constant associations between levels of attainment on the one hand, and social class and parental education on the other hand. Parental education (especially mother's education) is a better predictor of attainment than

Registrar General's social class. Figure 3 on page 291 shows different proportions of young people from different social classes staying on. For all social classes there have been rises in staying-on rates and some narrowing of the gaps between social classes. There has also been some narrowing of the differences between social classes in attainment at 16. It should be noted that these gaps remain substantial and that there has not been a corresponding narrowing in attainment at 18.

Analysis of the proportion of young people entering higher education according to social class shows that there was no narrowing between 1978 and 1988. Figure 4 on page 291 shows that parental education is as important as social class as a factor influencing whether a young person enters higher education.

Pupils are coming from smaller families. There was a rapid fall in the proportion of school leavers between 1977 and 1991 who had three or more siblings. Figure 5 on page 292 shows that this fall has been particularly evident in social classes III–V.

Spatial aspects and the growing social gap
Some of the features of the 19th century education system in the relationship between schools and their communities remain, including the following:

- substantial differences between Roman Catholic and non-denominational schools in social composition, attainment and added value;

- substantial differences between the old grammar schools and other schools, even though all are now comprehensive;

- 'contextual' effects on attainment, attributable to the social background and mix of the pupils.

We should be aware of the historical interaction between

judgements about the educability of local communities and their response to what education has to offer. There is evidence that despite the social mixing implied by comprehensivisation in Scotland, there has been a polarisation of outcomes across schools. The mixing of classes may have reduced differentials but the mixing has been partly prevented by parental choice legislation. Those who are disadvantaged are more extremely disadvantaged than before. Deprivation of the neighbourhood seems to add to other social background factors with a negative influence on outcomes. It is possible to link census data to school outcomes via postcodes – this has been done by Garner and Raudenbush in the *Journal of Sociology of Education*. This shows that the immediate physical and economic circumstances of the home, such as the level of deprivation in the neighbourhood, have a strong effect on outcomes. They conclude that ' . . . policies to alleviate educational disadvantage cannot be focused solely on schooling but must form part of a broader remit to tackle social deprivation in society at large.'

Unemployment among parents has hit disadvantaged areas much worse than the rest of Glasgow and very much worse than the rest of Scotland. Pupils in these areas get less education and there has been a fall in the last four years in the proportion of school leavers participating in any course or training. This substantial polarisation of outcomes is particularly strong for boys in these areas, partly caused by the collapse of YT. The picture is not quite as depressing as this suggests, for the following reasons:

1 despite constant social class relativities, deprivation affects fewer pupils since there is a decreasing proportion in the adversely affected social classes;

2 constant relativities matter less across high spans of attainment, and there is evidence of an overall rise in educational outcomes;

3 the evidence shows that parental education matters and

will affect inequality as the population in general becomes better educated;

4 social background is a multivariate concept and the Registrar General's classification is not a good measure in representing the disadvantages that really matter (for example, unemployment bears differently on different social classes);

5 educational interventions can change social class relativities.

Note on ethnic minorities by John Gray (Youth Cohort Study)
The YCS is carried out in England and Wales and therefore captures more data on ethnic minorities. YCS results show similar patterns to SYPS, such as increasing participation in education across the social classes, partly driven by increased parental education. There have been higher levels of participation amongst ethnic minorities, in particular Afro-Caribbeans (see Figure 6, page 292). Labour market factors may have contributed to this, but so have increasingly high expectations, aspirations and a strong belief that staying on will pay off. This trend towards a narrowing of the gap is not so apparent for exam scores or numbers of high scoring passes. At 18+, however, ethnic minority young people have greater difficulties in getting jobs, so the investment they make in education is not sustained in the labour market.

Discussion
In 1991, 15% of school leavers lived with only one parent, but this does not tell us about those that live away from home. There is evidence from Kathy Kiernan's work that young people from single-parent homes leave home earlier. There is no evidence of any variation in this amongst ethnic groups, although it should be stressed that family relationships are an important influence on decisions about whether to stay at home or not. The prognosis for children from broken families is poor (as is shown by the widening gap in HE entry) and the

proportion of those in this situation is increasing. However, it is likely that being from a single-parent family is correlated with other factors of disadvantage such as poverty or living on peripheral estates.

What remedial strategies can be suggested for the particular problems of boys (such as those in Glasgow following the demise of YT)? There is a problem of 'masculine' views of what work should be like, leading to alienation from the types of job that are available in areas of regeneration. Another problem is that young people can see the value of continuing education, but do not feel that it is 'for them'.

We must try to guarantee progression within the education system. Despite rising levels of attainment for all groups, there are certain kinds of progression that are dependent on the position in a queue. It must be asked whether the combination of the 16+ exam and the school leaving age is worthwhile in terms of the incentives it offers for progression.

Inequalities will never disappear. The Commission should be careful not to paint too deterministic a picture of the relationship of social class and educational outcomes, or else teachers might see themselves caught in a 'trap' and low expectations of the limits of young people's potential could have a negative effect. It is better to consider the substantial overlaps in ability between social classes, and differences in school effectiveness where phenomena are more susceptible to manipulation by policy makers.

To what extent is innate ability a determinant of educational outcomes? There is no way of answering this question. The effects of social class are 'net' of individual differences, but differences in attainment due to social class widen, even at the stage of primary education. It is better to look at talents and motivation: the key concept is growth rather than individual differences.

Have there been any comparisons of the results of these two surveys with results for education and social mobility in other countries? Surveys have been conducted in other countries and the results seem to parallel one another. Differentials in performance between schools are greater in the UK than anywhere else in the world. However, between-school variance in outcomes in Scotland has declined substantially over the last 10 years.

Schooling – John Gray and David Jesson

Reorganising the system: comprehensive reform
It was emphasised that educational reforms can work but not if they are half-completed, in which case the process of reform may well weaken. Comprehensivisation is an example of a half-completed reform. It is now giving way to a statement from the centre that the Government cannot guarantee standards and that parental choice will be the mechanism to ensure standards in individual schools.

How should a comprehensive system be defined? Major issues emerge about definitions of a comprehensive school: what a school is called and what are its aspirations are two separate matters. Even in Scotland, no school in a major conurbation can be described as comprehensive.

Are some studies more credible than others? There have been seven major studies of this subject. The YCS and SYPS work is unique in that it uses information based on individual pupils rather than aggregated data.

Did comprehensive reform improve achievement levels? The answer to this question differs according to the definition of 'comprehensive' one is using and according to the quality of the data. When a strong definition is used along with high quality data, it is shown that comprehensive reform in Scotland, where it was vigorously pursued, led to results that had been desired by policy makers. The system performed at least as well in terms of traditional indicators as a selective system and there are tentative signs that it might have been performing in a superior fashion. The independent sector has only militated against the advantages of the comprehensive system where it is a large sector, such as in London. Where the sector is small, the results in effective comprehensive schools are comparable to those of the independent schools.

Did comprehensive reform reduce differentials in performance? The evidence from Scotland is that class differentials were reduced. The situation in England and Wales is more patchy: 96 different policies were pursued with varying levels of vigour.

Variations within the system: school effectiveness
How large are variations between schools in their impact on academic performance? Systemic reform has dropped out of favour. Researchers are more interested now in how institutions function within frameworks, in other words school effectiveness and in particular the improvement of failing schools. LEA strategies for failing schools have often involved replacing the manager. The work on school improvement shows that it is often also necessary to change a substantial proportion of the staffing. Moreover, it may be that we value some of the more traditional aspects of schooling too highly and that the difficulties of closing down schools and possibly reopening them six weeks later are too high. Both surveys show sizeable variations in effectiveness. The difference in added value between the top 25% of schools and the bottom 25% is about two exam passes. How significant this is depends on the context, for example, the requirements of HE institutions. There remains a continuing debate about whether schools are effective to varying degrees for different types of pupils.

Does it matter who you go to school with? The evidence suggests that it does matter, although of course there are limits to how far schools can be made effective through adjustment of intake. David Raffe argued that one can do a lot about this by restricting market choice. Research in Fife shows that attempting to increase the social mix and spread the advantage of contextual effects results in a narrowing of differences in outcomes and also of contextual effects themselves. This may also have been affected by the fact that the authority mixed staff from high and low status schools. Teacher expectations are another important influence on outcomes.

Do some types of schools retain a competitive edge? There is evidence that this is the case for denominational and voluntary-aided schools. One possible explanation is that this is due to differences in values affecting the performance of the pupils, although this is not convincing. A more plausible explanation is that where values are *shared*, achievement is more likely to be high. In any case, there is a need to have a broader view of achievement and to think carefully about how we offer strategies for schools, allowing individuality irrespective of intake. What is clear is that there are several routes to excellence within a broader framework.

Desmond Nuttall said that he had found that girls-only schools in London retained a competitive edge. John Gray said that this may be true but that he was not convinced that this is a like-with-like comparison: there may be different types of parents with a corresponding effect on performance.

How are parents choosing between schools? The Scottish evidence is better on this subject due to the implementation of stronger legislation in the early 1980s. It shows that pupils tend to 'emigrate' from disadvantaged areas, with a zero-sum chase after pupils with appropriate backgrounds (see Figure 7, page 293). Pupils move towards more effective schools if one includes gains of contextual effects in the analysis. Adler's work shows this to be particularly the case for the large cities, but the SYPS shows that this also occurs on the national scale. More choice is exerted by middle-class parents than working-class parents, but this is mainly explained by their choice of independent schools rather than maintained schools. Parents' choices were 'rational' but five years out of date. Not only does one parent's choice make things worse for another but the extension of parental choice might well lead to a smaller group of top schools and more unsatisfied customers. A preferable approach is to raise the standards of as many schools as possible and reduce differentials, so that choice is less important.

Desmond Nuttall reminded the seminar that often the pupil

has a strong role in the choice and that the Commission should not ignore the family dynamics that make up the choice of a school. There is evidence that working-class children, who have more influence on choice than middle-class children, are more susceptible to peer-group pressures and myths; hence working-class parents do not make as 'rational' decisions as middle-class parents. It was pointed out, however, that feedback from older pupils may be a good thing. John Gray hoped that teachers will not see themselves as 'hung, drawn and quartered' by a system that does not value their efforts.

Managing the system: performance indicators
If you know where you are headed, then there are more chances of raising achievement. We should rediscover the power of institutions to change perceptions and outcomes.

What principles should inform the construction of performance indicators? Indicators have two main roles: first, to give a snapshot of where we are, to allow comparisons between, say, schools at any point in time; secondly, they should indicate the direction and extent of institutional change over time. The DFE league tables allow a photograph of the steady state. As for the numbers of indicators, there should be a balance between having a comprehensive list that covers a wide range of outcomes and the credibility to be gained from having relatively few in number.

How can the implications of new measures of performance be explored in an open way? Indicators provide reasons for schools with lower levels of achievement to look at their practices and procedures. They provide a benchmark for measuring own performance against that of others and for monitoring movements over time. As a crude measure they reflect intake. This makes the interpretational framework that is applied to the league table approach crucial. Most surveys see youngsters as people who are 'operated on'. The YCS asks the pupils themselves about their experiences. It deals with truancy. Figures are available for a range of definitions of truancy and the results are worrying, as indeed they are for negative attitudes to school. Andrew McPherson provided some figures for Scotland (Figure 8, page 293).

Do schools which perform well in terms of one performance indicator perform equally well in terms of others? The data show correlations between attitudes towards school and examination scores, staying-on rates and truancy. Despite this correlation it is a dangerous assumption that a single measure could capture all of the outcomes of schooling. Schools differ in their rankings on each of these measures.

Changing assessment: the case of GCSE
The YCS is useful in judging the effects of GCSE because it has cohorts that took both the old exams and the new one. Has GCSE changed young people's attitudes to school? There has been a noticeable rise in positive attitudes. Has GCSE influenced youngsters' propensity to stay on? Yes, probably (see Figure 9, page 294), although it coincided with some other changes. Has GCSE altered the relationship between performance at 16 and A level? O level was a better predictor of A level than GCSE. Desmond Nuttall pointed out that this might not be the case when the format of assessment in GCSE changes in 1994. Michael Austin pointed out that this does not take account of the growth of BTEC. It was answered that the YCS has shown growth in both A levels and BTEC.

Post-compulsory provision – David Raffe

Why have full-time staying-on rates been rising?

1   Push from social background

- Compositional change: higher proportion of population in social classes I and II, more educated parents.

- Changes in attitudes and expectations of all social groups.

2   Push from compulsory schooling

- Rising attainments at 16, and pupils with a broader range of achievements are staying on, and the rise in attainments is fastest amongst the lower attainers.

- GCSE/Standard Grade enables more pupils to succeed.

- TVEI: there is little evidence about the effects of TVEI, although it is likely that it has had indirect effects in making school more attractive to a wider range of pupils.

3   Pull from post-compulsory education

- Demography/'spare capacity': the size of the relevant age cohort has fallen, although the true nature of the relationship between the demand for places and supply of places is not clear in post-compulsory education.

- Easier access to higher education – the expansion of HE has opened up more opportunities. Evidence from Scotland shows that demand for places has been responsive to supply.

- Courses: there have been various innovations in the provision of vocational courses such as BTEC and NVQ.

4   Pull from the labour market

- Declining ageism: 16 year olds had previously been preferred by employers. This prejudice against those that stayed on, especially males, has probably diminished, resulting in a declining pull from the labour market at age 16. This trend was held to be particularly true for Scotland.

- Declining attraction of YT, which originally provided an attractive alternative to staying on in full-time education, but its fall in popularity has had the effect of making full-time education a relatively more attractive option.

- Unemployment: there is a view based on evidence from

cross-sectional analysis that rising unemployment increases staying on rates (the 'discouraged worker' effect), although the opposing view that it reduces the importance of qualifications is also often held. The evidence from England and Scotland conflicts on this point, with a strong positive correlation in Scotland between unemployment and staying-on rates.

- Benefit changes: the removal of the entitlement of 16–17-year-olds to benefit has probably boosted staying-on rates – interestingly, this occurred in the same year as the introduction of GCSE.

5   Credentialism (or 'virtuous spiral')

- The higher the proportion of young people with qualifications, the more difficult it will be for those who do not have qualifications. This might make obtaining qualifications some sort of norm.

What have been the effects of initiatives in vocational education and training (VET)?

1   YT(S)

- Changes and continuities: there have been numerous shifts in policy in this programme.

- Impact on level and distribution of VET have meant that most people get something.

- Problems have usually concerned duration and quality rather than quantity.

- Diversity of clients, functions and routes – YT has not been a single uniform programme but an umbrella for a wide range of different schemes.

- Internal stratification, related to internal/external labour market.

- YTS had a positive effect on employment but not on earnings or on the external labour market (i.e. it did not help young people to find a job outside the scheme).

- Training credits may have been more successful in breaking the continuity of attitudes. Evaluation has shown that they do not have the negative image of YT; hence, a motivational block may have been broken. However, there is not much evidence yet that they have done much to improve young people's aspirations. The evidence also suggests that young people have not been exercising choice.

2 TVEI pilot scheme

- Effects are variable across schools.

- Negligible average effects on 'hard' outcomes such as attainment, staying on and employment.

- More effect on 'soft' outcomes such as increasing self-confidence of pupils. TVEI brought about substantial 'process-orientated' changes in education, a 'loosening-up' type of role.

- Tentative evidence of 'technical' stream emerging where pupils go on to technical jobs.

- Student reactions: students like the content of TVEI and dislike its context (i.e the status of the scheme), views being more positive among females and the less qualified.

3 Modularisation/National Certificate

- A single modular framework has many advantages. It can cover different institutions, cater for a diversity of students and purposes, increase the coherence of the system (e.g. between YT and FE) and can increase responsiveness.

- Student reactions were similar to those of TVEI students.

- Low status, especially in schools where it was more popular amongst lower achieving pupils. It was often taught in different (and possibly more 'progressive') ways compared with Highers, thus reinforcing its low status.

- 'Institutional logic' stronger than 'intrinsic logic': little effect on total participation, inequalities, etc. The institutional logic is stronger because the intrinsic logic is premised on the qualifications at the end, which have insufficient 'market value'.

- Little 'compensatory' role: the National Certificate does not help out people at the bottom but is of most benefit to those in the middle range of ability.

- Problems of recognition of modular 'currency' beyond schools. This results in the problem of students finding they are required to repeat areas of study after leaving school.

Conclusion: some general issues

1 Instrumentalism and 'rationality' of young people's decision-making: importance of offering both opportunities and incentives as a fundamental part of the education system.

2 What the labour market demands is not necessarily what it needs. This may be a case of 'market failure'. We should consider the relationship between needs, expectations and demands, which will often be very different.

3 Institutions and structures do matter. There are limits to such 'outcomes' approaches as the NVQ model which might be considered naive in this respect. There is also a problem of institutional coherence in a mixed model.

4 Must differentiation always be hierarchical? It might be

possible to have 'horizontal' differentiation achieved through rigid tracking (each track having its own identity as in Germany), flexible tracking or a unified system.

5   Can a single framework cope with coherence and flexibility?

6   Will staying on still be an issue in the 21st century? Great Britain's problem is participation at 18+: HE is currently the only option, whereas other education/training options might be preferable. We do not have enough post-18 non-advanced education. It should be noted that Germany is shifting towards starting apprenticeships at 18+.

Discussion
The Commission should set its sights beyond the current expectations of employers. If employers rewarded qualifications, this would improve the situation. The main drawback of increasing the proportion of young people with qualifications is that the position of people without qualifications will get worse: international studies show around 11% in a 'relatively' deprived position. Nevertheless, employers must be encouraged or persuaded to value qualifications.

There may be benefits in delaying qualifications so that young people can catch up. For example, the Bangladeshi community almost deliberately defers GCSE until Year 12, partly as a result of cultural attitudes. There is evidence that Afro-Caribbeans catch up with whites by the age of 19, suggesting the need for a less 'age-locked' mentality. Our system, however, has disincentives for staggering qualifications.

It is notable that there is a higher proportion of Scottish students entering HE via access courses than is the case in England. Take-up of HE, of course, depends on finance.

However, when the value of student grants declined in the 1980s, there was no increase in the association between social background and HE entry. 'Aspirations are very sensitive to opportunities.'

List of those attending

Chair: Professor Peter Mortimore (Associate Commissioner, Research Committee)

Professor Andrew McPherson (Associate Commissioner, Research Committee)
David Raffe (CES, Edinburgh University)
John Gray (QQSE Research Group, Sheffield University)
David Jesson (QQSE Research Group)

Sir John Cassels (Director of the Commission)
Professor Jeff Thompson (Commissioner, Research Committee)
Professor A.H. Halsey (Associate Commissioner, Research Committee)
Professor Desmond Nuttall (Associate Commissioner)
Michael Austin (Associate Commissioner)
Chris Hayes (Associate Commissioner)

Gill Courtenay (SCPR)
Barry Hedges (SCPR)
Louise Blakey (Employment Department)
C. McKay (Scottish Office)
Pamela Anderson (Northern Ireland Office)
Ailish Murtagh (Northern Ireland Office)
Dr. Wendy Keys (NFER)

COMMISSION STAFF:
Barry Wakefield
Janice Robins
Sue Taylor
Josh Hillman
Gwynneth Rigby
Sarah Banks

Figure 1: Eighteen year olds by social class, Great Britain.

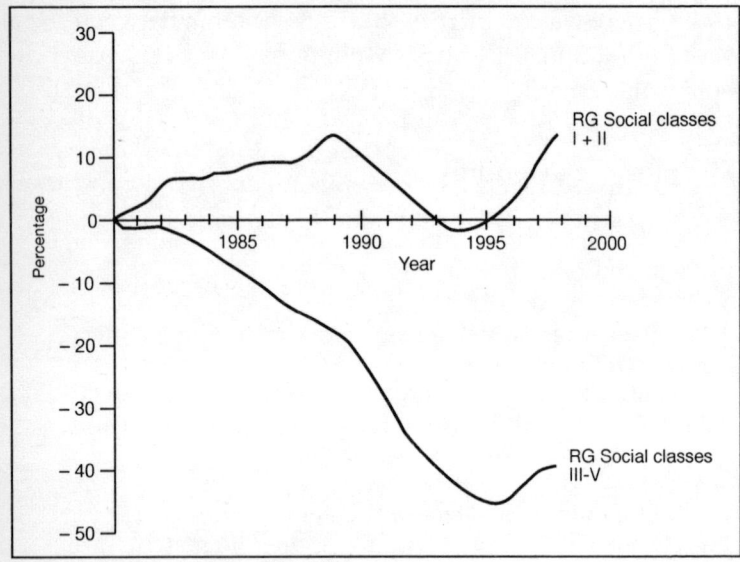

RG Social classes I + II

RG Social classes III-V

Source: Working Paper, The Royal Society (1983)

Figure 2: School leavers with at least one parent schooled to 16+ years, Scotland.

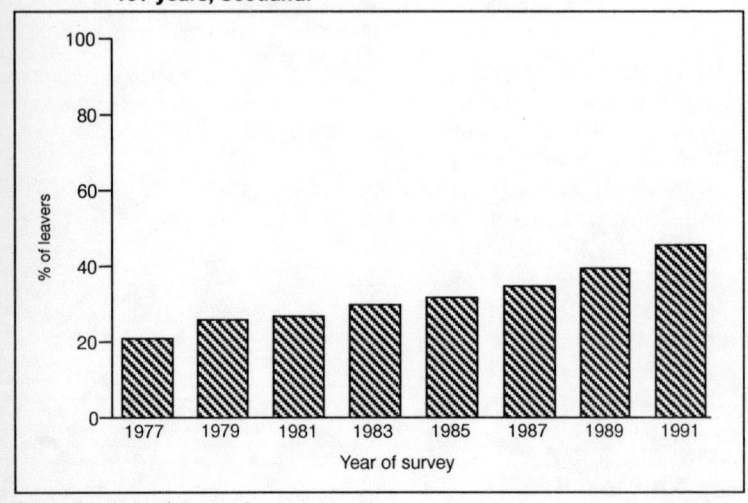

Source: Scottish Young People's Survey

Figure 3: Proportion staying on to end of fifth year or after, Scotland.

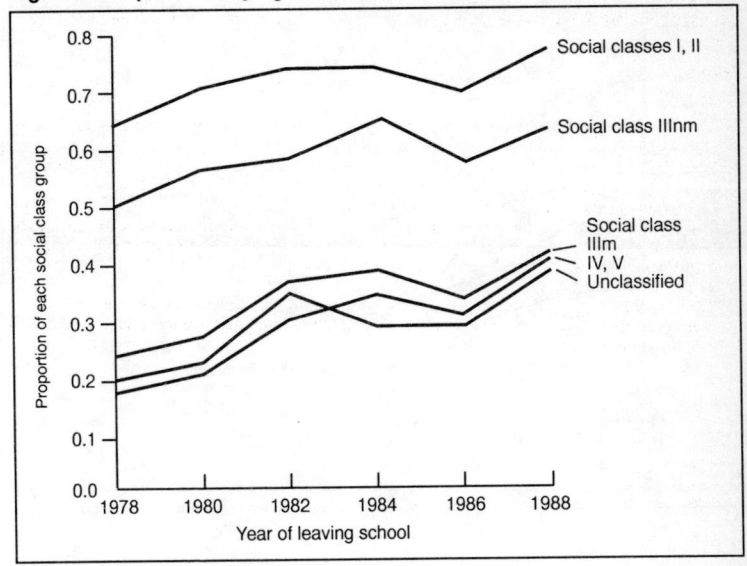

Source: Scottish Young People's Survey

Figure 4: Proportion entering any higher education.

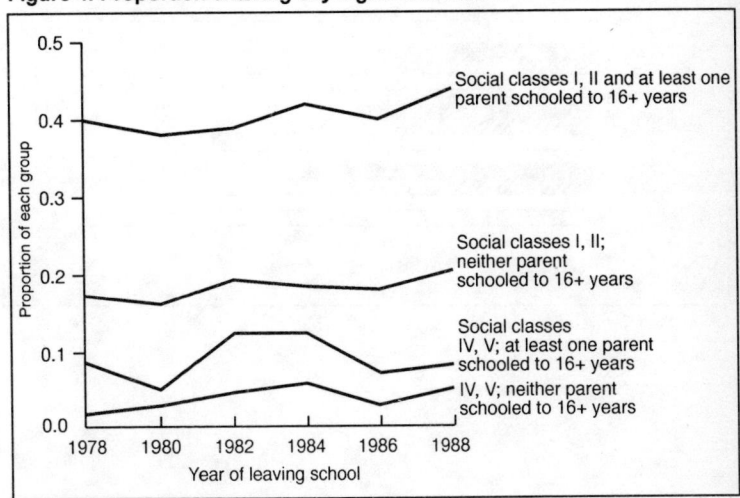

Source: Scottish Young People's Survey

Figure 5: Mean number of siblings.

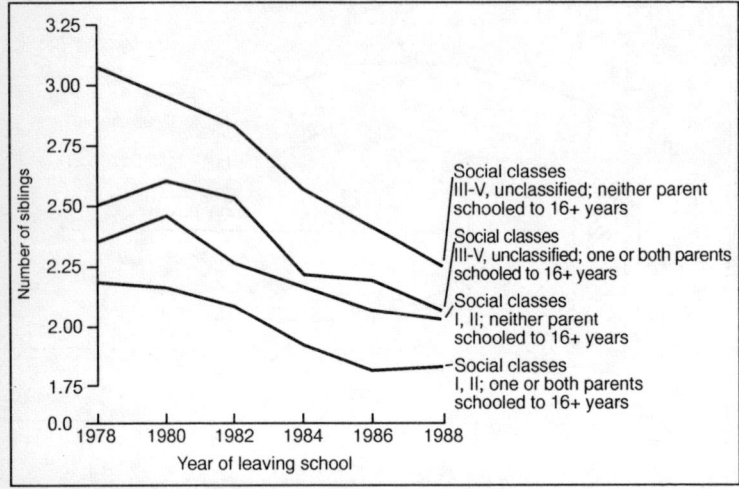

Social classes III-V, unclassified; neither parent schooled to 16+ years

Social classes III-V, unclassified; one or both parents schooled to 16+ years

Social classes I, II; neither parent schooled to 16+ years

Social classes I, II; one or both parents schooled to 16+ years

Source: Scottish Young People's Survey

Figure 6: Participation in full-time education beyond the minimum school leaving age by ethnic group, England and Wales.

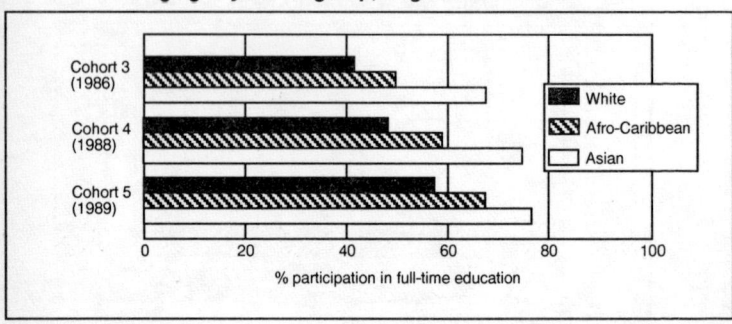

Source: Youth Cohort Study

Figure 7: Proportion of pupils not entering their local state secondary school, by father's social class, Scotland.

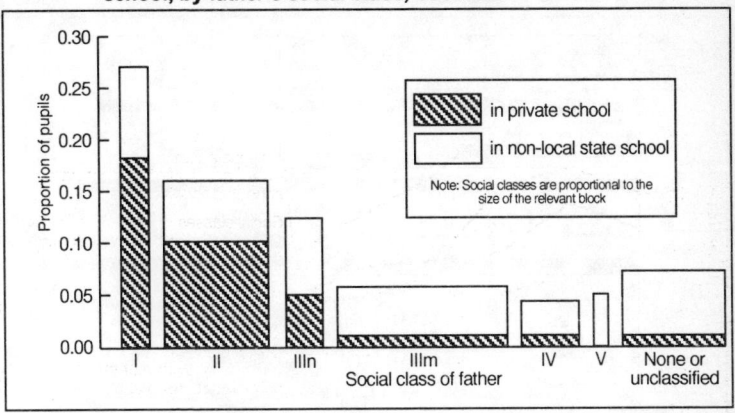

Source: Scottish Young People's Survey

Figure 8: Percentage of leavers indicating that they had truanted, Scotland.

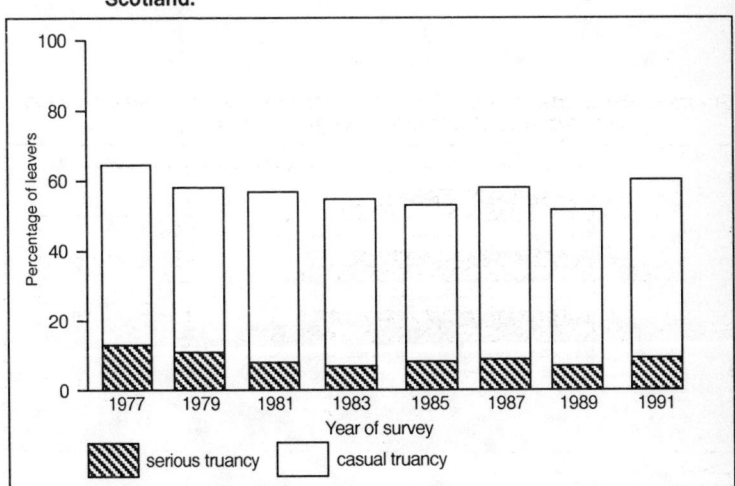

Source: Scottish Young People's Survey

Figure 9: Participation in full-time education by qualifications achieved at 16+, England and Wales.

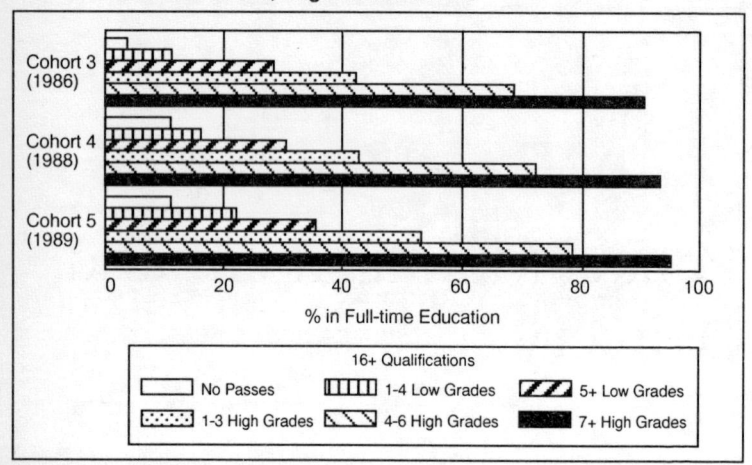

16+ Qualifications: No Passes, 1-4 Low Grades, 5+ Low Grades, 1-3 High Grades, 4-6 High Grades, 7+ High Grades

Source: Youth Cohort Study

III

Policy, Management and Delivery

25. Answers by the Department for Education to Questions posed by the National Commission on Education

A Note by the Department for Education, March 1993.

Before School

Q1. The Commission has received evidence from various quarters that there should be access for all children of 3 and 4 whose parents so wish to publicly-funded early childhood care and education of high quality. How high a priority does DFE attach to this? How strong is the case for a review of provision as argued by Sylva and Moss (NCE Briefing No. 8)?

As the Commission will be aware, child care is the responsibility of the Department of Health and questions on child care policy should be directed to them. As regards educational policies, the Department considers that priority has to be accorded to the statutory school age range, and that the extent and forms of provision for younger children are appropriately determined by local authorities and schools. Within this frame, substantial growth – which the Department welcomes – has taken place over the last decade. The numbers of under 5s in maintained nursery and primary schools in England rose between 1981 and 1991 from 428,000 to 604,000, and over 50% of the 3- and 4-year age group now attend maintained or independent schools. Following publication of the Rumbold Committee report[1] in 1990 the Department has taken every opportunity to promote the educational improvement of the largest care provider, the playgroup movement. From a figure of £179,000 in 1990–91 its grant to the Pre-school Playgroups Association will rise to £887,000 in 1993–94.

Primary Schools

Q2. *What more should be done to ensure that all children capable of it reach a satisfactory level of attainment in written and oral English and in the use of numbers by Key Stage 2? Should more use be made of learning support staff and voluntary helpers to achieve this?*

A. THE PRESENT POSITION AND POLICY

1 The primary policy instrument for raising standards of attainment in all stages of compulsory schooling, and in all subjects, is the National Curriculum and the investment that has gone with it. For all subjects, *curriculum Orders* specify statutory attainment targets for learning and programmes of study to be taught, and *assessment Orders* specify arrangements for measuring pupils' achievements against the attainment targets.

2 The attainment targets comprise statements of attainment at 10 levels, making it possible to chart each pupil's progress throughout his or her school career. Once all the assessment arrangements are in place, there should be a reliable baseline for the measurement of pupils' achievements from year to year. In the past this has been a notoriously difficult comparison to make.

3 Without reliable and objective 'baseline' performance measures pre-dating its introduction, it is difficult to assess the initial impact of the National Curriculum on standards. Moreover, in terms of educational lead times the NC is still at an early stage of implementation. OFSTED's recent 'overview' report is therefore properly guarded about the effect to date of the NC on standards overall. Nevertheless HMI/OFSTED's reports on the implementation of the National Curriculum in the core subjects in the first two years do provide evidence that some improvements in the teaching of *English* could already be discerned.

4 Inspection evidence may be compared with the results of the first NC assessments of the attainment of pupils at

age 7. Again little can be learned from the first year's results alone, since the NC assessment system is in principle criterion- rather than norm-referenced, and the proportions of pupils attaining different levels at the end of Key Stage 1 were not predictable. However, the comparison between the first and second year of testing may show changes with suggestive significance for the early implementation of the NC.

The picture for mathematics

5 The National Curriculum ensures that pupils are taught a balanced curriculum that gives proper attention to all aspects of mathematics, including numerical skills. It requires pupils to develop a range of methods of calculation, including mental calculations, pencil and paper methods and the use of electronic calculators and other mathematical tools.

6 The NC requirements for mathematics encourage a balanced approach to calculation and set challenging targets for pupils of all ages and abilities. International comparisons have tended to show that in comparison with other branches of mathematics, and mathematical skills, handling numbers is not one of the strongest features of our pupils' performance. By making explicit the attainments expected of pupils in number, the NC should help to redress the balance and overcome this relative weakness.

7 The evidence from HMI/OFSTED does not point clearly to any improvement in mathematics generally. The testing evidence, however, points to some improvement over the first year of the introduction of the NC. In 1991 the first statutory tests for 7-year-olds showed that 72% of pupils achieved or went beyond level 2 – the standard expected of the typical child at this age – in mathematics. This rose to 78% in 1992. The proportion of 7-year-olds reaching level 2 in the *number* attainment target in 1991 was lower than for mathematics as a whole, at 55%. This was still the case in 1992, but there was a significant improvement to 63%. Moreover, HMI noted in its report

on the 1992 assessments that tests had begun to challenge teachers' expectations of what pupils could attain and so to exert a significant influence on teaching. In particular, they observed more work on mental arithmetic.

The picture for English (including writing and speaking)

8 The English Order identifies attainment targets for speaking and listening (AT1), reading (AT2), writing (AT3), spelling (AT4), and handwriting (AT5). The requirements for AT1 build on the best practice in the development of oral (and aural) skills that has developed over recent years, with the stimulation of the oracy project promoted by the Department and the NCC. The requirements for the writing AT mark stages in the progression of the ability to construct and convey meaning in written language 'matching style to audience and purpose', and require, in the higher levels, the ability to write in a wide variety of forms.

9 In September 1992 the Secretary of State announced that a review of the English Order would be undertaken by the National Curriculum Council, with the Curriculum Council for Wales. The aim of the review is to strengthen the statutory requirements and to define these with even greater precision and clarity. A revised Order is expected to take effect in schools from August 1994 for 5–14-year-olds, and August 1995 for 14–16-year-olds.

10 OFSTED/HMI reports on the first two years' experience point to many benefits from the introduction of National Curriculum English, including a rise in standards in some aspects of primary English teaching. Teachers have responded to the challenge, and improved planning and teaching provision has been evident. The experience of National Curriculum assessment procedures has helped teachers match their teaching to their pupils' strengths and weaknesses. In oral work, the National Curriculum has led to an improvement in opportunities, and high standards were observed. Standards in writing, though

widely satisfactory, were less high than in the other attainment targets, especially at Key Stage 2, but there were signs that closer attention was being given to handwriting.

11 In the case of English, however, the KS1 testing results did not show any significant change between the first two years. The 1992 finding that 77% of 7-year-olds had reached or gone beyond the expected level of 2 compared with a 1991 figure of 78%. In writing, the corresponding 1992 figure of 66% represented a fall of 12 percentage points, but this was thought to be attributable to a tightening of the rules on punctuation rather than any real decline in standards. For *reading* the corresponding figure went up by 5 percentage points to 76%.

B. SCOPE FOR FURTHER ACTION

Reading Recovery

12 In January 1992 a national trial of the 'Reading Recovery' intervention, pioneered in New Zealand, was announced, with grant under the GEST programme to support expenditure of £10 million over three years. To this Ministers have now decided to add a further £750,000 in 1993–94. The trial is being conducted in inner city schools in 20 local education authorities. The programme targets children who at age 6 are having difficulty in learning to read and write. (Although this particular remedial intervention has been given the title of 'Reading Recovery', that title is a misnomer since it is equally directed at difficulties with writing.) These children are given individual attention by a specially trained teacher for half an hour each day for an average of 16 weeks. Current evidence (mainly from New Zealand) suggests that most participating pupils reach average levels of attainment in literacy in their class by the time they enter Key Stage 2.

Use of voluntary helpers

13 The use of voluntary helpers is organised at local level. It is a tradition in early reading, but not in mathematics. In

the present financial year the Department is making a grant of £50,000 to the Volunteer Reading Help (VRH) organisation to enable it to expand its operations. VRH is a national charity which links volunteers with children who need help and encouragement with their reading. Primary school teachers choose the children to be helped. Each volunteer usually works with three children, regularly spending half an hour twice a week with each. Volunteers need no formal qualifications, but they are interviewed and trained by VRH before being introduced to the schools.

Resource requirements

14 The Government has already earmarked substantial additional resources for the implementation of the National Curriculum and its associated assessment arrangements; in the current financial year alone, grants are being made available to support expenditure of some £176 million. This is on top of some £390 million expenditure supported between 1989 and 1992. It is up to LEAs and individual schools to decide how to apply for these grants and how to deploy the resources available in the light of local priorities and needs. More generally, it is recognised that support staff can make an important contribution to successful work in the classroom, but their employment is a matter for local decision.

Q3. For many years the Senior Chief HMI's Annual Report has expressed disquiet that pupils of average ability and above are not given sufficient learning challenge in the later years of primary school. How can this be put right? Should at least one foreign language be taught at primary school?

The National Curriculum, which is only this year being taught in its entirety to pupils in Key Stage 2, is intended to raise teachers' expectations through setting out clear national targets for children's learning. In addition, by specifying learning objectives within a ten-level scale, the curriculum allows pupils at all stages of education to work at the highest level of which they are capable, whatever their age.

The National Curriculum will not in itself ensure that work is matched properly to individual pupils' abilities. That must remain a task for teachers. But the National Curriculum provides a framework within which teachers can assess their pupils' progress and use the information gained to match work more precisely to children's abilities and aptitudes, and to plan challenging work which will stretch them and encourage further progression.

This issue was addressed in the discussion paper, *Curriculum Organisation and Classroom Practice in Primary Schools*, by Professor Robin Alexander, Jim Rose of HMI and Chris Woodhead of the National Curriculum Council, published in January 1992. The Government has commended this report to teachers and schools and will continue to press for improvements where necessary.

Following two reports on the primary curriculum and teaching methods from the NCC and OFSTED, the Government has announced a five-point strategy for improving primary education. The reports have been circulated to all involved in primary education; OFSTED have been asked to report progress in a year's time; school prospectuses will have to set out the policy of each school on classroom organisation, curriculum planning and teaching methods; and new criteria for primary ITT are to be brought forward in the spring.

On the question of modern languages in primary schools, the Government recognises the desirability, in principle, of as early a start as possible to language learning and accepts that it is possible to lay the foundation for foreign language learning in primary schools by developing children's communication skills and understanding of the nature of language. They have not, however, made the teaching of a modern foreign language compulsory in primary schools. Nor do they plan to do so. The curriculum requirements at KS2 are already under review because it is considered by teachers to be overloaded.

Even if there were space in the primary timetable, the

Government's first priority must be to increase the number of secondary school pupils studying a modern foreign language to a worthwhile level of fluency. Since there are not at present enough teachers qualified to teach modern languages, recruitment and training efforts concentrate on remedying the shortage of language teachers in secondary schools, in special schools and in middle schools which are now required to teach modern foreign languages for the first time.

Primary schools which have the necessary staffing and other resources are, however, free to introduce their pupils to a modern foreign language now, once they have satisfied the requirements of the National Curriculum.

Secondary Schools

Q4. Does DFE favour the provision by schools which so wish of more work-related and/or practically oriented courses from age 14 onwards?

The Government has since the early 1980s promoted the development of work in the curriculum which is not only related to particular vocations, but is more relevant generally to the world of work, by emphasising a range of skills and knowledge, both basic and practical, which are relevant to the needs of industry, through the Technical and Vocational Education Initiative (TVEI). The National Curriculum builds on this by designing provision which is relevant to adult life, whether generally or in relation to employment.

The individual subject Orders of the National Curriculum have been designed, where appropriate, to bring out practical 'making' skills, as well as knowledge and understanding. The Technology Order is being reviewed to make that emphasis on the practical clearer and to ensure that the provision permits easy progression on to more directly vocational courses post-16.

The National Curriculum is intended to offer a broad and balanced foundation in a wide range of skills, knowledge and understanding to pupils, whatever their aptitudes and abilities, during compulsory schooling. The Government recognises, however, that some pupils have clear career aspirations before 16. Schools have for some time offered specifically vocational courses to 14-year-olds, and the Government is happy to see such provision continued, over and above the National Curriculum requirements.

The Government has therefore introduced an element of flexibility in the National Curriculum requirements for 14–16-year-olds, by continuing to require full courses to be taken in the core subjects of Mathematics, Science and English, but permitting short courses only to be taken in Technology, Modern Foreign Languages, History and Geography, and by lifting the requirements on schools to take Music and Art at that stage. This provides space for pupils to study either additional academic subjects outside the National Curriculum, relevant to their future career – for example, GCSE courses in a second modern language or economics – or to take vocational courses, which might be accredited towards the achievement of General National Vocational Qualifications (GNVQs) or National Vocational Qualifications (NVQs). Since all National Curriculum study at Key Stage 4 above Level 4 has to be assessed by means of a nationally recognised qualification, in practice many pupils taking a short course, particularly in Design and Technology or Technology, will combine these with a vocationally oriented element to make up a full GCSE. Syllabuses of this type are currently being developed.

Q5. Employers insist strongly that children at school should acquire core competencies, which include such things as written and oral communication, team-working, the ability to reason critically, adaptability and self-confidence. What is the DFE's view on how such competencies are best taught and how attainment in them can be assessed?

It has always been the case that school education has, in

addition to developing children's academic knowledge and understanding, aimed to inculcate skills which are relevant to work and indeed to all aspects of adult life.

In recent years, the teaching of communication skills and numeracy has become more explicit in English and mathematics teaching, and throughout the curriculum where these skills are applied in other subjects. Increasingly, the same is becoming true of skills in information technology.

The Government believes that pupils should also develop other personal skills through their education. In general these skills are taught through work in subjects, by use of teaching and learning styles which support such development. The National Curriculum provides opportunities for the use of such learning styles, and in some instances the Orders make specific reference to them. Teachers can build on the development work undertaken through TVEI.

Work experience, of course, plays a part in developing more general personal skills, and good preparation for work experience helps to ensure that pupils recognise the skills which they have, and how they will be used in a working environment.

The application of generic skills such as literacy and numeracy will continue to be assessed in the context of pupils' work in the various subjects of the curriculum, and in particular through public examinations. This is the reason for an insistence that GCSE marking across all subjects should take account of pupils' ability to spell correctly, as one part of an assessment of communication skills.

Skills which cannot easily be assessed in this way may need to be assessed through teacher assessment, and recorded separately on a record of achievement. The Government has consistently promoted the use of such records, which are designed to ensure that the range of pupils' skills and abilities are recorded.

Post-16

Q6. Would DFE like to see all, or virtually all, young people continue in education in order to achieve qualifications at 18? Should full-time education provide the only route post-16 or should there also be an alternative employer-based route involving colleges part-time?

DFE (and ED) Ministers support the National Education and Training Targets to underpin a better qualified workforce and community. The targets for foundation learning include:

- by 1997, 80% of young people to reach NVQ Level II or its academic equivalent of four or more GCSEs at grades A–C;

- by 2000, 50% of young people to reach NVQ Level III or its academic equivalent of two or more A levels.

Ministers very much welcome the fact that the proportion of young people choosing to remain in education and training beyond 16 is increasing; they expect this trend to continue, and have taken steps to encourage it and to ensure that it is based on firm foundations.

The Further and Higher Education Act 1992 establishes in law that full-time education opportunities should be available to all 16–18-year-olds who wish to take advantage of them. The recent Public Expenditure settlement provides the resources necessary to sustain over the next three years the expansion of the new Further Education sector which will be in place from April 1993. The Government has made clear to the Further Education Funding Council that they attach particular importance to the achievement of an increase in participation of 17-year-olds in full-time education and training.

Furthermore, Ministers are committed to the establishment of a range of good and well-regarded qualifications which will allow each young person to pursue a course of study appropriate to their abilities and ambitions. A levels and AS are well established and widely available. National Vocational Qualifications (NVQs) are widely available in some occupational areas, and coming on stream very quickly in most others. The early signs are that the new General NVQs (GNVQs), introduced from September 1992, have made a popular and successful beginning.

Against this background, Ministers consider that it remains primarily for the young people themselves to decide whether they wish to continue in education and training post-16, and whether any such study should be full-time or work-based. Youth Training already provides one mechanism for work-based study, and Ministers will continue to work to ensure that young people can choose among a full range of effective and attractive options.

Q7. How can greater flexibility and choice be opened up in learning post-16 (or perhaps post-14)? Are there useful lessons to be learned from the current Scottish approach (rather than the two-track approach proposed by Howie) or from the International Baccalaureate?

The Government's primary objective for education up to 16 is to ensure that all pupils acquire, by the end of compulsory schooling, a broad and balanced range of skills, knowledge and understanding, as the basis not only for adult life, but for responding flexibly to the further education and training demands arising from the rapidly developing needs of industry. DFE Ministers have already revised the requirements of the National Curriculum for 14–16-year-olds to provide opportunities not only to achieve that broad and balanced education, but also to begin to exercise a degree of choice in the depth to which they address subjects beyond the core of the NC, and the range of vocationally related courses available leading on to post-16 training and qualifications. It would not be possible to offer greater flexibility for 14–16-year-olds without endangering the fundamental learning which all pupils need pre-16, whatever their abilities, aptitudes and career aspirations.

DFE and ED Ministers wish to ensure that young people are able to choose the form of study and qualification which is right for them beyond compulsory school age. Much work is currently under way to ensure that post-16 qualifications offer greater choice and flexibility than in the past.

GCE A levels continue to be a successful and respected option among post-16 qualifications, serving well those for whom they were designed. Where schools and students wish to make use of them, Advanced Supplementary (AS) examinations offer a mechanism by which A level work can be broadened while retaining the same mode of study and common standards.

Ministers are confident that these three broad qualification pathways, once fully established, will provide significant choice, flexibility and breadth for young people.

Ministers are naturally interested in academic and vocational education in Scotland and the current debate about its future development. However, the Scottish education system (including its interaction with Higher Education) is historically very different and the potential for read-across is correspondingly limited.

It is for local authorities and individual schools and colleges to decide whether they wish to offer the International Baccalaureate, taking into account the staffing and other financial implications, the capabilities of students, and the scope which A levels and AS, GNVQs and NVQs already provide for high quality attainment.

But Ministers recognise that the traditional three A-level path is not suitable for or attractive to all those wishing to continue their study post-16. From September 1993 General National Vocational Qualifications (GNVQs) will be available in an increasing number of schools and colleges, and Ministers expect that they will provide a high quality study programme which develops young people's knowledge, skills and understanding in a broadly occupational context and thereby keep open the options of higher education and good jobs thereafter. (A GNVQ at Level 3 is broadly comparable to 2 A levels, and in some cases students may wish to combine it with an A level or AS, or with further GCSEs.) The more job-specific NVQ offers a further option, mainly for those young people already in employment who wish to improve their skills.

Governance

Q8. To whom precisely are the governing bodies of LEA-maintained schools and of grant-maintained schools accountable? Does the DFE envisage any substantial change in this accountability if more schools become grant-maintained?

The governing bodies of grant-maintained schools are statutory corporations with charitable status. The governing body is directly accountable to the parents of registered pupils at the school, not only through a governors' annual report and an annual parents' meeting, but also through its responsibility to deal with questions and complaints that parents may address to them. Ultimately, the governors must also account to the Secretary of State.

Governing bodies of LEA-maintained schools have been given a number of duties and a range of powers to enable them to carry out those duties. The LEA may also have delegated powers and duties to the governors, which will be detailed in the Articles of Government for the school. Any interested person can complain to the Secretary of State if he believes that a governing body is acting 'unreasonably' in using its powers, or is failing to carry out its duties properly. If the Secretary of State agrees that the complaint is justified, he can direct the governing body to take whatever action seems to him to be best.

Under LMS provisions governing bodies have responsibility for deciding how to spend the budget for their school. If a governing body gets into serious difficulties with its budget, the LEA can in the last resort take away that body's financial responsibilities until it seems safe to restore them.

Legislation has also made governing bodies more accountable to parents. Governors must prepare an annual report for parents and hold an annual meeting for parents, which is designed to allow discussion of the annual report and how the governing body, the head teacher, and the LEA have carried out their responsibilities since the last report. If there are enough parents present they may pass resolutions on issues which must then be considered by the governors, the head teacher or the LEA as appropriate.

The DFE does not anticipate any change in the accountability of the governing bodies of LEA-maintained schools or of grant-maintained schools as more schools become grant-maintained.

Q9. How does the DFE expect to avoid a situation in which grant-maintained status, parental choice and open enrolment lead to more favoured schools in effect choosing the pupils (and the parents) more likely to be well-motivated towards education, and hence to 'sink schools' developing from those less popular?

Popular schools have always been oversubscribed – they will continue to be required to allocate places on the basis of published admissions arrangements which must be clear and objective. For a comprehensive school, whether LEA-maintained or GM, these arrangements cannot include more than a very limited amount of selection without the publication of formal proposals to change the character of the school. The Department recently issued for consultation a draft circular giving guidance on admissions policies.

Parents are increasingly aware of their right to say which school they prefer and are sent information on which that preference can be based. Schools which are less popular have every incentive to improve to attract pupils. The increased accountability introduced through annual reports from governors to parents, publication of performance tables, and inspection reports every four years, will mean that parents and the local community can themselves press for improvements where necessary.

For that small number of schools at risk of failing their pupils, the current Education Bill includes new measures to secure improvement. But where parental choice leads to the concentration of surplus places in a particular school it may be that closure is the right option.

Teachers

Q10. Now that there is general support in the teaching profession for the establishment of a General Teaching Council (for which revised proposals have recently been published), does the DFE now favour this move towards professional self-regulation with appropriate lay representation?

The Government set out its position on a General Teaching Council (GTC) in response to the Education Select Committee in 1990, which made clear that it was not persuaded by the arguments in favour of a GTC. A GTC would not improve on present arrangements for such matters as teacher supply and teacher discipline.

The Government stands by that response, having read carefully the latest proposals of the GTC proponents and found nothing new which could persuade it to reconsider that view. In particular no convincing arguments have been advanced that a GTC would perform the statutory functions claimed for it more effectively than they are performed at present. The Secretary of State has however suggested that the profession might set up its own associations, perhaps along the lines of the Royal Colleges in the health service, which would not have statutory functions but would be able to offer authoritative advice on issues of professional concern. This could go a long way towards satisfying teachers' legitimate ambitions for professional bodies to enhance their status, and could command more widespread support outside the profession, raising public appreciation of their work.

Q11. Does the DFE accept that every child has the right to be taught each subject in the National Curriculum by teachers professionally competent to teach it? Even today, in a severe recession, there are shortages of teachers qualified to teach certain subjects, especially in S.E. England. What can be done to ensure that such shortages become a thing of the past, whatever the state of the labour market?

The Government acknowledge the crucial importance of ensuring that all pupils are taught by people who are knowledgeable and skilled in the required subjects at every level of the National Curriculum. Policies for recruitment and training will continue to be directed at that objective. The Secretary of State intends to build on the reforms in initial training introduced by his predecessors and to find ways of improving the quality of teachers already in service.

On recruitment much has already been achieved. There are still some pockets of shortage, but in the last couple of years we have seen a marked improvement in teacher supply. Between 1990 and 1992 vacancies in the teacher force of 400,000 have fallen from 6,500 to fewer than 2,000. The tables on pages 320–321 show how few vacancies now exist even in the traditional 'shortage' subjects. Over the same period, applications to initial teacher training courses have been buoyant and recruitment to courses is up by over a third. Applications for courses in shortage subjects are at a healthy level, and ITT institutions have the opportunity to pick the best quality and most promising candidates.

Ministers accept that they cannot afford to relax these efforts. Since 1986 the Government has introduced a wide range of measures to improve recruitment and retention and encourage qualified teacher returners. Many of these measures are targeted on shortage subjects and most are still in place. A range of distance learning materials has been funded and developed to improve the quality of serving teachers and returners in shortage subject areas. A very substantial investment has been made by way of specific grants for in-service training and for helping mature people make an effective start after taking a career break. Measures to attract mature entrants include the Open University PGCE which will begin to bear fruit in the mid-nineties with an annual output of about 1000 newly qualified teachers. Many of these mature entrants will concentrate on secondary shortage subjects or on mathematics and sciences at primary level.

Q12. School-based initial teacher education to be effective requires training and cover for mentors. Does DFE acknowledge that lasting reforms in this area require extra resources for the schools involved?

Circular 9/92 sets out new criteria for initial teacher training. These criteria indicate the conditions on which the Secretary of State is prepared to approve courses leading to a teaching qualification. One of the key new requirements in the circular is to extend the minimum time to be spent by student teachers on the premises of schools which operate in partnership with colleges and departments of education. The new criteria apply to courses for secondary school teachers. New requirements for primary school courses are still under consideration: the Secretary of State expects to propose changes in April 1993.

Circular 9/92 recognises that partner schools will incur costs over and above those which they have previously borne in providing teaching practice for student teachers. These costs will have to be covered by colleges and university departments from the grants which they receive from the Higher Education Funding Councils and from their fee income. The net extra costs are likely to vary according to local circumstances, depending, for example, on arrangements for providing reciprocal help to partner schools by way of professional advice, teaching support or access to libraries and laboratories. There is to be no uniform tariff for calculating the money to be transferred from HE institutions to schools. The circular indicates that there should be local negotiation on the basis of clear statements about the new roles and responsibilities of partner schools.

Colleges and departments of education receive, on average,

about £3,750 for each secondary PGCE student in training. An additional £6 million was made available for 1992–93 to meet the net extra costs incurred during the transition to the new arrangements. The transitional funds were intended to meet extra costs including release time and supply cover for teachers with specific responsibilities, both for their own preparation and for time spent training students. For 1994–95 the Funding Councils have been asked to make their own judgement of the transitional costs and to allocate grants accordingly. The costs to schools and the resources transferred to them will be closely monitored over the period up to the deadline by which all courses are to be adapted to meet the new criteria.

Higher and further education

Q13. Does DFE consider that there is a lack of even-handedness in the financial support available on the one hand to students entering full-time degree courses and on the other hand to students entering other higher and most further education courses at 18+?

No. Students on designated full-time and sandwich courses which lead to a first degree or comparable qualification, or to the HND or DipHE (which are regarded as being equivalent to the first two years of a degree course), and on full-time and part-time courses of initial teacher training can get financial support from mandatory awards and loans. The system – consisting of a means-tested maintenance grant, non-means-tested loan, and the payment of the student's tuition fees – underwrites one opportunity for people, regardless of age or sex, to undertake a full-time first degree or comparable level course. Loans (but not awards) are available for second or subsequent higher education courses. These arrangements share costs more equitably between students, their families and taxpayers, and are justified on the grounds of the length and cost of the investment for the taxpayer and the rate of return from higher education to the individual and to society.

The introduction of student loans from 1990/91 allows the Government to reduce in real terms, over time, direct public expenditure on grants, yet increase the overall resources available to students.

Students on other, non-designated, courses of further and higher education can apply for a discretionary award from their local education authority (LEA). There are no nationally-prescribed rates and conditions, and LEAs can choose which students and courses to support and at what level. Full-time higher education students on courses not designated for mandatory awards purposes may also be eligible for a loan, but loans are not available to students on further education courses or (initial teacher training students excepted) higher education students attending part-time. Support for further education or part-time study is discretionary because this gives the flexibility required to meet the much wider range of full- and part-time modes of attendance, students' needs and local circumstances, and thus facilitates expansion on an affordable basis. Part-time students, for example, are often in employment and receive financial help from their employers. Part-time students also retain entitlement to social security benefits.

Full-time or sandwich students in further and higher education can also apply to their college for financial help under the Access Funds. Colleges use the Funds to provide selective help at their discretion to students who have serious financial difficulties or who might not otherwise have been able to afford to enter higher education. The Government considers that Access Funds allow for limited resources to be targeted where the need is greatest, representing value for money for the taxpayer.

Q14. How can rapid increases in HE provision, coupled now with those in FE, be funded on a scale that avoids the risk of loss of quality?

The Government has provided substantial increases in the

level of funding for higher education in recent years. It has recently announced a record level of spending of over £4 billion on higher education in England in 1993–94.

The record shows that an expansion in student numbers can be achieved without loss of quality and with increased efficiency. Full-time equivalent student numbers have increased by 80% since 1979. More than one in four young people are now entering HE compared with only one in eight in 1979. Much of the increase in student numbers during this period took place in polytechnics and colleges. HMI have reported that these institutions raised their teaching quality while substantially reducing unit costs. The proportion of first and second class honours degrees awarded by universities and polytechnics and colleges increased steadily during the 1980s.

The effects of the rapid expansion in student numbers will, nonetheless, need to be kept under review. In the Autumn Statement, the Government assumed a period of consolidation in HE over the next three years. This pause in the drive for growth will provide an opportunity to take stock and allow institutions to build on their considerable achievements.

The Government has asked the Higher Education Funding Council for England (HEFCE) to look at ways in which higher education might be provided more cost-effectively.

There is, however, no room for complacency about quality. Universities and colleges have responded collectively to the need for quality audit arrangements for the new unified higher education sector by setting up a Higher Education Quality Council. The new Council will audit institutions' quality assurance systems and also promote quality enhancement in institutions. It will pursue the further development of credit accumulation and transfer, and access courses.

A structure is also being established for external assessment to ensure that there is proper, independent reporting on quality. The HEFCE is under a statutory duty to secure the assessment of the provision which it funds or is considering funding. Following pilot assessments in the spring, further test assessments were carried out in the autumn culminating in the launch of the assessment programme proper this year. The HEFCE has appointed a Quality Assessment Committee and is in the process of recruiting assessors for this important task.

Turning to the further education sector, the Government's aim is to increase participation by young people and adults in high quality education and training. The Government's expenditure plans for education gave top priority to further education.

Increased funding will allow for a 25% increase in student numbers in FE over the next three years.

The Secretary of State has made it clear, however, that his concern is not just with increasing participation but with raising levels of attainment and developing quality. In his launch letter of guidance to the Further Education Funding Council of 17 July 1992 he stressed that the Council should seek to maintain and enhance quality by relating funding to its assessments of quality. In his address to the Council's first national conference on 9 December 1992 the Secretary of State said: 'The aim must be to ensure that all the many different types of study that are undertaken in FE are fit for purpose and of high quality'. By relating funding to quality assessment (for which the Funding Council will be responsible under the Further and Higher Education Act 1992), the Secretary of State expects that increased participation will be achieved without any loss of quality.

Finally, for both further and higher education it is important that students, their parents, and employers have a clear statement about their entitlements and the services available for them. The Government therefore intends that further and higher education should be brought within the Citizen's Charter initiative. Work is in hand on preparing Charters which we plan to publish in the spring.

Q15. Does DFE consider that as the nation becomes more prosperous people will want proportionately more of GDP to be spent on education? Can any broad statements be made about how responsibility for funding education might shift as time goes on as between taxpayers (national and local), employers, parents and learners themselves?

United Kingdom public expenditure on education as a percentage of GNP is higher than that in Germany or Japan (the most recent figures, for 1989, show the percentages as 4.6, 4.1 and 4.2 respectively). But there is always pressure for more expenditure on education. The Government's task is to ensure the best possible value for money from the resources which can be made available, taking into account other claims on public spending.

The Government has no present plans for shifts in funding responsibilities.

Department for Education
March 1993

Reference

1 *Starting with Quality*, the Report of the Committee of Inquiry into the Quality of the Educational Experience Offered to 3- and 4-year-olds. Chaired by Mrs Angela Rumbold CBE MP. HMSO; 1990.

Vacancy[1] rates in maintained nursery and primary schools by grade and main age group of deployment: 1988 to 1992, England.

	Vacancies as a percentage of teachers in post[2]					Number of Vacancies
	1988	1989	1990	1991	1992	1992
All vacancies	1.4	1.8	2.1	1.9	0.6	1,074
By grade:						
Head or Deputy Head[3]	1.3	1.7	1.9	1.7	0.7	293
Head	..	..	1.7	1.5	0.6	128
Deputy Head	..	..	2.1	1.9	0.9	165
Main scale teacher	1.4	1.8	2.2	1.9	0.6	781
By main age group of deployment[4]						
Nursery	1.7	2.3	2.4	2.0	1.1	94
Infant	1.7	2.2	2.5	2.4	0.8	356
Junior	1.2	1.5	1.9	1.5	0.5	342
More than one age group	..	..	..	..	..	282

[1] Advertised vacancies for full-time permanent appointments (or appointments of at least one term's duration). Includes vacancies being filled on a temporary basis.
[2] Teachers in post include full-time regular teachers in (or in secondment from) maintained nursery and primary schools, plus the primary portion of full-time regular divided service, peripatetic, advisory, remedial centre and miscellaneous teachers.
[3] Prior to 1990 head and deputy head vacancies were not separately identified.
[4] The breakdowns of teachers in post by grade and main age group of deployment have been estimated from the 1987 Primary School Staffing Survey. For the purpose of calculating the vacancy rates, vacancies for 'more than one age group' of deployment have been divided between the three age groups in proportion to the numbers of vacancies specific to those age groups.

Vacancy[1] rates in maintained secondary schools by grade and subject: 1987 to 1992, England.

	\multicolumn{6}{c}{Vacancies as a percentage of teachers in post[2]}	Number of vacancies
	1987	1988	1988	1990	1991	1992	1992
All vacancies	1.2	1.0	1.3	1.5	1.1	0.5	824
By grade:							
Head teacher		1.0	1.9	1.4	0.8	0.3	17
Deputy head teacher	0.6	0.7 1.0	1.5	1.0	0.7	0.4	39
Head of department		0.6	0.8	0.8	0.6	0.4	157
Below head of department	1.5	1.1	1.4	1.8	1.3	0.5	611
By main teaching subject[3,4]							
Mathematics	1.2	0.9	1.2	1.2	0.9	0.4	73
Computer studies	3.8	2.7	2.9	2.2	1.5	0.3	5
Sciences:							
Chemistry	1.0	0.8	1.0	0.8	0.8	0.3	14
Physics	1.7	1.0	1.3	1.0	0.9	0.2	10
Biology	0.8	0.9	0.8	0.6	0.5	0.1	8
Other and combined sciences	1.2	1.1	1.3	3.0	1.8	0.6	49
All sciences	**1.2**	**1.0**	**1.1**	**1.6**	**1.1**	**0.3**	**81**
Languages:							
French	1.0	0.8	1.3	2.1	1.6	0.9	91
German	0.7	1.0	0.8	1.6	2.5	1.4	33
Other languages	2.2	2.8	6.7	6.4	7.1	3.6	38
All languages	**1.1**	**1.0**	**1.6**	**2.3**	**2.2**	**1.2**	**162**
English	0.9	0.9	1.1	1.4	1.2	0.4	88
Drama	2.2	1.9	2.5	3.1	1.9	0.4	7
History	0.7	0.5	0.7	1.0	0.8	0.3	21
Social studies	0.9	0.8	1.1	0.7	0.8	0.2	6
Geography	0.9	0.7	0.8	1.0	0.8	0.5	42
Religious education	1.3	1.2	1.3	2.3	1.4	0.7	29
Craft, design and technology	1.4	0.9	1.0	1.2	0.8	0.4	40
Commercial and business studies	2.3	1.8	1.8	1.8	0.8	0.3	12
Art or light craft	0.7	0.6	0.7	0.9	0.7	0.2	19
Home economics or needlework	1.1	1.0	0.6	0.9	0.4	0.2	19
Music	1.9	1.7	2.2	2.8	2.4	0.9	41
Physical education	1.3	1.0	1.2	1.7	1.1	0.3	33
Remedial education	1.7	1.3	1.7	2.0	1.5	1.0	52
Careers	2.0	1.8	1.5	3.4	2.2	0.2	1
Other subjects and combinations of subjects	2.0	1.5	2.4	2.0	1.6	0.6	38
Total vacancies (numbers)	2,508	1,995	2,424	2,778	1,977	824	

See Notes on p.322.

Vacancy[1] rates in maintained secondary schools by grade and subject: 1987 to 1992, England.

Notes

[1] Advertised vacancies for full-time permanent appointments (or appointments of at least one term's duration). Includes vacancies being filled on a temporary basis.

[2] Teachers in post include full-time regular teachers in (or on secondment from) maintained secondary schools, plus the secondary portion of full-time regular divided service, peripatetic, advisory, remedial centre and miscellaneous teachers.

[3] The breakdowns of teachers in post by grade and main teaching subject have been estimated from the 1984 and 1988 Secondary School Staffing Surveys. Estimates for 1987 are derived by interpolation between the two surveys. The breakdowns for 1989–1992 are assumed to be the same as in 1988.

[4] Prior to 1988, head and deputy head vacancies were also included in the breakdown by main teaching subject; thereafter they are excluded. This change is allowed for in the calculation of vacancy rates.

26. Pupils and Schools

A Position Paper by Josh Hillman for the National Commission on Education, April 1993.

- 'It is the responsibility of the Government and the education service to provide pupils everywhere with the same opportunities. The reality all too often is that some pupils are deprived of that right.' (DFE White Paper, *Choice and Diversity*, 1992.)[1]

- 'If the worst of our schools can be brought to the standard of the best, or even of the good, many of the problems of our society will be removed.' (Brighouse and Tomlinson, 1991.)[2]

- 'The best prospect for the system as a whole is to reduce differences between schools in effectiveness.' (John Gray at *NCE Research Committee Seminar*, 1992.)[3]

- 'Growing diversity in education will be one of the features of the 1990s.' (DFE White Paper, *Choice and Diversity*, 1992.)[4]

- 'Comprehensive reorganisation has helped to make schooling better and fairer in the past decade, and could do more in these directions.' (McPherson and Willms, 1988.)[5]

- 'The aim of the early advocates of comprehensive education – to improve the opportunities available to less academic pupils and to those from the lower social classes – has not been achieved.' (Marks, 1991.)[6]

- 'Parents should not have to accept second best within a local authority monopoly of free education.' (Kenneth

Baker, North of England Conference, 1988.)[7]

- 'Parents acting on their behalf and given a free market will seek out what they want for their own children, not for anybody else's children.' (Sexton, S., 1990, quoted in Miliband.)[8]

- 'Reformers would do well to entertain the notion that choice is a panacea . . . with the capacity *all by itself* to bring about the kind of transformation that, for years, reformers have been seeking to engineer in a myriad of ways.' (Chubb and Moe, 1990.)[9]

- 'School choice . . . must be viewed as a way to *supplement* not *supplant* the network of local schools.' (Carnegie Foundation, 1992.)[10]

Introduction

This paper deals with the organisation of schools in the maintained system and the factors that determine the distribution of pupils amongst schools. The particular school that a pupil goes to makes a difference to the quality of the education he or she receives and to his or her attainments and life-chances;[11] two different schools can elicit equally desirable outcomes for pupils through very different means;[12] the experience of children is substantially influenced by who their fellow pupils are.[13] These facts cannot be disputed. They have informed policy making concerned with one of the most important subjects in education: which pupils should go to which schools? Yet despite several policy shifts in recent decades, in particular relating to types of schools, there remains great confusion as to the best way forward and a refusal of some very old debates to disappear. The controversy and confusion is reflected in the quotations above.

There has been a tendency amongst policy makers to view secondary school organisation and choice of school separately. Policy in the former has been concerned with creating a *system* that might respond to differences and similarities in ability, aptitudes and interests across the pupil population. Policy in the latter has been concerned with the scope for allowing an *intervention* in that system to secure benefit for an individual pupil and to affect the system through the exercise of choice. However, the two subjects are integrally bound: policies and their effects in either are dependent on policies and their effects in the other. This paper attempts to combine them.

The conceptual framework which binds the two subjects is the dichotomy of the State and the market and how they structure supply and demand of a particular good.[14] The State and the market are vehicles for the arbitration of possibilities that impinge on the life of the individual, sometimes for the good, sometimes for the bad. How these relate to each other in pupils and schools, how they have operated in the past and how they might be used to improve the education of all pupils in all schools is the subject of this paper.

A universal entitlement?

Since World War II policy has increasingly allowed pupils of compulsory school age to be entitled to a common and accepted amount, type and standard of education. The 1944 Act established the universal right of free secondary education for all young people. In 1965, Circular 10/65 initiated the replacement of a selective system of secondary schooling with comprehensive schools.[15] In the mid-1970s the school leaving age was increased to 16, thus extending the opportunity for all young people to take public examinations. In 1986, the GCSE examination was introduced to replace the system of O levels and CSEs, which was seen as divisive. In 1988, a national curriculum was provided for by legislation to define a large part of the total amount to be taught in maintained schools. Assessment procedures now incorporate centrally devised tests at four key stages, one of whose intentions is to attempt to institute national standards of school performance, information on which will be publicly available.

All of these reforms have helped to develop some notion of

a universal entitlement for young people. However, despite them, research shows that differentials in school performance and parents' perceptions of them are extremely high.[16] This is partly due to differences in social class composition between schools and LEAs but it is also partly because the UK is still a long way from having a common system of schooling. Whilst LEA-maintained co-educational primary and comprehensive secondary schools are the norm, many pupils have a different type of schooling.[17]

- In 1992 in England, about 11% of secondary pupils and a very small number of primary pupils in the maintained sector were educated in single-sex schools, although these figures have been declining.

- 24% of pupils in the maintained sector were educated in voluntary schools, usually denominational.

- 23% of pupils of secondary age were in non-comprehensive schools, with around 150 grammar schools in 28 authorities educating 3.4%.

- There are no grammar schools in either Scotland or Wales, but there were 70 in Northern Ireland in 1991, educating 38.6% of pupils of secondary age.

- In 1992, 6.6% of pupils in the UK were in independent schools.

There are wide differences in raw attainment between these categories of school. For example, in England in 1992, 86.9% of grammar school pupils obtained five or more grades A–C at GCSE, as compared to 74.5% for independent schools and 34.3% for comprehensive schools.[18] These differences are important factors in determining the popularity of schools. Even within the comprehensive sector, there are wide variations in the popularity of schools, partly reflecting real or apparent differences in school effectiveness.[19] For example, many perceive voluntary schools as superior to LEA-maintained schools.

Recent policies have distorted perceptions of school effectiveness, and have possibly increased differences in effectiveness itself resulting in wider variations in school popularity. First, the Government has increased the variety of schools: it has created two new types of school, the grant-maintained school and the City Technology College; it has suggested various other new types of school, such as Technology Schools; and it has also supported independent schools through the Assisted Places Scheme. It is likely that these other types of school, as a whole, will continue to be of higher status than those run by the local authority. Second, there is evidence that increased parental choice of school through open enrolment has increased social segregation in schools and has widened differences in school performance.[20] Third, league tables of schools using 'raw' examination results provides misleading indicators of school effectiveness which are likely to cause further distortions.[21] Fourth, the recent decision by the Secretary of State to allow a grant-maintained school to select all of its pupils by ability will create the first new grammar school for over 20 years.[22] If carried out on a wider scale, this policy shift could also have a polarising effect on school performance.[23] Likewise, the concept of specialised or 'magnet' schools carries with it the danger of superimposing the status hierarchy of subjects onto schools and subsequently allowing a form of selection 'through the back door'.

Community schools

Schools are one of the most important focal points for communities.[24] The maintained system has traditionally been a local one, despite general improvements in transport, with individual schools serving a fairly well-defined neighbourhood. This has particularly been the case in more sparsely populated areas, where there may only be one or two feasible options. Geography, more than any other factor, has informed decisions about which pupils should go to which schools. In policy terms this has manifested itself in the use of catchment areas, which are still used by most authorities and also so far by most grant-maintained schools.

There are some clear advantages to a school attracting pupils from its immediate vicinity. Some of the negative effects of competition with other schools can be avoided, such as the development of a self-perpetuating hierarchy of schools, disincentives for co-operation between schools, and staff having to put time into 'selling' the schools to potential parents.[25] The enriching effect of a strong community dimension of a school's work is also often stressed,[26] including for example greater opportunities for schools to involve parents in their activities. Neighbourhood schools also minimise time-wasting and often expensive travel time for children.

There are also disadvantages to the notion of the neighbourhood school. First, a situation where a school is a monopoly provider can lead to complacency and lack of dynamism.[27] Secondly, in deprived areas the imposition of a catchment area can rule out certain pupils of high ability and motivation who might raise standards in that neighbourhood school.[28] Thirdly, keen and well-off parents are more able and willing to make arrangements for their children to attend a school outside the immediate vicinity of their home. Fourthly, these parents are also more able and willing to move house in order to be in a particular catchment area, thus further expanding their range of available schools and perpetuating the problems of creaming.[29]

It is also worth asking exactly what we mean by 'community'. It may be a geographical neighbourhood but for some people it might imply a collectivity with a common interest.[30] Which sub-communities justify special treatment is a subject that goes beyond the scope of this paper.[31]

Selection and comprehensive reform

There has not been nor will there be in the foreseeable future a truly comprehensive system of secondary schooling throughout the UK. The existence and indeed success of selective schools, mainly in the independent sector but in some parts of the country in the maintained sector, and the interaction of population patterns and parental choice of school make full comprehensive reform an unattainable aspiration. For this reason, implementation of the ideal of genuine comprehensive reform cannot be judged a success or a failure. Even judgements about the success of the policy as implemented are hindered by an astonishing lack of large-scale research into what was without doubt not only a major educational reform but also an important social reform.

The rationale behind the comprehensive reforms was that a system where schools serve children of all abilities would promote both higher overall educational attainment and more desirable social outcomes than a system where children were segregated by ability. Some reasons for this were as follows:

1 selection procedures were seen as unreliable tests of academic potential which discriminated against late developers;[32]

2 equality of opportunity for grammar school places did not exist across different LEAs[33] nor even within LEAs since the 11-plus examination was seen to embody a social class bias;[34]

3 grammar schools were perceived not only to have more able pupils and higher academic standards but also to have better access to public examinations, more resources, better teachers and generally higher status[35] – all qualities much in demand from a growing proportion of those not selected;

4 educational and non-educational peer group effects of pupils on each other[36] mean that the segregation of more able pupils has a negative effect on less able pupils, thus further increasing inequalities.

Few people believed that comprehensive reorganisation would not be able to address these points. What was more in doubt was its ability to provide a challenge for pupils of high ability.[37] Unfortunately, the question as to the effects of reorganisation cannot be answered satisfactorily. The research that has been conducted has been limited and of varied quality, and has focused almost exclusively on attempting to evaluate the impact of the reforms on attainments measured by examination results, an almost impossible task. It is worth looking at this research briefly.

Research into comprehensive reform

The central question which researchers have asked is whether comprehensive reorganisation has reduced inequalities in educational attainment, in particular the close association of social class with attainment, and whether this has been at the expense of overall standards, or indeed whether the latter have even improved.[38] The first thing that must be said is that research into comprehensive reform faces certain problems, some of which have been partially addressed by research methodology and some of which have had to be ignored. Some examples are cited below.

1 There has never been a proper comprehensive system in the UK: the reform is incomplete, since many LEAs still have selective secondary schools, and even those that fully reorganised often have voluntary and independent schools that have greater potential to attract pupils of high ability.

2 Data on performance relate to individual pupils rather than to the system as a whole:[39] an important distinction, since changes to a particular school have an effect on all surrounding schools.[40]

3 Changes in secondary school organisation have stimulated other trends in school choice, for example choice of independent school or moves to boroughs that retain selective systems.[41]

4 Allowance should be made for the problems of

adjustment faced by secondary modern schools converting to comprehensive status. First, like the former grammar schools, they had to adjust teaching styles for mixed ability intakes.[42] Secondly, they had to attempt to transcend their lower status and attract pupils, parents, teachers and resources despite their previous image.[43] Thirdly, they had often not previously entered any pupils for public examinations.[44] Fourthly, it takes at least four or five years before the school *can* be fully comprehensive.[45]

5 The examination system has had an academic bias so that large numbers of pupils have been excluded from contributing to school attainment, regardless of the quality of the school. This makes comparisons of the performance of schools very difficult, especially if they are different *types* of school.

Given these qualifications, it would be foolish to base policy prescriptions for secondary school organisation solely on an analysis of research into the subject. However, it is worth mentioning what the results of various studies have been. The research from Scotland, where comprehensive reform was introduced more vigorously than elsewhere in the UK,[46] used a strong definition of 'comprehensive'.[47] It showed that the policy had resulted in both a raising of overall standards and an equalisation of opportunities and attainments. Some of the more important detailed findings were as follows:

- reorganisation reduced social segregation but differences between schools in terms of social composition remain high;

- between-school variations in social composition themselves vary greatly across the country with, for example, more segregation in the larger cities and less in the New Towns;

- social class has had less of an influence on attainment since reorganisation, particularly at the lower and middle levels of attainment;

- an average pupil, in terms of social background, attained more in 'uncreamed' schools and schools that had pupils of relatively high ability and social advantage;

- variations between schools in the effect of their social composition on attainment were very similar for pupils from different social backgrounds or levels of prior attainment, suggesting a 'zero-sum game' for the net effect of social composition, with the advantage and disadvantage accruing to individual pupils cancelling each other out overall;

- schools tended to improve their attainment levels the longer they had been comprehensive.

The Scottish work requires two notes of caution. First, Gray and Jesson[48] have argued (as indeed have McPherson and Willms themselves)[49] that the research does not provide certainty as to how much the improvements during the period they examined are due to comprehensive reform or to other explanations.[50] Secondly, Heath has argued that although the Scottish data show a reduction in the *absolute* differences in attainment between social classes[51] they do not show a statistically significant decline in the 'relative competitive success of the classes in competing for the opportunities available'.[52] In other words, there has been no change in the relative chances of pupils from different social classes achieving a particular level of attainment and hence the positional advantage of the higher social classes has not been eroded. This is a fair point but it ignores the great advances made in the educational *experiences* of those of *all* social classes, making positional advantage less decisive in determining access to key educational experiences. Heath also fails to mention the relative decline in the size of the working class. This decline has two implications: first, a smaller proportion of the population is adversely affected by class disadvantage; and secondly, it has contributed to an increase in the relative disadvantage of that sector of the population thus making fair competition in educational opportunities more difficult.

Studies in England and Wales have not been so statistically robust and have dealt with a comprehensive system at an earlier stage of development.[53] Marks and Pomian-Srzednicki suggested that selective systems have a slight advantage over comprehensives[54] and Steedman suggested no significant difference,[55] in terms of overall levels of attainment, once background factors were taken into account. What is fascinating is that no single study showed a decisive difference either way.

All of the studies have shown that differences in attainments between schools of the same type are far greater than differences between the various types of school.[56]

Parental choice of school

Parents' expectations of their ability to choose schools for their children are rising. This is partly due to education having a higher profile and greater publicity for information about individual schools. It is also due to legislation in the 1980s shifting power in the allocation of pupils from the education authority to the parent.[57] Open enrolment prevents LEAs from imposing intake limits on schools and requires the LEA to admit a pupil to a school chosen by the parent if there is room.[58] It is worth looking briefly at the arguments that lie behind this policy approach.

- People are much more conscious of their right to choose between two or more providers of a good or service. Why should not schooling be the same?

- By allowing parents to 'shop around', emulating the purchase of consumption goods, competition is introduced into school provision, since schools' funding becomes dependent on their ability to attract 'customers'. Every school is now required to publish its examination results, and also usually produces a prospectus. Through these mechanisms, competition might be instrumental in raising standards.

- The fact that the school has been chosen might mean that the child and parent feel a greater allegiance to that school and work harder to make it effective.

These are all important points but there are various constraints on choice of school which reduce its scope and meaning in the real world and lead to the conclusion that in practice, 'choice' is only an expression of preference. These include:

- lack of good information for parents and children about the available options, and especially about what is best for the particular child;

- differences in the ability and motivation of parents and their children to take advantage of the choice that is available;[59]

- differences in the number of available options so that in some rural areas there is only one feasible option for a secondary school and in some inner city areas there may be more than twenty possibilities;

- inability of schools to expand and contract at will with the consequence that a popular or over-subscribed school will be doing the choosing as well as the parents;

- negative effects of the exercise of choice on less popular schools, effects which may constrain choice for the future since these schools will be less able to attract funding and may either become under-resourced or even close down;

- effects of market forces on small schools which (like corner shops competing with supermarkets) have certain attractions and may even be extremely popular with some 'customers', but despite this may be unable to compete and have to close down, thus restricting an important aspect of school choice;

- the fact that increased choice requires a certain amount

of 'slack' in terms of the number of places available in
the system as a whole, a requirement which runs
counter to attempts to improve efficiency (and hence the
choice of good schools) through the removal of 'surplus
places';

- the fact that school improvement is not an instant
process and parental choice is informed by out-of-date
information.

Research into parental choice
Open enrolment has not been in place for long enough in
England and Wales for the results of the research on its effects
to be reported. However, the policy was introduced seven
years earlier in Scotland, and its impact has been fairly well
researched. The findings have been as follows:[60]

- the right to exercise an alternative choice to the
designated school has been exercised by 14.9% of
parents of primary school children and 11.5% of parents
of secondary school children;

- these figures are higher in urban than rural areas and are
increasing year by year;

- better educated parents and those of higher social class
were more likely to have exercised their choice;

- school preference as a whole is informed less by
educational considerations than by geographical and
social considerations;

- on most occasions when choice is actively exercised, the
local school is being avoided;

- formerly selective schools in middle-class areas with
pupils of higher socio-economic status are gaining pupils
as a result of the legislation, whereas schools in deprived
areas are losing pupils;

- parents rely on fairly limited information, and there is a tendency for 'bandwagon effects' to occur;

- the interaction of these effects of open enrolment with the introduction of formula funding is likely to perpetuate and even increase inequalities, since schools that are losing pupils will also lose resources – the market is thus tilted against those that suffer disadvantage (even of a temporary nature);

- there is a danger of a two-tier system developing, particularly in large cities, with a serious threat to equality of educational opportunity.

The interaction of the ideals of community schools, comprehensive reform and parental choice

What has emerged is that the notion of a community school, the ideal of comprehensive education and encouragement of choice of school are all bound up in a complex relationship where they are often working against each other. A community school where the neighbourhood is not socially heterogeneous may not have a broad enough social or ability mix to be comprehensive.[61] Choice, when exercised, is often used to escape from the local school, working against the community school ideal.[62] Parents are tending to use their choice to take their children out of disadvantaged areas with a 'zero-sum chase' after schools taking in pupils with appropriate backgrounds,[63] a tendency running counter to attempts at comprehensive reform.

It is clear that pursuit of any one of these three laudable ideals is liable to have negative effects on one or both of the others. Within our existing structures, policies relating to the placement of pupils in schools will embody some sort of trade-off. The last section of this paper attempts to suggest a framework within which potential conflict can be resolved in a way in which pupils, parents, teachers and policy makers at all levels co-operate to the benefit of all.

Conclusions and recommendations

Note: This section makes reference to new organisations recommended in the Commission's report *Learning to Succeed:* a Department for Education and Training; Education and Training Boards (which would replace Local Education Authorities); and Community Education and Training Advice Centres.

(a) Provision of an entitlement to quality
All children should have a universal entitlement to high quality education. This will be partly achieved through an improved national curriculum and the unification of GCSEs, A levels and vocational qualifications into a single 14–18 framework to which all young people will have access. It will be partly achieved through the work of a high quality teaching force. It will be partly achieved through a more sensible approach to the level and distribution of resources in education with the introduction of fairer funding formulae, both from central to local government and from local government to schools. It will be partly achieved through strenuous efforts on the part of all levels of government – the Department for Education and Training (DET), the Education and Training Boards (ETBs) and the governing bodies – to ensure that all schools are able to provide suitably for all pupils, whatever their background or ability.

An education system offering a diverse range of provision is something to be celebrated as long as it does not prevent equal opportunity for *all* pupils to have access to high quality education. Research shows that once background factors of intakes to schools are taken into account, there are no significant differences in attainments between various types of school; indeed, differences between schools of the same type are greater. Large differences in raw examination results between schools do not necessarily reflect differences in their effectiveness, but they do affect differences in popularity. No child should have to go to a school that might be termed a 'sink school' but at present there is a perception that a large number of these schools exist. Attention to these schools should be an immediate priority. Some of the recommendations in this paper might help by first preventing a downward spiral and then 'levelling-up' standards in these schools.

(b) Allowing schools to build on their strengths
This levelling-up does not imply a move towards uniformity. A vast quantity of research evidence shows substantial differences in the *characteristics* of schools and it might be expected that these will become even more noticeable as powers and responsibilities are delegated to the school level. Every school has strengths and weaknesses of which those who have contact with the school may or may not be aware. In the future, not all secondary schools will provide identical options and courses. The menu of the curriculum will be too diverse for this to be feasible, nor would it be desirable, given differing local needs and wishes and uneven capabilities of individual schools to provide quality tuition and facilities for particular provision. The concept of universal entitlement for pupils might be put into practice without precluding schools, where they wish, from developing particular strengths or specialisms. All schools, including independent schools, will provide the core curriculum but may well differ in the amount of attention they devote to particular parts of that core or to other parts which they offer besides. If a reasonable balance is struck then the dangers of 'back-door' selection should be avoided.

It will help to increase access to wide curriculum choice if links between neighbouring schools (perhaps including independent schools) and colleges are improved, including exchanges of both students and teachers. If the ETB feels that a particular aspect of the curriculum is not sufficiently catered for in its area then it will be able to invite schools and colleges to submit proposals for putting this right.

(c) Challenging expectations of pupils

The development of an 'extended hierarchy'[64] of good, middling and bad schools must be severely discouraged. This entails ensuring that all schools are able to teach effectively the full range of pupils which they admit. The big question mark against this is whether all pupils can be suitably challenged in mixed-ability schools. HMI have argued that very able pupils 'are often insufficiently challenged by the work they are set' and may be underachieving even if they obtain better than average results in tests and examinations.[65] It has been demonstrated that with imagination, good planning and support, schools with a broad intake can provide very successfully for gifted children, without streaming, which carries the danger of limiting expectations. When specific attention is given to their needs, there is often a general enhancement of the quality of teaching and learning and a raising of the expectations and standards of all pupils.

The answer to this is to create choice *within* schools for pupils rather than between schools. The broad-based, non-age-related and modular curriculum for 14–18-year-olds will allow flexibility for all students to take control of their own learning programmes. For some, the ability to 'fast-track', move up a year for a particular subject and take extra options will be important; for others the need will be to move more slowly and consolidate progress as they go along with extra learning support. Some options, such as technical subjects or less commonly taught languages, may involve work on another site. In the case of primary schools, this may be a secondary school; in the case of secondary schools, it may be a college or university.

(d) Harnessing choice for the benefit of all

Pupils and parents now have the expectation that they have a large degree of influence over which school the pupil will attend and that their choice should only be rejected for a very good reason. The most conclusive of these will be that the school has more applications than it can accept and that priority has been given to other applications strictly in accordance with its admission rules. In such a case, pupils and parents expect to get their second choice and so on. It would not be desirable to attempt to remove these expectations.

However, on the basis of evidence from both this country and abroad, increasing parental choice of school can have unacceptable consequences. These stem from the fact that the effect of choice is not restricted to the pupil that the choice relates to. It impacts on the other pupils in the school that is chosen, and also on those in the schools that are not chosen, as was shown earlier in this paper. Schooling is not a consumer good where supply and demand are mediated by price and where actions in the 'market place' provide incentives and opportunities for providers to respond to their own popularity or unpopularity. Their popularity or unpopularity is partly driven by *who* their customers are. It is also perpetuated by its own financial implications in a context where money follows pupils. In a system where parental choice has primacy and where no interventions are made in the exercise of that choice, inequalities are increased and social segregation encouraged.

Choice must be harnessed for its positive rather than its negative effects. This cannot be done while its exercise appears to be in conflict with efficient planning of education, with increasing numbers of over-subscribed and under-subscribed schools. A system needs to be designed which simultaneously addresses the individual needs of children and such wider ends as equity, efficient use of resources and problems faced by less popular and failing schools. For these reasons, the decision as to which school a child should go to must result from a collaborative procedure between the pupil (with parents acting as 'agents'), the schools and the ETB.

(e) Provision of independent advice and guidance
The choices made by pupils and parents will be partly informed by improved provision of guidance and advice. This will be one of the functions of the Community Education and

Training Advice Centres (CETACs), locally based with an executive accountable to a board with representation from the ETB, primary and secondary schools, colleges, local business people and others. CETACs will act solely in the best interests of each individual pupil and will certainly not be free to give advice based on what would be administratively convenient for the school or the ETB.

Parents (on behalf of their children) will fill in a form expressing three choices of school (these may not all be in their own ETB) in order of preference and will send it to their own ETB and any other ETB included in their selection. The ETB will act as an admissions agency, both for maintained schools and the voluntary schools in its area. Each school will aim to fill 90% of its available places, and the ETB will have the right to fill 10% of the places of each school according to well-defined and published criteria (drawn up in consultation with the CETAC). Otherwise, pupil choice of school will have primacy in the sense that first preferences will be automatically accepted when the school is not over-subscribed.

It is too much to hope that the service provided by the CETACs alone will resolve all problems since schools will continue to vary in popularity. In some cases, independent advice may even exacerbate this, although it can be expected that it would combat expectations or beliefs about schools which run counter to the facts. The aim should be that the work of the CETACs will enable *all* pupils and parents to have access to the sort of guidance and advice that will steer them towards making the right decision for their first preference of school and indeed their other choices.

(f) A coherent policy for over- and under-subscribed schools
There will also be new arrangements for when schools are over-subscribed. Every school will draw up simple, clear and published sets of criteria which will come into play in these circumstances. These criteria will be drawn up in consultation with the ETB and will ultimately be approved by the ETB (which should itself consult the CETAC). Each school will

apply the criteria in their established order to all those pupils who have given the school first preference, until its 90% share of places is filled. It is likely that the criteria will include proximity to the school (to enhance the community link), attendance of a sibling, special needs of the pupil, and in the case of denominational schools, the religious faith of the pupil. As with all other schools, the ETB will have the right to apply its published criteria to fill the remaining 10% share of places in over-subscribed schools. In cases where parents feel disappointed about the decision that has been made they may use their right of appeal to an appeals board whose ruling will be final.

A school which is substantially under-subscribed[66] may not necessarily be a failing school: it may be a successful school in a depopulated area for example. The ETB must judge if a school is under-performing and then require it to submit plans for improving its future performance and standing, and once these have been approved (with or without amendment) the school will be required to implement its plans. The ETB will have the ability, within strict limits, to provide extra resources to enable remedial action to be taken by the school, and may also wish to introduce advisers or consultants, encourage the appointment of a new headteacher or senior management team, and in more serious circumstances, with all else having failed, close down the school with a view to reopening it as a revitalised institution.

Summary

All children should have a universal entitlement to high quality education. This has not been brought about by wholesale changes in the types of school that exist or by reliance on a particular mechanism (such as 'market forces') to supply a panacea. Indeed, in the current system, increasing diversity and choice have tended to *conflict* with this entitlement. Much more is to be hoped of reform of the curriculum and of the actions of individual schools, possessed of a high degree of autonomy but working co-operatively rather than competitively within local education and training networks that seek to provide every pupil with the most suitable education and to raise standards for all.

Notes and references

1 Department For Education (1992). *Choice and Diversity: A New Framework for Schools*. HMSO.
2 Brighouse, T. and Tomlinson, J. (1991). *Successful Schools*. IPPR.
3 Presentations at the National Commission on Education Research Committee Seminar on the Youth Cohort Study and the Scottish Young People's Survey, 1992.
4 See note 1.
5 McPherson, A. and Willms, J.D. (1988). *Comprehensive Schooling is Better and Fairer*. Forum, 30, 2.
6 Marks, J. (1991). *Standards in Schools*. Social Market Foundation.
7 Baker, K. (1988). *Speech to the North of England Conference*. 8/8/88.
8 Miliband, D. (1991). *Markets, Politics and Education*. IPPR.
9 Chubb, J. and Moe, T. (1990). *Politics, Markets and America's Schools*. Brookings Institution.
10 Carnegie Foundation for the Advancement of Teaching (1992). *School Choice*. Carnegie.
11 See note 3.
12 See note 8.
13 McPherson, A. (1992). *Measuring Added Value in Schools*. NCE Briefing No. 1. See also note 3.
14 Hindess, B. (1987). *Freedom, Equality and the Market*. Tavistock.
15 LEAs were required to submit plans for reorganisation. There was no compulsion for them to initiate comprehensive reform.
16 Walford, G. (1992). *Selection for Secondary Schooling*. NCE Briefing No. 7. See also notes 3 and 13.
17 DFE (1993). *Statistics of Schools*. GSS; Central Statistical Office (1993). *Regional Trends*. HMSO; and Department of Education, Northern Ireland.
18 DFE (1993). *GCSE and A/AS Examination Results*. Statistical Bulletin 15/93.
19 See notes 3 and 13.
20 Adler, M. (1993). *An Alternative Approach to Parental Choice*. NCE Briefing No. 13; Adler, M., Petch, A. and Tweedie, J. (1989). *Parental Choice and Education Policy*. Edinburgh University Press; Echols, F., McPherson, A. and Willms, J.D. (1990). *Parental Choice in Scotland*. Journal of Education Policy, 5, 3; and Willms, J.D. and Echols, F. (1993). *Alert and Inert Clients: the Scottish Experience of Parental Choice of Schools*. Economics of Education Review, 11(4).
21 See note 13.
22 Queen Elizabeth Grammar School, Penrith, Cumbria.
23 Ball, S. (1990). *Markets, Morality and Equality in Education*. Tufnell Press.
24 The term 'community school' as used in this paper refers mainly to a school providing for the pupils in its immediate neighbourhood, and

should not be confused with the designated community schools such as those in Cambridgeshire and Leicestershire which make provision for education of the whole community as well as serving their own pupils.
25 See note 23.
26 National Commission on Education (1993). *Report of the Working Group on Effective Schooling*. Unpublished paper.
27 Tooley, J. (1992). *The 'Pink-Tank' on the Education Reform Act*. British Journal of Educational Studies, XXXX, 4.
28 Garner, C. and Raudenbush, S. (1991). *Neighbourhood Effects on Educational Attainment: a Multilevel Analysis*. Sociology of Education 64 (October); Maguiness, H. (1991). *Educational Opportunity: the Challenge of Under-Achievement and Social Deprivation*. Paisley College Local Government Centre; and Willms, J.D. (1986). *Social Class Segregation and its Relationship to Pupils' Examination Results in Scotland*. American Sociological Review, Vol. 51 (April).
29 This is accentuated by the fact that borders of catchment areas have often had a marked influence on house prices at the local level.
30 For example, a Catholic school appeals to a particular subset of a wider geographical neighbourhood.
31 For example, the question of whether Muslim schools should be given voluntary-aided status.
32 See note 16.
33 See note 16.
34 McPherson, A. and Willms, J.D. (1986). *Certification, Class Conflict, Religion and Community*. Research in Sociology of Education and Socialisation, 6. See also Willms, J.D. in note 28.
35 Willms, J.D. and Kerckhoff, A. (1992). *Selective Schooling and Value for Money*. Draft.
36 See note 13.
37 It should not be ignored that some pupils feel more comfortable and perform better when they are relatively successful compared to their fellow-pupils, whereas others benefit from being below average and stimulated by more able pupils or even being a bit 'out of their depth'.
38 This paper does not examine research into secondary school organisation from abroad, in particular the Scandinavian countries, where unlike Western European countries there has been an aspiration to universal comprehensive education.
39 Heath, A. (1984). *In Defence of Comprehensive Schools*. Oxford Review of Education, 10,1.
40 For example, let us say that an LEA has five grammar schools and converts four of them into comprehensives. The remaining grammar school will become even more selective; comprehensive reform of the other four will actually improve the results of that school, regardless of anything within its own power. Also see note 28.
41 See notes 16 and 39.
42 Gray, J. and Jesson, D. (1989). *The Impact of Comprehensive Reforms*. In Lowe, R. (Ed.) *The Changing Secondary School*. Falmer Press.
43 McPherson, A. and Willms, J.D. (1987). *Equalisation and Improvement: Some Effects of Comprehensive Reorganisation in Scotland*. Sociology, 21, 4.
44 Burnhill, P., Garner, C. and McPherson, A. (1990). *Parental Education,*

Social Class and Entry to Higher Education 1976–86. Journal of the Royal Statistical Society, 153.
45 Paterson, L. (1991). *Trends in Attainment in Scottish Secondary Schools*. In Raudenbush, S. and Willms, J.D. (Eds.) *Schools, Classrooms, and Pupils.* Academic Press.
46 McPherson, A. (1992). *Schooling*. In: Dickson, A. and Treble, J. (eds.), *A Social History of Modern Scotland since 1914*. John Donald.
47 See notes 5, 34, 43, 44 and Willms, J.D. in note 28.
48 See note 42.
49 See note 43.
50 Such as changes in public examinations, rising participation rates and developments in the youth labour market.
51 Heath, A. (1991). *Educational Reform and Changes in the Stratification Process in Great Britain*. In: Leschinsky, A. and Mayer, K. (eds.), *The Comprehensive School Experiment Revisited*. Peter Lang.
52 Heath, A. and Clifford, P. (1990). *Class Inequalities in Education in the Twentieth Century*. Journal of the Royal Statistical Society, 153.
53 See notes 16 and 42.
54 Marks, J. and Pomian-Srzednicki, M. (1985). *Standards in English Schools: Second Report*. Sherwood Press.
55 Steedman, J. (1983). *Examination Results in Selective and Non-Selective Schools*. National Children's Bureau.
56 See notes 3 and 16.
57 See note 20.
58 The LEA has no role in admissions to grant-maintained schools.
59 See note 20.
60 See note 20.
61 See note 28.
62 See note 20.
63 See note 3.
64 See note 16.
65 HMI (1992). *The Education of Very Able Children in Maintained Schools.* HMSO.
66 It should be noted that policies towards over-subscribed and under-subscribed schools are not symmetrical issues.

27. Multicultural Issues and Educational Success

A Discussion Paper for the National Commission on Education by Sue Taylor, Janice Robins and Robin Richardson, November 1992.

Introduction

There is a clear expectation in the Commission's vision of the 21st century that *everyone* should have the opportunity of a good education. In order to gain a better understanding of what this might mean in the context of a society characterised by ethnic and cultural diversity, a Working Group of the Commission organised a meeting on October 1st 1992 with a group of people experienced in the field of multicultural education and race equality. The meeting was chaired jointly by Margaret Maden, County Education Officer, Warwickshire and a member of the Commission, and Robin Richardson, Director of the Runnymede Trust. The names of participants at the meeting are listed on page 359.

The aims of the meeting were:

> To advise the Commission's Working Group on the main themes and principles which need to be addressed with regard to race equality and cultural diversity, if the Commission's key issues are to be properly considered, and in particular, to assist in the preparation of a discussion paper for a meeting of the full Commission.

This paper represents the outcome of the meeting on October 1st. It reports the concerns expressed at the meeting and indicates the recommendations which participants wished to make to the Commission. These concerns and recommendations relate chiefly to the following areas:

- recent legislative developments
- school admission procedures and selection within schools
- teachers' expectations
- teacher recruitment and training
- school governors
- the curriculum
- school inspection and monitoring arrangements
- parents
- post-compulsory education and training
- resources
- the place of multicultural issues in the Commission's report.

Recent legislative developments

It will be important for the Commission to have a view of the extent to which recent legislative developments (the Education Reform Act 1988; the Further and Higher Education Act 1992; the Education (Schools) Act 1992; and the recent White Paper, 'Choice and Diversity') provide a framework which will lead to progress in education and training for ethnic minority people.

There was support at the meeting for the view that recent legislative developments will result in a framework which offers at least the potential for schools to be improved. Positive aspects include the entitlement of all pupils to a common curriculum; the attention given to curriculum planning and to clarity about objectives; pressure on educational institutions to be publicly accountable and to raise standards; the requirement to measure attainment; the increased rigour of monitoring, inspection and evaluation; the serious intention to provide information to parents and other lay people; and the greater involvement of school governors.

Despite this note of optimism, however, there remains a serious concern that, unless measures to ensure equity and social justice are *explicitly* built into the new structures and practices developing in education, there will be no benefit for certain pupils, families and communities. Indeed, it is possible that the situation will get worse for significant numbers of people. If certain sections of society do become increasingly disadvantaged in the education system, the principal victims, in terms of their numbers, will be those who are already affected by social disadvantage – the 20% or so of people who live in poverty, as officially defined, i.e. in households where the income is less than half the national average. Many – but definitely not all – ethnic minority pupils are within this 20%. They will be even more adversely affected than their white counterparts if the new education system is not only inexplicit about social justice but also colour-blind as well. At the same time, it has to be remembered that ethnic minority people who are *not* disadvantaged by poverty may nevertheless suffer as a result of discrimination.

The need to give explicit attention to issues affecting ethnic minority pupils is reinforced by the view expressed at the meeting that multicultural education issues are no longer accorded the high priority by policy makers, managers or teachers which they received, say, in 1986 or 1987. Some participants were deeply disillusioned about the lack of progress in changing attitudes in society. These feelings are supported by evidence gathered from local education authority advisers and inspectors by the National Foundation for Educational Research,[1] which revealed 'a general perception . . . that the national educational and political climate was ideologically unpropitious' for multicultural and anti-racist education, often resulting in the denial of support and resources at local level. It cannot be stated too strongly that multicultural education should be for all pupils at all ages, from very young pre-school children upwards, not just a subject to be taught in areas with high ethnic minority populations. All young people need to learn to value different cultures from their own, to gain an understanding of what they have in common, and to recognise one another as equal citizens.

In brief, the Commission is asked to consider two main tasks. They are separate from each other, but inter-related. First, and more importantly, there is a need to build into the education system specific measures to ensure equity and social justice. Second – and as part of the first task – there is a need to address specifically issues of ethnic and cultural diversity, and ways of combating, reducing and removing racism and racial discrimination. Celebrating cultural diversity, and at the same time providing opportunities for learning about shared values, would be one approach to tackling racism in education.

School admission procedures and selection within schools

Very careful attention needs to be paid to school admission procedures. Two particular developments emerging from recent and proposed legislation give cause for concern: (a) the increasing reliance on parental choice of school as a lever for raising standards and (b) the encouragement given to greater diversity in educational provision, for example through specialised institutions. Most participants at the meeting felt that parental choice and diversity in institutional provision would not work in the best interests of ethnic minorities. There is a perception that certain schools will increasingly select pupils, and that they will select with criteria which discriminate against working class families in general and against ethnic minorities in particular. It is alleged for example that open enrolment in Scotland has led to a more segregated school system. Schools use such criteria as 'Will this child fit in with our ethos?' and 'Does the family have sufficient cultural capital?' Answers to questions such as these are bound to be subjective and are very likely to have a discriminatory outcome: 'cultural capital' for example tends to be regarded as greater among white, middle class people.

Selection *within* schools also needs to be closely examined. Processes of banding, setting and streaming in secondary schools, and similar though less visible processes of group formation in primary schools, may have the effect of restricting pupils' opportunities. The way in which pupils are 'channelled' into particular courses of study, and the quality of the advice and guidance offered to ethnic minority pupils, should also be given careful attention.

Teachers' expectations

Many of the concerns expressed at the meeting relate to the skills, training and attitudes of teachers and to the support available to them. Teachers' expectations of ethnic minority pupils (as of working class pupils) were said to be too often too low and their attitudes towards pupils' abilities and behaviour patterns too narrow. The Commission is urged to adopt the idea of 'unlimited potential', implying that teachers should be determined to find ways of continually improving individual pupils' achievements.

There is evidence that teachers tend to allocate ethnic minority children to low streams or to classify them as having special educational needs, when their main requirement is for additional English language support. Without this kind of support, some ethnic minority children may be unable to demonstrate their strengths in Standard Assessment Tasks (SATs), with the result that they are assessed below their actual skill level.

Teachers have not only been imbued with inadequate concepts of 'ability', but may also make no distinction in practice between 'ability' and 'acceptable behaviour', with the consequence that their expectations of certain pupils are based on pupils' behaviour, rather than on their learning. It was claimed that teachers' notions of acceptable behaviour might be culturally biased. Closely related to the question of acceptable behaviour is the major issue of the disproportionate number of suspensions and exclusions among ethnic minority pupils, particularly Afro-Caribbean boys. This is a problem which must be tackled: schools cannot be regarded as effective if large numbers of pupils are being excluded, and pupils who are not in school are denied the opportunity of an effective education.

Teacher recruitment and training

Steps should be taken to recruit – and support – more teachers from ethnic minority communities. As well as providing valuable role models for pupils, such teachers are likely to have crucial 'intercultural' skills which are much-needed in the profession as a whole. They are likely therefore to be able to help schools to become more 'culturally inclusive', both in their curriculum and in their general organisation; and they are also likely to have a significant impact on staffroom cultures and on key decision making.

Although there is certainly a need for more black teachers in schools, participants at the meeting stressed that the main issue is not that of colour, but of recruiting (and equipping) teachers with appropriate skills to meet the needs of ethnic minority pupils.

Governors have a vital role to play in the appointment of staff (as well as in ensuring that their schools monitor the ethnic composition of the teaching establishment). It is therefore very important indeed that governors should receive high-quality training, advice and support for these aspects of their work. Although local education authorities currently have a duty to ensure that governors comply with employment law, impressionistic evidence from around the country suggests that since the introduction of local management (LMS), some governors have *not* been fair in their recruitment practices.

Teacher training is an area of great concern. At the heart of the matter is the need for change in teachers' attitudes, which are based on deeply embedded cultural values and are resistant to change through training. It was suggested at the meeting that more progress has been made in introducing multicultural issues into initial teacher training in BEd courses than in PGCE courses, though there was also concern that the time available for dealing with multicultural issues in the PGCE might be limited under the new arrangements for school-based training. Associated with the school-based element of initial training is the risk that in schools which are inexperienced in handling multicultural issues, or where discriminatory attitudes are entrenched, trainee teachers will not receive adequate preparation.

Some scepticism and even despair was expressed at the meeting with regard to efforts to retrain teachers through in-service training (INSET), but it was acknowledged that continual learning was necessary, both for heads and classroom teachers. Ideally, in-service opportunities should be thoroughly school-focused, since the traditional style of teachers 'going off on a course' has rarely proved effective in changing teachers' practice in relation to multicultural issues. Work carried out in Birmingham in the 1980s on the whole-school management of change has shown that it is possible to alter teachers' approaches towards multicultural issues, by focusing on changing their professional strategies, rather than tackling the question of values head-on.

The use of clear performance indicators in teacher appraisal could also help to improve teachers' skills in this area – indicators concerned, for example, with teachers' ability to work effectively with support teachers; to distinguish racial harassment from general bullying; and so on. It would be helpful to make the use of INSET opportunities by teachers a matter for discussion in their appraisal interviews.

It is hoped that the Commission will be able to support moves to create additional posts to assist classroom teachers. Such moves would be beneficial in improving the resources available to meet the ESL needs which some ethnic minority children have.

School governing bodies

School governing bodies (as well as headteachers) play a crucial role in ensuring that their schools pay heed to issues of equality and social justice. To perform this task well, they need external support: to ensure for example that governing bodies are representative of their communities and have the appropriate background and skills to enable them to respond to ethnic minority concerns in the recruitment and development of heads and teaching staff. There is a feeling that unless government funding is specifically targeted for governor support and training, other demands within the school are likely to take precedence.

Curriculum

The Commission should not assume that if ethnic minority concerns relating to 'structural' issues such as selection and admission are resolved, all will be well. The way in which ethnic minority interests are reflected in the curriculum is also vitally important. From comments made by participants at the meeting, it is clear that teachers do not always exploit the opportunities available to them to give the curriculum relevance and life for all their pupils. In other words, the curriculum needs to become 'culturally inclusive'. Historically, far too many pupils have experienced the curriculum as something which excludes them, and it can be argued that the national curriculum is just as 'exclusive' as previous provision.

A radical change in the structure of the post-14 curriculum would, according to participants at the meeting, serve the interests of ethnic minority children better than the present arrangements. Recommended changes include re-structuring key stages 4 and 5, with arrangements to overcome the academic/vocational divide and allow students to mix vocational and academic study. The abolition of A level, and the introduction of a more flexible, modular approach incorporating core, specialist and vocational options, is favoured. In terms of assessment methods, continuous assessment is felt to benefit ethnic minority pupils (as it does girls).

Within the work of the Commission, great emphasis has been placed on the need for schools to give attention to values, in the formal curriculum and in the development of a school ethos. It has been recognised that this is an area which is fraught with difficulty and one where the expectations placed upon schools by society at large are frequently unrealistic. Multicultural issues add a further dimension. Although it is assumed that schools can and should develop coherent value systems (and some would support the view that schools which do this will achieve better academically), ethnic minorities often feel excluded from the culture of the school. What is clear however is that schools need to achieve a better balance between the teaching of knowledge and skills, and the teaching of values. Schools should not lose sight of the idea of 'world citizenship' in teaching the values of equality, justice and freedom. The approach adopted by the Swann Committee,[2] which considered the kind of society we should strive towards, was commended to the Commission.

School inspection and monitoring arrangements

One message to emerge very clearly from the meeting is that the school inspection framework should be used in a positive way to monitor progress in race equality. A rigorous and comprehensive system of ethnic monitoring is essential, with co-ordination at regional (possibly LEA) and national level, and arrangements for follow-up action.

For example, data should be collected, interpreted and published on the following:

- examination entries and results
- school admissions, showing admissions to different types of schools
- the proportion of parents in different ethnic groups who obtain their first choice of school
- the composition of sets, streams or bands in a representative sample of schools
- truancy
- suspensions and exclusions
- post-school destinations, including work placements
- the composition of the teaching force
- the provision and take-up of in-service training in multicultural issues for teachers and governors
- the composition of governing bodies.

It is suggested that, too often, LEA inspectors do not possess the appropriate skills to enable them to evaluate how effectively schools are meeting the needs of ethnic minority children; inspectors need bilingual skills and also general 'intercultural' skills, or at least specialist support of this kind. Under the new arrangements for training inspectors, there is apparently no provision for training in multicultural issues: participants saw this as a serious omission.

Parents

Effective schools will give high priority to parental involvement, and will have a decision-making structure which enables parents' views to be taken into account. In a multi-racial community, schools will need to find successful ways of working with parents whose mother tongue is not English and who may not have any knowledge of the education system in this country. Schools also need to 'educate' parents: informing them of their rights and responsibilities, offering curriculum workshops and generally helping them to feel that they too have skills and knowledge to enrich their children's learning.

Post-compulsory education and training

Many of the issues addressed in this paper with regard to schools will also have relevance for the post-school sector: issues to do with access to courses, teachers' expectations, and the monitoring of provision are examples. Perhaps particular attention needs to be given to the question of access to further and higher education for ethnic minority girls. For many Asian/Muslim girls, formal education stops at the end of compulsory schooling, unless the school has a sixth form. Often, parents are reluctant to send their daughters to mixed colleges away from home. This may be an area where an expansion of local provision would be helpful, not only for school leavers but also for young women who might wish to return to education after marriage.

Sensitive employment training schemes would help to bring many young Asian/Muslim women (unmarried and married) into the employment market.

Resources

The adequacy and effective use of resources for education at all levels will be major concerns in the Commission's report. Many of the measures discussed in this paper would, if implemented, improve education for all pupils. The Commission is however urged to examine ways of ensuring that, where necessary, resources are effectively deployed to assist schools in areas of social disadvantage and those which require additional support for ethnic minority pupils. Funding issues which would merit investigation include:

- the effective use of the indicator for social disadvantage within the LMS formula

- the use of Section 11 funding.

The place of multicultural issues in the Commission's report

The Commission will need to decide how to treat multicultural issues in its report. The message of the meeting is that if the Commission is concerned with educational success for all, then multicultural issues must be reflected in every section of the report and not simply be allocated to a separate chapter. It is emphasised firmly that 'cultural diversity is a mainstream issue'. This is not to be taken as suggesting that a concern with multicultural matters can be regarded as implicit in the Commission's recommendations: wherever appropriate throughout the report, explicit statements about ways of improving educational opportunities for ethnic minorities should be made.

Choice of terminology in referring to multicultural issues will be a critical matter, since the whole area of race and equality is so politically contentious. On this point the meeting offered suggestions but did not reach unanimity. The present Government favours the general umbrella term 'equal opportunities' rather than specific reference to multicultural education or race equality; this was not felt to be an adequate term. In some cases, certainly, the needs of ethnic minorities coincide with those of others who are disadvantaged, for example as a result of poverty or class background, but in other cases it is important to draw attention to the special needs arising from ethnic minority status. It should also be remembered that, at times, needs will vary between ethnic minority groups, and between British-born ethnic minority people and recent immigrants.

The Commission is urged to choose terminology which suggests an education system that is 'inclusive' rather than 'exclusive'. 'Non-discriminatory provision' (in the legal sense) is one suggestion, and could be applied to the curriculum as well as to other aspects of provision; other suggestions are 'education in a culturally diverse society' or 'inclusive education'.

References

1. Taylor, M.J. (1992). *Equality after ERA? Concerns and Challenges for Multicultural Antiracist Education.* National Foundation for Educational Research.
2. Committee of Inquiry into the Education of Children from Ethnic Minority Groups (1988). *Education for All.* (Swann Report) HMSO.

Participants at the meeting

Mr Philip Barnet, Principal Officer of Education, Commission for Racial Equality
Mr Godfrey Brandt, Education Officer, Commonwealth Institute
Mr Tom Buzzard, Head, Willesden High School, Brent
Mr Carlton Duncan, Head, George Dixon School, Birmingham
Dr Jagdish Gundara, Head of Multicultural Education, Institute of Education
Mr Richard Holmes, Citibank – on secondment as Director, SE London Compact; member of the Working Group on Schools, Society and Citizenship
Mr Akram Khan-Cheema, Senior Inspector, Bradford LEA
Ms Margaret Maden, County Education Officer, Warwickshire LEA; NCE Commissioner; Chair of the Working Group on Schools, Society and Citizenship
Professor Bob Moon, School of Education, Open University; member of the Working Group on Schools, Society and Citizenship
Ms Giti Paulin, Advisory Teacher, Westminster College, Oxford
Ms Nargis Rashid, Co-ordinator, Governor Training, Birmingham LEA
Mr Robin Richardson, Director, The Runnymede Trust
Mrs Janice Robins, Secretary, National Commission on Education
Ms Sue Taylor, Research Officer, National Commission on Education
Professor Sally Tomlinson, Goldsmiths' Professor of Policy and Management in Education, Goldsmiths' College, University of London
Mr Barry Troyna, Department of Education, University of Warwick
Ms Angela Wood, Religious Education Inspector, City of Westminster LEA.

Apologies were received from:

Mrs Betty Campbell MBE, Head, Mountstuart Primary School, Cardiff; NCE Commissioner; member of the Working Group on Schools, Society and Citizenship
Mr Moeen Yaseen, Islamia Schools Trust.

28. Education in Northern Ireland

Discussion Paper by Josh Hillman for the National Commission on Education, October 1992.

Introduction

It was decided in the early days of the Commission's work that its terms of reference should cover all four countries of the UK. Andrew McPherson, in his response to the original 'key issues' paper of August 1991, provided several good reasons for including Northern Ireland in the remit. Aside from the fact that Northern Ireland is a small but significant part of the UK and will thus be affected by the proposals of the Commission, these included:

- the fact that comparisons of systems within the UK may be no less informative than international comparisons;

- the fact that Northern Ireland has been cited as an example of a successful traditional system with its retention of a bipartite secondary school structure and higher participation in post-compulsory education;

- the fact that 'core/periphery' issues, 'national identity' and issues of educational and geographical mobility may be more important after 1992.

This paper has three goals: firstly, to describe the education system in Northern Ireland; secondly, to display in both quantitative and qualitative terms the outcomes of this system in recent years; and thirdly, to focus on issues of particular interest, including the relationship between the allocation of pupils to schools and school effectiveness and equality of opportunity, and the place of education in a multicultural society. Two types of question arise for the Commission in the light of the insight that it receives into the situation in Northern Ireland. The first is the implication of the practice of education in the province for the whole of the UK. There are important lessons to be learned from the experience of Northern Ireland, in particular in relation to the effects of selection on educational participation and performance, to the social role of schools in the context of a divided community and to issues of the management and financing of schools. The second type of question relates to the ways in which the Commission can add value to debates about education that are specific to Northern Ireland.

A description of the education system of Northern Ireland

The education system of Northern Ireland is marked by a series of divisions. Most schools are either Catholic or Protestant, mirroring the cultural and political divisions at the root of the Troubles. Discussion in Great Britain and elsewhere about ethnic diversity and multiculturalism with respect to education is not directly relevant to Northern Ireland since the numbers from minority ethnic groups are so small and geographically dispersed. However, Northern Ireland has been faced with a specific form of multiculturalism that has prompted various initiatives in education that have the aim of making the province a more integrated society. The other important division in the education system in Northern Ireland which will be discussed at length in this paper is the separation of children by ability in secondary schools with the retention of a selective examination at 11-plus. This also has the indirect effect of dividing children on social factors. Children are often also separated by gender, particularly at secondary level, where in 1992, 38% of pupils were in single-sex schools.

Public education in Northern Ireland, other than university education, is administered centrally by the Department of Education (DENI) of the Northern Ireland Office, and locally by five Education and Library Boards (ELBs), less powerful versions of the British LEA. Unlike LEAs they are appointed centrally by the head of DENI. They were first appointed in 1973, the year of local government reorganisation, and are reappointed every four years following the District Council elections. Their membership consists of nominated representatives of District Councils, teachers, local community and church representatives, trade union nominees, trustees of maintained schools and other interested persons. Their duty is to ensure that there are sufficient schools of all kinds to meet the needs of their areas.

The Northern Ireland Higher Education Council (NIHEC) will come into being in April 1993 to work alongside the funding councils already established for England, Wales and Scotland in advising government on the planning and funding of higher education in Northern Ireland. The two Northern Ireland universities will not be directly represented on the Council.

The financing of education

Education spending in Northern Ireland is divided between DENI and the ELBs. The ELBs receive block grants from DENI to meet 80% of their expenditure excluding teaching costs, with a distribution determined by a 'relative needs exercise', a formula which is the subject of much dispute. ELBs are responsible for recurrent costs of all controlled and maintained schools, with DENI responsible for capital expenditure and also all costs of grammar schools.

Government spending on education in Northern Ireland in 1991–2 was £1,128 million, that is, 17.5% of spending by all Northern Ireland departments. This has fallen substantially since 1979–80 when the corresponding figure was 22%. Expenditure on education as a proportion of Northern Ireland GDP fell from 10.5% in 1980–1 to 9.7% in 1989–90. These figures are evidence that education is getting a lower priority than previously.

An examination of the breakdown of the education budget itself reveals large movements in the shares of education funds for different purposes. The share of educational funds going to the Education and Library Boards fell steadily between 1979–80 and 1986–7, from 41% to 35% but then rose to 37% by 1989–90. The slice going to teachers' salaries accounted for 37% at the beginning of the period, rose to 43% by 1986/7 and then fell back to 38% by 1989–90. Higher and further education rose from 15% to 17% and fell back to 16%. So, the first half of the 1980s saw a huge transfer of money from the ELBs to teachers' pay and post-compulsory education, but this process was somewhat reversed in the second half of the decade.

Spending per school pupil is similar in Northern Ireland to that in England, but spending per FE student is lower. There is evidence that there has been disproportionate funding in favour of the Protestant sector.[1] The first point is that the current arrangements for capital funding, by which voluntary schools receive up to 85% grant towards capital costs, result in a financial and administrative burden on Catholic schools, almost all of which are voluntary and so therefore have to raise the extra 15% themselves. As will be seen later in this paper, this issue has been partially addressed. There is also a gap in per capita recurrent funding between Protestant and Catholic schools to the disadvantage of the latter, although it is likely that this gap will be reduced by the introduction of LMS.

Much of the concern in Northern Ireland (as in the rest of the UK) about education cuts has centred round the deteriorating condition of buildings. Indeed, an analysis of recent trends shows that the expenditure on the capital building programme has been sharply reduced. Figure 1 on page 397 shows that it was not until last year that the amount of total capital expenditure reached the real terms level of the beginning of the 1980s. Aggregating the cutback in the first half of the decade, it can be seen that the total amount taken out of capital works in schools and colleges was more than £40 million.

The management of schools
The school system in Northern Ireland is highly complex. There are several different types of school management in Northern Ireland with different arrangements for DENI, the ELBs and the Boards of Governors of the schools. In all schools, since 1984, the representation of parents and teachers has been strengthened and that of the churches reduced. Resources are distributed on a formula funding basis linked to the local management of schools. There are four principal types of school, each of which contains important sub-divisions, but it should be noted that the system as a whole is currently under review.[2]

- *Controlled schools.* These are owned and managed by ELBs through Boards of Governors whose membership differs for the various types of school, but includes parents, teachers, Boards, and the Protestant churches. The schools do not deal directly with DENI, but rather through the ELBs. Protestant churches, which transferred their schools to the local education authorities, are guaranteed rights of involvement in the management of controlled schools. However, there is a new form of controlled school, the integrated controlled school, which provides an exception to this rule. The current and capital expenditure of these schools is met by the ELBs from funds provided by DENI.

- *Voluntary maintained schools.* These are owned by trustees (usually from the Catholic Church) and are managed by Boards of Governors which consist of representatives of trustees, parents, teachers and ELBs. The church representatives have been assisted more recently by a statutory Council for Catholic Maintained Schools (CCMS). It should be noted that while most schools in this category are Catholic, there is a minority of 14 Protestant, two other and three special schools which fall into the maintained school category. Recurrent expenditure is met by the ELBs, teachers are employed by the CCMS (in the Catholic schools) and capital expenditure is partly met (up to 85%) by DENI. In response to the unfairness caused by the restriction on DENI capital funding, a new category of voluntary school has been proposed which receives 100% capital grant-aid in exchange for DENI representation on the Board of Governors.

- *Voluntary grammar schools.* These are voluntary non-maintained schools also owned by trustees and managed by Boards of Governors, and can be either Catholic (usually particular religious orders) or non-Catholic (e.g. Protestant, the Royal schools and the Quaker schools). The constitution varies between schools but generally represents parents, teachers, DENI and the Boards. These schools receive block grants for recurrent funding from DENI and 85% capital expenditure from DENI. Voluntary grammar schools will also be able to opt into the new category of school to receive 100% capital grant-aid from DENI.

- *Grant-maintained integrated schools.* This is a new category of school which covers those schools that were originally independent and were purchased from the charitable trust with grant-aid from DENI. They receive all funding directly from DENI. The Northern Ireland Council for Integrated Education (NICIE) represents the interests and concerns of the integrated schools to DENI.

Teachers

There has never been a problem of low status of teachers in Northern Ireland, nor have there been serious teacher shortages. In fact, the average teacher vacancy rate is around 0.6%, a level low enough to be explained entirely by frictional movement. There are no special shortages in subjects or in the inner cities. The popularity of teaching as a career among young people in Northern Ireland can be illustrated by the ratio of applications to places available on initial teacher training courses. In 1990, before severe recession was easing teacher supply problems in England, this ratio was 5:1 for St Mary's and 6:1 for Stranmillis (the only two teacher training colleges, both in Belfast). Corresponding figures for English institutions are not available, but it is likely that they were much lower. Indeed, increasing interest in Northern Ireland teachers has been shown from Great Britain, particularly where and when there are shortages. These are all significant determinants of the quality of teaching in Northern Ireland.

Both Colleges of Education concentrate on the primary school sector, in respect of which four-year BEd courses and one-year PGCE courses are available. The training for teachers in secondary schools is provided, in the main, in the education departments of the universities, but four-year BEd courses are available in some subjects in the colleges.

Teachers in Northern Ireland are better qualified than their equivalents in Great Britain. In Northern Ireland, 56.5% of teachers were graduates as compared with 52.2% in England and Wales and 47.5% in Scotland, in 1989–90. The 1991/2 figure for Northern Ireland was 60%. Some of the difference between Northern Ireland and Scotland can be explained by the fact that in Scotland, male teachers are twice as likely as female teachers to be graduates, and two-thirds of teachers are female. However, a higher proportion of both male and female teachers in Northern Ireland have graduate status than in England and Wales.

Education reform

The Education Reform (Northern Ireland) Order 1989 entailed that Northern Ireland follow the main thrust of the English and Welsh reforms:

- *Curriculum and assessment*. There will be a similar, though not identical, common curriculum and pattern of assessment. Two statutory bodies are established: the Northern Ireland Curriculum Council and the Northern Ireland School Examinations and Assessment Council. These are responsible to the Department for the implementation of the curriculum and associated assessment arrangements.

- *Open enrolment.* Parents have a right to express a preference for the secondary school which they wish their children to attend and a child must be admitted to the preferred school, provided there is room at it. This has been extended to primary schools in autumn 1992.

- *LMS.* From last year, all schools and colleges are being funded on the basis of a formula based primarily on pupil numbers, but also taking account of size of school, accommodation costs and socio-economic disadvantage. All secondary schools and colleges will have delegated budgets with the Boards of Governors deciding on how to prioritise spending within that allocation.

- *Integrated education.* New opportunities are made available for Protestant and Catholic children to be educated together if parents wish. Existing schools will be able to become integrated schools and financial assistance will also be available to parents who wish to set up new integrated schools. There is more detail of this later in this paper, in the section on segregation and integration.

Pre-school education
Nursery education in Northern Ireland is provided either in nursery schools or in nursery classes in primary schools. The level of provision is slightly lower than in England: 46% of those aged 3–5 in 1991–2 in Northern Ireland received some education as compared to 48% in England. However, a large proportion of 4-year-olds in the province are enrolled in infant classes (as distinct from nursery classes) in primary schools. This is because compulsory schooling in Northern Ireland starts well before age 5 (see below). As a result, the proportion of 4- but not 3-year-olds receiving an early start to their education, either in nursery or primary schools, compares favourably with that in other parts of the UK. However, the question must be raised of whether a 4-year-old in primary school is receiving the appropriate kind of provision. The pupil-teacher ratio in nursery schools in Northern Ireland in 1991/2 was 24.5, higher than in England (19.1).

Primary schools

In many respects primary education in Northern Ireland is very similar to the rest of the UK, but there are some differences.

- The lower limit for compulsory schooling requires a child who reaches the age of 4 between 1 July and 30 June to start school by the following 1 September. However, a number of 3- and 4-year-old children, who have not reached the compulsory school age, are enrolled in primary schools where there are surplus places.

- A small number of pupils attend the preparatory departments of grammar schools.

- There is a higher proportion of small primary schools (fewer than 50 pupils) in Northern Ireland, although as in the rest of the UK, the number has fallen rapidly in recent decades.

- It has been commented that 'progressive' education has not made much headway in traditionalist Northern Ireland.[3]

The pupil-teacher ratio in 1991/2 was 22.6, higher than in England (22.2).

Secondary schools

The Northern Ireland Education Act of 1947 made provision for a tripartite system of grammar, secondary intermediate and technical intermediate schools, but the failure of the last to develop as intended resulted in the creation of a mainly bipartite system in the 1950s. It should be noted, however, that technical intermediate schools lasted longer than their equivalents in Great Britain, with some still operating in the mid-1970s. In setting up a selective system of education in the 1940s, the Ministry of Education's professed intention was that all children likely to benefit from a grammar school education should, regardless of parental income, have access to such a school. Whereas in the 1950s, two-thirds of all secondary places were in grammar schools, the rapid building of secondary intermediate schools meant that by the mid-1970s this was reversed with around two-thirds of places in secondary intermediate schools, and this is still the case.

In its 1973 report, 'Reorganisation of Secondary Education in Northern Ireland', the Seventh Advisory Council for Education recommended the elimination of selection at 11-plus leading to a restructuring of the educational system. Subsequently, in 1977, the Minister of State for Education formally announced a decision to do so but established a Working Party to devise an alternative transfer procedure for the interim period. The incoming administration in 1979 had no intention of implementing comprehensivisation in Northern Ireland, and so plans were abandoned. Issues of selective procedure are discussed later in the paper.

It should be noted that around 10% of Northern Ireland secondary pupils are educated within systems that do not involve selection at age 11. In the Craigavon district in County Armagh there are seven junior high schools in which selection for senior high schools is delayed until age 14. At that age, selected pupils go to senior high schools and pupils who are not selected go to technical colleges if in the Protestant sector, or remain in junior high schools if in the Catholic sector. In other districts, certain secondary schools have been designated as non-selective 11 to 16 or 11 to 18 schools by their ELBs. It is worth mentioning, however, that any school can determine its own admissions criteria, and of course the presence of a grammar school has implications for the admissions of all schools within accessible distance. In 1992, just under 39% of pupils in public sector secondary education were at grammar schools. This proportion has risen in recent years, possibly as a result of the introduction of formula funding which provides an incentive to grammar schools to accept more pupils.

The pupil-teacher ratio in secondary schools in 1991/2 was 14.5, lower than in England (15.5).

Special schools
The proportion of pupils in Northern Ireland with special needs is smaller than the UK average; more than two thirds of these are in special schools, slightly more than in England, much more than in Wales but much less than in Scotland. It should be noted that this was the picture in 1989–90 and that more recently there has been concern about the increasing demand for statementing and segregation, with large differences between the practices of local authorities. Figures for 1992 show 1.2% of pupils in special schools and a further 1.6% of primary school pupils in special units within primary schools. The pupil-teacher ratio in 1990–1 in Northern Ireland special schools was 6.9, which compares unfavourably with the UK average of 5.7.

Independent schools
There are only 17 (mainly primary) independent schools in Northern Ireland which cater for a tiny part of the school population (0.3% in January 1992).

Further education
After the recent amalgamation of the three Belfast colleges to form the Belfast Institute of Further and Higher Education, there are now 24 colleges in the province. This number remains twice the number of colleges one would expect to find in an area of comparable size and population in Great Britain. However, in February of this year, it was announced that FE will be rationalised in Northern Ireland with mergers reducing the number of colleges to 17 without the closure of existing college sites. The colleges currently range in size from 429 full-time equivalent students to 3,866, and therefore, compared to their counterparts in Great Britain, are quite small. Many small colleges in provincial towns see themselves as under threat from questions about the minimum size for college viability.

Most of these colleges are multi-disciplinary in nature, offering a wide range of academic and vocational courses, as well as organising adult and community education in outcentres which are often local halls. The colleges have traditionally provided technical elements of education which were uneconomic to provide in schools. The close integration between secondary and further education has continued, with link courses being provided in technical, business and catering subjects. Whether the relationship is maintained under local management remains to be seen.

The 1989 Education Reform Order, as in the rest of the UK, established college governing bodies with enhanced representation from business and commerce, and under schemes of local management, governors received powers to manage the budget for their college and to become more entrepreneurial in their approach. Boards were required to produce strategic plans for further education in their areas, to advise, support and deliver training programmes, in addition to acting as employing authorities.

In June 1990 the Department of Education for Northern Ireland issued a consultative document, 'Signposts for the 1990s – A Review of Further Education', which in the ensuing months initiated a debate on the future of further education in the province. Shortly after the Government's White Paper on Education and Training, DENI issued its proposals for further education in the province entitled 'The Road Ahead' and simultaneously announced that further education would remain within the control of the Education and Library Boards. The document underlined how circumstances in Northern Ireland differ significantly from those elsewhere in the UK. Firstly, its higher proportion of small colleges, while capable of operating as free-standing units, could bring disproportionately high administrative burdens. Secondly, with no separate sixth-form colleges it does not have Great Britain's 'self-contained' post-16 sector. The system of local provision within an integrated education service remains.

Within the province, the number of 16–19-year-olds, the traditional market for FE, is declining and is expected to continue to decline until the mid-1990s, but there has been an increasing proportion of young people within this cohort enrolling in FE. However, attention is now being turned towards increasing the participation of adults within FE. Some estimates suggest that up to 50% of adults in employment have not undertaken any education or training since leaving school. Many of these need new skills or the updating of old ones.

Higher education
The Lockwood Report (1965) extended the aims and principles of Robbins with more ambitious projections of HE participation which were in general achieved by the beginning of the 1980s.[4] However, the fact that over this period the student inflow to Northern Ireland was only 15% of the outflow meant that the number of HE places in Northern Ireland did not rise as much as anticipated. Moreover, the institutional pattern favoured by Lockwood, two universities and an advanced FE college, was not viable. In 1991/2, the age participation index for higher education in Northern Ireland was 30.4%, already not far off the Government's target of one in three by the year 2000 for the UK.

Higher education in Northern Ireland is provided by the Queen's University of Belfast (QUB), the University of Ulster (UU), and two Colleges of Education, Stranmillis and St Mary's, both in Belfast. In 1991/2, 76% of Northern Ireland full-time undergraduates enrolled at Northern Ireland universities, with 24% enrolling in universities in Great Britain. These proportions have not changed in recent years. In 1991/2, 83% of undergraduate enrolments at Northern Ireland universities were from Northern Ireland, 4% were from Great Britain, 11% from EC countries and 2% from other countries. The EC country enrolments have doubled in four years, to an extent due to a surge of entrants from the Republic of Ireland.

QUB provides a full range of undergraduate and postgraduate degrees over its nine faculties. In one sense, it is a flagship of integrated education: its student population divides 50/50 between Protestants and Catholics, although only a quarter of the staff are Catholic. However, on closer inspection it will be noted that subject choice differs greatly with Protestants favouring science and engineering and Catholics favouring humanities and law. Separatism also extends to social activities.

UU has seven faculties and as well as offering undergraduate and postgraduate degrees, it offers diplomas and professional qualifications. It also has a significant programme of non-degree courses leading to Higher National Diplomas. This reflects its origins in the merger in 1984 of a university and a polytechnic to become the first 'polyversity' in the UK, as does the fact that many of its courses are designed to suit the needs of industry, commerce and the professions. UU has nine years of experience of post-binary issues that might be of great interest to institutions in Great Britain.

In Northern Ireland, as a result of a combination of demographic and migrational factors, the universities have been much more forthcoming in opening their doors to non-traditional entrants than their equivalents in Great Britain. Even by 1985–6, 14% of students admitted to QUB and 22% of students admitted to UU were from FE colleges. This year a third of the undergraduates in UU are studying part-time. So in Northern Ireland, there has been both widened access to higher education and an increasing diversity of institutional provision, that has been ahead of the rest of the UK. This has been one of the factors contributing to the much higher participation in higher education shown in Figure 7 on page 400. These trends are likely to be enhanced by the fact that the two universities from the current academic year are reorganising their degree courses into a modular framework.

There has for a long time been concern that the Northern Ireland institutions suffer a loss of high quality students through migration to British institutions and to a lesser extent to institutions in the Republic of Ireland, a migration which is not offset by a flow of students from Great Britain into Northern Ireland institutions. There is a second process of migration where graduates are attracted by the higher average graduate incomes that can be found in almost all areas of the UK outside Northern Ireland. There is particular concern about the migration of graduates of subjects that are seen as important for economic development and of graduates of higher ability (as measured by degree class and A level results).

Training
The Department of Economic Development (DED) is charged with the responsibility for the development of the economy and for the provision of a skilled and trained workforce. Policy in training is formulated by DED with input from DENI when appropriate, and professionally supported by a newly formed Education and Training Inspectorate. The Training and Employment Agency, part of the 'Next Steps' initiative, manages job centres and government training centres, as well as directly supporting training on employers' premises and community workshops.

The Youth Training Programme (YTP), administered jointly by DENI and the Training and Employment Agency, is a two-year programme for all young people in the 16 and 17 age group. The education service within the province is also actively involved in training and the colleges provide an essential element of YTP, providing for 25.4% of the young people in training. Last year, the system of funding for this programme changed with the introduction of block funding. The system allocates one of five premium levels to each trainee, based on the level of the course being followed and the ability of the young person as tested in the final year at school. The provider then receives the finance attached to the premium level and from it must pay the trainee's allowance and provide the training. The outcome of this new funding system is that in 1990–1 in one board area, the number of trainees enrolled in colleges on YTP doubled, but the income generated was less than that received under the previous system, leading to allegations of training on the cheap. Other consequences have been reduced staffing levels, a higher profile for marketing and pressure on administrative procedures within colleges.

Outcomes of schools in Northern Ireland

Examination results

Detailed analyses of outcomes of schools in Northern Ireland are shown in Figures 2–7 at the end of this paper. The annual survey of school leavers confirms the view that the educational system in Northern Ireland produces extremes of performance, that is to say, disproportionately high numbers of pupils with either one or more A levels or with no qualifications at all.[5] The increase in the qualifications of school leavers in the last fifteen years is striking. There has been a substantial reduction in the number of youngsters leaving school with no qualifications, from 36% in 1974–5 to 9% in 1990–1. Particular increases have been seen during this period in school leavers with A levels, from 21% to 32%, and also in those with low grade O levels, CSEs or GCSEs or other qualifications.

These figures mask two very different systems with distinct trends. The overall minority of school leavers with one or more A levels becomes a large majority in the grammar schools, where 62% of leavers had this qualification in 1974–5, rising to 76% by 1990–1. In that year, 52% of leavers from grammar schools had three or more A levels. Figure 4 (page 398), showing the qualifications of leavers from secondary intermediate schools, shows where the rapid fall in those with no qualifications has been. The figure was 50% for 1974–5 falling to 13% by 1990–1. There has not, however, been a correspondingly rapid increase in those leaving secondary intermediate schools with A levels nor indeed with good O levels/GCSEs. Those with one or more A levels rose from 3% to 6%, those with five or more O levels/GCSEs (not including those with A levels) from 5% to 12%.

So unqualified leavers remain concentrated in the secondary intermediate schools, whereas those with A levels are concentrated in the grammar schools. This suggests not only that the extremes of performance reflect the system of selective schooling but also that the profile is shaped itself by the selective education. This profile can be compared with that of England. It might be argued that the figures for England are an aggregation of very different patterns within constituent LEAs and that some of these LEAs might have profiles similar to that of Northern Ireland. This is not the case, despite the fact that there is considerable variation in the profiles of LEAs. None of those LEAs that have high proportions of leavers with no qualifications had high pass rates of one or more A levels. Northern Ireland's examination performance has greater extremes than that of England, with more students leaving school with A levels, but also more students leaving school with no qualifications at all.

The difference between males and females in Northern Ireland is much greater than the difference in England. For example, 31% of girls in Northern Ireland achieve 2 or more A levels as compared to 25% of boys. The corresponding figures for England are 23% and 21%. Likewise, 12% of boys in Northern Ireland leave school without any qualifications as compared to 5% of girls. The corresponding figures for England are 8% and 6%. An explanation for this might be the fact that girls perform better in single-sex schools which are more common in Northern Ireland than in England, whereas boys are less affected by this characteristic of schools (in fact there is evidence that they perform better in mixed schools).

Destinations of school leavers
Analysis of trends in the destinations of school leavers in Northern Ireland in the last fifteen years shows that the proportion of school leavers going on to full-time higher education started from a high base (17% in 1974–5) and has only risen a few per cent to 22% in 1990–1. Meanwhile, there has been a massive increase in (younger) school leavers going

on to FE colleges full-time, from 11% to 33%. The proportion of school leavers in England going to full-time HE and FE was 17% and 28% respectively. Whereas in England, the same proportion of boys and girls go on to higher education, in Northern Ireland there is a 3% difference in favour of girls. Full-time FE is significantly favoured by girls as compared to boys in both Northern Ireland and England.

Assessment of Performance Unit studies
The APU surveys between 1978 and 1987 point to consistently higher achievement in mathematics by pupils in Northern Ireland at age 11 than all regions of England and Wales. This might be partly explained by the fact that Northern Ireland pupils have more homework. It should also be noted that pupils in primary schools in Northern Ireland achieve high proficiency in taking mathematics tests through rigorous preparation for the transfer tests. This could also explain why at age 15, Northern Ireland pupils are no longer ahead of their counterparts in England in most aspects of the subject. Northern Ireland pupils were also highest in the national rank order for reading and writing at age 11 although this small lead was lost by age 15. In science, Northern Ireland pupils were behind England but ahead of Wales at ages 11, 13 and 15. This is partly explained by the fact that schools in Northern Ireland give less time to science, but also by the fact that provision of resources in this area is relatively poor, both in the primary and secondary phases.

Secondary school organisation, effectiveness and fairness

Selection
The retention of a bipartite and selective system of secondary education in Northern Ireland has attracted the attention of critics of comprehensivisation, particularly outside Northern Ireland. They argue that the fact that the proportion of school

leavers in Northern Ireland with five or more O levels or GCSEs or one or more A levels has overtaken that in England and Wales can be partly attributed to the retention of traditional and 'successful' structures and values. Marks and Cox have looked towards public examination statistics in Northern Ireland to support their case that the retention of a fully selective system is linked with better performance. Despite these types of comparison, throughout the post-war period there has been a strong body of opinion within the Northern Ireland research community which believes that selection has been damaging, divisive and only more effective for a minority of pupils. As has been mentioned earlier in this paper, in the late 1970s the government intended to introduce comprehensivisation, a policy much influenced by this research.

It is extremely difficult to assess in a conclusive manner the relationship between systems of school organisation and outcomes in terms of school performance and fairness between different categories of pupils. Different researchers have used the Northern Ireland experience to show both the so-called benefits of a selective system and the so-called dangers. Part of the problem is that it is not clear what selective systems are being compared with. First, as is shown by Walford in NCE Briefing No. 7, there has never been a true comprehensive system in Great Britain and there has been a very wide variety of secondary school structures, with different starting ages, or separate sixth-form colleges, for example. Second, comprehensive schools are affected by the presence or absence of selective (including CTCs) or independent schools in the region. Third, intakes to comprehensive schools are affected by patterns of population and urbanisation in their catchment areas. Given the high correlation between the intake of a school and its examination performance, as shown by McPherson (NCE Briefing No. 1) and others, these factors prohibit accurate comparison between Northern Ireland and non-selective systems. However, it is possible to draw some tentative conclusions from studies of the interaction of selection and performance in Northern Ireland.

The issues raised by selection fall into two main categories with a great deal more research on the first category than on the second. The first category is the accuracy of the system in identifying able pupils, at whatever age they are tested. The second category is the relationship between the selective process and social justice. In recent years it has been found that transfer is socially biased, in that even if they had similar scores in the 11-plus tests, working-class children were less likely than middle-class children to be admitted to grammar schools. There is also some question about the fairness of the transfer procedure for girls, and the adequacy of grammar school provision for Catholics. All of these issues have generated several important research studies, mainly of a policy-oriented nature, and are discussed later in the paper.

Changes in selective procedures
Over the years, different procedures have been used in Northern Ireland to select pupils for non-fee-paying grammar school places.[6] Selection for Northern Ireland was introduced as a result of the 1947 Education Act (NI). Between 1948 and 1965 there was a Qualifying Examination with tests in English, arithmetic and intelligence. The first two were based on a prescribed syllabus. Partly in response to complaints about the distorting effects on the primary curriculum, and on the recommendation of the Advisory Council on Education, the Qualifying Examination was replaced in 1966 by the Selection Procedure. This used a combination of scores on two verbal reasoning tests and scaled teachers' rankings from the primary schools on general performance of individuals with particular reference to English and arithmetic.

In 1973, the Burges Report recommended an end to selection. Four years later, there was public acceptance of this course of action by the Minister of State, who declared his intention to phase in a comprehensive system. The Alternative Transfer Procedure, introduced in 1978, was a temporary measure. It lasted only three years, with non-attributable tests in different combinations of English, arithmetic and verbal reasoning. Primary school principals were allowed quotas, the basis for which also changed during the course of the three years.

In 1980, a return to 'attributable testing' was announced, with pupils awarded either an A, M or G grade. An A grade (around 20% of pupils) guaranteed a free place; an M grade (around 10% of pupils) was borderline and a G grade (around 70% of pupils) entailed the paying of fees for a grammar school place. Fee-payers amounted to around 10% of entry to grammar schools. Criticism of the wide variations in the allocation of M grade pupils resulted in a change to the system in the mid-1980s, with pupils either being awarded an E grade (27% of pupils) or an N grade (73% of pupils), with the former guaranteed a free grammar school place and the latter paying fees.

The Education Reform Order (1989) resulted in a further change to the system in 1990, with open enrolment giving schools greater powers in determining admission criteria.[7] Post-primary schools will be required to admit pupils on parental request up to the extent of their physical capacity. Only grammar schools, however, are allowed to take ability into consideration in specifying criteria for admission in order to prevent a hierarchy amongst other schools. A new grading system was introduced for the 11-plus exam, with 25% of pupils awarded a grade 1, 10% a grade 2, 10% a grade 3 and 55% a grade 4. No pupil is guaranteed a grammar school place but grammar schools must use this grade as their primary criterion. Those with a grade 1 can be fairly certain of gaining a place and places might be awarded to any pupil in another category, even with a grade 4. If they receive Departmental approval, grammar schools are able to admit below the level of full capacity where there are not enough pupils that reach the required standard. Fee-paying grammar school places were abolished.

The introduction of the national curriculum for Northern Ireland with attainment tests at 8 and 11 has presented great complications for the system of selection by grammar schools.[8] The original intention was that selection would be based on pupils' records of achievement in the common programme of study including scores on the Key Stage 2 assessments. However, these were not felt to be established nor finely graded enough to be used alone as a criterion for allocation. Yet requirements of pupils to sit both these assessments and verbal reasoning tests at age 11 were felt to be excessively demanding and it was also felt that the latter might distort the curriculum at Key Stage 2. The problems, in fact, go beyond this. Eleven-plus selection tests aim to be norm-referenced, in that they are used to allocate a limited number of places to grammar schools. Curricular assessment, however, is intended to be criterion-referenced, to use broad levels of attainment and to draw heavily on teacher assessment. Policy has changed several times on this matter in recent months and the latest line is that the verbal reasoning tests will continue alongside the new Key Stage 2 assessments.

Predictive efficiency of selective procedures
There have been several attempts by researchers to analyse the predictive efficiency of the different forms of selection that have existed in Northern Ireland by correlating the results of individuals in selection tests with measures of their later performance. There are several problems with this type of work: only in the last 20 years have substantial numbers of secondary school pupils sat public examinations, and even during the recent period were generally entered for fewer and often different (CSE) exams; transfer grades do not provide an accurate measure of performance in the selection procedures; and comparisons of selection procedures and pupils over time are complicated by other factors in the education system.

Several sources are relevant here, including the annual School Leavers Surveys, the reports of the Assessment of Performance Unit (APU), the research studies submitted to the Advisory Council for Education (ACE), the studies by the Northern Ireland Council for Educational Research (NICER) and numerous other independent research studies. In general, more recent forms of selection show no increase in accuracy over those of the 1950s. The research studies that used performance in later public examinations as a criterion suggest that between one in five and one in seven pupils are 'misplaced' by selection at age 11.[9] However, the significance of the outcome of selection for the life-chance of the individual has been reduced by the increase in the entrance of secondary school pupils for public examinations, including A levels, and the introduction of the national curriculum.

Submissions to the Advisory Council for Education:

- In the 1950s and 1960s, several research studies were submitted to the Advisory Council for Education (ACE), all concerned with the predictive efficiency of the qualifying examination in relation to performance of grammar school pupils in the group examinations known as the Junior and Senior Certificates.

- In 1955 it was observed that girls perform better than boys in the English and verbal reasoning tests.[10] This was the reason why they are treated separately in the transfer procedure (see later).

- In 1960 Patterson showed that the best single predictor of later success is the intelligence test.[11] Twenty per cent of qualified pupils failed to pass any exam and half failed to reach or pass the Senior Certificate, regarded as a truer measure of grammar school success. Moreover, two-thirds of border-zone cases failed to reach or pass the Senior Certificate. It was thus argued that the qualifying standard was too low and that the border-zone category should be eliminated.

Northern Ireland Council for Educational Research work:

- Wilson in 1969 looked at the proportion of grammar school pupils passing five or more GCEs, according to how they had qualified for grammar school. The results were as follows: qualifying examination (69%), review procedure (55%), Junior Certificate (33%), fee-paying unqualified pupils (4%). Those qualified by review from reorganised primary schools did as well as those from the qualifying examination. The conclusion was that the qualifying examination fails to take account of able pupils. Spelman (1979) found that selection at 11-plus brought about intellectual, social, and attitudinal differences between post-primary school intakes in a 1975 cohort. Using the same cohort, Wilson (1982) showed that performance in public examinations is better predicted by performance in the first year of secondary education than by the selection procedure.[12] He later (1985) showed a substantial difference between selected and non-selected pupils, rather than between different forms of selection.

- Gallagher found that selective status as determined by the grades awarded in the 1981 transfer procedure was the major determinant of academic performance.[9] However, 19.7% of the pupils awarded an A or M grade in the transfer procedure failed to reach the four O level criterion needed to gain or retain a free grammar school place for sixth form, while 14.7% of those awarded a G grade passed at least four O level equivalents. Overall, for 16.4% there was a 'mismatch' between transfer grade and performance at 16-plus.

- Wilson and Gardiner used the 1975 cohort study to compare pupils in the Craigavon two-tier system with other pupils in Northern Ireland.[12] They found that delayed selection at 14 on the basis of school performance was a better predictor of later school performance than the 11-plus test. More interestingly, they also found that within a selective school system, pupils selected at age 14 in senior high schools tended on average to do better at 16 than pupils enrolled at age 11 in grammar schools. It would be interesting to see a comparison of pupils at secondary intermediate schools and those who remained in junior high schools in the Craigavon district.

- Wilson and Spelman surveyed teachers on the organisation of secondary school teaching and their preference for alternatives.[13] They found that teachers in grammar schools were more likely to favour the status quo, and that those in secondary intermediate schools were almost all oppposed to the bipartite system. They found that teachers in Protestant schools were more favourably disposed towards selection than in Catholic schools. There was a general lack of enthusiasm for systems where there is no selection or for systems that vary locally according to preference, but there was almost consensus as to the positive merits of deferred selection at 14-plus or 16-plus. The most popular options were: first, 11–16 comprehensive system with separate academic sixth form colleges and technical colleges; second, 11–16 comprehensive system with sixth form colleges doing both academic and vocational options; and third, a two-tier system akin to the Craigavon arrangement with its junior high schools and senior high schools.

- Sutherland and Gallagher reported that over half of primary school teachers would prefer deferring the selection procedure and that the age rather than the principle of selection was of most concern. They also showed that the amount of preparation for the transfer procedure was far greater than that recommended by DENI, partly due to parental pressure and partly due to spiralling competition between schools. In general, teachers felt that there was a conflict between the transfer procedure, with its narrowing effect on the curriculum, and the implementation of Primary Guidelines to extend the curriculum of the upper primary school. They later turned to secondary education (1987) and claimed that the gap between the curriculum in grammar and secondary schools widens as time progresses, with grammar school pupils spending more time on sciences and languages and secondary school pupils spending more time on technical and vocational subjects. It should be noted that this study took place before the introduction of the national curriculum for Northern Ireland.

Equality of opportunity in the selection procedure
 (a) Geographical distribution. Grammar school places are not evenly distributed around Northern Ireland. For example,

Wilson found that an M grade (borderline) pupil had an 85% chance of a place in a Western Board grammar school but a 55% chance in the South East Board.[14] This type of inequality of opportunity caused by lack of access to grammar schools cuts across other types of inequalities subsequently described.

(b) Religion. NICER's analysis of intakes between 1981 and 1985 showed that 30.9% of secondary school pupils in the Protestant sector were in grammar schools as compared with 25.7% in the Catholic sector.[15] Two sets of reasons explain this discrepancy.

First, fewer Catholics than Protestants initially chose to enter grammar schools at the transfer stage – a significantly higher proportion of Catholic grade A and M pupils nominated non-grammar schools as a first preference as compared to Protestant pupils.[3] Wilson found that 9.1% of A grade pupils in the Catholic sector but only 2% in the Protestant were in other types of school.[14] Possible explanations for this trend include the following: problems of physical access to grammar schools in certain parts of the province where Catholics are concentrated; the fact that there are fewer Catholic grammar schools overall (30 Catholic to 44 Protestant); and the fact that there are more Catholic than Protestant secondary schools which have on their rolls at least 10% of pupils with an A or M grade.[15]

The second reason for the lower ratio for Catholics is that when the studies took place it was possible for the parents of pupils with a G grade to pay fees for their children to go to grammar school. There was a much higher level of admissions for Protestant fee-paying pupils, and this can no doubt be explained by the fact that they were in general in a better financial position. As many as 5% of Protestants with G grades were in grammar school as compared to 1.9% of Catholics.[16]

These two factors might have been partially offset by two other trends. First, a higher proportion of Protestant than Catholic grade M pupils were unsuccessful in gaining a grammar school place where one was sought.[15] Secondly, substantially more Catholics nominated Protestant grammar schools as first preference than vice versa.[3] The reasons for this are similar to the reasons why they are more likely to nominate non-grammar schools, caused by problems of access.

However, the discussion so far has only related to the initial choice of school. There is also a small net transfer from Catholic schools to Protestant schools from the age of 16 onwards, comprising a movement out of Catholic grammar schools into Catholic secondary schools and Protestant grammar schools, and a movement out of Protestant secondary schools into Protestant grammar schools. As a result, Catholics only represent 40% of grammar school *leavers*.[3] Only 26% of Catholic pupils leave school having attended grammar school for all or part of their secondary education compared to 35% of Protestant pupils.

If we consider the grammar sector and the secondary sector separately, Catholic pupils achieve a level of qualification as good as, if not better than Protestant pupils. Overall, Catholics leave school less well qualified than Protestants.[3] This could be partly explained by an imbalance in the proportions of Catholics and Protestants attending grammar schools. Moreover, Livingstone has shown that although profiles for pupils from Protestant and Catholic schools were similar in both grammar and secondary schools, the percentage of unqualified leavers was higher from Catholic schools (33%) than Protestant schools (26%).[3] Individual Catholic pupils do no worse than their Protestant counterparts within grammar schools or secondary schools, but the relatively poor provision of the high-achieving Catholic grammar schools has a detrimental effect on the qualification rate of Catholics as a whole.

It should be noted that this imbalance in the system has to an extent been responded to by the Government. In July 1992, the Education Minister approved development proposals for an additional 1,470 grammar school places under Catholic management, concentrated in Londonderry and Belfast. These issues are returned to in the section on segregation and integration.

(c) Social class. NICER studies have also shown that the selective structure of secondary education in Northern Ireland embodies a social class bias. In 1981, 46% of middle-class children qualified for a non-fee-paying grammar school place as compared to 22% of working-class children.[9] Of course, this might reflect differences in ability between the social classes, but there is reason to believe that this is not entirely true. For example, only one of the G grade pupils who were enrolled in grammar schools as fee-payers came from a working-class background and only one of the A grade pupils who did not claim their grammar school places was from a middle-class background. Three-quarters of middle-class M grade pupils but only half of working-class M grade pupils enrolled in grammar schools. Neither has this situation improved with the abolition of fee-paying places and the introduction of open enrolment. Sutherland found in 1990 that middle-class parents were far more likely than working-class parents to apply for and succeed in getting grammar school places for those children who had not achieved the top grade.[17] It is not yet known what the effect of the introduction of the more flexible procedure in the autumn of the same year had.

There are several possible explanations for this bias. First, questionnaires reveal that more middle-class (84%) than working-class parents (59%) wished their M grade children to attend grammar schools. Second, among those seeking grammar school places for their children, middle-class parents (84%) were more successful than working-class parents (59%). The reasons for this might be more favourable references from primary school headteachers, or better strategies of parents in ranking preferences.

(d) Gender. For years, treatment of the transfer tests into secondary education was different for boys and girls, since it has been argued that at age 11 boys are at a temporary disadvantage due to factors relating to physical maturity. Because of this, from 1968, selection tests in the province were processed to ensure that equal percentages of boys and

girls qualify for non-fee-paying places in grammar schools. At first, this was done by the adjustment of score, but after 1971 the two sexes were treated as separate populations, with girls requiring a higher score to qualify. Despite this, Wilson still found that more M grade girls than boys were enrolled in grammar schools.[14] The argument that girls enjoy an advantage due to accelerated development around the age of 11 was weakened by the aforementioned results of the School Leavers Surveys which increasingly show girls significantly outperforming boys in public examinations.[5] Following the involvement of the Equal Opportunities Commission, in 1988 the High Court ruled that boys and girls should not be treated as separate populations.

Segregation and integration

Segregation
The community divisions in Northern Ireland are reflected in the school system. Even before the partitioning of Ireland in 1921 the Catholic and Protestant school systems were separate.[18] Even now, the vast majority of pupils are educated in schools where either most or all of their fellow pupils are of the same religion. Although there is a common belief that this separation of the communities in the education system is an important source of the problems of the Troubles, there remains a vocal minority who argue that children should not be used as pawns in 'an attempt at social engineering' and that their cultural identity should not be tampered with. Moreover, it can be argued that the fact that segregated schools exist in societies where there is no conflict and yet in others where there is, means that they cannot be intrinsically divisive. The conclusion can only be that schools at a cultural level tend to reflect or perpetuate differences and conflict rather than cause them. To this should be added the important point that the system of maintained schools is one of the few institutions over which the Catholic community has self-control.

Various educational interventions have been suggested to improve community relations and eventually promote a less divided society. Some believe that this can only come about with the integration of the schools themselves. Others believe that initiatives to establish curricular change and contacts between schools within a segregated system would be more likely to have an impact. Of course, the two approaches are not mutually exclusive. Interestingly, there is some indication that much of the enthusiasm for change in the role of education comes from central government rather than the local authorities. This contrasts with the situation in England, where local authorities are usually seen as the level of government supportive of multiculturalism rather than the Department for Education.

Equality of treatment
Before dealing with initiatives designed to ease the problems of segregation, it is important to look at a body of work, culminating in the report of the Standing Advisory Commission on Human Rights (SACHR) on the human rights implications of education policies and structures in Northern Ireland.[19] One of the areas of particular interest to SACHR was equality of treatment for Protestant and Catholic schools. Much of the research for this was done by NICER, some of which has already been referred to. The main findings were as follows:

- Catholic schools are smaller than Protestant schools and hence have less pupil teaching space; there is also a lesser degree of specialist teaching space provision per pupil in relation to science and CDT;

- teachers in Catholic schools are slightly more likely to be qualified in the humanities or languages than in science or technology;

- in 1989, 10.1% of Protestants and 15.9% of Catholics left school without any qualifications; there are some large Catholic secondary schools in urban areas where very large proportions of male leavers have no qualifications;

- in 1988, 56% of grammar school pupils were in Protestant schools despite the fact that in the age band the population is distributed more or less evenly between the two communities; this is mainly due to a lack of grammar school provision in certain areas where Catholics predominate;

- the DENI curriculum survey showed that differences in curriculum patterns between Protestant and Catholic schools were smaller than the differences between grammar and secondary schools and between boys' and girls' schools; however, pupils in Protestant schools spent more time on science and technology, while pupils in Catholic schools spent considerably more time on Irish in the lower forms and RE throughout.

- although a bias in Catholic schools towards A levels in arts and humanities remains, the gap has been narrowing in recent years;

- attention is drawn to funding arrangements by which Catholic schools but not Protestant schools must make a 15% contribution to capital funding; as mentioned earlier in this paper, there is also concern that Catholic schools are receiving a lower level of per capita recurrent funding;

- the majority of parents were in favour of *comprehensive* education, held a positive view of the general idea of integrated education, and believed that the Irish language should be taught to those who wanted it.

It should be noted that the Government has already responded to two of these points. In July 1992, it was announced that 1,470 extra grammar school places under Catholic management would be provided in Belfast and Derry. As was mentioned earlier in the paper, the Government has also responded to research into the effects of capital funding arrangements by proposing a new category of voluntary school with 100% capital funding but a different composition of Board of Governors.

Integrated schools
An important development in attempts to address the issue of segregation has been the emergence of integrated schools. These have an admissions policy and a curricular programme that are aimed at attracting pupils from both sides of the divide and educating them in both traditions. The integrated schools began as voluntary and self-financing, and even attracted finance from overseas. The first integrated school was Lagan College, still a flagship for the movement. The next development was that integrated schools were able to achieve maintained status on the lines of the Roman Catholic schools. The movement for integrated schools originally insisted on there being a 40:60 ratio of the two religions in these schools, but this was abandoned when Brownlow High School in Craigavon became the first school to adopt controlled integrated status, despite only having 15% Catholic pupils and only two Catholic teachers.

After 10 years of integrated education there are now 2,840 pupils at 15 integrated schools. This amounts to only 1% of Northern Ireland's classroom population. The schools have proved more popular amongst Catholics: there are usually waiting lists of Catholics who cannot be admitted because Protestants are needed to maintain the 60:40 denominational ratio.

In the Education Reform Order, the Government stated a policy of encouraging the development of integrated schools and made provision for them to seek controlled status, or to opt out as grant-maintained schools. Arrangements have also been made for any existing school to have its status changed to 'integrated' if a majority of parents wishes, and if the school is prepared to reformulate its admissions and curricular policies accordingly. These schools will receive 100% of recurrent and capital funding from DENI. The Government has also indicated that it would be prepared to give preference to integrated schools for capital programmes and that those wanting to set up integrated schools 'from scratch' are eligible for substantial state aid.

The movement for integrated schooling has not, however, taken off. Only 1% of pupils in Northern Ireland are educated in integrated schools, and many people remain antipathetic to the movement. The Catholic Church has not been the single impediment to the introduction of integration. Protestant schools have been just as vociferous in the defence of single religion schools as Catholic ones. It seems that for the time being, initiatives *within* a segregated system have the major role to play.

Curriculum and other initiatives
Schools have in many cases developed a more positive role with initiatives to bring together pupils from Protestant and Catholic schools in learning, community service and recreational activities, recognising the fact that, in cultural terms, the children have much more in common than that which separates them. Leisure activities have provided good opportunities for contact between children, and for example, community youth sports teams have been set up with members from both sides of the religious divide.

These initiatives began at the local level and developed into a structured programme of joint educational activities called 'Education for Mutual Understanding' (EMU). The notion of EMU has emerged out of a series of curriculum initiatives and research over 20 years.[20] It has involved a search for ways in which the possible consequences of separation at school level can be ameliorated. The aim was that children should be made aware of the value positions held by the various groups in society. This aim was promoted and specifically funded by central government, delivered through LEA involvement and supported by HMIs and local authority advisers and field officers. Confidence has thus been built between schools in very separate communities. It led to the demand for the curriculum to incorporate these ideas so that the subject did not simply become a non-academic, non-examinable and non-prestigious option, and so that it could extend beyond low-ability classes and hopefully involve parents.[21]

The statutory Orders on cross-curricular themes were issued in June 1992. The new Northern Ireland curriculum is taking account of the experience of EMU in order to encourage cross-community contact, given that in general, segregation will continue for a variety of deep-seated reasons, including ghettoised housing. Two of the cross-curricular themes which have been specified to inform all subjects are 'Education for Mutual Understanding' and 'Cultural Heritage'. The former encourages pupils to accept differences and appreciate the interdependence of communities. The latter begins by looking at local culture for the youngest pupils and then broadening its perspective, with political and civil discontent, and relationships between the Protestant and Catholic communities a constant theme. Both subjects are designed to foster tolerance across the sectarian divide. Schools are expected to include these dimensions in their programmes for most subjects in accordance with guidelines drawn up by task forces appointed by the Northern Ireland Curriculum Council.

It is early days to assess the impact of EMU, although it is clear that there have been some teething problems and that much work is needed to provide a clearer conceptual framework for its implementation, with improvements in co-ordination, training and evaluation.[22]

References

1 Cormack, R.J., Gallagher, A.M., and Osborne, R.D. (1991). *Religious Affiliation and Educational Attainment in Northern Ireland: the Financing of Schools in Northern Ireland.* Paper for Standing Advisory Commission on Human Rights (SACHR).
2 DENI (1993). *Educational Administration in Northern Ireland: a Consultative Document.* DENI.
3 Osborne, R.D., Cormack, R.J. and Miller, R.L. (eds.) (1987). *Education and Policy in Northern Ireland.* Policy Research Institute.
4 Lockwood Report (1965). *Higher Education in Northern Ireland.* Report of

the Committee appointed by the Minister of Finance (Cmd. 480). HMSO.
5 DENI (various). *Statistical Bulletin*. DENI.
6 Sutherland A.E. (1990). *Selection in Northern Ireland: from 1947 Act to 1989 Order*. Research Papers in Education, 5,1.
7 DENI (1988). *Education in Northern Ireland: the Way Forward*. DENI.
8 DENI (1992). *Transfer from Primary to Secondary School: 1993–4 and Beyond*. Consultation paper.
9 Gallagher, A.M. (1988). *Transfer Pupils at 16*. NICER.
10 Advisory Council for Education (ACE, NI) (1955). *Selection of Pupils: Secondary Schools: Second Report*. HMSO.
11 ACE, NI (1960). *Selection of Pupils: Secondary Schools: Third Report*. HMSO.
12 Wilson, J.A. and Gardiner, T. (1982). *Progress at 16*. NICER.
13 Wilson, J.A. and Spelman, B.J. (1977). *The Organisation of Secondary Education*. NICER.
14 Wilson, J.A. (1986). *Transfer and the Structure of Secondary Education*. NICER.
15 Cormack, R.J., Gallagher, A.M., Murray, D. and Osborne, R.D. (1992). *Curriculum, Access to Grammar Schools and the Financing of Schools*. Paper for SACHR.
16 Wilson, J.A. (1985). *Secondary School Organisation and Pupil Progress*. NICER.
17 Sutherland A.E. (1992). *After a Term in the New School: Evidence from a Parental Postal Survey*. NICER.
18 Dunn, S. (1990). *A Short History of Education in Northern Ireland: 1920–1990*. Paper for SACHR.
19 SACHR (1992). *Seventeenth Report for 1991–2*. HMSO.
20 Richardson, N. (1992). *Roots If Not Wings! Where Did EMU Come From?* Keynote paper at 'EMU in transition' conference.
21 DENI (1990). *Education for Mutual Understanding*. Papers from Stranmillis College conference.
22 Smith, A. and Robinson, A. (1992). *Education for Mutual Understanding: Perceptions and Policy*. University of Ulster.

Other sources

Cormack, R.J. and Osborne, R.D. (1983). *Religion, Education and Employment: Aspects of Equal Opportunity in Northern Ireland*. Appletree Press.

Cormack, R.J., Osborne, R.D., Reid, N.G. and Williamson, A.P. (1984). *Participation in Higher Education: Trends in the Social and Spatial Mobility of Northern Ireland Undergraduates*. Final Report, SSRC Funded Project HR6846.

Darby, J. (1978). *Northern Ireland: Bonds and Breaks in Education*. British Journal of Educational Studies, 26(3).

DENI (1988). *Education in Northern Ireland: Proposals for Reform*. DENI.

DENI (1993). *School Performance Information, 1991–2*. DENI.

Dunn, S. (1986). *Education and the Conflict in Northern Ireland: a Guide to the Literature*. Coleraine: Centre for the Study of Conflict.

Dunn, S. (1986). *The Role of Education in the Northern Ireland Conflict*. Oxford Review of Education, 12(3).

Fulton, J. (1982). *Education in Northern Ireland*. In: Cohen, L., Thomas, J. and

Manion, L. (eds). *Educational Research and Development in Britain, 1970–1980.* NFER-Nelson.

Government Statistical Service (1991). *Education Statistics for the United Kingdom.* HMSO.

Harbison, J.I. (ed.) (1989). *Growing up in Northern Ireland.* Stranmillis College.

McEwen, A., Salters, J. & M. and Agnew, U. (1992). *Integrated Education: the Views of Parents.* School of Education, Queen's University.

McKernan, J. (1981). *Transfer at 14: a Study of the Craigavon Two-Tier System as an Organisational Innovation in Education.* Belfast. Northern Ireland Council for Educational Research (NICER).

McKernan, J. (1982). *Constraints on the Handling of Controversial Issues in Northern Ireland Post-Primary Schools.* British Educational Research Journal, 8(1).

Murray, D. (1985). *Worlds Apart: Segregated Schools in Northern Ireland.* Appletree Press.

Osborne, R.D. (1986). *Segregated Schools and Examination Results in Northern Ireland: Some Preliminary Research.* Educational Research, 28(1).

Osborne, R.D., Miller, R.L., Cormack, R.J. and Williamson, A.P. (1988). *Trends in Higher Education Participation in Northern Ireland.* Economic and Social Review, 19(4).

Spelman, B.J. (1975). *Developments in Post-Primary Education in Northern Ireland: a Research Perspective.* The Northern Teacher, 11(4).

Wilson, J.A. (1983). *Developments in Secondary and Further Education in Northern Ireland.* The Northern Teacher, 14(1).

Education in Northern Ireland 397

Figure 1: Capital expenditure on education, Northern Ireland, 1980-1 to 1990-1.

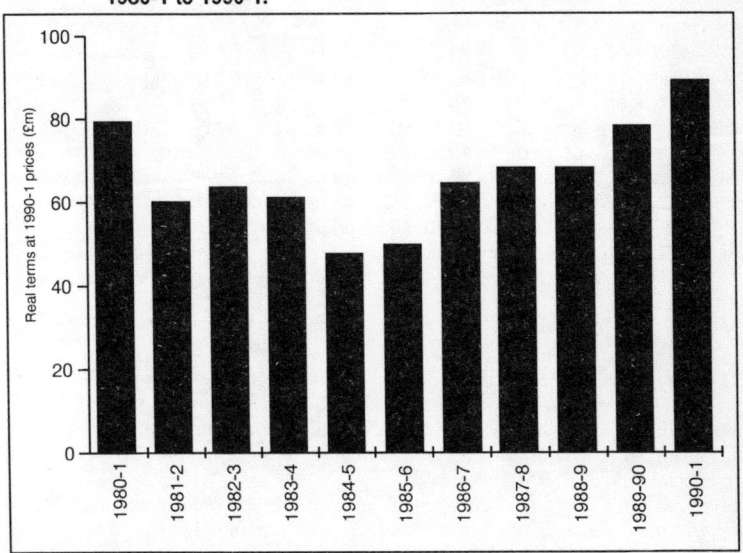

Source: Department of Education, Northern Ireland (various)

Figure 2: Highest qualifications of leavers from all schools, Northern Ireland.

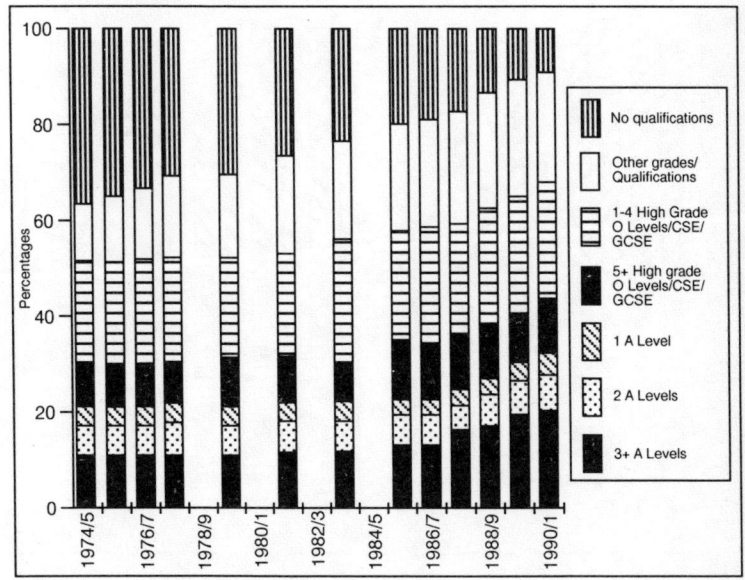

Source: Department of Education, Northern Ireland (various)

398 *Insights into Education and Training*

Figure 3: Highest qualifications of leavers from grammar schools, Northern Ireland.

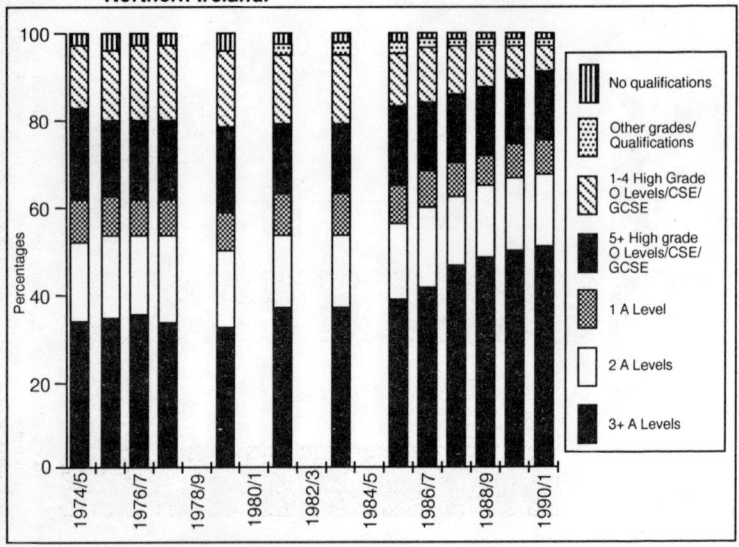

Source: Department of Education, Northern Ireland (various)

Figure 4: Highest qualifications of leavers from secondary schools, Northern Ireland.

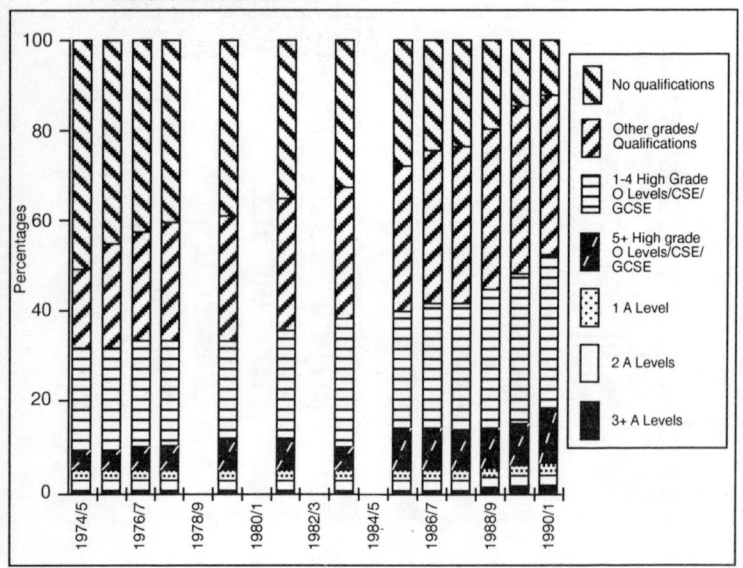

Source: Department of Education, Northern Ireland (various)

Education in Northern Ireland 399

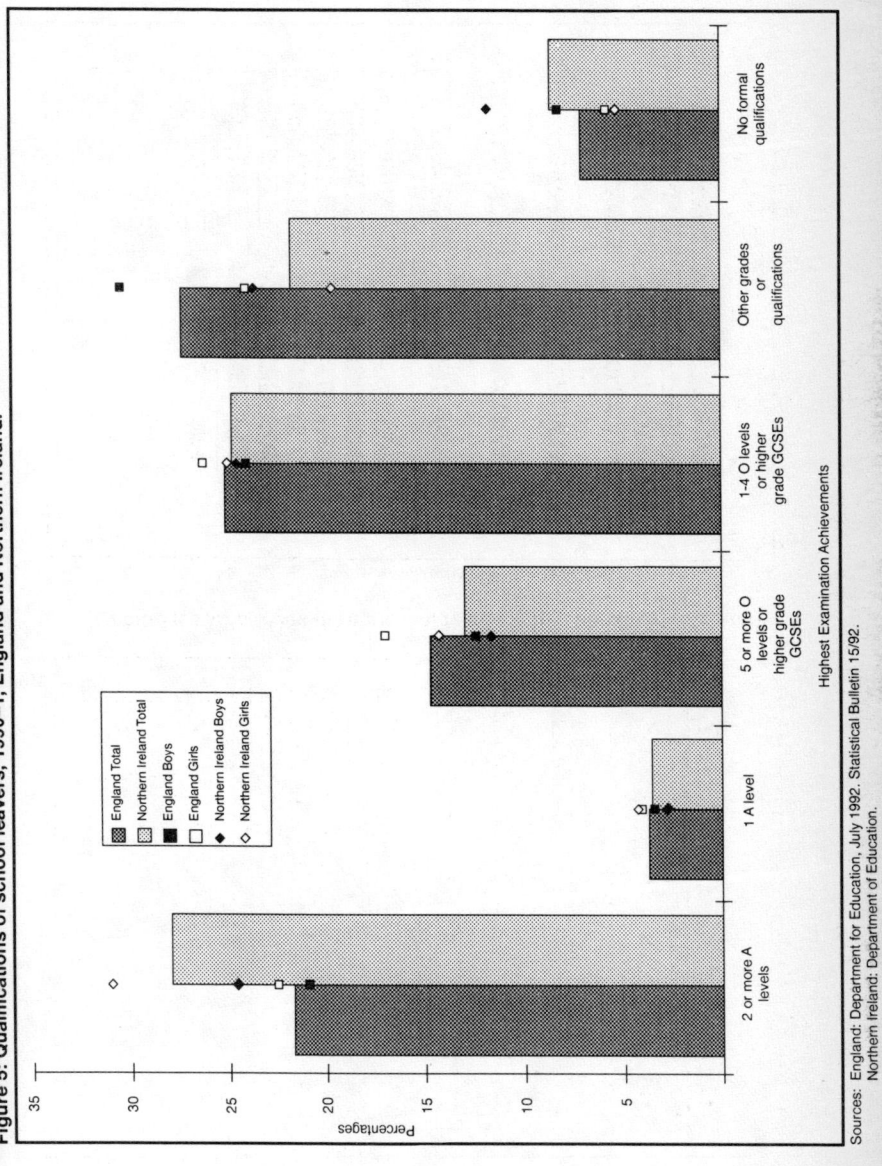

Figure 5: Qualifications of school leavers, 1990–1, England and Northern Ireland.

Sources: England: Department for Education, July 1992. Statistical Bulletin 15/92.
Northern Ireland: Department of Education.

400 *Insights into Education and Training*

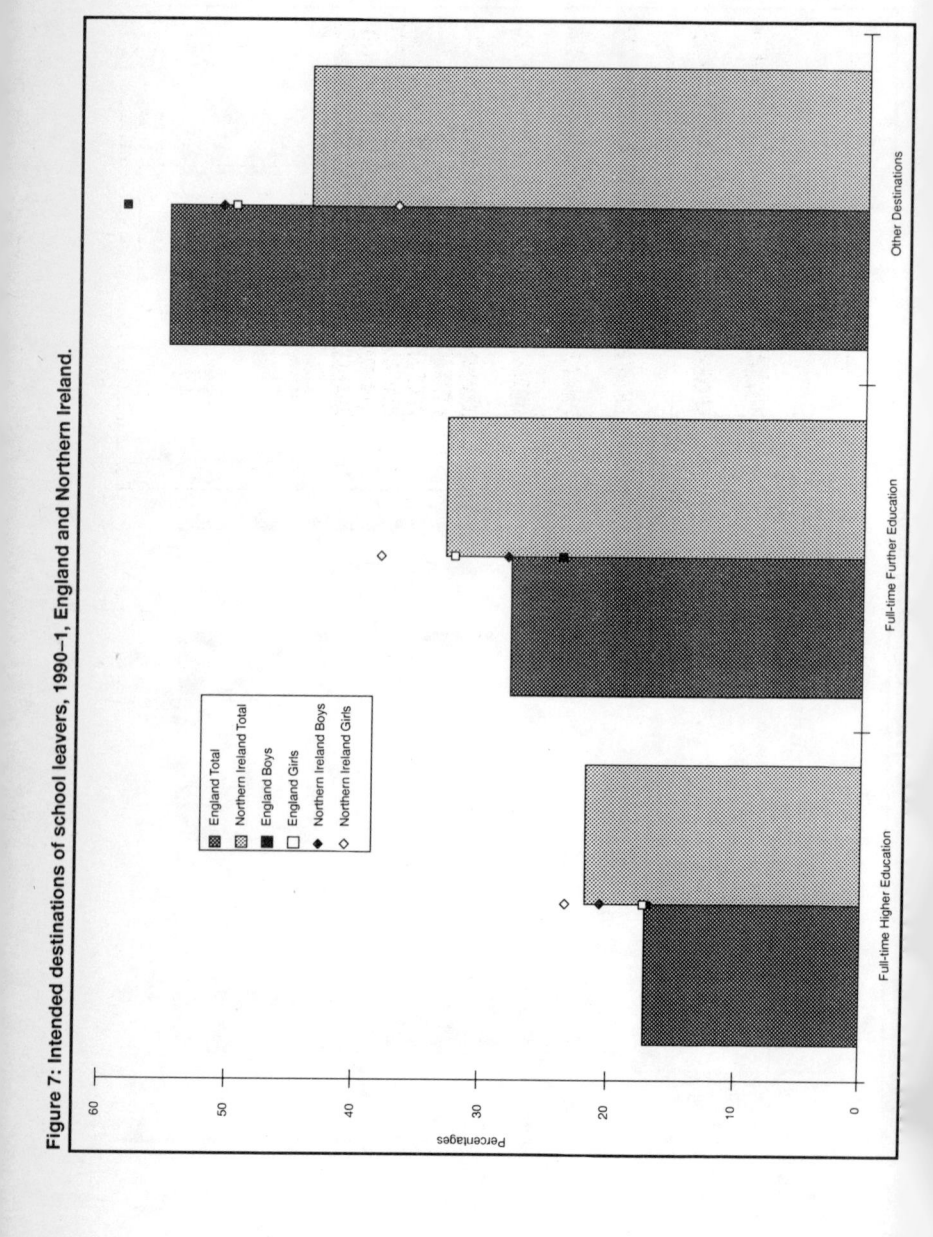

Figure 7: Intended destinations of school leavers, 1990–1, England and Northern Ireland.

Figure 6: Destinations of school leavers, Northern Ireland.

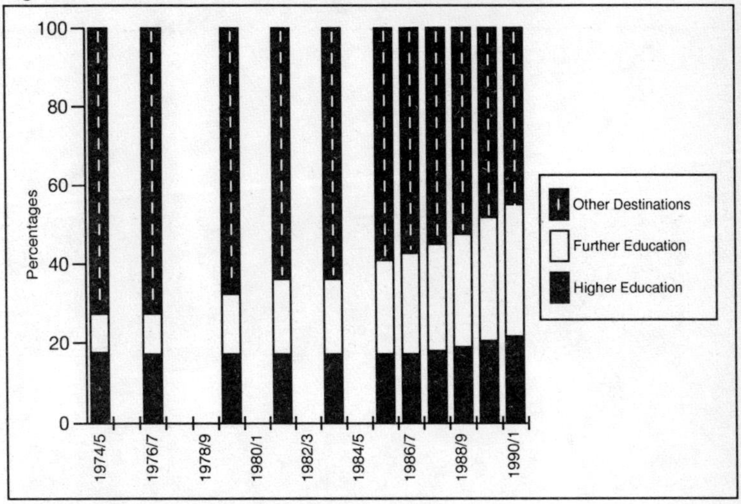

Source: Department of Education, Northern Ireland (various)

29. Independent Schools

Position Paper by Josh Hillman for the National Commission on Education, January 1993.

Recent trends in independent schools

Introduction

Before 1870, all schools in Britain were private, that is, independent from the State. In that year, the growth of the maintained sector began, with the State attempting to plug the gaps between private, voluntary and charitable provision. As in most other countries, Britain's education had mainly been provided by churches and other charitable bodies, but Britain was unusual in eventually incorporating the bulk of denominational schools within the maintained sector. Legislation in 1870, 1902 and 1944 has resulted in a situation where maintained denominational schools now contain 17% of all pupils. This has meant that Britain has a relatively small private sector in education and this simple fact is a major reason for the élite nature of those schools. In most countries private schools provide for religious, ethnic and cultural diversity. In Britain they provide an often high-powered preparation for a significant proportion of the future members of high-status occupations. However, most of the argument about the role of private schools in the reproduction of élites relates mainly to a small group of schools, often known as the public schools, a minority within a minority.

'Independent schools' is an umbrella term for a sector which incorporates such diverse institutions as the old 'public schools', many of the former direct grant schools, preparatory schools, a wide range of religious, special and small schools. There are different regional patterns with former grammar schools more concentrated in the North and boarding schools in the South-East. Independent schools do not make up a coherent sector and the schools are as much, if not more, in competition with each other as with the maintained sector, and meanwhile headteachers are keen to provide distinctive educational experiences in this 'marketplace'. Indeed, it is probably fair to say that quality varies as much in the independent sector as in the maintained sector. Certainly, there is more diversity of character in the independent sector than in the maintained sector, with the latter unable to provide such a range as Eton, Summerhill and the various proprietary and profit-making private schools dotted around the country. Having said that, although the Headmasters' Conference (HMC), an association formed in 1871, represents a small minority of independent schools, it has been said that they 'form a model for much of the independent sector'.[1]

Independent schools
In 1992, there were 2,271 independent schools in England, that is, 8.4% of all schools. Of these, 1,372 were members of the Independent Schools Information Service (ISIS) of which 233 were in HMC and 245 were in the Girls Schools Association (GSA). The total number of independent schools has been roughly stable for the last six years, having fallen by 70 in the previous three years. This, however, conceals the fact that the number of independent schools with fewer than 150 pupils has fallen (in particular those with fewer than 50 pupils), while the number of schools with more than 200 pupils has risen substantially. This is a continuation of what Halsey describes as 'the tail and not the head . . . withered'. Although most independent schools claim some sort of religious affiliation, this is a *raison d'être* in only a minority of the schools and rarely does it constitute a link between schools through a central religious organisation. The independent sector is much smaller in Scotland (3.1% of schools in 1989–90), Wales (2.9% of schools) and Northern Ireland (1.4% of schools).

The survival of independent schools depends on both parents meeting their costs and governments permitting their existence.[1] Their popularity has probably been increased by the phasing out of selective maintained schools, overt ideological support from the present Government for the independent sector, and serious concern among parents about declining quality in the maintained sector. Although independent schools are often described as a traditional sector, they have had to respond quite fundamentally to post-war developments in the education world in that:

- higher staying-on rates in the maintained sector and increased access to higher education have put more academic pressure on independent schools;

- parents, governors and others have become much more interested in what goes on in schools and as a result they have had to become more open institutions;

- some of the hallmarks of independent schools have faded and continue to do so, including the combined cadet force, chapel, the house system, the study of Classics, the cult of athleticism, corporal punishment, fagging;

- the demands of institutions such as universities, the civil service, the armed forces and business have changed in terms of their expectations of the quality and type of previous educational experience;

- there have been threats of changes in government policy on independent schools, including abolition.

Independent schools have responded to these developments partly by concentrating more on academic outcomes, as will be seen later in the paper. There has also been a closing of ranks within the sector as a defence against threats. ISIS was founded in 1972 and the Independent Schools Joint Council (ISJC) in 1974, with identical memberships, to provide facts and advice to member schools and to publicise the value of independent education and the dangers of state monopoly to the nation.

ISJC also provides a service of accreditation of new member schools, review and inspection of member schools and consultancy. The requirements vary across the associations within ISJC; for example, HMC have their own validation processes. Inspection teams are led by a former HMI and include a practising head from the same association as the school. HMI itself has been able to inspect any independent schools as and when it chooses, and has often done so, with two or three independent schools a year receiving full inspection reports. OFSTED's four-year cycle will not be obligatory for independent schools, but there has been some discussion of inspection for schools with assisted places.

Independent school pupils

In 1991, 565,900 pupils attended independent schools in England, if those under the age of five are included, that is, 7.4% of the total school population. Table 1 shows trends in the last forty years in independent schools' share of pupils of different ages.

Table 1: Pupils in independent schools in England (1951-1991), by age group.

Percentages (and numbers)

	Age group of pupils			
	5-10	11-15	16+	All 5+
1951	6.9 (249,400)	11.1 (266,800)	37.9 (49,600)	9.2 (565,900)
1961	5.7 (222,700)	8.8 (276,300)	28.1 (71,100)	7.8 (569,400)
1971	4.0 (192,200)	7.7 (254,100)	18.2 (76,100)	6.1 (519,900)
1981	4.7 (187,300)	6.6 (250,400)	17.8 (68,200)	6.2 (501,000)
1991	5.4 (193,700)	8.6 (239,800)	18.7 (77,200)	7.6 (510,700)

Source: Derived from Statistics of Schools (England).

The table shows a decline in the share of the independent sector in all three age groups up to the late 1970s, a trend which had begun well before the Second World War (there had been 2½ million pupils in private schools in the 1850s).[2] There was a large fall in absolute numbers for the age group 5–10, despite the increase in the birth rate, mainly as a result of the growing popularity of maintained primary schools. The absolute numbers for 11–15 fluctuated around a mean, but the share fell due to increases in the size of the cohort, the raising of the school leaving age in the early 1970s and almost certainly greater selectivity and rapid increases in fees in independent schools. In many senses there was little incentive for successful independent schools to expand in response to increased demand.[3] For the 16+ age group there was a large rise in absolute numbers but a fall in the share, for the same reasons as for the 11–15 age group, coupled with substantial rises in staying-on rates in maintained schools. The independent sector share increased in all three categories in the 1980s, partly because social classes I and II expanded as a proportion of the whole population and did not experience such rapid falls in school-age population, but also due to government policy, as will be seen later in the paper.

Of the 565,900 pupils in independent schools in 1991 (the figure including those under the age of 5), 47% were girls but of the 105,170 boarders only 37% were girls. Boarders have declined as a proportion of independent school pupils from 23.1% in 1984 to 18.6% in 1991, with a corresponding shift from full boarding to weekly boarding. Over half (52%) of pupils attending independent schools in 1991 were in the South East (including Greater London) whereas only 35% of pupils overall were in this area. In the South East 10.9% of pupils were in independent schools as compared with 3.6% in the North and 7.6% nationally. The figures for Wales (2.6%), Scotland (4.3%) and Northern Ireland (0.3%) were all well below the UK average. Scotland is also interesting for the variance within its own borders. In 1987, 11.5% of pupils in Lothian were in independent schools (17.2% of secondary pupils), whereas the corresponding figures for Borders, Highlands and all of the islands were well under 1%. It is also worth noting that in Scotland there are twice as many pupils in independent secondary schools as in independent primary schools,[4] a much wider ratio than that shown for England in Table 1.

The most interesting and controversial demographic information about independent schools relates to social class, but it is here that the statistics are most difficult to obtain. The only large-scale inquiry used the results of the Oxford Mobility study to investigate the social class of males of different ages in 1972 who had been to independent schools.[5] It was found that although the middle class was in a large majority in independent schools and the working class in an even larger majority in maintained schools, in all eight social class categories the majority had been to maintained schools. In the HMC schools 66.7% of pupils had parents in the 'service' (professional and managerial) class as compared to 13.7% in the whole population, 27.0% in the 'intermediate' (clerical, artisan, technician) class as compared to 31.4% in the whole population, and 6.3% in the working class as compared to 54.9% in the whole population. The Public Schools Commission (1968) found that over 90% of pupils had parents in professional or managerial jobs and only 1% had parents who were manual workers.[6] Kalton (1966) found that the direct grant schools were just as socially selective, although here of course the social selection is more indirect, resulting from greater selection by ability.[7] Fox (1985) surveyed boys' schools only and found that 69% of boys had fathers in the service class with the manual class almost absent.[8]

International comparisons of private schools
Few attempts have been made to compare private sector provision of education in the UK with other countries. The studies that do exist show a remarkable diversity, both in the size of the sector and in its role.[9] In the Netherlands, 72% of children at secondary level attend private schools, as compared to 2% in Sweden. In between this are the USA (12%),

Canada (4.8%), Australia (25.8%) and West Germany (5.8%).[4] However, comparing these figures is unrewarding since such factors as state support for private schools, private contributions to maintained schools, state provision of religious education, and the degree of élitism in private schools differ so much between countries. Private schools must be seen in a historical and sociological context and in particular in relation to the maintained sector. Comparing private schools in isolation across countries is not a worthwhile or meaningful exercise.

The boundary between independent and maintained schools

So far, this paper has made the implicit assumption that there are two distinct school sectors: maintained and independent. This has never been the case, with for example, state grants to private charity schools in the nineteenth century, central government scholarships to direct grant schools after 1926 and payment of private fees by LEAs ever since LEAs were established. Also, many denominational schools receive large contributions to the upkeep of the fabric from church funds. It is a particularly false assumption in the 1990s, by which time central government policy has created new categories of schools to bridge the divide, has increased government expenditure on private education and has encouraged private expenditure within the maintained system to the extent that some have argued that it is neglecting its statutory responsibilities. It is difficult to quantify the total extent of these cross-subsidies and it is not clear how accountable the expenditure on both sides is. All of these developments are part of what has been called the 'blurring of the boundary' between maintained and independent provision,[10] which, by reducing a psychological distinction, has almost certainly made the concept of 'privatisation' in education[11] acceptable to more people.

New categories of school

- City Technology Colleges are a small group of independent schools established by the Government, where recurrent costs are paid by DFE but the schools are totally independent of the LEA and are not obliged to follow the national curriculum or to follow other schools regulations. Parents are expected to agree to keep their children at a CTC until they are 18. The original intention was that Government would provide an equal share of capital costs with charity and companies, and would pay recurrent costs.[12] Lack of interest amongst larger corporations meant that the outside sources were only expected to contribute 20% of capital costs, once the CTCs were proposed. Even this reduced target was not reached by some of the CTCs, as was shown in a written answer in Parliament (12/3/92). The Government spent £58 million on recurrent and capital costs in 1990–1. There are now 15 CTCs and this looks like being the final total.

- Grant-maintained schools are non-fee-paying maintained schools, subject to the national curriculum, which are in many senses modelled on independent schools. Indeed in Margaret Thatcher's original speech announcing this new policy she said that they might be able to charge fees as well as operating their own admissions policies. In the end this was not the case, although their freedom from the locally-elected tier of government, and the extremely powerful role of the governing body, particularly in respect of budget control, make them a type of half-way house. Some have even seen their establishment as an interim step towards full privatisation.

Public subsidy of independent schools. I: the Assisted Places Scheme

The origins of APS
The initiative that encouraged the APS policy originated from the direct grant schools in the early 1970s when their fear of abolition became real. The APS, in a sense, restored the

principle of the direct grant schools whose grants were indeed phased out from 1975, with 120 of the 170 schools in England and Wales opting for independence. These schools were surviving very well by the beginning of the 1980s, but the Conservative Government felt that they, and other independent schools, should extend their provision to 'help the academic needs of pupils whose talents might not otherwise be catered for'. In fact, the APS was intended to go beyond the direct grant system in improving the mechanism by which children from poor homes might attend academically excellent schools.

Direct grant schools came about in 1926 when a Circular decreed that schools could not receive grants from both central and local government. They were the grammar schools which received grant directly from central government and children could transfer to them at age 11 either on scholarship awards or on payment of fees. They had to have at least 25% places as free places for pupils not previously in direct grant or independent schools. This figure was always exceeded and was over 60% in 1970, with a quarter of the others only paying partial fees. Direct grants were phased out by the Labour Government from 1975 and the schools were given the choice of opting for independence or joining the maintained sector. Of the 50 which chose the latter course, nearly all were Catholic schools that had offered substantial majorities of free places.

The Scottish equivalent of direct grant schools were called grant aided schools of which there were 29 in 1969 and whose grants were also phased out in 1975. There were some major differences between the two types of school. Grant aided schools did not have to set aside a fixed number of places for local authorities and 80% of pupils paid full fees and 13% paid part of their fees in 1968.[13] Also, grant aid was not driven by a per capita formula but rather by non-capital expenditure. Moreover, their grants were phased out much more rapidly from 1975 and many were struggling by the time of the change of administration in 1979. In many senses grant aided schools were much more part of the independent sector than direct grant schools and were seen to offer independent education at reduced prices.[4]

Like direct grant and grant aided schools, the APS creates a bridge between the independent and maintained sectors, but covers a wider and more varied range of schools. The former direct grant schools provide around half of the places and certainly before their abolition had been more socially mixed than other independent schools. Some direct grant schools could be found in prosperous neighbourhoods backed by rich foundations with highly selective intakes, but many were located in relatively deprived areas such as in Lancashire. The social class composition of APS pupils is similar to that of pupils in direct grant schools in the 1960s, but the latter included around 30% of pupils paying full fees. It is therefore likely that the social background of those with scholarships at direct grant schools was more representative than APS pupils. The APS is, in this sense, less successful than the former direct grant schools in widening access to high performing schools.

The principles of APS
The APS in England and Wales was part of the 1979 Conservative manifesto and of the 1980 Education Act. Its aim is to transfer high ability pupils from maintained schools to selected independent schools, helping their parents with tuition fees and expenses on a means-tested basis, using a sliding scale for 'relevant income'. Its introduction in 1981 represented the only education policy of the period that increased government expenditure, which is ironic in view of the chronic underfunding of the maintained education sector at that time.

The APS was presented not as a policy to support independent schools but rather to help individual pupils by extending parental choice, restoring real academic opportunities to bright children and protecting them from the perceived 'levelling-down' of comprehensive reorganisation. In this sense it is supposed to be a scholarship ladder, although it is clear that the privatisation element of the policy remains a powerful motivating force for the Government.

Having said that, there is a sense in which the APS represents a nationalisation of scholarships to independent schools. It has had a substantial effect on participating schools' own bursary funds: some have suspended their own schemes entirely, leaving the capital to accrue interest for future contingencies (such as helping APS parents if the scheme is abolished); others have used their bursary funds for boarding fees for APS pupils; others have used the funds to subsidise parents of pupils already in the schools, who are not eligible for APS but are not considered well-off. This substitution of funds is a murky area which may well need attention, given that all APS schools have charitable status.

The selection of the individual schools to participate in the scheme was a fairly rigorous process with the 470 schools that applied in 1980 being graded with HMI advice. However, the planning of the overall pattern of assisted places does not seem to have been done on a rationally planned basis. Decisions were made quickly about individual schools that applied according to range and size of sixth form, examination outcomes and percentage going on to higher education. There are signs that the scheme has been aimed particularly at former direct grant schools (as noted earlier), areas where there are no grammar schools and inner cities. There are many independent schools that receive substantial support through APS provision, and in some, as many as half of the pupils benefit from APS. The scheme has often been described as a 'lifeline' for some schools (Griggs, Walford).[14] However, it is not just self-preservation or financial opportunism that have encouraged the independent schools to support the scheme. It is also their desire to be more associated with the maintained sector and the mainstream of educational policy.

The APS scheme operated differently in Scotland, where comprehensivisation had advanced more rapidly. As a result, parental choice was stressed more than academic selection. Other differences were the inclusion of the last two years of primary school (partly due to the high age of transfer) and the absence of fixed entry ages. It should also be noted that APS gives a higher level of support for independent schools in Scotland than in England and Wales, since it is funded according to the school-age population of Scotland, despite the fact that the independent sector is much smaller in Scotland than in England and Wales.

Facts and figures
Nearly 300 independent secondary schools now take part in the scheme in England and Wales, with 33,296 places available in the academic year 1991/2. Nearly all of the available first year places were taken up in that year. Over 60% of the pupils admitted through the scheme are taken by the former direct grant schools. The scheme cost DFE £78 million in the last financial year (1992–3). The DFE has a 'residual control' over the fee levels of the participating schools.

The pupils

- *Ability*. Although the Government has been active on the financial side of the scheme it has taken a very *laissez-faire* attitude to selection of pupils. As a result, all participating schools have different approaches to the selection of APS pupils and there is no overall information on this subject. Some schools have used the same selection criteria that they use for full fee-paying pupils. Some schools have made allowance for the lack of coaching and other ways in which potential APS pupils may be disadvantaged, by requiring a lower standard of entry. Other schools have a higher threshold for APS pupils. This relates only to those pupils recruited from the maintained sector. Following a compromise with the independent schools, the terms of the APS require a minimum of 60% of places to be awarded to pupils who have received at least the whole of the previous year of their schooling in the maintained sector. Most schools have not met this target for sixth form entry, but the Government has allowed a trade-off between age groups, to allow schools to remain within the terms of the scheme.

- *Parental income.* There may be some abuse of the means-testing arrangements at the margins, where bursars are not in a position to ascertain income where the parent is self-employed, cohabiting or receiving funds from an ex-spouse. However, in general, the scheme seems to be targeted well at those with low income. In this sense, the policy is preferable to a return to direct grant schools. In 1991/2, for example, the parents of 41% of pupils entering the scheme received full remission of fees which means that they had incomes of less than £9,000. In 1987, the average income of parents of APS pupils was £8,516, compared with a national average income for the equivalent year of £11,073. However, the parents of one third of the APS pupils in that year had above-average income.

- *Social background.* There have been various studies of the social background of APS pupils. MORI (1991), however, found that 60% of their sample were in the clerical and professional classes and 16% in the unskilled manual classes or with the lowest level of subsistence.[15] They also found that in 32% of cases income was less than £8,715, with school fees paid entirely by the Government, and that 7% of pupils were Asian. The social class figures were not out of line with those of earlier (and smaller) surveys. Douse (1985), using a small sample of 200, found that no pupils came from ethnic minorities but 19% had a parent who had been recently or was currently unemployed, 41% came from single-parent families, 32% had one or more parents who were graduates and 84% could be categorised as middle-class.[16]

Table 2 overleaf is from Edwards et al (1989).[17] It shows the occupational status of the fathers of APS pupils in a sample of pupils and in a sample of parents.

The researchers also found that 40% of the pupils were from one-parent families, as compared with a figure of less than 10% for pupils in general. They found examples of parents with new partners with very high incomes. They also found that 68% of mothers and 51% of fathers had had an independent or selective education and that 50% of fathers

Table 2: Occupational status of fathers of APS pupils.

Percentages of sample

	Service Class I	Service Class II	Intermediate Class III	Intermediate Class IV	Intermediate Class V	Working Class VI	Working Class VII	Unpaid
As reported by pupils	11.9	38.1	10.2	15.3	8.5	6.8	2.5	6.8
As declared by parents		54.4		27.8			6.6	7.8

Source: Derived from Edwards, A. and others (1989)[17], Tables 8.3 and 8.4.

and 60% of mothers had had a formal post-school education. Over one third had five or more O levels (compared to 16% in a national sample) and just under one third had one or more A levels (compared to 8% in a national sample). It is notable that nearly 70% of single parents of APS pupils had been to academically selective schools. Edwards et al attempt to explain this by suggesting that class-related social, cultural and educational factors inform the choice of opting into the APS and even more importantly enable some parents to recognise its possibilities and execute them more advantageously. For this reason, income is much too limited as evidence for disadvantage.

There is some evidence that a substantial minority of APS pupils would have attended independent schools anyway. Douse gauged from headteachers that 30–40% would have done so,[16] and the Assisted Places Committee found in 1984 that a third of new APS pupils were already in independent schools.

There is a further piece of evidence to suggest that the APS may not be targeted at those who would benefit most. MORI, in a survey commissioned by ISIS, found in August 1991 that 44% of adults aged 18 or over were aware of the APS.[18] There were large social class and regional differentials. There was much greater awareness amongst those in social classes AB (69%) and C1 (56%) than amongst C2 (37%) and DE (28%). There was greater awareness amongst those in the South (53%) than amongst those in the North (38%) and the Midlands (39%).

Implications of APS practice

There seems to be some truth in the rather extreme formulation that APS provides 'real financial assistance to relatively impoverished but educationally aware members of the *petit bourgeoisie*'.[1] Even the HMC were worried that the purposes of the scheme would be frustrated if the beneficiaries turned out to be confined to 'distressed gentlefolk'. It is clear that the notion of disadvantage used in the original justification of policy has been narrowed to refer only to income. Edwards et al have pointed to the 'unreliability of "relevant income" as a guide to the cultural and educational situations of families', partly caused by the increase in the number of single-parent families.[17] The APS has also benefited many children from the 'submerged middle class' already with substantial 'cultural capital' such as the clergy who may lack gross income but certainly not other social and cultural advantages. The APS may well be another case of the middle class taking advantage of a reform ostensibly introduced for the benefit of more socially disadvantaged groups.

The reasons for parents opting into the scheme are usually related to academic selectivity rather than independence or social exclusiveness, and although there is no research evidence that shows any advantage of the APS for individual pupils, it is very likely that the selection does help those pupils (see NCE Briefing No. 7) as does the fact that on average, pupils in independent secondary schools have over 65% more spent on them than their counterparts in maintained schools (see page 432).

There are strong arguments, however, why the scheme might be harmful for the maintained system as a whole. The sponsored withdrawal of some of the most academically able pupils from the maintained sector not only lowers the performance of maintained schools, but reduces their ability to attract those parents concerned about the 'critical mass' and makes the possibility of improved performance in the future more difficult to achieve. There may even be cases where, to fend off this competition, comprehensive schools have to concentrate appeal on the most able pupils, thus distorting their own intentions. In short, the APS introduces selection by the back door out of the maintained system, reducing the chances of comprehensive schools having a full range of abilities amongst their pupils, thus exacerbating their problems. It might also impede the planning of LEAs and in extreme cases make maintained sixth forms unviable.

On a wider scale, the APS is an indictment of the maintained system by government in the sense that it gives a signal that the maintained sector is second best and inadequate for bright pupils. The scheme can only be said to be complementary to maintained schools if one believes comprehensives cannot cater for bright children. Otherwise, it competes with maintained schools and may even raise standards in independent schools, widening attainment differences between the sectors. The fact that the scheme represents state funding of independent education makes the transition to independent education less traumatic for parents, breaking down moral as well as financial disincentives for transfer. The APS operates on a fairly small scale, but aside from its direct detrimental effects on individual maintained schools, it may also have indirect effects in sapping the morale of the maintained sector.

It might be said that at £78 million a year (less than 1% of all government expenditure on secondary schools) the APS is not worth arguing about and that any attempt to reduce or remove the support that it gives would be seen as so undesirable by independent schools that it might damage relations between the two sectors. But as specific education expenditure by central government, it is not such a small amount. In the same year (1992–3), DFE expenditure on Grants for Education Support and Training (GEST) for raising standards in inner city schools was £4 million, and for training for all special needs in schools was £4.6 million. Public expenditure on APS, if transferred to the maintained sector and applied sensibly, would result in significant improvements.

Public subsidy of independent schools. II: charitable status

Independent schools and charitable status
All independent schools, unless they are run for profit, are eligible for charitable status. In 1985, 56% of independent schools had charitable status. Since 1974 they have been financially accountable to the Charity Commission rather than the DFE. The change was not just for reasons of efficiency but was intended to make the control judicial and separate from policy considerations. As the Conservative spokesman said at the time, the change was intended 'to make the public schools immune from political interference'. Some schools, such as Eton and Winchester, are exempt charities and cannot even have their accounts scrutinised. Exemption (which is also enjoyed by GM schools) is not from the law of charity but from the supervision of the Commission. The accounts of GM schools are scrutinised by the National Audit Office.

Benefits for the schools
Independent schools are exempt from paying VAT, regardless of their status. Charitable status allows the following tax concessions: rates relief; exemption from corporation tax, income tax, capital gains tax, inheritance tax, stamp duty; tax concessions for donors; and tax relief for covenants.

Independent schools can also receive free advice from the Charity Commission on how to maximise their financial benefits. It has been estimated that the loss of charitable status would add approximately 5% to costs. Whether this would be fed through into fee levels would depend on the economic climate. Of course, the ability to make up this loss through fund-raising would be reduced. ISIS have estimated the financial benefits of charitable status (tax concessions etc.) to the independent school sector to amount to £41.3 million, which they claim is more than counterbalanced by charitable giving by the schools (mainly bursaries) amounting to £55.4 million.[19]

Is private education a charitable purpose?
Parliament has never legislated about the meaning of charity: this has been left to the courts, with the Charity Commissioners undertaking the administration with case law guidelines. The 1601 Statute of Charitable Uses still forms the basis of an attempt to define a charity legally. Most defences of the charitable status of independent schools are expressed as tautologous phrases about the status quo. According to the Charity Commission there are three key characteristics of a charity;[20] a charitable purpose; assets assigned to that purpose; and protection of the purpose and the assets.

What exactly is meant by 'a charitable purpose'? Educational institutions or funds can be charities provided that they have the necessary element of public benefit which justifies the concessions to which they are entitled.[21] The implication of this in charity law is that the beneficiaries must be a subgroup of the general public, rather than a private group (i.e. one defined with reference to a particular individual or company), unless they are poor or in financial need. The key issue, then, is whether a sufficient section of the community benefits.

ISIS claim that a range of community needs is satisfied, for example SEN, specialist subjects, curriculum innovation and suchlike. But this argument ignores the fact that this is not a commitment to planned provision. Moreover, stressing this type of aspect of the charitable activities of independent schools mistakes the basis of the present legal position, which is that schools are charities because of their wider goals rather than the ways that they function or the specific needs they address. The issue of charitable status is not just about financial concession but is also about broader ideological and symbolic support and status. Yet most attacks on charitable status have concentrated on who benefits rather than what activities should be defined as charitable.

Enquiries into charitable status

- In 1965, Anthony Crosland established the Public School Commission, which as the Newsom Commission (including two public school headteachers) reported in 1968 and proposed the abolition of all charitable privileges for independent schools.[6] They stated that there was no justification for the benefits, and that an anomaly had arisen through the complexities of English charity law. The institutions, and indirectly those that pay fees to them, are being subsidised by the tax-payer despite the fact that they are in general relatively wealthy. For example, endowments mean that fee-payers are being relieved by tax-payers of some of the true cost of what they are buying, while the tax-payers are not even aware of the contributions they are making. The reforms that the Commission suggested were not backed by strong political will.

- The 10th Report of the House of Commons Expenditure Committee criticised the failure to define a charity and suggested that the overriding criterion should be the adoption of 'purposes beneficial to the community'.

- The Goodman Committee did not recommend any great changes, although Ben Whitaker's minority report argued that charitable status should be concentrated on institutions concerned with the deprived and the disadvantaged, so as to prevent the redistribution of wealth from the poor to the rich.

Despite the fact that all schools have the same basic purpose, that is to educate the pupils that have been entrusted to them, some schools have charitable status but others do not. For example, two independent schools may seem, from a superficial viewpoint, to be similar in their objectives, but one might be a profit-making business and the other a charity. Moreover, the Charity Commission does not see the education of the wealthy as being any less valid a charitable purpose than the education of the poor. Indeed, Robin Guthrie, the Chief Charity Commissioner, has stressed that charities are defined by their purpose, e.g. to advance education, and there need be no reference to the poor.[20]

Public subsidy of independent schools. III: other government expenditure

Aided Places Scheme
This scheme was also introduced in 1981 and provides assistance with fees for pupils at six music and ballet schools which is means-tested but more generous than Assisted Places and is also available for boarding fees. In 1992/3 the DFE spent £6 million on this scheme.

LEA place-buying
There are a number of pupils in independent schools with some or all of their fees paid for by Local Education Authorities (LEAs). Many of these have special needs. The number was substantially reduced in 1976 by forcing authorities to seek approval from the Secretary of State for each place. While most were approved, fewer were offered in practice. The 1980 Education Act reversed this by allowing LEAs to pay for as many places as they wanted without even having to submit the plans to the Secretary of State.

In 1990–91, LEAs spent £174 million on places in independent schools. In January 1992, 7,633 pupils in ISIS schools were receiving contributions to fees from LEAs. Of these, 5,514 were in HMC schools. These figures may seem high but they represent a rapid fall in recent years. For example, the corresponding figure for ISIS schools in 1982 was 19,904. The reduction has been driven by the introduction of APS and also by financial constraints on LEAs. However, the rate of reduction of LEA expenditure on places for independent schools has been less than the rate of increase of APS since the introduction of the latter.

Although there is often not adequate maintained provision, LEAs sometimes use boarding, denominational and special needs (including being gifted) as reasons for supporting pupils where there *is* adequate maintained provision. Some LEAs also subsidise independent schools through fares for visiting parents overseas, use of advisers, loans and meals provision.

Boarding school allowances
The children of military and diplomatic personnel are entitled to free education including boarding fees, irrespective of whether or not they are stationed overseas. Provision of places in LEA boarding schools has been cut by nearly one half in the last twelve years due to financial pressure, resulting in a substantial increase in the number of pupils in independent boarding schools receiving allowances. In 1988, 16,287 pupils in ISIS schools were receiving contributions to fees in this way, as compared to 10,416 in 1982. Public expenditure on boarding school allowances in 1990–91 was £115 million.

Teachers
Independent schools do not make any contribution to the cost of training the teachers that they recruit. Many of their teachers also use the state superannuation scheme, and participate in in-service education and training provided by the State and government-sponsored international exchanges.

Other subsidies
There are various ways in which independent schools receive help from other government departments. For example, some of the funds from schemes such as City Challenge, City Action Teams and Task Forces have supported projects in independent schools. The Department of Trade and Industry has funded schemes providing computers for all schools, including independent schools, even those that already have substantial facilities.[22]

Private expenditure on maintained schools

In recent years, the assumption that statutory education provision in the maintained sector should be provided by government funds has been challenged. HMI reports have shown very clearly that maintained schools are under-funded and that repairs and maintenance, books and other essential teaching and learning materials have particularly suffered. One of the most important consequences of this is that maintained schools are increasingly relying on financial and other contributions and donations from parents and charities and from business and industry. There have been numerous newspaper reports of schools fund-raising to prevent teacher redundancies and of charities such as Children in Need and Telethon being asked for money by schools for basic educational requirements.

It was estimated in 1991 that each year parents and trusts contribute between £80 million and £100 million towards the support of the maintained system, with a further £50 million to £130 million coming from industry and commerce. Many schools use such contributions for essentials such as teachers' salaries, buildings and equipment and there is evidence of an inequitable distribution of these funds in favour of schools in richer areas.[21] It is likely that this trend is reducing the psychological distinction for parents between paying for education in independent and maintained schools.

Outcomes of independent schools

Why do some parents choose independent schools for their children?
The choice invariably relates to the outcomes of independent education, whether they be academic, social, cultural or eventually financial, but the research evidence on this question is extremely limited. What emerges from the existing literature is that there are essentially two types of parents: the traditional and the pragmatic. The former do not question their choice whereas the latter have made a more informed

decision and would use the maintained system if they felt that it was better. The shift away from social exclusiveness related to the growth of the less expensive end of the market, and the growing predominance of day pupils may have reduced deep-seated inter-generational adherence to independent schooling.[5] The fact that there is a fair amount of movement between the independent and maintained sectors suggests the dominance of the pragmatists, although it has been argued that the phasing out of grammar schools might gradually polarise the sectors.[23]

- Fox (1985) found that one third of her sample of parents had an unquestioning commitment to independent education and that the most common reasons for choosing independent schools amongst the remaining two-thirds were 'getting on better in life', 'providing academic advantage' and the ability to 'develop character and foster discipline'.[8]

- Johnson focused on those parents who could be said to have opted out of the maintained system and found that the most common reasons for choosing independent schools were the phasing out of selective schools and the associated perception of comprehensive schools as not being able to offer an adequate education for children of high academic ability.[24]

- MORI carried out a survey of parents of children in ISIS schools and found that the most common reasons for choosing independent schools rather than maintained schools were a higher standard of education, dissatisfaction with maintained schools, better discipline and more individual attention.[25]

- West interviewed a small sample of parents of pupils in nine primary schools in Islington who had considered independent secondary schools.[26] She too found that quality of education was the most frequently given reason for choosing independent schools, followed by the high ability of their child, higher expectations in independent schools and reputation and experience of maintained schools.

There is a growing emphasis on academic achievement as measured by examination results by both users and providers of independent education,[1] and there is plenty of anecdotal evidence to back this up. Indeed, there is evidence that this is a trend that was occurring as far back as the 1930s.[27] Independent schools have responded to the growing pragmatism evident in parental choice by losing much of their educational and ritualistic peculiarities and are likely to stress exam success. Maintained schools have been obliged to follow this trend and this has led, in the view of some commentators, to 'a genuine convergence of the experiences of schooling'.[23] However, this has not been to the benefit of maintained schools. MORI found in 1991 that 54% of adults believe that educational standards are lower in maintained schools than in independent schools, and 11% believe they are higher in maintained schools.[18] The breakdown into social classes is interesting here. It shows that 63% in social classes A, B and C1 believe that standards are lower in maintained schools, as compared to 50% in C2 and 47% in D and E.

Examination results
Independent school pupils, at an aggregate level, achieve significantly better examination results both at 16 and 18. Statistics on examination attainments in England are given in Appendix A. It is interesting to note that the 13,700 16-year-olds who attended grammar schools within the maintained sector performed even better than the independent school pupils. Of the grammar school pupils, 88.1% achieved five or more grades A–C and only 1% had no graded results. For A level achievements of all school leavers in 1991 there is an even more marked pattern of higher independent school attainment. A higher proportion of the 14,600 leavers from grammar schools (77.1%) achieved at least one A level as compared to the independent schools, but fewer achieved three or more (54.8%).

Trends in these figures over the last 30 years show significant improvements in A level performance in both the independent and maintained sectors. The former started from a much higher baseline and has made particular headway in achievements of three or more A levels, the key to the high prestige universities. In this sense, inequality between the sectors has increased. Trends in this key variable using odds ratios measure the relative chance that pupils entering independent or maintained types of schools will achieve three or more A levels. Between 1966 and 1981 these odds widened, although during the last decade they have started to fall again, mainly due to extremely rapid increases in staying on in maintained schools during that later period.

The independent sector's share of certificates for 16-year-olds has fallen over the last 30 years, as has (to a lesser extent) its share of those leaving school with 1 or more A levels. However, in the last 20 years the share of the independent sector in school leavers with three or more A levels has risen. Such comparisons overestimate the success of the independent schools in high performance at A levels, because the figures relate only to school leavers and hence ignore the increasing number of students who take A levels at FE colleges. In the 1980s there was a substantial shift of A level students within the maintained sector from schools to colleges, and when this is taken into account, the rising share of the independent schools remains but is not quite as high.

Post-16 participation in education and training
There is a higher staying-on rate at age 16 amongst independent school pupils. It should be noted that the staying-on rate for the 13,700 16-year-olds at grammar school, included in the maintained sector, was similar (83.2%) to the independent school figure. It has been suggested that it is this difference in staying-on rates that explains the superior examination performance of the independent sector, rather than superior teaching or greater resources.[3] Over a quarter of the age cohort of 16-year-olds are now in FE colleges, not far short of the proportion in maintained schools, and many of these are studying for A levels. Independent schools specialise

almost purely in A levels. This year, maintained schools have introduced BTECs and so any comparison of the outcomes of the independent and maintained sectors will have to go beyond the single outcome of A levels.

Participation in higher education
Many studies have demonstrated how pupils at independent schools are more likely to aim for, and enter, higher education. We have already seen that the performance in exams at 16 and the related decision to stay on for A levels favours the independent schools. However, even those who do take A levels in independent schools achieve better scores than their maintained sector counterparts, as shown by the A level performance of those applying to universities in 1991. Unfortunately, equivalent figures are not available for the former polytechnics, although we do know that in 1991, 7.8% of applicants and 5.2% of those admitted to polytechnics were from independent schools. The disproportionately high number of successful applicants to universities from independent schools is not due to any bias in the selection process between independent and maintained schools; the acceptance rates of each of the categories of point scores are similar between the sectors. This is not, however, the case for those applying from FE or HE, but that is not the subject of this paper.

School differences between independent and maintained schools in university entrance are small when social and initial ability factors are controlled for. Both the Robbins and Franks Reports found that the standards of Oxbridge entrants from maintained schools were higher than those from independent schools in terms of A level grades.[28] They also found differences between former independent and maintained school pupils in the distribution of degree classes, with independent day schools having a disproportionately high number of Firsts, maintained schools having a low number of Thirds and independent boarding schools a low number of Firsts and a high number of Thirds. Since those reports, Oxbridge has become more meritocratic in the sense that it places a high premium on A level grades, generally accepting those with very high grades.

Oxford University appointed the Dover Committee which reported in 1983. The Committee examined the A level scores of university entrants and found that there should be more pupils from maintained schools in Oxford.[29] This does not necessarily reflect any bias: the high fliers from maintained schools might not necessarily see Oxbridge as the best option, as compared to those from independent schools. The Committee did show, however, that applicants from maintained schools in general were less likely to choose Oxbridge and that the success rate amongst those who do apply is lower. Since we do not know how the A level scores of individual students relate to their applications and admissions we cannot form a precise view about the meritocracy of Oxbridge. However, what the Dover Committee did show was that the differences in outcomes between former maintained and independent school pupils once at Oxbridge, noted by Robbins and Franks, had vanished.

Elite occupations
Much of the criticism of independent schools has been concerned with the domination of positions of power in British society by the privately educated, and a multitude of studies has shown the grip that major public schools have had on recruitment to élite occupations.[30] Table A 2.11 in the statistical appendix illustrates this. Although the phenomenon has declined in some occupations (such as the civil service and the clergy) it has actually deepened in others (such as some of the armed forces). The 1984 figures are confirmed in a separate study[31] which shows high proportions for the judiciary (83%), ambassadors (69%), bishops (59%), bankers (70%) and civil servants (50%).

To posit that these professions are biased in favour of the privately educated or even that independent schools in some sense prepare pupils for élite positions immediately runs up against a series of problems. First, those who reach these positions might have done so regardless of the type of school that they attended, on account of their social class, family background or connections. Second, trends in recruitment operate with a long time-lag: for example, it takes around 30 years for a graduate to become a permanent secretary. The recent expansion of higher education and other changes will not show through for some time. Third, the success of independent schools in providing members of élite occupations, shown in the table, may be as much to do with the success of independent schools in getting pupils into Oxbridge, from where the same studies show an equally significant proportion of élite professionals are recruited.

Explaining the outcomes of independent schools

The previous section showed substantial differences in several outcomes of independent and maintained schools. This section examines some of the possible explanatory factors. The higher performance of independent schools in terms of raw examination results is due to a complex blend of input and process factors which it is almost impossible to analyse, but some discussion is necessary.

Pupils that enter the schools

The most crucial task in any attempt to explain differences in outcomes of schools is to isolate school effects from the effects of social class and family background and, related to this, to take account of the initial ability of the pupils entering the schools. There has not been a serious attempt to compare independent and maintained school pupils with similar family and home backgrounds.

What we do know is that there are substantial differences in the intakes of independent and maintained schools. The independent sector takes on pupils of a higher level of ability in general since so many independent schools (especially secondary schools) have entrance examinations which can be extremely rigorous. NCE Briefing No. 1 states that 'studies typically find that about half of the variation among pupils in attainment in public examinations can be predicted from, or statistically "explained", by pupils' attainment on entry to secondary school'. This would suggest that the selective powers enjoyed by many independent schools have a substantial influence on examination results a few years later. This is enhanced by the APS which takes highly selected pupils out of the maintained sector, adds to the success of the independent sector and thus widens the difference between the two.

Ability of pupils at 11 or 13 is highly correlated with social background indicators such as parental occupation and education, household size, and characteristics of neighbourhood. These are 'also correlated with progress' of pupils (NCE Briefing No. 1). Earlier in this paper, some indication of the social background of pupils in independent schools was given and it was shown that this has hardly been affected by the introduction of the APS. It seems clear that independent schools have a significant advantage over maintained schools in that their pupils are of higher ability to start with, and have better conditions to make progress, such as parents who are more likely to be in work and to be better educated, better living conditions, more space to do homework and suchlike.

Unit costs

In general, independent schools are much better resourced than maintained schools. Unlike maintained schools they have been able to cope with rising costs by increasing their fees well above the rate of inflation. For example, school fees in ISIS schools (80% of independent school pupils) increased in 1991–2 by 12.0%, having gone up the previous year by 12.6%. The Retail Price Index for those years rose by 4.1% and 9.1% respectively. Average termly fees in January 1992 were thus £1,258 for day pupils and £2,875 for boarders.

These fees varied widely, from £350 to £3,850.

These fees cannot be contrasted with unit cost figures for maintained schools in order to compare expenditure on pupils in the two sectors. The independent school fees do not take account of the substantial endowment funds possessed by some schools, support from the Government through APS and suchlike, nor profits enjoyed by the schools, and whether they are directed towards shareholders or towards reinvestment in the fabric of the school.

A comparison of unit costs in independent and maintained schools is shown in Table 3, using the figures from the Government's Expenditure Plans Departmental Report for the maintained sector and the annual survey of costs in independent schools that is undertaken by a firm of chartered accountants.

Table 3: Unit costs in schools, 1983-84 to 1990-91, England.

£

	1983-4	1984-5	1985-6	1986-7	1987-8	1988-9	1989-90	1990-1
Primary								
maintained	770	802	840	941	1003	1077	1177	1262
independent	1104	1347	1398	1543	1584	1848	2010	2317
Secondary								
maintained	1025	1094	1165	1345	1547	1691	1837	1926
independent	n/a	n/a	1715	1908	2314	2556	2872	3206

Sources: DFE Statistical Bulletins 13/92 and 13/93; MacIntyre and Co., Independent School Cost Surveys.

The overall increase in unit costs in primary schools during the period was 64% for the maintained sector and 110% for the independent sector, increasing the difference between the sectors from 43% to 84%. The overall increase in unit costs in secondary schools during the period 1985–86 to 1990–91 was 65% for the maintained sector and 87% for the independent sector, increasing the difference between the sectors from 47% to 66%.

Pupil-teacher ratios
The most important advantage for independent school pupils that stems from the differences in unit costs mentioned above is in the amount of contact that they have with teachers. Unfortunately, it is not possible to compare class sizes in the independent and maintained sectors directly, but figures are available for pupil-teacher ratios in schools which give a good indication (Table 4).

Table 4: Pupil-teacher ratios by type of school.

	England	Wales	Scotland	N Ireland	UK
Maintained					
primary	22.2	22.3	19.5	22.8	22.0
secondary	15.5	15.4	12.2	14.9	15.2
Independent (all)	10.8	9.8	10.4	11.0	10.7
All schools	17.3	18.2	15.2	18.1	17.2

Source: Regional Trends 1992.

The table provides only a rough guide, because there is no figure for all maintained schools which would be comparable to the figure for non-maintained schools (which includes both primary and secondary age pupils). However, Mortimore and Blatchford point out in NCE Briefing No. 12 that the overall effect of the independent schools on the 'all schools' row is minimal, reducing the figure for England from 17.4 to 17.3. Therefore, we can conclude that on average teachers in maintained schools in the United Kingdom each have approximately 60% more pupils than their counterparts in the independent sector.

Teachers
There is no evidence available on the relative quality of teaching in the independent and maintained sectors. It is probable that the better-known independent schools are able to be more selective in their appointment of staff. This is partly because many good teachers are likely to be attracted by the

better conditions of these schools, in terms of the motivation of the pupils and the physical conditions to work in. It is also partly due to the fact that some independent schools are able to attract teachers with salaries above the maintained sector scales, as was found by the Interim Advisory Committee on teachers' pay in 1988. In a small sample, most schools were sticking fairly firmly to the scale, but several were paying as much as £5,000 more.

Walford has argued that in many senses teachers in independent schools have more of the characteristics of professionals than their counterparts in the maintained sector.[32] They are often called 'masters' and 'mistresses'; they are more likely to be Oxbridge-educated and have higher degrees; they are more likely to write books; they have a lower turnover. However, Walford suggests that in recent years 'deprofessionalisation' has occurred amongst independent school teachers (as with maintained school teachers) with a greater emphasis on examination outcomes, 'curriculum delivery' and management, with financial constraints on schools, and with a narrowing gap in salaries between independent and maintained school teachers.

What remains the case is that teachers in independent schools probably have higher expectations of their pupils than their maintained sector counterparts and, as is well known, higher expectations themselves are often translated into attainment.

Working environment and facilities
Much has been said in recent years about the poor physical condition of school buildings in the maintained sector. Independent schools have not really had to face this problem. Comparable figures are not available but it is unlikely that in the maintained sector anything like £546 per pupil was spent on new buildings and improvements to buildings and equipment in 1991. This was the case for ISIS schools, with a figure of £836 for HMC schools, although it should be noted that a number of these schools are boarding schools.[33]

Independent schools also enjoy superior facilities, both for teaching and for extra-curricular activities such as sports, music and drama. In 1985 the ratio of computers to pupils was 1:260 in maintained schools and 1:26 in independent schools (Walford).[14] It is likely that similar differences would be noted in science laboratories, CDT centres and books.

Independence
All the causal factors for differences in outcomes mentioned so far have related either to the pupils entering independent schools or to the resources of those schools, together with some relating to teachers. Apart from some of the points about teachers, none of these advantages relate to the independence of independent schools per se. This is an important point, because advantages, if any, relating to independence are the only ones that cannot be transferred wholly to the maintained sector (although GM status is a partial attempt to do so).

This paper can only tentatively suggest some of the possible advantages in this area that are enjoyed by independent schools, although attempts are being made to introduce some into the maintained sector and some could just as easily be seen as disadvantages:

- governing bodies are more powerful, but nothing is known about the differences in the quality of governing bodies in the independent and maintained sectors;

- freedom from government constraints on curricular and pedagogical innovation;

- ability to expand or reduce size, negotiate contracts, spend less than income and invest the difference, and transform own character.

The effect of independent schools on maintained schools

Earlier sections compared the outcomes of the independent sector with the maintained sector and suggested some factors which might account for the difference. This section adds a new dimension by suggesting that the independent sector may itself have effects, both positive and negative, on maintained schools. There has been a fair amount of debate about whether independent schools are competitive with or complementary to the maintained sector. In general, it can be said that the positive effects of independent schools relate to their complementary nature and the negative effects to their competitive nature, although some would claim that competition should raise maintained school standards.

Positive effects

- *Raise overall standards* and thus spur on the maintained sector to better performance. There may be an element of truth in this, especially now that outcomes of schools are becoming so well publicised and parents encouraged to use this information to help their choice of schools. However, the outcomes in which schools 'compete' are limited and are biased against maintained schools, which have very different intakes of pupils and also a wider range of post-16 courses.

- *Prevent a state monopoly on education* and thus ensure choice and diversity of provision. It is true that a monopoly is prevented but there is nothing to prevent choice and diversity within the maintained sector, as the Government seems keen to emphasise at present.

- *Allow innovation* which can cross over into the maintained sector (e.g. computer education, new teaching techniques), although this, of course, is not one-way.

- *Provision of types of education that are scarce or unavailable in maintained schools.* Some independent schools make provision for children with boarding, artistic and other special needs. There are also a number of independent small schools, whose *raison d'être* is to be small rather than independent. In all of these cases the reason that independent schools are complementary is restricted provision of a certain type of education in the maintained sector. Meanwhile, in mainstream education, independent and maintained schools are certainly in competition for pupils.

- *Sharing of facilities.* ISIS gathered information in autumn 1991 from 1,088 independent schools (over three quarters of its members) about the extent to which they share their facilities with other schools and the local community. Eighty-four per cent of the schools had charitable status; and 4.9% of all schools reported that maintained schools used their facilities once or more a week, 18.2% less than once a week and 77% never. Of those that allowed maintained schools to use their facilities, 65.1% did not charge, 18.6% charged a nominal fee, 7% charged for cost only and 9.2% charged for profit. The most used facilities were sports and physical education facilities, where 8.1% of schools allowed maintained schools to use the facilities once a week or more, and 23.6% allowed use less than once a week. The corresponding figures for educational facilities were 1% once a week or more, and 7.2% less than once a week. The survey also showed that around one in ten schools were involved in co-operative arrangements with maintained schools, such as shared classes, shared use of teachers and teacher exchanges. Unfortunately, the survey did not examine independent school use of maintained facilities.

- *Saves money for the maintained sector* by educating the children of parents who have already contributed to maintained education through the tax system. ISIS continually stresses that 'at least £1 billion a year is saved . . . in day to day running costs alone' by parents with children at independent schools paying twice. This is a rather curious argument which ignores the wider social benefits of education, for it assumes that a certain portion of taxes is destined for the education of the tax-payers' own children. In a sense, it implies that those without children should ask for their money back for the taxes that they have paid which were not spent on the education of children that they do not have!

Negative effects

- *Take valuable resources away from the maintained sector*, such as motivated pupils, good teachers, parents willing to get involved in the school and speak out for the maintained system with a personal incentive, and of course government money. 'The private market starves the comprehensives of the resources they need to attain high standards'.[5]

- *Dangers of undermining the comprehensive system* by attracting high ability pupils away, with a vicious circle effect on the parents of other high ability pupils. The extension of this is the sort of situation that is seen in some of the larger cities in the United States where a middle-class 'flight' away from the inner city maintained schools to independent schools has taken place, lowering standards in those maintained schools and increasing differentials in outcomes between the two sectors. There are signs of this happening in this country; indeed, the OECD has recently shown that school performance differentials are larger in England than in any other OECD country.

- *Narrow the ground on which maintained schools are judged.* More and more, maintained schools are being forced to compete with independent schools on terms of performance very much set by the latter. For example, the publication of post-16 achievements in this year's school performance league tables was restricted to A levels, despite diversification of courses in the maintained sector and the unsuitability of A levels for the majority of children. Even more worrying is the danger that promotion of parental choice, celebrated most fervently in the independent sector, will relegate the social aspects of schooling.

- *Perpetuate the class system* by transferring economic status, social position and influence from generation to generation. 'One of the central charges levelled at the public schools . . . is that they are integral to the process by which a closed ruling class perpetuates itself over time'.[23] It might be questioned whether schooling exercises a significant independent influence or whether it simply provides a context for the 'obtaining and augmenting of social capital'. However, independent schools do allow the segregation of a significant proportion of future decision makers and children of current decision makers. This creates the situation where these decision makers have little knowledge of, or commitment to, state education. There is a related danger of independent schools being isolated from the rest of society. For example, it has been shown that a substantial majority of teachers in independent schools themselves went to independent schools.[7]

- *Undermine the confidence and morale of the maintained sector.* In many senses, the maintained sector, in competing with the independent sector, is fighting a losing battle due to its relative shortfall in the resources that go to make a good school. Its inferior performance in terms of raw examination results promotes the view that something that is paid through private means is better.

The way forward

Conclusions
This paper shows that independent schools are a small but highly élite sector of schools in Britain, although there has been a significant blurring of the distinction between independent and maintained education in recent years. On several important measures, independent schools in aggregate perform much better than maintained schools, and the paper outlines some of the factors which might have contributed to this discrepancy, and suggests that the independent sector itself may have had an effect on the performance of the maintained sector.

It is often argued that independent schools have an influence on the education system, and indeed on much wider aspects of British society, that is wholly disproportionate to the size of the sector.[34] If one were designing an education system from scratch it is highly unlikely that one would even consider the possibility of having some children educated in independent schools and some in maintained schools. However, that is the situation that we are in now, and there is no doubt that some independent schools provide very fine educational experiences for those who are fortunate enough to attend them.

The central problem faced by the Commission is to make recommendations about independent schools that are both desirable and politically feasible. This paper has shown that independent schools and 'quasi-independent' schools cause some fundamental problems for the maintained system and it is suggested that the situation could worsen. However, short of the abolition of independent schools, there is very little that can be done to affect this situation, which goes beyond tinkering within the context of co-existence. The political and legal obstacles to abolition are well known, although it should be stressed that private education, where it conflicts with the rights of others (as certain sections of this paper imply happens at present), is not a fundamental right. An important fact that should be borne in mind is that in 1991, 70% of adults disagreed with abolition (although it is notable that this figure has fallen gradually from 78% in 1983).[18] More than half of supporters of the Labour Party in 1991 disagreed with abolition.

The Commission may well make recommendations that, if put into practice, would boost the performance of maintained schools and enable them to compete more effectively with the independent sector. Most of these recommendations will be improvements to the maintained system and will not relate directly to independent schools. However, the Commission will wish to consider ways of reducing government support for independent schools in order to make more of a 'level playing field'. There are two problems with accepting this type of solution too complacently. The first is that a revamped maintained sector and reduced government subsidy for independent schools is likely to 'crowd out' the weaker rather than all independent schools, with an even more élite independent sector as a result. Second, and related to this, the stronger independent schools will be able to respond to reductions in government subsidies and in the differential in resources between the sectors, by finding other ways of preserving their advantage, such as raising their fees, thus enhancing their élite status further and restricting the social background of their intake. What is certain is that if great improvements were made to the maintained sector, there would be a strong possibility of a virtuous spiral occurring and independent schools would have to become a sector offering much more of a clear alternative to the maintained system.

Recommendations
The following is a list of possible recommendations that might be considered.

1 The APS should be phased out. First, it gives a signal from government that maintained schools are not adequate to cope with the education of pupils of high ability. Second, it extends the process (in this case with government sponsorship) by which independent schools attract children of high ability from maintained schools, thus restricting the range of ability of pupils in maintained schools through the undermining of 'critical mass'. Third, it is not well targeted at children from deprived backgrounds: some of the children would have attended independent schools regardless; and a large proportion of the others, although they may well have parents with income below the national average, are relatively advantaged in social and cultural terms. Fourth, central government expenditure on the scheme, although relatively small, could be more usefully applied to improving maintained schools, especially if targeted carefully and spent efficiently. The phasing out of APS should not be an isolated policy but should be accompanied by measures to improve the maintained sector, in particular its capacity to educate pupils of high ability.

2 LEAs should be prohibited from paying independent

school fees except where there are special needs (as determined by the 'statement' procedure) and no satisfactory alternative exists.

3 The charitable status of independent schools should be examined in the context of the charitable status of schools in general. It is obviously undesirable that LEA-maintained schools cannot have charitable status while independent schools can. To extend charitable status to all schools risks an unequal distribution of the benefits amongst schools to the detriment of schools that are deprived to start with. But to remove the charitable status of independent schools might give them less incentive to legitimise that status through less socially divisive activities. Some independent schools, especially SEN schools, do deserve the subsidies entailed by charitable status, but there is certainly room for improvement in the trade-off between charitable status and community benefits from independent schools. There are clearly problems with the law of charity as it stands which go way beyond the scope of this paper.

4 A wide-ranging investigation of boarding provision is necessary. In particular, LEAs' cutbacks in maintained provision should be questioned, given the growing dependence of the armed forces and the civil service on independent provision.

5 There should be serious consideration given to extending the national curriculum and national assessment arrangements (in whatever form they may be recommended) to independent schools to ensure that the 'entitlement' involved is extended to all children in the country. This would also encourage organisations such as HMC and GSA to take an active interest in national systems of curriculum and assessment. The argument that independent schools alone should have freedom to innovate and experiment is special pleading which is insulting to maintained schools.

6 There should be more formal arrangements for inspection of independent schools to make them more

accountable for public funding, and for greater application of state regulation and quality assurance to those schools.

7 The CTCs should be nationalised. Private sources have accounted for only a small amount of their capital funding and none of their recurrent costs. Their powers to select pupils should be removed and they should be encouraged to share their specialist scientific and technological facilities with maintained schools.

References

1 Salter, B. and Tapper, T. (1985). *Power and Policy in Education.* Falmer Press.
2 Glennerster, H. and Wilson, G. (1970). *Paying for Private Schools.* Allen Lane.
3 Halsey, A., Heath, A.F. and Ridge, J.M. (1984). *The Political Arithmetic of Public Schools.* In 32.
4 Walford G. [ed.] (1989). *Private Schools in Ten Countries: Policy and Practice.* Routledge.
5 Halsey, A., Heath, A.F. and Ridge, J.M. (1980). *Origins and Destinations.* Clarendon Press.
6 Public Schools Commission (1968). *First Report.* HMSO.
Public Schools Commission (1970). *Second Report.* HMSO.
7 Kalton, G. (1966). *The Public Schools: a Factual Survey.* Longman.
8 Fox, I. (1985). *Private Schools and Public Issues.* Macmillan.
9 Boyd, W.L. and Cibulka, J. [ed.] (1989). *Private Schools and Public Policy: International Perspectives.* Falmer Press.
James, E. (1987). *Public Policies Toward Private Education.* World Bank.
Mason, P. (1992). *Independent Education in Western Europe.* ISIS. See also 4.
10 Walford, G. [ed.] (1991). *Private Schooling.* Paul Chapman.
11 Pring, R. (1988). *Privatisation.* Educational Management and Administration, 16,2.
12 Walford, G. and Miller, H. (1991). *City Technology College.* Open University Press.
13 Walford, G. (1987). *How Important is the Independent Sector in Scotland?* Scottish Educational Review, 19,3.
14 Griggs, C. (1985). *Private Education in Britain.* Falmer Press.
Tapper, T. and Salter, B. (1986). *The APS: a Policy Evaluation.* Journal of Educational Policy, 1,4.
Walford, G. (1990). *Privatisation and Privilege in Education.* Routledge.
15 Independent Schools Information Service (1991). *Assisted Place Pupils.* ISIS.
16 Douse, M. (1985). *The Background of APS Students.* Educational Studies, 11, 3.
17 Edwards, A. Fitz, J. and Whitty, G. (1989). *The State and Private Education:*

an Evaluation of the APS. Falmer Press.
18 MORI (1991). *Attitudes to Independent Schools*. British Public Opinion (Nov. 1991).
19 Davison, R. (1992). *Good Neighbours*. ISIS.
20 Mountfield, A. (1992). *The Charitable Status of Schools: What Needs To Be Done?* Directory of Social Change.
21 Mountfield, A. (1991). *State Schools: a Suitable Case for Charity?* Directory of Social Change.
   Robson, M. and Walford, G. (1989). *Independent Schools and Tax Policy under Mrs Thatcher*. Journal of Education Policy, 4,2.
22 Walford, G. (1987). *How Dependent is the Independent Sector?* Oxford Review of Education, 13,3.
23 Tapper, T. and Salter, B. (1984). *Images of Independent Schooling*. In 32.
24 Johnson, D. (1987). *Private Schools and State Schools: Two Systems Or One?* Open University Press.
25 MORI (1987). *Attitudes of Parents Towards Independent Education*. Gabbitas, Truman & Thring.
26 West, A. (1992). *Choosing Schools*. Centre for Educational Research, LSE.
27 Heward, C. (1984). *Parents, Sons and their Careers*. In 32.
28 Franks Report (1966). *Report of the Commission of Inquiry into the University of Oxford*. Clarendon Press.
   Robbins Report (1963). *Report of the Committee on Higher Education*. HMSO.
29 Dover Report (1983). *Report of the Committee on Undergraduate Admissions*. Oxford Colleges Admissions Office.
30 Boyd, D. (1973). *Elites and their Education*. NFER.
   Reid, I., Williams, R. and Rayner, M. (1991). *The Education of the Elite*. In 10.
31 Reid, I. (1986). *The Sociology of the School and Education*. Fontana.
32 Walford, G. (1984). *British Public Schools: Policy and Practice*. Falmer Press.
33 Independent Schools Information Service (1992). *Annual Census*. ISIS.
34 Labour Party (1980). *Private Schools: a Labour Party Discussion Document*. Labour Party.
   Labour Party (1981). *TUC-Labour Party Liaison Committee Statement on Private Schools*. Labour Party.
   McClelland, V.A. (1986). *Private and Independent Education*. Aspects of Education 35, University of Hull Institute of Education.
   Roker, D. (1992). *The Private Sector of Education in Britain*. Educational Studies, 18,3.
   Sampson, A. (1992). *The Essential Anatomy of Britain*. Hodder & Stoughton.

30. Managing the Education System

Extracts from Written Evidence to the National Commission on Education by the Society of Education Officers, February 1992.

Introduction

The Society of Education Officers welcomes the establishment of the Commission and the opportunity to make some initial comments to help the Commission with its work. The Society is particularly pleased to see the wide-ranging remit and the lack of association with any particular political group. The Society very much identifies with the Commission's vision and targets.

The Society considers the following general points to be extremely relevant:

- The Commission needs to step back from the populist assumptions that guide so much contemporary comment about education. Assertions need to be challenged and the true facts established.

- The Commission will need to be in the business of changing our national culture in two main respects: first, we tend to undervalue education and training in this country, and secondly, we have the unfortunate national characteristic to denigrate what we have – even when much of it is good and provides a solid basis for change.

- The high political profile of education in recent years is in many ways welcome. However, the Commission will need to watch the downside of this trend – i.e. simplistic approaches to short-term 'fixes' and the tendency to devalue professional advice. At present there is great pressure for politicians to 'do something' even if they do not know what and to whom!

- The Society hopes that the Commission will point to the continued value of people and organisations working in partnership (rather than in competition) for the good of the education service and those served by it. There is an urgent need for a clearer definition of the roles of some of the major partners, especially the Department of Education and Science, local education authorities (LEAs) and school governing bodies.

- The Commission will need to be wary of the rosy view that we had a golden age of education and that we need to replicate this. *What we need to do in the future has to be both better and different* – previous education and training systems since the war have not placed this country in a leading position amongst our competitors.

- The Society would like to see any major proposals emanating from the Commission fully justified and backed by evidence, and taking a long-term view of the country's needs.

- The Society is unhappy with a number of aspects of the current tendency to apply 'market forces' to schools and colleges. Whilst not against healthy competition, the Society is acutely aware that market successes will also mean market failures. We cannot afford any failures where pupils and students are concerned.

- Pupils who are disadvantaged and have special educational needs require particular attention.

- Any changes to the infrastructure of the education service, and particularly LEAs, need to be treated with caution and from an evolutionary, not revolutionary, point of view. LEAs, over the years, have been responsible for initiating many major innovations, e.g. financial devolution to schools. It is the Society's view that there is a strong case for locally responsible and accountable bodies somewhere between Whitehall and the individual school/college. If this tier of management is removed and/or changed too quickly it will be a recipe for chaos and a block to the introduction of any necessary changes to education.

- In the Commission's introductory paper there is much talk, and rightly so, of 'quality'. The Commission will have done a valuable job if it can make a major contribution to the definition of quality (as opposed to quantitative targets) and the definition of entitlement for pupils and young people.

- The Society believes that it is the role of the national education service to prepare children and young people for the multi-ethnic, multi-faith society which they will be entering, and to promote attitudes favourable to concepts such as equal opportunities, environmental awareness, personal, social and health education.

The future framework of management for schools

A basic framework of national government, local authorities (or successor intermediate bodies) and representative governing bodies with delegated budgets is necessary to run a coherent system.

The role of an intermediate body
The intermediate body (hereinafter referred to as 'local authority') need not be the present system of LEAs, but there needs to be something. Examples of functions that neither Whitehall nor individual schools can effectively cover include strategic planning and resourcing, special needs, curriculum support and advice, headteacher appraisal, inspection, admissions policy and the resolution of parental complaints and grievances.

The local community as a whole must have a say in the running and resourcing of the local school and college system.

The need for local democracy and accountability is fulfilled by an elected local authority.

Inspection and advice
The local authority must retain the right, indeed the duty, to inspect,[1] if necessary with national guidelines and subject to accreditation by Her Majesty's Inspectorate. In addition, local advisory services are important in the identification and dissemination of good practice. If the Government's new inspection arrangements and the trend to delegate more LEA budget to schools diminishes such services, it will be a major blow to good practice.

Partnership not market forces
The notion of unbridled market forces needs to be replaced by constructive partnerships of all the major players. The marketplace brings success but also failure. Young people cannot be allowed to fail.

Market forces, with money following pupils, are not necessarily factors that aid continuity and progression in education. In this area, there is no substitute for planning across the system as a whole. Continuity and progression can be enhanced by the existence of a local authority with a planning and co-ordinating function.

Danger of fragmentation
Current Government policy could easily cause the disintegration of the present system without an alternative system in place to promote continuity and progression.

We support full but sensible delegation to schools – not, however, a slavish adherence to delegating items better dealt with by a local authority and preferred as such by most schools.

Taking a wider view, the fragmentation of the school system down to individual institutions may not help European integration. Local authorities can develop European strategies for local areas and relate more easily to their equivalent bodies in Europe.

Co-operation between the independent and maintained sectors
Each sector should respect the other and feel able to share good practice. *Both* sectors should be subject to the same legislation on the national curriculum, assessment, the publication of examination results and inspection.

The very considerable resources owned by independent schools could be used more often to take forward developments that would be of use to all schools.

Policy on the curriculum and qualifications

Defining the national curriculum in subject terms is a major lost opportunity because it plays down relevance as opposed to breadth and balance, and undervalues cross-curricular themes. What has happened to the concept of a broad entitlement curriculum, which has been diluted of late, particularly by changes at Key Stage 4?

The Commission may wish to analyse why some groups are so concerned to retain 'A' levels in their present form. A modular system (as in Scotland) with parity of esteem for academic and vocational subjects is what the UK needs, both on educational and on economic grounds. 'A' levels do *not* constitute the required 'gold standard'. A Scottish or Baccalaureate approach – broader but still rigorous – is necessary. The Commission is recommended to examine the Higginson Report and recent CBI documents, as well as the experience of competitor countries: they do not justify support for the 'A' level system.

Managing the teaching profession

Teacher recruitment
The best people will not be attracted into teaching as a career until it has the status and payment commensurate with being a profession. Teachers' pay is simply not good enough, but

other matters like public esteem, teaching conditions and professional development opportunities are also important. The acid test of successful teacher recruitment will be when graduates are overheard saying: 'I am not sure I am good enough to be a teacher'. The job of teaching, done well, is extremely challenging and is vital to the wellbeing of the nation. It should be so recognised. In our view the formation of a General Teaching Council is long overdue. Government should take the lead in changing the national culture on attitudes to teachers. It must reverse its tendency to subject teachers to a barrage of both overt and implied criticism and to expose them to too much destabilising and rapid change.

Initial teacher training
The training of teachers needs to be a careful balance of academic study, child development and practical application. There is no doubt that the classroom experience element should be increased: this should include structured observation, working with small groups, and whole class work. However, 'training schools' should *not* take over the whole function of teacher training institutions in the higher education sector. There is a danger of 'de-professionalising' teacher training to the extent that teachers will be regarded even less as professionals and be seen instead simply as 'classroom technicians'. The expertise of the HE training institutions must not be lost. The assessment of teacher training should be carried out by tutors from the training institutions, a tutor from the school, and by the relevant classroom teacher. National guidelines would be helpful.

Professional development
Professional development is crucial not only for individual and career development purposes but also from the point of view of the development of schools. There should be a mix of development on the job, opportunities to attend events and courses with teachers from other local schools, and occasional chances to attend regional and national events, as well as to

take part in longer-term courses leading to accreditation. For those aspiring to management positions in schools, management development on a structured, LEA-wide basis should be available.

Professional development programmes need to take account of a wide variety of individual needs, for example to gain further qualifications, take a refresher course, retrain in new skills, or join a course for 'returners' to the profession.

Both schools and LEAs need resources at their disposal to provide in-service training opportunities. The delegation of all such resources to school level will be detrimental to overall provision and could lead to professional development becoming parochial. Funding arrangements should allow schools and local authorities freedom to relate professional development to their own strategic development plans.

Good schools

Good schools arise from good teachers, good resources and well motivated pupils and parents – given good backing by governors and local authorities and well managed by competent headteachers. *All* schools need to be good in this sense. Closing bad schools is no solution, as this wastes building resources and disadvantages pupils in the process. Research should be conducted into what constitutes a good school, backed up with facts rather than the current vogue for dogma.

Note

1 The Society believes that this should still apply, notwithstanding the introduction, from 1993/4, of new inspection arrangements administered by the Office for Standards in Education (OFSTED).

31. The Quality and Training of Teachers

Speech by Professor Eric Bolton CB to a National Commission on Education Conference in Shrewsbury, 30 January 1992.

The conditions for quality

Deciding which are the crucial factors influencing the quality of education is neither easy nor straightforward. There is a link between resources and quality, but it is complex and indirect; more money; more teachers; more equipment; more materials do not lead automatically to higher quality education. An adequate level of resources is nevertheless required, even though the meaning of 'adequate' varies from one aspect of the curriculum to another. For example, the effective teaching of physical sciences is difficult to envisage and achieve without adequate laboratories and sufficient equipment and materials to enable experimentation and application. Similarly the pressing need to equip our pupils and students with the knowledge and skills needed to gain competence and confidence in the use of the new information technology cannot be developed as fully as we now expect without equipment such as calculators, micro-computers, word processors or the software that goes with them.

So, resources do matter; they are important factors in quality education. But a fact constantly revealed by inspection, research and ordinary common-sense experience is that the most crucial factor at the heart of high quality learning is high quality teaching. Invariably, high quality teaching is synonymous with high quality teachers. Yet here again there is a link with resources. All teachers do better given appropriate resources. Yet poor teachers will not be made good simply by being paid more, or by being given additional and/or different resources. Good teachers can, for a time at least, overcome the most awful conditions and desperate shortages of resources. But they cannot, and/or will not, continue to do that indefinitely.

Sooner or later the constant uphill struggle, allied to a growing feeling of being undervalued, will militate against many good teachers persevering with high expectations in the face of inimical circumstances.

Types of teachers

What then are the characteristics of good teaching that impinge upon high quality learning by pupils and students? If they can be identified, can they be measured and/or assessed or appraised; and how, once identified, are they to be spread more widely through the system? Robert Witkin categorised teachers into three broad groupings as follows:[1] the utterly hopeless; the 'pied-pipers'; and the rest.

- *The utterly hopeless,* always a very small minority of the teaching force, are a kind of full-stop to any and all worthwhile developments in education. They should never have become teachers; have no feel for, or affinity with it and cannot be improved much, or at all.

- *The 'pied-pipers'* get their name from the poem by Robert Browning that tells in verse the story of the Pied Piper of Hamelin whose pipe-playing initially charms away the plague of rats affecting the town and then, when he is not paid for his work, he charms and leads away all the town's children. Thus pied-piper teachers, also very few in numbers, are those naturals, who are often idiosyncratic, and always charismatic, that children will follow anywhere. Once again there is little to be done with, or about such teachers: they can and do break all the rules and yet succeed, and they are as different from each other as chalk and cheese. They can sometimes be dangerous, like Miss Brodie in Muriel Spark's novel *The Prime of Miss Jean Brodie,* but they are always exciting, stimulating and challenging. It is the pied-pipers we remember in adult life when so many of us recall that particular teacher who changed our perception of ourselves, of our abilities and aspirations.

- *The rest* refers to the large majority of teachers who, like professionals anywhere, take their work seriously; want to do well in it; are interested in and concerned about their pupils and students, but teaching is not the be-all and end-all of their lives. They do not spend every waking moment thinking, talking and becoming better informed about education. It is this large majority of the profession that can be influenced and helped to enhance the quality of their teaching; to bring about desired changes in curricula; and to develop new and improved patterns for the organisation and delivery of teaching and learning.

Good teachers and good teaching

And so, leaving aside the utterly hopeless, and noting the presence of the pied-pipers (sustaining their efforts and curbing their excesses where we can), what seem to be the characteristics of good teachers and of good teaching capable of generalisation and of spreading more widely through the education service? From the welter of studies and evidence over time the following general characteristics emerge:

- they like children in general, though not all individual children equally, but set out to treat them all even-handedly;

- they are well informed about child development, physical, intellectual and emotional; and are conscious of the great range of individual variation, of progress and set-backs and of plateaus and sudden spurts that constitute human growth towards maturity;

- they know something about what they are teaching and they are interested in and enthusiastic about their subject. They are well qualified. Formal qualifications do matter as does teachers' willingness to keep up to date and well informed;

- they maintain high expectations of individual pupils and students in terms of behaviour and of performance, and place high value on qualities such as perseverance, rigour and integrity as well as upon imagination and creativity in their pupils' work.

These general characteristics link with observable processes and practices in class and lecture rooms as follows:

- good teachers are in control and, varied as are their ways of achieving this, they are, and are seen to be, just and fair by their pupils;

- lessons are well prepared; learning is efficiently and effectively managed, as are time and resources; the resources are suitable and available when needed and the optimum available time is devoted to the tasks in hand;

- what is expected of the pupils and students is made explicit and is understood and good teachers constantly review and check that such is the case;

- good teachers use, and are competent and confident in using, a wide range and variety of teaching styles and approaches and can move effortlessly from one to another as the situation demands;

- praise, used appropriately and taking many forms, is much more prevalent than are criticisms and sanctions;

- good teachers are confident and competent enough to seize the opportunities of the moment; to recognise the potential of building on the unplanned comment or event. In short they are assiduous collectors of 'ill-considered trifles';

- teaching and learning are matched to the age and

aptitudes of the pupils yet are also challenging and demanding;

- pupils are actively involved in the learning process and are not simply passive receivers of wisdom from on high.

In addition the vast majority of teachers' work alongside each other and with their pupils and students is in institutions. Consequently good teachers are:

- aware of the place of their subject in the whole curriculum and its inter-relationships with other subjects. They also recognise that, while guarding their subject's interests, their demands need to be reasonable and take account of the compromise necessary if the curriculum as a whole for each pupil is to be broad and balanced, and to constitute an educationally worthwhile entity;

- continually involved in discussion and debate with their peers about their subject, broader educational issues, the health and vitality of the institution and about quality and standards;

- good adult role models for their pupils and students and capable of developing and maintaining appropriate relationships with their peers and their pupils that are neither overly autocratic nor too permissive;

- reliable and trustworthy professionals in that they are punctual, regular in attendance, conscientious etc.;

- active participants in and initiators of activities in the wider school community that contribute to the raising and widening of pupil/student aspirations, to the social cohesion of the institution and its sense of collective identity and to the personal and social development of the pupils and students.

Implications for training and development

The implications for the initial and continuing training and professional development of teachers are clear. Devising schemes and programmes for carrying them out smoothly and effectively is not so straightforward, affected as they are by strongly held philosophical, professional and political views about teaching and its influences on the here and now and on future generations.

The first hurdle is to attract 'good' people into teaching. That means making it an attractive career. Pay and conditions of service are important in that; but so, crucially, are the status and standing in our society of teaching as an activity and as a profession. The former of those has not been too badly handled in recent years, though the position of teachers in mid-career is still where the economic shoe pinches badly.

Status and standing are quite different matters. Over the past two or three decades, as national interest in, and concern about our education service has grown, teachers and the teaching profession have been under sustained and increasingly sweeping criticism. Some of that was justified but much of it bears all the signs of politicians, employers and society at large looking for scapegoats. The general outcome is that, while individual teachers still find great satisfaction and worth in what they do day-to-day, they feel that teaching itself is badly regarded by society at large. That is a serious problem, and it affects recruitment to the profession quantitatively and qualitatively.

We are experiencing promising recruitment at the moment but, given the uplift in the economy that must surely come one day, that could be reversed: we could face serious supply problems.

Given that we continue to attract bright, capable and enthusiastic people into teaching, we need to train them well and to sustain their professional development throughout their careers. Initial training is much in the news at the moment and it is clear that the routes into teaching are becoming more varied, and that schools and colleges are set to become more actively involved in the training.

The first of those places a premium on the need to control the quality of the output. That requirement in turn demands that there exists broad agreement about the range of qualities and competences that should characterise the beginning-teachers who enter our schools and, one hopes, influence their induction training at the end of their initial training. That distinction between initial training and induction begins to look unclear. As the form of initial training changes and becomes more varied, spotting the join between it and induction will become increasingly difficult.

Questions about maintaining and enhancing quality are also raised by the accelerating movement to base some part of initial training, over and above teaching practice, in schools and colleges and to actively involve teachers in those schools in the training. There can be little doubt that schools and teachers potentially have a great deal to offer to teacher training. There is equally little doubt that, well planned and adequately provided for, partnership schemes have much to offer to the participating schools and teachers. None of those benefits will be realised, however, unless both partners are enabled to play their full part and do so effectively.

Crucial to that will be clarity about where overall responsibility lies for ensuring that courses are coherent, cohesive and of high quality. That coherence needs to bring together the range of expertise that exists in training institutions. It needs to unite schools and institutions, and progressively lead the students from absolute beginners to competent and confident new teachers, aware of much still to be learned and experienced, but with the beginnings of personal rationales as teachers, soundly based on the skills and capacity to organise learning and teach children.

Implications for induction and in-service training

Induction for new teachers has long been an unsatisfactory aspect of the education service generally. In what has come to be HMI's favourite adjective, it is at best 'patchy' in quality and incidence. The imminent abolition of the legal requirement for new teachers to serve a period of probation has emphasised the need for decent induction programmes. Once again in a world of the local management of schools (LMS), of grant-maintained schools (GMS), city technology colleges (CTCs) and of new teachers being able to undergo induction in independent schools, there is both scope and a need for co-operation between training institutions and schools and colleges in the development and provision of induction programmes for individual and groups of schools.

Induction itself may not in future be so clearly distinguishable from initial training as more training of all kinds is likely to be based in the schools. That being so, active partnership in initial training between schools and training institutions is well placed to provide both a basis for, and a means of, building induction programmes that, in significant parts of what they do, are of benefit to trainees and to new teachers at one and the same time. In addition, a firmer and more formal partnership between training institutions and schools should make possible a sound platform for closer and better-focused links to develop in in-service education for serving teachers and in school improvement programmes.

Clearly, as individual schools and colleges become increasingly autonomous, decisions about priorities for in-service and school improvement fall to them, taking into account, of course, any nationally set priorities. At the same time, indeed as a direct consequence of increased school level autonomy, LEAs and the services they provide are rapidly diminishing.

Quite how much INSET, and what form of it, individual schools will need and be able to provide is not yet clear. Some larger schools are beginning to build up their own training programmes and capacity and, as ever, some are more or less optimistic than others about the future of such provision. It is clear though that it will be at the level of individual schools that need and priorities for INSET and school improvement will be decided. While training establishments have a key role to play in assisting schools to identify needs and, once identified, in working with them to tackle the issues or problems effectively, the days when the teacher trainers set the agenda for INSET courses are gone. The writing was on the wall with the emergence of Education Support Grants and the Local Education Authority Training Grants Scheme. Since then, the scene has moved on at an accelerating rate, and whatever else is unclear about the future in education, there can be little doubt that for some time to come most important decisions about priorities and spending will be made at individual school level. That being so, one of the few remaining agencies able to operate across groups of schools are the higher education training institutions. Provided what they have to offer is based on a shared identification of need, an agreed notion of what's to be done and an active partnership in doing it, the training institutions could play an important and constructive role in helping schools individually and in groups to tackle INSET and school improvement programmes efficiently and effectively.

Conclusion

While the 'right' number of teachers in the 'right' places at the 'right' time are necessary requirements for education to take place at all, it is the positive characteristics of individual teachers and their teaching, and how generally they apply to the whole teaching force, that impinge, for good or ill, on pupil performance.

Consequently, while political and legislative frameworks, adequate funding, organisational planning and curricular guidelines are necessary, without effective ways of developing the characteristics and qualities associated with effective teaching in the majority of our teachers, and broadcasting them throughout the system, they will do little to improve the quality of the educational experience and thereby the performance of our pupils and students.

It is those individual teachers that we need to affect if we are to raise standards. It is that issue which politicians, administrators, teacher-trainers and teachers need to address if they are intent upon raising the quality of what goes on in schools and colleges. Without the presence of high quality teaching, neither abundant resources nor ingenious achievement tests, nor even the sticks and carrots of rewards and punishments, will bring about a lasting and real improvement in educational quality and the standards of performance achieved by pupils.

Reference

1   Witkin, R.W. (1974). *The Intelligence of Feeling*. Heinemann Educational Books Ltd.

32. Quality in Primary Teaching

Speech by Professor Charles Desforges to a National Commission on Education Conference in Birmingham, 12 March 1992.

Introduction

The focus of my paper is on quality teaching with particular reference to primary schools. I will make and elaborate on four points. First, I will argue that we have in our primary schools a very high quality teaching profession. Secondly, I will show that children are, by nature, extraordinarily good at learning. Third, I will suggest that the outcomes of schooling are disappointing and fourth, that quantum leaps in quality are essential and possible but they will take courage and vision the like of which we have not seen in education since 1944. I set out briefly a view of quality teaching in the light of these observations.

My four points are, of course, generalisations and should, perhaps, be surrounded by caveats and qualifications. In the space available to me, however, I intend to proceed boldly and directly in an argument which I believe to be the high road to quality teaching.

A quality profession

The Commission's pursuit of quality is timely and I am confident it will be relentless. But in the search for quality it must not be assumed or implied that we are without quality. Primary teachers have decades of collective achievement for which they might be justly proud. The historical record will show significant teacher-led developments in the quality of classroom life since the 1950s. Several academic areas of study have been radically reconceptualised in favour of more challenging intellectual work:

- nature study, for example, prevalent in the 1940–60s, has become thoroughgoing science; life cycles, observations and sketching have given way to the demand for operational thinking and experimental design;

- 'number' and the manipulation of routine four rules calculations has become mathematics – the mindful exploration of patterns and relationships between quantities;

- 'painting' has become art, the newer approach requiring even the youngest children to consider composition and technique;

- in advance of the national curriculum, whole new areas of experience had been worked into the primary programme including the use of micros and the study of design/technology.

These progressions to increased mindfulness were, by and large, grassroots achievements initiated by classroom zealots and spread by word of mouth by teachers looking to increase intellectual challenge in ways practicable under classroom conditions. Primary teachers have also responded to centrally driven initiatives. The national curriculum is up and running in Key Stage 1. New assessment techniques have been mastered and implemented – to no good end as it turned out. But the willingness and the work devoted to doing their masters' bidding has been clearly evident in teachers' responses to DES innovations.

Teachers have secured enormous 'customer' satisfaction. Research conducted by my colleague, Dr Martin Hughes, indicates that 90% of parents of KS1 children rate teachers somewhere between very good and excellent, an achievement the best high street stores or corporate organisations cannot match.

These achievements have been against the odds of unhelpful social and managerial change. The drop in the birth rate in the 60s and 70s led to school closures and amalgamations with all the attendant disruption and insecurities. A generation of wise old teachers was hurried out of the profession on early retirement schemes. And the greater part of two generations of energetic young teachers is missing as a consequence of cuts in teacher training programmes in response to anticipated reductions in pupil numbers. Massive social changes in the 70s and 80s in regard to drug abuse, unemployment, divorce and homelessness have not left young children unscathed. A battery of related problems has been brought into schools.

These massive disruptions to security and continuity – long considered to be foundation principles in the education of young children – have since been exacerbated by large-scale, persistent and rapid managerial changes to primary schooling. These changes have included the introduction of directed time, of the national curriculum, of LMS and of burdensome assessment and reporting arrangements. This last factor alone, in the shape of KS1 summative assessment, robbed teachers of 15% of their teaching time in 1990–91.

In the face of enormous social, economic and managerial changes teachers have shown outstanding abilities to learn and to adapt. They have exhibited endless tenacity. These are qualities essential to the achievement of educational aspirations.

Quality learners

If teachers are impressive, young learners are more so. Research on pre-school children shows that almost all of them are extremely good at learning. This is neither the time nor the place for a thoroughgoing review of relevant research literature.[1] But I am prepared to assert without fear of sustainable contradiction that all normal children have and exercise capacities for logical thinking, creativity and pattern recognition which they use to impose order on their experience and to create meaning in their social, material and intellectual world.

The most accessible evidence for this claim comes from studies of how young children learn their home tongue. This is a remarkable achievement, completed in all its important respects by the age of 5 or 6 years. A moment's reflection on common experience of the language of young children exposes its power and creativity and provides ample evidence of their generative learning capacity. Of course children vary in their accomplishments in language use. Some come to school unwilling to speak. But none comes without language or without the learning processes implicit in the mastery of speech.

It should be emphasised that mastery of spoken language is not a special case of learning. There is plenty of evidence of unremarkable pre-school children making remarkable progress in writing, reading and mathematics. Sufficient is known about these accomplishments for teachers and parents to be optimistic about what might be achieved in the early years of schooling through the provision of a quality intellectual environment.

Achievements in classrooms

The enduring debate about standards of attainment in primary schools is well known and inconclusive. On the one hand, until the mid-1980s at least, British primary school teachers had an international reputation for 'state of the art' practice. HMI and independent academic researchers have documented high levels of industry and commitment. People work hard in classrooms. Pupils learn how to cooperate, how to manage time and materials and how to take responsibility for their activities. In the primary age range children are predominantly interested in their work and happy to come to school to do it. On the other hand, persistent doubts are expressed about standards of achievement in basic skills, particularly in comparison with those of children in countries billed as our economic competitors or in comparison with a previous 'golden age' of education.

It has proven fruitless to pursue this debate in terms of evidence from test scores. This is in part because such evidence is always open to multiple, plausible interpretations by honest commentators. More importantly, test scores are an exceedingly impoverished measure of the quality of educational achievement. If the National Commission's deliberations could somehow procure the 3–4 points increase in test scores necessary to bring English children to the top of international league tables, teachers' anxieties might very well be alleviated but it would be an empty, even a distracting achievement. It would be empty because achievements in classrooms across the world, given what we now know about children as learners, would best be described as modest. It would be distracting because it would stand to reify the assumptions behind the psychometric assessment of learning, and these assumptions are part of the array of forces limiting ambition and sustaining mediocrity. Such assumptions include the notions that all worthwhile learning objectives can be specified and therefore measured and that objectives can be organised into levels of difficulty. The first assumption sustains the attitude that 'if we cannot measure it we will not teach it'. The second sustains the notion of basic skills and the practice of introducing young children to simple routines, leaving difficult 'thinking' activities until later. This practice entirely ignores the pre-schooler's capacity for thoughtful learning established earlier.

Limitations in classroom learning are manifest everywhere. Whilst the achievements of school children are not to be dismissed they are nonetheless characterised by certain limitations. The most salient of these is a general lack of capacity to apply concepts and skills evidently acquired securely. Employers and HMI have noted for at least 100 years that so much school learning is 'inert knowledge'. Children find it inordinately difficult to transfer their hard-earned understandings to use on practical, everyday, out-of-school problems.

Quality learning, that learning which, under the purposive control of the learner, can be applied in a variety of contexts for a range of problems, requires the capacity on the part of learners to transfer knowledge. Knowledge transfer has been described as the Holy Grail of schooling. Quality teaching has to proceed on the assumption that the quarry is not quite so elusive. But it most certainly has proven to be difficult to secure.

I should note in passing that there are some experts who do not agree that teachers are faced with a difficult, even a resistant problem. There are those who feel that the extensive use of 'tried and proven' teaching techniques, particularly those involving the transfer of knowledge by the use of expert didactic methods, would be sufficient to procure a significant increase in educational standards. And there are others who insist that the spirited use of public accountability through the publication of test scores would focus teachers' minds and practices on test score increases. The fact is that these methods have been tried ruthlessly in the past in Britain and are currently pursued in the US. They have certainly been tried and tested. They have also been found desperately wanting. The popularity of these methods is sustained by rhetoric. It has no basis in empirical evidence.[2]

Significant improvements in the modest levels of attainment in schoolrooms will require a better understanding of classroom teaching than that which underpins current official efforts to raise standards. And they will demand a radically different view of learning.

Learning and the structure of classroom experience

The following brief case studies should illuminate the problem.

- Sam is five years old. He enjoys school and he particularly enjoys maths. Observed during a series of maths activities, he was seen to work extremely hard at the tasks in the commercial scheme used in his classroom. This work predominantly involved drawing objects to make up sets and then colouring the objects in the set. When asked what the work was all about he said 'colouring'. He called his maths work-book his 'colouring book'.[3] Sam's view is quite common amongst 5- and 6-year-old pupils.

- A teacher set out to get her class of 8-year-olds to understand the socially negotiated origins of laws. She asked them to pretend they had been shipwrecked on a desert island and to sort out a set of rules and sanctions to determine people's behaviour. The class worked attentively on this project. They animatedly discussed the rules they would need. They reported clearly to their teacher. Later, when they were asked what they thought they had learned one said she felt she had learned what to do if she were shipwrecked. Another thought she would never take another boat trip. They had missed the abstract content of the teacher's lesson.[4]

Scenes like these are common in classrooms. They raise some extremely important questions about the relationship between experience and learning. They call into question the validity of the old slogan, 'I do and I understand' and they challenge us to think again about the assumed link between hard work and learning.

Of course, in the scenes described, the children were learning something. But they were not learning what their teacher intended. Rather, the children appeared to have a much more immediate view of their activities. Their interpretations – and what they carried away as learning – were related directly to the activities in which they had engaged.

Edwards and Mercer reported several detailed case studies which expose the gap between classroom experience and learning.[5]

- In one class, some 10-year-olds had been set up to explore the periodicity of a pendulum. In the teacher's

mind was the aim that the class would discover, or
re-invent, the scientific principle of control of variables.
The teacher had given the pupils a range of pendulums
made of different lengths of various materials. They also
had a range of bobs. The children worked intensively on
the problem but it was clear to the teacher that they
were altering several variables at once, thus precluding
their understanding of the factors affecting the rate of
the pendulum and manifesting their lack of progress
towards understanding the principle of control. The
teacher, feeling he was running out of time, asked each
group to alter only one variable so that each would have
something to report to the class at the end of the lesson.
This they did. They discovered that the length of the
pendulum was the factor which determined the rate of
swing. When asked why they only altered one variable
at a time however they each said, in different ways,
'There were four groups and four things so we did one
each'. Clearly, they had not learned the notion of
control. They had learned how to manage classroom
work.

It is important not to make too much of a few case studies but it consistently appears that young children focus on the working practices of their activities in making direct interpretations of them. In their efforts to make sense of their classroom experience the working practices are much more salient than abstract ideas. Colouring, discussing, managing materials and time and reporting back are important matters to sort out in the eyes of these children. What they learn from classroom experience is how to do work, how to be neat, how to finish on time (or sometimes how to spin work out) and how to tidy away.

It is not surprising to observe that children find it very difficult to use their experience in classrooms on problems which require the generalisation of knowledge and skills met there. For example, APU surveys have shown that most 12-year-olds can solve '225 ÷ 15'. But they find it difficult to answer word problems such as 'If a gardener has 225 bulbs to set equally in 15 beds, how many bulbs will there be in each bed?' Many do not realise that this is a division problem. Learning in classrooms is often constrained to the particular formats in which it has been met. Generalisation or knowledge transfer is consequently extremely limited.

The problems of the relationship between experience, learning and knowledge use or transfer are serious challenges to schooling. Schooling is premised on the concept of transfer. We are supposed to learn in school bodies of knowledge and skills which we can then use elsewhere. The fact that large numbers of pupils find this extremely difficult is a serious challenge to teachers. The challenge often comes in the form of accusing teachers of letting standards fall or failing to meet standards set. Teachers are charged with not working hard enough or, perhaps, not working their pupils hard enough. In this view more work should lead to more learning which would lead to more transfer. Plausible though this perspective is, it is clear from the case studies reported above that rather than leading to more learning it could lead to less. Putting more pressure on classroom workers is likely to urge them to focus even more on working practices rather than conceptual content. It is working practices that get tasks finished. Further emphasis on a production line approach to classroom work is likely to exacerbate the limitations of classroom learning. A solution to the challenge of classroom learning and transfer of knowledge might have to involve 'doing different' rather than 'doing more'.

In the face of this challenge, some workers (e.g. Seely Brown et al) have suggested a fundamental rethink of the problem, starting with a re-conception of the nature of knowledge.[6] Forms of teaching, they argue, are intimately linked to conceptions of knowledge. Traditional schooling, they suggest, is based on a view of knowledge as a 'self-sufficient substance . . . independent of the situations in which it is learned and used'. The aim of schooling is to transfer this 'substance' into the minds of children. 'The activity and context in which learning takes place are thus . . . merely ancillary to learning – useful but fundamentally distinct and even neutral to what is learned'. Seely Brown et al argue that this view of knowledge and its acquisition is no longer tenable. They suggest that recent research in developmental and social psychology and in anthropology indicate that knowledge is not separable from the activities and situations in which it is produced. 'Situations might be said to co-produce knowledge through activity. Learning and cognition . . . are fundamentally situated'. By 'situated' they mean that knowledge is an inseparable part of the activity, context and culture in which it is used and generated.

This view of knowledge as socially situated has important implications for our understanding of subject matter knowledge and for how classroom experience might be managed to help children acquire such knowledge. From this perspective, bodies of knowledge (e.g. physics, history) are generated by communities of scholars. Their concepts are not fixed quantities. Rather they are a 'product of negotiation within the community'. Communities of scholars are intimately connected through the work they do. But they are also bound by 'intricate, socially constructed webs of beliefs, which are essential to understanding what they do'. To understand an academic subject is to appreciate how the community of scholars in the subject uses the tools (i.e. the concepts and working practices) of the domain. Understanding involves entering the community, adopting its perspectives, appreciating how the world looks from within the culture of scholars in the domain. In the terms of Seely Brown et al, learning is a process of enculturation. 'Unfortunately students are too often asked to use the tools of a discipline without being able to adopt its culture. To learn to use tools as practitioners use them, a student, like an apprentice, must enter the community and its culture.'

In the main, schools deny pupils the opportunity to engage with the cultures of academic domains. Whilst pupils meet and use some of the tools of academic discipline, the pervasive culture in which they use them is school life itself. 'The ways schools use maths formulae or dictionaries are very different from the ways in which practitioners use them . . . students may pass exams (a distinctive part of school cultures) but still not be able to use a domain's conceptual tools in authentic practice.' This is a way of explaining the lack of transfer of knowledge and procedures learned in school. In order to achieve authentic practice, learners must be engaged in authentic activity. 'Authentic activities then, are most simply defined as the ordinary practices of the culture.'

Quality teaching

Quality teaching must engage children in activities authentic to the setting in which they will be used. And yet, these authentic activities must necessarily be enacted for the most part on school premises. I have been accused, in this argument, of attempting to resurrect the educational thinking of John Dewey. This is only half right. Certainly there is a strong family resemblance between the 'real problem' solving approach to learning advocated by Dewey and the 'situated cognition' identified by Seely Brown. But there are major differences too – especially in the role demanded by the teachers and learners.

In a modern statement of the matter, there is no element of discovery learning. Authentic intellectual activity is to be taught, mainly through modelling. The teacher plays the role of a coach and the pupil becomes an apprentice. Pupils proceed, after witnessing models of good intellectual and practical performance, to engage in a great deal of carefully constructed practice. In this practice they must be encouraged to be mindful of the intellectual processes engaged. This is achieved partly through reflection and partly through a demand for articulation. To meet these challenges teachers would be required to apply their familiar skills of explaining, describing, modelling and coaching to the realisation of objectives more ambitious and certainly more practical than mere knowledge transfer.

The implications for curriculum organisation and for

teacher training are radical. In regard to curriculum organisation the academic disciplines model is seriously wanting in terms of identifying the ranges of intellectual behaviour we might desire children to master. For example, 'data handling' in mathematics is a narrow and rarefied sample of the challenge of data handling in the extra-school culture. The conception of a discipline in terms of 'concepts, skills and attitudes' is misleading since it says hardly anything at all about the working practices of people in the discipline and it is the working practices which reveal how a discipline is used. When a pupil learns the concepts, skills and attitudes of a mathematician, small wonder that they cannot 'do' or apply mathematics. The recently constructed national curriculum would stand in need of radical reconception, in terms of both content and organisation, if it were to form a basis for learning transfer.

In regard to teacher training, as I have noted already, it would be essential to nurture traditional skills of explaining, describing and managing. But the contents of explanation and description would alter significantly. What would stand in need of explanation and description would be intellectual processes and the working practices of disciplined enquiry. Teachers would either need to be masters of these working practices (of historians, of artists, of accountants) or to be able to recognise, recruit and manage suitable surrogates.

Summary

I have argued that children are remarkably good at learning and that in the light of this, school achievements are modest at best. We might expect radically better outcomes from schooling. The natural learning capacities of all children warrant a grander vision for schooling than that currently upheld. I have suggested that current conceptions of the curriculum and of 'standards' are counterproductive to quality learning and the proposed approaches to the issue of 'low standards' (including public accountability through test scores) have failed in the past, will fail again and are dangerously part of the problem.

I have argued that the central challenge of schooling is to procure the transfer of learning gained in the culture of the classroom to settings outside the classroom. I have suggested a conception of curriculum, teaching and learning that should help us achieve this. I accept that its enactment would take a great deal of research and development work.

An important part of my argument is that we have a teaching profession which could rise to this challenge. Their track record for meeting managerial demand is unimpeachable. What is regrettable is that teachers' managers (at all levels) have set challenges which are part of the problem rather than part of the solution to the nurturing of high quality learning in classrooms.

Notes and references

1 Desforges, C. (1989). *Understanding Learning for Teaching*. Westminster Studies in Education, 12.
2 The effort to raise educational standards through the publication of standardised test scores has been applied vigorously in the US for many years. There is now extensive evidence that it has massively failed. See, for example, the entire December 1989 issue of Educational Researcher (18, 9), and Educational Researcher, 20, 5, (1991) containing papers by Haladyna, Smith and Paris. For a discussion contrasting the rhetoric and the reality of standardised testing see Ellwein et al in Educational Researcher, 17, 8, (Nov 1988).
3 Desforges, C. and Cockburn, A. (1987). *Understanding the Mathematics Teacher*. Falmer Press.
4 The relationship between classroom activity and learning has been extensively called into question. For recent work see note 3 and Edwards, D. and Mercer, N. (1987). *Common Knowledge*. Methuen. See also Marshall, H.H. (1988). *Work or Learning: Implications of Classroom Metaphors*. Educational Researcher, 17, 9.
5 See Edwards and Mercer (note 4).
6 Seely Brown, J., Collins, A., and Duguid, P. (1989). *Situated Cognition and the Culture of Learning*. Educational Researcher, 18, 1.

33. Teaching 9–11-Year-Olds

Written Evidence to the National Commission on Education from Robin Peverett on behalf of the Incorporated Association of Preparatory Schools (IAPS), November 1992.

Introduction

In our view, the term 'primary' has tended to obscure the fact that within the 5–11-year-old age range quite different teaching methods may be needed. The primary years are not a single entity: it would be more practical to consider Years 5 and 6 (age 9–11) as a separate division, more closely allied to Years 7 and 8 than to Years 3 and 4.

Class teachers and specialist subject teachers

At the recent primary seminars organised by the National Curriculum Council it was clear that primary teachers were strongly attached to the concept of the class teacher throughout the primary age range. They felt protective towards 'their' pupils and would only consider the introduction of a specialist teacher if the class teacher were present as well. IAPS can understand this attitude, but does not believe that it is valid. Pupils aged 9–11 are mature enough to cope with several teachers. They may benefit from fresh approaches, and there is the possibility that having specialist teachers could be a relief for a pupil who does not have a good relationship with the class teacher.

The national curriculum has increased the extent of subject knowledge required by upper primary teachers. At a recent conference of the National Association of Head Teachers, primary heads felt that they were all likely to have a few pupils who would be at Level 6 by the time they left primary school. IAPS does not believe that it is possible for one teacher to have the degree of expertise in up to 10 subjects to enable gifted pupils to reach such high levels. It would be normal for all teachers to be able to cover English, history, geography; most would be able to cover art and PE; some would be able to cover technology (including information technology) and religious education. In future, proper initial training of teachers should enable them to cover all of the subjects mentioned. Music, and the higher levels of maths and science would, however, require a degree of specialism. If, as IAPS recommends, the teaching of a foreign language should be statutory from the age of 9, this would be an additional area of specialism until it could be covered by initial teacher training (ITT).

Implications for subject coverage and initial teacher training

IAPS believes that the best way forward is for teachers within a primary school to become co-ordinators of particular subjects. Each would be responsible for the overview of a subject, for arranging in-service training as necessary, for updating staff on new subject initiatives, for checking that the subject was properly covered in each topic and that there was real progression, for advising other teachers about the most effective way to teach the subject, for producing clear subject documentation, and, where necessary, for teaching the subject at the highest level.

It is accepted that this would create difficulty in very small primary schools. IAPS believes that such schools may not be able to exist for very much longer, unless their structures and resources are reviewed.

The main implications for ITT are the need for an acceptance of the different requirements of teachers of pupils in Years 1–4 and of teachers of pupils in Years 5–6; the need to ensure that each primary teacher has a specialist subject that could be taught to Level 6; and the need to consider providing training in the teaching of a foreign language from Year 5.

Advantages of setting classes by ability

The National Curriculum Council primary seminars demonstrated the resistance that exists among primary teachers to the concept of subject setting by ability. In part this stems from a lack of clarity about the difference between *streaming* (children divided into ability groups in which they learn all subjects) and *setting* (children divided into ability groups for a particular subject). Although teachers were quite happy to allow pupils to work at their own pace, so that some would be well ahead of others, they felt that setting would in some way humiliate, and so hold back, the less able. The experience of IAPS does not support this, although it concedes that even in non-selective preparatory schools the ability range will be less wide than in many maintained primary schools.

Our experience has shown that:

- Less able pupils are often inhibited by the presence of very able children. They are reluctant to ask questions for fear of ridicule and may receive less attention from a teacher kept busy with the demands of able pupils.

- Able pupils are frustrated by the lack of real challenge in a mixed ability group.

- Less able pupils make greater progress, achieve better understanding, and gain an improved self-image, when working in a set suited to their ability.

- Able pupils respond to the challenge and competition within a high ability set, and reach higher standards.

- IAPS has found little evidence that pupils of differing ability learn from each other in class. The less able do not seem to be inspired by the example of the able, and the able do not progress by helping the less able.

IAPS believes that at primary level such setting by ability is only essential in mathematics, although it can be useful in other subjects, especially the teaching of modern languages. Recent reports by H.M. Inspectorate (on mathematics, English and science at Key Stages 1–3 of the national curriculum; on special needs; and on the education of very able children in maintained schools) have highlighted the lack of progress in mathematics.

Setting would in our view help *all* pupils, from those with special needs to the very able. We believe too that such setting can help to ensure that the teacher is suited to the pupils. In broad terms less able pupils require a patient and supportive teacher with understanding of their problems. The able require a knowledgeable and challenging teacher who has a deep interest in the subject.

The reluctance to consider specialist teaching and setting in mathematics stems, we think, as much from a mistaken philosophy as from problems of organisation and administration. Nevertheless we concede that primary schools do have particular problems to overcome, including resources. All schools will be helped by the clear presentation of the possibilities in *Curriculum Organisation and Classroom Practice in Primary Schools* (Alexander, Rose and Woodhead, 1992, paragraphs 146–150).

34. The Preparation, Selection, and Development of Headteachers

Discussion Paper by Josh Hillman for the National Commission on Education, December 1992.

Headteachers

One of the central messages which the Commission is receiving is that there are large and widening differentials between schools in their effectiveness. It is universally acknowledged that the quality of leadership is the single most important determinant of school effectiveness. This has always been the case, particularly in Britain where heads have such a major role. But the dramatic reforms which have affected schools in recent years have made significant demands upon headteachers and have increased the importance of adaptability and ability to manage rapid change. In particular, certain powers have been decentralised from the local education authority to the governing body and the headteacher. Accountability, especially for financial decisions, has in theory been sharpened.

Yet the process by which potential headteachers are identified early in their careers, selected and prepared for the role, remains highly unsatisfactory. There is a huge diversity of practice, some of which is admittedly on the right lines, but most of which is ad hoc to say the least. Selection tends to take place in an arbitrary manner, and the provision of high quality training both before and after appointment is erratic and certainly not guaranteed by resources. To put the scale of this subject into perspective, in the year to March 1991 there were newly appointed headteachers in approximately 480 secondary schools, 1,950 primary schools and 140 special schools. Early retirements may have made the numbers in that year artificially high, but every year a significant number of schools undergo a change of leadership with a newcomer experiencing the responsibilities and isolation of headship for the first time.

It is also being recognised that leadership must not just come from the individual known as the headteacher but that it is the responsibility of the whole senior management team of the school. In particular, the role of the deputy head or deputy heads has been widened to take on many of the management and leadership tasks that were previously seen as being in the ambit of the headteacher. Moreover, many of the individuals that make up the senior management team are likely to become headteachers in the future and their future success in this role is partly shaped by their experiences in their current roles.

This paper summarises the research on the preparation, selection and development of headteachers, identifies the requirements in view of the central but rapidly evolving role of the headteacher, and suggests some ways forward. Since most of the research, descriptions of local practice and legislative changes referred to in the paper apply to England and Wales, the conclusions and recommendations should not necessarily be taken to apply to the United Kingdom.

The importance of the role of the headteacher
Shortly after his period as Secretary of State for Education, Keith Joseph claimed that a good headteacher is the 'closest thing to a magic wand' for a primary school. There are very few, from the practitioner to the researcher and the policy maker, who would dispute that claim as being true for *all* types of school. Indeed, this point is made in various ways by many of the organisations submitting evidence to the NCE. For example, Tim Brighouse states that 'all the literature and research confirms the importance of headteachers and their senior team as agents for school improvement'. AMMA say that: 'The role of the headteacher, in our view, is not only an essential element in the governance of schools but it is also the

headteacher's leadership which most crucially determines an ethos which favours effectiveness'.

HMI reports such as 'Ten Good Schools' and 'Secondary Schools: an Appraisal' have stressed the importance of good leadership with clear aims and associated objectives. The former explained that the one thing that all ten schools had in common was a good head. Recent annual reports from HM Senior Chief Inspector of Schools have stressed that 'good leadership and a clear sense of purpose at all levels were evident in schools of high quality', but that 'the management of schools leaves much to be desired. In only about a third of those inspected was senior management judged to be particularly effective'. Specific examples of mismanagement have included the following: failure to supplement 'the aims in the development plan with the detailed objectives necessary to translate them into effective practice'; 'preoccupation with low-level administrative and organisational matters'; 'failure to translate policies into practice'. The school effectiveness literature mirrors much of this:

- *Rutter et al* (1979) stressed that 'obviously, the influence of the headteacher is considerable', but that 'no one style was associated with better outcomes'.

- *Reid et al* (1987) stressed the importance of leadership in shaping effective schools. Different leadership styles can be equally effective, but the most successful are likely to be non-authoritarian and facilitative, so that all teachers are continually involved in the improvement of the practice of the school.

- *Mortimore et al* (1988) found that 'various aspects of the head's management style were found to be associated with effects on pupils' educational outcomes', in particular 'purposeful leadership of the staff'. They also found that 'indicators of the head's positive leadership, especially in connection with academic matters, were related significantly to particular aspects of teacher behaviour . . . found to be associated with more effective teaching'.

- *Sanday* (1990) said that an analysis of the research findings on effective schools leads to the conclusion that 'the single necessary factor is the leadership role of the head'. He goes on to stress the importance of extracting the maximum benefit from a change of headship, by training for headship and by the induction and support of the head after appointment.

- *Smith and Tomlinson* (1990) conclude that one of the main influences on the success of a school is the leadership and management by the headteacher.

- *Brighouse and Tomlinson* (1991) remark on successful schools going into decline 'after the appointment of an inadequate headteacher or one in which leadership becomes ineffective'.

The changing context for headship

The role of the headteacher has changed. This is partly due to changes in the school system such as in school size, composition and organisation, and more recently in the location of responsibility between central and local government and the schools themselves. Furthermore, the increased powers given to governing bodies have substantially altered the relationship between headteachers and governors and have also created confusion in their respective roles. Meanwhile, there has been a change in the conception of leadership, from what Weindling and Earley (1987) call the 'autocratic headmaster tradition' to the 'leading professional and chief executive' who is supported by a senior management team and aims to empower that team, other staff and of course the pupils.

The Hay Management Report prepared for the National Association of Headteachers (NAHT) in October 1988 on the changing roles and responsibilities of headteachers and deputies clearly illustrated the shift away from predominantly professional towards managerial tasks. The conditions of service document of the Teachers Pay and Conditions Act (1987) and the Education Reform Act (1988) both stressed the managerial duties of headteachers and the Hay Management

Consultants concluded that in most schools, LMS alone would increase the headteacher's job by 15% and that in many this figure would rise to 30%.

The findings of the report have been borne out in the intervening years, with the role and responsibilities of headteachers in a state of flux and sometimes confusion. They have been modified by major Education Acts increasing powers of parents and governors and altering the responsibilities of LEAs. Implementation of the largely imposed national curriculum has necessitated regular curriculum meetings and constant disruption of the timetable by in-service training, often removing teachers from the classroom for days at a time. At times and places of teacher shortage, this has caused real problems for headteachers in finding supply and cover teachers. It has often necessitated their using deputies or even filling in themselves. Headteachers have also had to adjust to the notion of appraisal of teachers and more frequent testing of pupils. The increased powers of governing bodies have had implications for the appointment and dismissal of teachers, and LMS has forced responsibility for the management of resources towards the headteacher.

The Government, both in its legislation and through the speeches of ministers and even the Prime Minister, has stressed that successful implementation of its reforms depends on leadership of schools by experienced, dedicated and highly motivated headteachers. However, it might be said that there has not been nearly enough policy that can put this into practice. Surveys have shown that the level of stress in headteachers is high and that this could be lowered by adequate training and support. Steps must also be taken to ensure that the increase in the managerial responsibilities of headteachers does not lead to a neglect of their role as leading professionals. The Commission, before making recommendations about the preparation, selection and development of headteachers, will have to define precisely the role of the headteacher that it sees as being applicable in the 21st century.

Equal opportunities in headship

Table 1 shows figures for March 1990 for the gender of teachers and headteachers in England and Wales.

Table 1: Teachers and headteachers in maintained schools, 31 March 1990, England and Wales.

Numbers and percentages

	Male	Female	Total
Primary:			
Teachers	34,619 *(19%)*	144,119 *(81%)*	178,738 *(100%)*
Headteachers	11,218 *(51%)*	10,614 *(49%)*	21,832 *(100%)*
Secondary:			
Teachers	107,424 *(52%)*	99,015 *(48%)*	206,439 *(100%)*
Headteachers	4,111 *(80%)*	1,028 *(20%)*	5,139 *(100%)*

Source: Department of Education and Science. Statistics of Education: Teachers in Service, England and Wales 1989 and 1990.

How much the wide discrepancies shown are due to unfairness in the preparation and selection procedures for headship and how much due to other factors is not known. However, the figures should be borne in mind throughout the reading of this paper because there is much that is relevant to the narrowing of the gender differences.

There are no national figures for numbers of ethnic minority teachers, let alone headteachers. At a rough estimate there are between two and three per cent ethnic minority teachers, and a negligible percentage of headteachers. Again, this highly undesirable situation might well be improved by some of the recommendations of this paper.

The preparation of headteachers

There have been important advances in headteacher preparation in recent years and it is probable that instances of new heads arriving at their desks alone and in the dark are now rare. However, there is a rather ad hoc system of headteacher preparation in Britain which contrasts with the system in other countries, in particular the US, where there is compulsory certification (see later). One of the implications of the possible application of the Management Charter Initiative to education is that in order to become a headteacher one will have had to pass courses. Most researchers and practitioners do not find this possible way forward appropriate but recognise other important ways in which the current situation can be improved. OFSTED's emphasis on the criteria for school management within its inspection arrangements is likely to improve the situation. Each inspection team must include someone with an understanding of school management and the inspections might well be an important means of stimulating schools to improve practices.

Several organisations submitting evidence to the NCE urged us to recognise the preparation and development of headteachers as an area of major importance, for example:

- AMMA recommended increased resources for 'management training for headteachers and intending headteachers which stresses the nature and skills of educational leadership and to secure beneficial outcomes from teacher appraisal'. It referred to the 'notoriously patchy' national picture in relation to training opportunities for headteachers and potential headteachers and urged the Commission to support this area as a 'major target for funded in-service training in management'.

- HMC argued that the management training of potential heads and deputies is an area of weakness. 'Headteachers have considerable and increasing responsibilities, for which their previous pedagogical experience will have trained them erratically. An educational "Staff College" is an investment worthy of serious consideration.'

- NUT recognised that people should be trained for a post before taking up appointment, in particular deputies and heads.

- SHA describes the preparation and on-going professional development of headteachers as requiring 'urgent and systematic attention', such as an entitlement to adequate resources for development once in post. It expresses concern that senior staff are often unwilling to spend money on their own professional development now that money for INSET is devolved to schools.

- GPDST suggested the development of the profession of school administrator on the lines of the American model, so that administration could be carried out by professionals and teachers could advance to positions of responsibility 'without losing touch with the classroom'.

Research into headteacher preparation

The bulk of the literature that exists focuses upon ways of ensuring that the best candidates are selected and subsequently receive adequate training, in particular for management responsibilities. Very little has been written about preparation for headship by obtaining appropriate experience and academic qualifications during a career, or about preparation for a leadership role in pedagogy and curriculum.

- The Audit Commission (1986) examined management training. Historically, headteachers have had little management training even though they control and deploy considerable capital assets, staff, stock and annual budgets. The Commission therefore recommended the development of management courses for aspiring heads. Once such courses were available, no teacher should be considered for a deputy headship until he or she had successfully completed the appropriate middle-management course. LEAs and governors should have regard to formal qualifications of teachers in considering fitness for appointment and on appointment a new headteacher should attend a refresher course before taking up the post.

- Everard (1986) in his study of management in schools noted the lack of any underlying strategies and a reliance on chance. He was 'disturbed' by the low level of training to which the majority of those in management positions had been exposed in terms of both quality and quantity.

- Earley and Baker (1989), reporting for NFER on the experiences of 250 headteachers five years after appointment, found that most view their jobs as becoming increasingly difficult because of the welter of new initiatives. Looking back over the first five years, heads felt that newly appointed heads had been through traumatic appointment procedures, were given inadequate training, felt cut off from the LEA and had little support from deputies. In many cases they had not had an induction programme and some had not even been allowed into the school before taking up the post.

- Earley and Baker (1989) in a study of senior staff noted a common complaint that they were being launched into a job with little, if any, introduction or preparation. They linked this with a high rate of turnover and a worsening shortage of good quality and experienced teachers in such schools. Seven out of ten LEAs reported that they had difficulties during the past two years in drawing up short lists for vacant headships. Most gave the reason as a shortage of high calibre applicants. Numbers applying for headships had also decreased over the past five years at the same time that numbers of heads applying for early retirement were increasing. LEAs also reported difficulty in retaining heads due to increased pressures of the job, greater management responsibilities and 'panic' about LMS. There was also reference to the problems of maintaining morale.

Preparation before headship

Headship training is only part of the development of good management in schools and it is important that it should be seen as such. Weindling and Earley (1987) found that headteachers felt that they learned things at every stage in their careers which would later help them as heads. The question of the stage at which teachers should begin training for headship is difficult. One of the main messages that comes across from the School Management Task Force work is that every teacher is a manager, and this might suggest that training for managerial positions should begin at ITT and will reap benefits as soon as teaching begins. However, there is a large body of knowledge and skills which is necessary only for the headteacher. Few people decide to be headteachers until they become deputies, and one cannot completely train someone to be a head before they do the job. The general point seems to be that there should be a three-stage preparation. First, *some* pre-headship training is necessary. Second, once in post the new head needs support and induction to cope with the huge transition from being a deputy. Third, even the most experienced heads benefit from INSET, especially something like peer assisted learning. There are some who believe that the competence approach provides a common language for a whole career approach to management training.

There are significant differences in the requirements for the preparation of primary and secondary heads. In secondary schools the main learning period is as a deputy or as part of the senior management team. At this stage, the teaching load tends to fall to around 50% with the remaining time directed towards managerial tasks. Meanwhile the 'sphere of influence' of the new deputy within the school grows rapidly. Management training is helpful for heads of department, and headship training is best begun when the potential head is a deputy.

Primary schools are much smaller, so deputy heads have much heavier teaching loads and tend to do managerial tasks in their spare time. The transition to headship is thus a much more sudden change than it is in secondary schools. However, it is becoming increasingly common for primary schools to have senior management teams with the head, the deputy and some curriculum post holders. All these people need some management training, and headship training should begin at the deputy head stage.

Using the period of deputy headship for preparation
Headteachers have more influence than anybody else on the management development of deputies and other senior staff. Of course, problems emerge where the head does not think that the deputy is up to the job or, even worse, where the head does not want to lose the deputy. Weindling and Earley

(1987) argued that LEAs need to improve the use of the period of deputy headship as a preparatory stage for headship. They noted a very common view that the most valuable preparatory skills were acquired as a deputy head but that few heads had attempted to prepare their deputies for future headship, nor when they were deputies had they received enough preparation for their future role from their heads. They then suggested ways that preparation for headship at the deputy head stage could best be improved:

- heads to take a more active and conscious role in the grooming of deputies;
- heads to rotate deputies' job responsibilities to ensure wide management experience;
- deputies to spend more time standing in for heads;
- deputies to attend governors' meetings (with observer status);
- deputies to participate in more management courses;
- deputies to have greater opportunities to visit and even be seconded to other schools and industry.

Baker (1992) adds to this list by suggesting that the 'grooming' will involve:

- a commitment to an induction programme for new deputies, including co-operation with the organisers on school-based tasks and on-the-job experience;
- allowing release during school hours for courses;
- more sharing of decision-making in the senior management team.

He also draws attention to arrangements in some LEAs for

peer group support for deputy heads, generally with input from advisers, inspectors and officers and funding through Grants for Education Support and Training (GEST). Some authorities also allocate places on external management courses, such as at the Educational Assessment Centre (EAC) in Oxford.

In their follow-up study to the 1987 book, Earley, Baker and Weindling (1990) found that 'the training provision for senior managers provided by LEAs was reported to be patchy and lacking in coherence', and that there was a feeling that management training and development should be extended to all staff with management responsibilities, particularly given the rapid changes which all schools are undergoing.

It can be concluded that the headteacher's role in preparing deputies for headship should be made more explicit. Deputies can learn a great deal through watching a head at work, but they should also be encouraged to acquire a wide range of experience including chairing groups, planning the curriculum and suchlike. It is not common enough for deputies to be included in management training programmes alongside headteachers in order to develop skills for present roles or to prepare for future leadership. The role of the head in preparing deputies should be made part of the content of the head's training.

The selection of headteachers

Most of those in the education world believe that at certain key events professional interventions are crucial. The selection of a new headteacher for a school is one of these. There is, however, research evidence that much current practice in this country has *not* been very professional and plenty of anecdotal evidence that the situation is deteriorating. SHA, for example, in its evidence to NCE says that 'The ill-organised progress candidates make towards headship and the ad hoc arrangements which prevail for appointment reflect little credit upon the profession'. The selection of headteachers is very closely related to the preparation and the development of headteachers. They are all stages in the attempt to ensure that individuals fulfil a crucial role with efficiency and effectiveness and both selection and development are very much affected by the nature of that role. Some preparation will be necessary for potential heads who will be assessed for each appointment. Some development will be necessary after the selection process has taken place.

There has been a very haphazard approach to the selection of headteachers in this country. Problems include the following: patronage in selection panels; lack of a clear idea of what qualities are required in headteachers; and highly variable means for the exchange of information between employers and applicants for posts. Moreover, as SHA (1983) noted, the information on potential heads that is held by LEAs is only useful for them when comparing candidates from *within* the authority. The lack of a coherent and structured professional approach is indefensible in an increasingly complex educational system and there seems to be a case for greater uniformity in many of the procedures. Some examples of this can be found later on pages 505–507. It should also be mentioned that one of the most important requirements for ensuring that we have high quality headteachers in the future is the ability to identify leaders before they have worked in leadership positions. The key to this is often prediction rather than assessment, in particular where deputies are ignorant of the general management of the school because headteachers have not given them this experience.

Current practices compare very unfavourably with those of other large organisations, in both the public and private sectors, such as the civil service and major banks and corporations, many of which undertake highly rigorous assessment and training programmes as personnel move into senior management positions. They also compare unfavourably with systems of selection and training of headteachers abroad, as will be seen later in the paper.

Of course, appraisal of teachers is now being implemented,

and if it is carefully integrated with in-service training and career development then some of the criticisms of the way that headteachers have emerged in the past might be addressed. But teachers will in all likelihood be assessed as teachers, and the skills of potential headteachers will be ignored and not catered for in the identification of training needs.

Research into headteacher selection
The bulk of the literature on the selection and training of headteachers is concerned with the qualities that comprise effective leadership and there is no doubt that some of this academic work filters through into LEA interview guidance sheets and suchlike. In recent years the literature has tended to focus on ability to manage change, and in particular change emanating from central government policy shifts. Research into the appointment of headteachers was very rare until the last decade. There is a general feeling in the educational world that appointments are not carried out systematically, either within LEAs or between one LEA and another. Part of the reason for this has been the closed door approach which has prevented researchers from having a clear view of the process as it stands.

1. *Project on the Selection of Secondary Headteachers.* From 1980 to 1983 the DES funded what was the first research on headteacher selection, known as the Project on the Selection of Secondary Headteachers (POST). The aims of the research programme were fourfold:

1 to establish the range of procedures and instruments currently deployed in the selection of heads;

2 to contrast this practice with the procedures of executive selection used by industry and the public services and education services elsewhere;

3 drawing on the best practice both within and external to

the LEAs, to develop alternative selection strategies and tools and monitor their use;

4   to make recommendations on how LEAs could and should improve their practice.

The POST project was written up in a book by Morgan, Hall and Mackay (1983). They found that procedures had changed little since the beginning of the century and that selection remained 'an exercise in group power relations' with conflict between selector groups encouraging control and patronage, political or otherwise. Their main findings indicated that selectors had a meagre knowledge of the job and used undeclared criteria; the roles of different groups of selectors were ambiguous and non-job-related factors dominated the selection decision. The decision-making process was primitive and interviews were ill-planned and unstructured. Interviews themselves, the main tool of the selection procedure, were found to have low or nil predictive value.

Selection was found to be an introverted process in the sense that it ignored important developments in the selection of senior managers outside the education service and of headteachers abroad. The researchers blamed arbitrary and amateurish procedures on the culture of education, where there is a common view that these developments are irrelevant to education, where personality is seen as more important than management, and where a 'hunch' is seen as a more valuable indicator than more objective criteria of ability to do the job. In short, the dominant characteristic of procedures that had to be overcome was that 'nothing be made explicit'. The research team advocated the open use of clear criteria related to the practical requirements of the job and more sophisticated tools and procedures.

Assessment techniques that were commended included:

- *analogous tests* where specified job-related skills can be assessed;

- *peer group assessment* where experienced headteachers could be used to comment on the suitability of candidates;

- *appraisal systems* for senior staff to ensure that references are reliable and relevant;

- *senior management courses* where potential heads can be exposed to the skills and demands of headship in a context away from the actual appointment procedure;

- *training of selectors* in specific institutions on job analysis, selection procedures and appraisal systems;

- *clearly defined roles for each selector group* with LEA officers given special training and responsibility for extracting all of the relevant evidence and presenting it to selection panels; education committees to have sub-committees dealing with headteacher development and appointment; and school governors to be responsible for ensuring that the particular needs of the school are taken heed of in the preparation of the job specification and in the main selection procedure itself;

- *external experts in selection procedures* to be brought in as consultants;

- *more standardised procedures to improve the present idiosyncratic approach*:

— factors relating to ability to carry out post responsibilities should be formalised;

— all candidates, internal and external, should be assessed according to the same formulae;

— evidence should be recorded in writing and added to at each stage of the selection process, instead of starting afresh after each elimination hurdle;

— candidates should be able to visit the school informally before the first interview;

- assessment should not take place during this visit or on any social occasions;

- selection officers should be trained and should then organise training and briefing for members and governors;

- all panellists should meet for a prior briefing on the interview format, candidates' performance so far, the allocation and order of questions, mode of assessment and the final decision-making process;

- clear definitions of the roles of all members should be agreed by all parties at this stage;

- an LEA officer should be made responsible for all headteacher appointments and should assemble all relevant evidence, help the committee determine job criteria systematically, obtain evidence of the candidates' competence in agreed areas and produce complete profiles of each candidate for the members as an aid to their final decision.

At the National Conference on Headteacher Selection which followed the publication of the report there was a reasonable consensus of agreement with the main findings and recommendations of the POST project, in particular the following points:

- LEAs should identify and provide opportunities for the development of those with headship potential;

- selectors should meet early to consider requirements and arrangements;

- candidates require fuller exposure to the schools.

2. *Audit Commission.* 'The way that a school is managed by its headteacher and governors is perhaps the single most powerful influence on the nature and quality of the education it

provides. It follows therefore that LEAs and governing bodies should devote very considerable time and resources to selecting headteachers . . .' So spoke the Audit Commission in 1986. It went on to describe the selection of headteachers as being in general need of urgent improvement, and in some cases 'evidently a shambles'. The Commission found that the candidates were not examined on a practical basis and had little peer group assessment and that LEA officials had a meagre amount of training in interview techniques. Assessment criteria were found to be implicit, unstated and variable and few job-descriptions or required skills lists were available. Political conflict and patronage were observed. Final interviews were often unstructured, decisions were arrived at in an unsystematic, rushed, chaotic and often inappropriate manner.

3. *National Foundation for Educational Research.* Weindling and Earley (1987) studied the whole cohort of secondary heads who took up post in England and Wales during the school year 1982–3. Eighty per cent of these appointments were new heads, their average age was 42, only 13% were women, most had been deputy heads for around five to seven years, and only 10% were internal appointments. Selection was only a subsidiary topic of the study and the researchers mainly concerned themselves with the first few years of actual headship. Like the POST team, the NFER researchers pointed to considerable variety across LEAs in the appointment process and a large element of chance in the procedures. They did suggest, however, that the POST team had painted too pessimistic a picture and unlike the POST team their criticism was of some, rather than all, LEAs.

Recent legislative changes in the selection procedure
The ways in which headteachers were appointed were many and various until the Education Act 1986 came into force. In some LEAs the governors had no say at all, unless the chair of governors was allowed to take part. In others,

the whole governing body, which might amount to more than 20 people, interviewed aspiring heads. It was only in voluntary aided schools that governors could have the final say. The Education Act 1986 secured for governors an equal voice in the decisions. Governors could not be outnumbered by the LEA representatives on the joint selection panel (at least three of each) and any decision reached had to be by a clear majority of the whole panel, with no casting votes. The Education Reform Act 1988 set out new arrangements for headteacher selection for schools with delegated budgets. When schools do not have delegated budgets, the provisions of the 1986 Act apply in an altered form. The implications of this for different types of schools are as below.

Maintained schools with delegated budgets:

- vacancy must be advertised throughout England and Wales;
- governing body must set up a selection panel;
- CEO or representative may attend relevant meetings to offer professional advice but only governors can vote;
- governors must consider CEO's advice before reaching conclusion;
- decision of panel must be endorsed by governors;
- LEA must appoint recommended candidate unless he or she fails to meet legal requirements on qualifications or health.

Maintained schools without delegated budgets:

- LEA makes the actual appointment but all aspects of selection are in hands of panel;
- schools' Articles of Government will determine the composition of the panel;

- CEO or nominee has right to attend all proceedings and offer advice;
- decision of panel is reached by simple majority with no second or casting vote;
- if no decision made then LEA can re-advertise the post;
- if LEA decides not to appoint recommended candidate, panel must make a different recommendation, having re-advertised if necessary.

Voluntary aided schools with delegated budgets:

- governors must fill the post in accordance with provisions set out in the Articles of Government (usually to advertise, short-list, interview and then appoint);
- governors decide whether to allow CEO or nominee to attend meetings to offer advice;
- LEA cannot give directions concerning educational qualifications or prevent appointment;
- governors must ensure that successful candidate meets standards of qualifications, health and fitness specified in Education (Teachers) Regulations;
- if governors cannot reach a decision, Articles will probably provide for them to re-advertise the post.

Voluntary aided schools without delegated budgets:

- arrangements set out in the Articles may allow CEO or nominee to attend meetings of governors when they discuss appointment, to offer advice;
- if LEA not satisfied with educational qualifications of candidate that governors want to appoint, it can prohibit the appointment and governors must then make another selection having re-advertised if necessary.

Assessment Centres

Assessment Centres have been widely used by both the public and private sectors (including the Armed Services) to inform the management development and selection of senior personnel. The system of Educational Assessment Centres (EACs) was devised by the National Association of Secondary School Principals (NASSP) in the USA and has been in operation for about 15 years in the USA and Australia. It evaluates the headship potential of deputies using a model that provides a profile of the candidate's strengths and weaknesses.

In the majority of cases, the process occurs for potential principals and is used by districts in the selection of principals and for professional development. The system requires a ratio of assessors:candidates of 1:1, hence it is very expensive. Written reports are produced on each candidate followed by verbal feedback on strengths and weaknesses. The EAC process provides senior managers with a detailed profile of their current level of performance across twelve key competences for school leadership (for a discussion of the competence approach see pages 513–514). This profile can then be used by the participant, alongside other sources of evidence like appraisal discussions, to plan a programme of further professional development.

The EAC process is based on four key stages:

1 identification of the management competences required for success as a head;

2 design of job-related exercises to assess the competences;

3 assessment of performance;

4 further professional development.

This fourth stage includes assignment to a mentor, an idea which is discussed later in this paper.

The Oxford scheme

The EAC in Oxford was set up in 1990 on the NASSP model. The Centre has been in a pilot phase (1990–92) supported by a four-way partnership between the profession (SHA), higher education (the former Oxford Polytechnic), industry (BT, the Post Office, Rover and ICL) and government (ED and DFE), with clients from both the independent and maintained sectors. The Centre is accredited by the NASSP although the scheme has to an extent been 'anglicised'. Twelve management competences required in a successful head were identified: problem analysis, judgement, organisational ability, decisiveness, leadership, sensitivity, stress tolerance, oral communication, written communication, range of interests, personal motivation and educational values. The assessors are either heads, those with headship experience, or senior education officers and advisers who regularly work with senior teams in schools. The assessors undertake a rigorous training course and there is a possibility of failure. The exercises that participants perform include leaderless group discussions, in-tray exercises, video observation, role-playing, fact-finding exercises and interviews.

The evaluation report by Derek Esp and Malcolm Young Associates reviewed the early development of the project and commended the quality of the assessment methods, the assessor training and the mentor training. Their criticism was of two of the competences: range of interests (for whose inclusion they said there was no theoretical justification); and motivation (for which they suggested a change in the interview method). The evaluators noted the desire of users of the Centre to develop a network of these centres, possibly at a regional level. They recognise that the type of provision is expensive but note that this level of investment is made in most large enterprises, and that funding need not necessarily come solely from the public sector.

The evaluation report was not, however, able to determine how well the Assessment Centre predicted the ability of future headteachers. Studies of NASSP Assessment Centre candidates showed very low predictive powers of the centres in terms of performance in subsequent jobs and one study even found 'few significant correlations'. Whether or not the Oxford Centre has improved on its American counterparts has yet to be shown, although it is early days and major adjustments are still being made. The main problem with the scheme is its very high cost, mainly in terms of time away from the job for both assessors and candidates. It would only be worth pushing the scheme on a widespread basis if it could be shown that the system was giving reliable evidence about how candidates might perform in the real world.

It is interesting that the Oxford approach was endorsed by the School Management Task Force despite the fact that in general it favoured on-site development activities. It is possible that the experience of the Assessment Centre may have already influenced the selection procedures of schools and LEAs. The latest development in the EAC is that it is attempting to extend the competences to cover educational and pedagogic leadership and management values. SHA has asked the Commission to consider the virtues of the EAC approach.

A uniform procedure: the way forward?
The research into headteacher selection seems to suggest two important things. First, that procedures might benefit from greater uniformity, or at least a large degree of common elements across and within LEAs. An example of this being put into practice is in the nursing profession, where there are now uniform forms and procedures for all vacancies. Second, there is a need for greater openness and accountability in the system of headteacher selection and a subsequent dissemination of good practice. This section discusses what these points might imply for various aspects of the process at its various stages.

- *Advertisements and job descriptions.* At present, practices vary widely in terms of location of advertisements of posts, information contained and time allowed for application. It would probably not be feasible to standardise practice in the location of advertisements, but there is no reason why there should not be a basic set of information to be included in all advertisements and a minimum interval for the obtaining of further literature and the submission of an application. This further literature should include a detailed, comprehensive and up-to-date package of information about the school and a full job description for the vacant post.

- *Standard application form.* Non-standardised forms encourage subjective viewpoints and can be time-consuming, whereas curricula vitae are often distrusted by employers. A common application form would allow consistent input, minimise discrimination, allow candidates to send in photocopies and allow standardised classification. For example, teachers would always be able to give details of INSET and suchlike. However, it might also encourage candidates to recycle applications for several posts without thinking about them individually. It is clear that there is a need for a balance in this which might be achieved by imposing minimum criteria for application forms. An alternative might be to allow candidates to comment on their fitness for the unique requirements of a particular post in a special supplement which would allow governors to pose school-related questions. This would allow both governing bodies and potential heads to focus very clearly on how they see the responsibilities for a particular post.

- *References.* At present some references are confidential, some are written by LEA officers, some by headteachers. The POST project found that references in general did not relate very well to the skills and knowledge required by headship, and they designed a reference questionnaire which was piloted but not subsequently used on a widespread basis. Whether this related to the quality of the particular questionnaire that they used is not known.

- *School visits.* There could be greater opportunity for

short-listed candidates to visit the school informally and meet staff and pupils.

- *Selection panels*. As well as including high level representatives from the LEA and from the governing body, panels might also include, in a consultative role, a head of a similar school, perhaps even in the same area. There is an argument for the head who is moving on and his or her senior staff to be able to express an opinion during the selection process for the successor. In its oral evidence to the Commission, SHA put forward the idea of an independent assessor taking part in the selection process, possibly in the context of a GTC.

- *Governors*. There is a GEST category for the support and training of governors. Training in the selection of headteachers has not been a prominent use of these funds, in comparison with informing governors of their rights and obligations under new legislation and of the implications of LMS. Governors require basic training in the techniques of interviewing and should proceed according to previously decided objective criteria.

- *Interviews*. No research has been undertaken on the question of whether interviews are good predictors of future performance. Some have argued that too much premium has been placed on the interview in the selection process. For example, SHA in its evidence to NCE says that 'Interviews, on their own, have a very low predictive validity in getting the right person for the job' and that 'unstructured interviews are little better than the toss of a coin'. The sorts of skills which are assessed are very important but group discussions and written submissions allow the assessment of other sorts of skills which are also valuable, and perhaps interviews should form a less major part of the selection process.

- *Decision making*. There needs to be more time for reflection both for the panel and for the decision of the successful candidate. POST and others have commented that current arrangements make it very difficult for successful candidates who get cold feet about a school to refuse the post.

The development of headteachers

Induction of new heads
The induction of headteachers is not compulsory, but when offered the chance, almost every head will choose it. A high quality induction programme will involve elements before, at the point of and after appointment. Despite awareness and acknowledgement of the considerable tasks that are faced by new heads, few authorities have formal induction schemes. In 1988, the National Development Centre for School Management Training carried out a survey of all LEAs in England and Wales and found that only 25% of authorities were providing induction programmes for new headteachers. More recently, Baker (1992) found a range of provision 'from the ad hoc (particularly for newly appointed secondary school headteachers) to the highly structured two-year programme'.

Weindling and Earley (1987) found that 16% of new heads did not feel adequately prepared for headship but pointed to great room for improvement in the rigour of systems of induction for new heads. They noted that 60% of new heads had moved to a different LEA to take up post yet only a quarter of LEAs provided an induction course lasting more than one day. They stress that research shows the importance of a well constructed induction programme and suggest ways that LEAs might improve their practice:

- allow more time for heads to visit the school before appointment and talk to the outgoing head and staff;

- require outgoing heads to produce a full written report on the school;

- plan carefully-organised introductory visits to LEA offices;

- provide practical induction courses of several days designed to address the needs of new heads, possibly through consortia of LEAs;

- produce handbooks outlining LEA personnel and procedures (at the time of research 38% of LEAs did this);

- allocate to each new head a 'mentor' head for the first couple of years (at the time of research 14% of LEAs did this), so that new heads can seek advice from another head, rather than an LEA officer, if he or she so wishes.

In their follow-up study, Earley, Baker and Weindling (1990) expressed concern about the fact that many LEAs still failed to provide induction courses for new heads and that many heads are still not allowed into their new schools until the first day of appointment. They found that many of their recommendations and exhibits of good practice had not spread very far although they noted a growing recognition that senior managers need a 'coherent lifelong pattern of development'.

Likewise, Baker (1992), reporting on current practice, shows that only some of the 1987 recommendations have filtered through to only some of the LEAs. For example, despite the fact that the researchers recommended the handbook of procedures and contact names and that new headteachers find the handbooks helpful, only a small number of the authorities surveyed adopt this idea. Once again, it emerges that there is a remarkable diversity of practice across those LEAs that were operating induction programmes. In certain LEAs there is a genuine attempt to provide strategies that are flexible enough to meet the needs of individual new headteachers. These include:

- participation in a management development programme (sometimes including other members of the school senior management team);

- adviser/inspector support (in particular, early contact);

- introduction to the education office and other personnel;

- allocation of a 'contact' headteacher and/or officer (see mentoring, page 514);

- invitation to attend a peer support group (for example through local headteacher associations, consortia and clusters).

A change of headship is often a huge spur to the effectiveness of a school but schools require a degree of stability and continuity which are helped by giving the new head plenty of documentation relating to the school's last few years. Certainly, before term starts, the new head needs time with the administrative and teaching staff so that the learning curve can begin before the pupils' learning takes place.

Training courses
At present there is a wide diversity of providers of training programmes for headship.

- *Higher education institutions.* These tend to provide more theoretically-based courses such as MAs and MBAs. They also provide shorter courses which attempt to integrate theory and practice through work that can be applied in the school but discussed in the HE institution.

- *LEAs.* They run management courses which are more practically-based.

- *Groups of deputies.* These are usually area-based and organise training (often supported by the LEA) for themselves, and buy in consultants etc. Some even have inspectors for management development.

- *Industry.* Companies which organise courses often give places to potential headteachers.

In the past, headteacher training was largely the responsibility of LEA officers and inspectors and they still remain the most valuable source of knowledge and expertise for governing bodies, although legally the governing body need only listen and need not necessarily accept advice. LEAs have increasingly taken steps to define clearly the role of the headteacher.

Although successful approaches may differ, some LEAs are developing programmes that may provide a useful starting point for new headteachers and become an important tool of accountability, particularly in relation to headteachers' role in resource management. It is important to note that courses are optional and the pattern of provision is very mixed across LEAs and even across schools within LEAs, although there is good practice in many parts of the country.

BP's project on coping with change is described in 'Training the Consultant' (1988). It found that the problems being faced by the education service could be best served by good management and that LEA management training programmes needed to become better planned, less 'one-off', and better integrated within a wider management strategy or policy. A survey of headteachers in Essex revealed the need for better induction training within a context of personal development and support. Subsequently, five authorities became committed to the project with headteachers being seconded for training and subsequent assistance in on-going development.

The Local Education Authorities Project is a larger management training programme which was developed by a consortium of 15 LEAs with five modules covering such issues as change, staff development and resource management, using video and audio materials provided by the BBC. There are also dozens of management courses available at Institutes of Education, LEAs and the Open University, which seemingly vary greatly in quality.

There is now central government support for LEA work in these areas through GEST activity category 1C: *Training For School Management*. This concentrates on the more practical elements of headship, such as running accounting systems, appraisal systems and suchlike rather than adopting a theoretical view of the relationship between leadership and effective schooling. This GEST activity has led to the establishment of management development centres in some authorities with, in some cases, induction training and post-service training for headteachers.

One problem is that courses tend to deal with short-term issues relating to government imperatives so that most headteachers will now have regular training sessions on the national curriculum, LMS and staff appraisal. Headteachers are increasingly finding that they also need training in finance, budgeting, marketing, public relations and working with governors. These are all important, although some could be delegated in a large school to a bursar or similar member of staff. Headteacher development might better incorporate broader themes, such as school culture, management of change, strategic planning and leadership.

From next April, INSET money will be delegated to the schools themselves and it is not clear what the effects will be. There is likely to be more detailed planning at the school level and possibly a move from institution-based training to on-site training by consultants.

The School Management Task Force

The School Management Task Force (SMTF) was set up on 1st January 1989 to report on school management and the needs of those with responsibility for it and to propose a range of practical measures.

They recognised the substantial and increasing responsibility of headteachers and expressed surprise that the only qualification for headship is teaching experience. They pointed to other countries where candidates are required to have successfully completed management training courses, have had a minimum length of management experience or have completed written examinations. They did not propose a master's degree as a minimum qualification as in the United States but they did suggest that 'accreditation of both relevant management experience and additional study be given urgent attention'.

They recommended provision of systematic support and training for induction to *all* management posts, but accepted that the development of headteachers was the major responsibility. Their approach concerned itself more with support inside and local to the school than with off-site training. Of course, the view that development should be based in schools assumes that all schools have a reasonable level of competence in this area.

The competence approach to school management
Competence may be defined as the ability to perform work activities to the standards required in employment. There are some who believe that an approach based on competences is appropriate for the education world and that a national set of standards can be provided for school managers in line with those already existing in parts of industry, commerce and the public sector. It is important to note that the competence approach can take many forms and there is a multitude of models in operation. Not only can the list of competences differ but so can the procedures for following up an evaluation of an individual's performance. Some approaches involve concentrating on deficiencies; others involve building on strengths and providing damage limitation for weaknesses, for example by choosing other personnel to compensate.

A pilot project has been carried out by School Management South, a regional consortium of 14 LEAs, with the identification of a mission statement, roles to achieve it and performance criteria to define the characteristics of competent performance of the component tasks. The schools which participated did so mainly for the purposes of self-assessment and institutional review but there are some involved in this work who would like to see it linked with the Management Charter Initiative.

The competence approach has also been used by the Education Assessment Centre in Oxford and by the North West Education Management Centre in a two-year pilot scheme for a consortium of 17 LEAs, with observers at a management development centre giving feedback to participants about how identified competences might be developed and practical management skills enhanced. Cleveland LEA has used an alternative American competence approach, as has the University of East London for the development of heads and for selection boards' assessment of applicants.

There are conflicting views about the value of this approach and about the fields of education in which its application might be appropriate. There are many, especially in the US (where this approach is very common), who believe that the competence approach cannot adequately reflect the complexities of school management or of professional development. Moreover, some of the American research casts serious doubts on its validity and utility. There are two major works on this subject that will shortly be published in this country and firm conclusions should await their findings.

Headteacher mentoring
Mentoring has been used in industry for years. Headteacher mentoring is different. In industry middle and junior managers are groomed by senior managers for their career enhancement. In headteacher mentoring those that are mentored are already headteachers, and are mentored by another head who is simply more experienced. HMI (1987/8) suggested that attachment to a mentor might prove an appropriate way to help new heads. The Inspectorate uses the mentor system itself. Informal arrangements, where a new head is in contact with the previous head of the school or another head, are not a new thing. Formal arrangements were not so common until recently: Weindling and Earley (1987) found that 14% of LEAs had such systems. The SMTF (1991) found that this had risen to about 50%. These systems vary greatly in terms of the criteria for pairing, the roles of the mentors and the amount of funding that has been put in.

In the most rigorous systems, the mentor guides and supports the management development of the new head by a planned programme of on-the-job experience, possibly supplemented by off-site experience, and linked to regular meetings for analysis, reflection and further planning. The mentor is an experienced and established headteacher who is deemed successful according to strictly laid-down criteria. The mentor will come from a different school where there is no conflict of interest. The 'protégé' will be a newly appointed head with carefully identified needs.

At the end of 1991, the mentoring scheme was launched on the advice of the SMTF to support new headteachers. The pilot scheme is running from January 1992 to March 1993 on a regional consortium basis: there are 10 regional consortia in England (based on the Task Force areas), one consortium for Wales and one consortium for the grant-maintained schools. The consortia are required to make bids for resources to fund the scheme and the allocations do not go to individual LEAs but to the consortia themselves. The SMTF advise consortia on how best to formulate bids and this has resulted in a greater degree of uniformity in the arrangements than before. In fact, virtually every LEA is taking part. From next April there will be a new GEST category for headship mentoring. The more long-term intention is that there will eventually be an entitlement scheme.

The mentoring is intended for headteachers in their first year. The DFE has recommended that there be 50 hours of contact between the mentor and the new head during the year. It is providing £1000 per pair for relief costs. The total cost of the scheme will be £4 million. The SMTF favours the use of peer assisted learning or work shadowing to enhance the mentoring process and it wants headteachers to run the schemes. The LEA INSET co-ordinators are very much involved, but the chair of the steering group must be a headteacher, so that heads have ultimate control. Otherwise, the Government does not mind how the training takes place.

The general impression so far is that the scheme is going well in some areas but not so well in others. Worries that co-operation between heads would be difficult in a climate of competition between schools have in fact proved unfounded, according to anecdotal evidence. Although the LEA seems to be the ideal agency to administer the scheme, there could be interesting developments in cross-LEA mentoring. There is also a case for experimenting with cross-phase mentoring. It will be difficult to separate mentoring from appraisal by peers. It has also been suggested that mentoring could go on longer, say for 18 months to two years.

International comparisons

International comparisons of headteacher preparation
1. *The United States*. A structured academic and technical Masters programme in Educational Administration must be successfully completed before application for a principal's or even an assistant principal's post is permitted, in all States except Michigan. As in Britain, there is a recognition that good teachers do not necessarily make good administrators. However, the American system at least ensures basic and advanced training in accepted management skills, even for those who appear to be brilliant and gifted headteachers to start with. Certification does not ensure quality but it is a starting point in preparing headteachers for their role and in monitoring what preparation is received.

However, there has been extensive criticism of the provision of these pre-service courses in the US, both from practitioners and from participants. A recent survey found that half of a sample of over a thousand administrators rated their training as only fair or poor and on-the-job training was rated as the most significant element in administrator preparation. There would have to be much stronger arguments than the American experience for the introduction of certification procedures in this country.

2. *Europe*. Derek Esp studied the preparation of headteachers in Scandinavia, the Netherlands and France. His conclusion was that 'Britain is failing to train its headteachers'. He found two common assumptions in the continental countries: first, that leadership can no longer be exercised on the basis of experience and natural ability alone; second, that the whole school should be allowed more autonomy to develop its own

response to local needs and circumstances. All of the countries had substantially invested in impressive training programmes for almost all headteachers.

The French in particular provide a three-month partly residential course for teachers appointed to deputy headship or headship, and ten-day courses for those with previous administrative experience. The Swedes provide 25 days over a period of two years, divided into short residential sessions. The Danish provide four residential periods totalling 21 days in the first year plus three more residential sessions over a total period of four years. Norway and the Netherlands have similar arrangements.

International comparisons of headteacher selection
International comparisons of headteacher selection are rare and out of date. Those dissatisfied with procedures in this country should take comfort from the fact that we are not the worst. In Luxembourg the staff of a secondary school elect one of their number and the appointment is then confirmed by the Grand Duke!

Derek Esp studied the selection of secondary school headteachers in the Netherlands, France, Sweden and Denmark. He found that the British selection procedures were widely admired in these countries, although it should be noted that the study took place before the legislative changes in the second half of the 1980s. His main findings were as follows:

- small countries often dispense with formal interviews because they know the applicants;

- industrial legislation and trends towards greater participatory democratic practices have led to a sophistication of selection procedures and a slowing of the process;

- teachers have been worried by the trend to put selection in the hands of lay people, even where professional educators and members of elected school boards have retained a final veto;

- there have been some interesting experiments (e.g. in Haarlem) enabling pupils, parents and teachers to draft preliminary views on the needs of their schools and involving them in the preliminary stages of interview.

The French have an interesting system in which teachers apply to be included on the promotion list and are then interviewed by the *inspecteur d'académie* who makes a recommendation for inclusion or not on the list. As well as this power to sift, the *inspecteur* has freedom to devise and use a variety of selection procedures, and local practice varies.

Since that study took place there has been a common trend in all of these countries towards delegating responsibilities from central government to local government and in turn from local government to the schools themselves. In Sweden, the local authorities have delegated power to the schools at differing paces. Malmo has given extensive responsibilities to the schools and their governors, including headteacher selection.

Germany has a highly rigorous system of headteacher selection which is conducted by professional inspectors and involves a range of exercises including the following:

- candidates are placed in the situation of observing a teacher in a class and are asked to comment on this observation;

- they are required to sit a written examination on education law;

- they are asked to chair a meeting.

International comparisons of headteacher development
1. United States. Headship development in the US has evolved from the 'amateur' stage, which is still evident in the UK, to the business management and 'school executive' stages which

many in the UK are now trying to emulate. Programmes for the licensing of teachers as administrators are approved by the government. This gives respectability to a distinct branch of management science and encourages a body of administrative research to be built up, contributing to the field of social science. An accepted licensing standard has ensured uniformity and transferability between States with courses taking place in evenings, at weekends and in the summer holidays, based on credit requirements. The options within the courses are a mixture of 'field-based' internships and university-based elements.

As well as certification for principals, there has been a whole range of innovations for their development in the United States. Weindling (1990) provides an extremely comprehensive and reasonably up-to-date review of practice in the US. It covers such innovations as assessment centres, the competence approach to management, 'National Leadership Centres', Peer Assisted Leadership (PAL), Case Records and mentoring schemes. Of course, many of these ideas have crossed the Atlantic, but it is worth noting how much further advanced the Americans are in recognising the developmental needs of headteachers and attempting to address them.

PAL is of particular interest and has been highly successful in helping principals to reflect on their practice. It involves pairs of principals shadowing each other as non-participant observers followed by reflective feedback. It has been tried out on heads in Britain who found that it helped reduce the isolation that is inevitably felt by most heads. It is particularly beneficial for heads in their first few years and could easily form part of the mentoring process.

2. *Europe*. In recent years, the French have invested more in the continuing education of headteachers, whilst retaining the programmes mentioned in the section on preparation for headship. In France, the Netherlands and Sweden a national training team is in each case charged with the task of co-ordinating, developing and evaluating the training. The members are usually teachers, inspectors and educational

psychologists on secondment. The balance in content between administration and human relations differs between countries according to the level of devolution in the system. In almost all cases, headteachers were given ample opportunity to take part in planning their own training, and moreover, courses were flexible enough for heads to address the needs of their own schools and to develop their own strengths. In general, participants are not evaluated, except in Denmark where 'credits' have salary implications.

The conclusions that emerge from international comparisons of headship development are that schemes which train heads in the context of their own schools' requirements and link training to developments in the school, seem the most likely to produce improvements. Successful courses of development abroad allow heads to address their own strengths and weaknesses, with trainers developing links with individual schools. In smaller countries such as the Netherlands this is fairly straightforward, with a national staff college taking on this role.

Conclusions and recommendations

The preparation, selection and development of headteachers in this country is best described as haphazard. There is plenty of good practice to be found in various locations but little is done to encourage it to spread. There is no crisis but there is great scope for improvement and this should not be shirked, given the fact that the quality of leadership has the single greatest impact on school effectiveness. There is still too little commitment to management courses for heads and potential heads when resources are restricted; and not enough LEAs have high quality induction programmes. There is a lack of appropriate mechanisms for the identification of good managers early enough in their careers for them to be properly prepared. Selection procedures vary enormously: they are often not nearly professional or rigorous enough and too often chance, patronage and highly subjective 'hunches' are allowed to influence decisions.

Moreover, the erosion of many of the powers of local education authorities and indeed their possible demise have implications for preparation, selection and development which may well be undesirable. Legislation has strengthened the role of governors and weakened that of LEA advisers and officers in the selection process. A move from professional to amateur practices and criteria in the process may be resulting in poor choices in many schools. This situation is not helped by woefully inadequate training for governors. LEAs have been the main provider and co-ordinator in programmes of headteacher development. Financial constraints on local government and delegation of many of their responsibilities to individual schools have made it difficult for headteachers to find the time or money for training either for themselves or for their deputies and other staff. It is also not clear who might take over the role of the LEA in this area in the event of its dissolution.

The following is a possible set of recommendations:

1 **Preparation, selection and development of headteachers must not be seen in isolation from each other or from staff development in general.** The selection and development of headteachers must be seen as buttresses within the whole system of management and professional development in schools. Leadership is no longer seen as embodied in a single individual but rather in a team. Preparation for headship needs to begin at the stage of initial teacher training, with the recognition of the importance of management skills throughout a career. Good potential heads need to be recognised earlier and given the opportunity to develop those skills which might stand them in good stead if and when they attain headship and indeed before.

2 **An educational management development centre (EMDC) should be set up with a wide remit to**

include management development before and after headship appointment, assessment and research.
The centre might have a central body but would probably best be organised on a regional basis, due to the size and non-uniformity of the UK. Its governing body could include GTC representation; indeed, if a beefed-up and 'non-conservative' professional body is recommended, it might be run solely by that body. The centre or centres would need government funding, at least initially. There are various possibilities for the organisation of the regional centres: they could be based in selected universities; operated through the Open University network; or organised by consortia of LEAs. The centre would be responsible for management training for senior staff including deputies and heads. It might have a role in assessment, on the lines of a refined Educational Assessment Centre approach. It would be able to provide external professional assessment for selection panels for headteachers for schools. A strong research remit and input from managers outside the education world would ensure that the centre is dynamic, innovative and responsive to developments.

3 **Better use of the period of deputy headship for preparation for headship.**
There must be an entitlement for headteachers to have a satisfactory amount of preparation for their role, before, at the point of and after their first appointment. The period as deputy is the most useful learning time and all deputies should be entitled to preparation for promotion if they want it. One of the principal responsibilities of the headteacher is the development of staff and this must be stressed in their training. Headteachers should take a more explicit, active and conscious role in preparing their deputies for headship, mainly through on-the-job experience but also through off-site and on-site development, mediated by the EMDC.

4 **The professionalisation of the selection procedure.**
There is a need to move towards a more professional system for selection of headteachers. Selection panels must include governors, who can ensure that the

successful candidate is appropriate for the specific nature of the school and is able to work constructively with them on appointment. However, professional advisers should not be on the sidelines when candidates are being assessed or when decisions are being made, because they can bring great knowledge and experience to bear on the process. They need to be present at all stages of the selection process and should have voting rights as well. These professionals may be from the LEA or whatever intermediate tier exists between central government and schools, but might also come from the EMDC. GM schools should buy in this service from the EMDC or even the LEA. Training for governors in headteacher selection, possibly through the EMDC should be a top priority for resources.

5 **Basic requirements for the selection process.**
As a corollary to this professionalisation, procedures need to be made more uniform or at least minimum requirements laid down in terms of the information that goes out about a post, the information that comes in about the candidate and some of the practices of the selection panel. For example, all panels must have in front of them appraisal reports, going back as far as possible, including information about the extent of experience of, and standard achieved in, management duties. They should also have detailed and up-to-date references.

6 **Entitlement to a comprehensive induction programme including mentoring.**
New heads should be entitled to an induction programme that not only addresses general issues of headship but is also geared towards the particular needs of the authority, the school and of course the individual head. The headship mentoring scheme should also be made an entitlement and might be extended from one year to 18 months or two years. It is important that the mentors themselves receive high quality training and funding for cover in order to fulfil their role properly. Peer assisted learning might also form a useful part of the mentoring process and possibly be integrated with the process of headteacher appraisal.

7 **Entitlement to continued and broad training after induction.**
At the end of this induction period heads should still be entitled to a certain amount of training in order to address their own needs and cope with change. These needs will be identified through appraisal, personal development plans and perhaps assessment of competences. There should be a shift in the emphasis of headship development away from financial and marketing subjects, which might be delegated, to more wide-ranging areas, such as the development of school culture and creating a positive climate and ethos, curriculum and pedagogic leadership, staff development, strategic planning and the management of change. None of the entitlements mentioned need be specified too rigidly, or else they might have an adverse effect on the dynamism of the system. Once again, the EMDC would be expected to take a lead in outlining the entitlements and ensuring that they are able to be fulfilled.

8 **All new developments to be properly monitored and evaluated.**
As part of this process, good practice should be recognised and disseminated. OFSTED would seem the most obvious body to take on this role.

Bibliography

1 Audit Commission (1986). *Towards Better Management of Secondary Education*. HMSO.
2 Baker, L. (1992). *Preparation, Induction and Support for Newly Appointed Headteachers and Deputy Heads*. NFER.
3 Bevan, S. and Stock, J. (1992). *Staying a Head: a Survey of Headteachers*. IMS Paper No. 229 for NAHT.
4 Bolam, R. (1991). *The Effectiveness of Schooling and of Educational Resource Management*. OECD.
5 Bolam, R. (1991). *Curricula in Educational Management*. Department of Education, University College of Swansea, Wales.
6 Bolam, R. (1992). *Administrative Preparation: In-service*. In: Husen, T. and Postlethwaite, N. [eds.]. International Encyclopaedia of Education: 2nd edition, Pergamon Press (forthcoming).
7 Brighouse, T. and Tomlinson, J. (1991). *Successful Schools*. IPPR.
8 Carter, D. (1988). *The Appointment and Selection of Headteachers*. Education Management Information Exchange, NFER.
9 Daresh, J. and Playko, M. (1992). *Induction for Headteachers: Choosing the*

Right Focus. Educational Management and Administration, Vol. 20, No. 3.
10 DES (1986). *Education (No. 2) Act.* HMSO.
11 DES (1988). *Circular 7/88, Education Reform Act: Local Management of Schools.* HMSO.
12 DES (1989). *Circular 18/89, Education (Teachers) Regulations.* HMSO.
13 DES (1992). *Statistics of Education: Teachers in Service 1989 and 1990, England and Wales.* HMSO.
14 Earley, P. and Weindling, D. (1988). *Heading for the Top: the Career Paths of Secondary School Heads.* Educational Management and Administration 16.
15 Earley, P. and Baker, L. (1989). *The Recruitment and Retention of Headteachers: the LEA Survey.* NFER Interim Report for NAHT.
16 Earley, P. and Baker, L. (1989). *The Recruitment, Retention, Motivation and Morale of Senior Staff in Schools.* NFER for NAHT.
17 Earley, P., Baker, L. and Weindling, D. (1990). *Keeping the Raft Afloat: Secondary Headship Five Years On.* NFER.
18 Earley, P. (1992). *The School Management Competences Project: Final Report.* School Management South.
19 Eraut, M. (1988). *Learning About Management: the Role of the Management Course.* In: Poster, C. and Day, C. (1988). Partnership in Education Management. Routledge.
20 Esp, D. (1980). *Selection and Training of Secondary School Senior Staff: Some European Examples.* Education, 17th October 1980.
21 Esp, D. (1992). *Educational Assessment Centre Project: Stage 1 Evaluation Report.* School of Education, Oxford Polytechnic.
22 Esp, D. (forthcoming). *Competences for School Managers.* Kogan Page.
23 Everard, K. (1986). *Developing Management in Schools.* Blackwell.
24 Green, H., Holmes, G. and Shaw, M. (1991). *Assessment and Mentoring for Headship.* School of Education, Oxford Polytechnic.
25 Green, H. (1992). *Leadership, Values and Site-Based Management.* Paper for BEMAS Conference in Bristol.
26 Her Majesty's Inspectorate (1977). *Ten Good Schools.* HMSO.
27 Her Majesty's Inspectorate (1988). *Secondary Schools: an Appraisal by HMI.* HMSO.
28 Her Majesty's Inspectorate (1992). *Education in England 1990–1: the Annual Report of HM Senior Chief Inspector of Schools.* HMSO.
29 Howson, J. (1992). *Pay Rise for Heads Pays Off?* School of Education, Oxford Polytechnic.
30 Kelly, A. and Wallace, E. (1988). *Selecting a Head.* School Governor, March 1988.
31 Lowe, C. (1987). *Education Act 1986: Implications for School Management.* SHA.
32 Lowe, C. (1988). *Education Reform Act 1988: Implications for School Management.* SHA.
33 Morgan, C., Hall, V. and Mackay, H. (1983). *The Selection of Secondary School Headteachers.* Open University Press.
34 Mortimore, P. et al (1988). *School Matters: the Junior Years.* Open Books.
35 Mortimore, P. and J. [eds.] (1991). *The Primary Head.* Chapman.
36 Mortimore, P. and J. [eds.] (1991). *The Secondary Head.* Chapman.
37 National Conference on Headteacher Selection (1984). *Record of Proceedings of Conference held on 27th February 1984.*

38 OFSTED (1992). *Framework for the Inspection of Schools*. HMSO.
39 Reid, K., Hopkins, D. and Holly, K. (1987). *Towards the Effective School*. Blackwell.
40 Rutter, M. et al (1979). *Fifteen Thousand Hours: Secondary Schools and Their Effects on Children*. Open Books.
41 Sanday, A. (1990). *Making Schools More Effective*. Warwick University.
42 School Management Task Force (1990). *Developing School Management: The Way Forward*. HMSO.
43 School Management Task Force (1991). *Mentor Scheme for New Headteachers: Notes of Guidance for Regional Executive Groups*.
44 School Management Task Force (1991). *Mentor Scheme for New Headteachers: Information Pack*.
45 School Management Task Force (1991). *Regional Conferences on Mentoring for Newly Appointed Heads: Background Papers*.
46 Secondary Heads Association (1983). *The Selection of Secondary Heads: Suggestions for Good Practice*. Occasional Paper No. 2.
47 Smith, D. and Tomlinson, S. (1990). *The School Effect*. Policy Studies Institute.
48 Taylor, F. (1989). *Planning a Head*. School Governor, March 1989.
49 Topple, S. (1991). *The Remuneration of Headteachers in Schools with Delegated Budgets under LMS*. Hay Management Consultants for NAHT.
50 Wallace, M. and Hall, V. (1989). *Management Development and Training for Schools in England and Wales: an Overview*. Educational Management and Administration, 17, 4, 163–75.
51 Weindling, D. and Earley, P. (1987). *Secondary Headship: the First Years*. NFER.
52 Weindling, D. (1990). *Current Developments in the Preparation and Support of US Principals*. Create Consultants, Commissioned by School Management Task Force.
53 Witters-Churchill (1991). *University Preparation of School Principals*. School Organisation, Vol. 11, No. 3.

35. Undergraduate Perceptions of Teaching as a Career

Summary of a Survey by Josh Hillman for the National Commission on Education, June 1993.

Introduction

This paper summarises the findings of a study conducted by the National Commission on Education. The objectives of the study were to obtain from final year undergraduates information relating to their career choices, influences on these choices, criteria in choosing careers and their perceptions of a selection of careers, in particular, teaching. At the end of November 1992, questionnaires were completed by students expected to graduate in the summer of 1993 in five general subject areas in a range of universities across the United Kingdom. Heads of faculties took responsibility for ensuring a good response rate in their departments. There were 1,428 responses, giving a response rate of approximately 60%. Responses were well distributed by type of university, region, gender, age, subject of study and type of previous school or college.

General career intention of students

The students indicated their most likely course of action after finishing their degree course as follows:

- Embark on career requiring further qualifications 40.6%

- Embark on career not necessarily requiring further qualifications 36.1%

- Undertake further study not necessarily leading to specific career   18.4%

- Other   4.8%

Students at former polytechnics were less likely to intend to embark on a career requiring further qualifications. English students and maths students felt more need to take vocational qualifications after completing their degrees; engineering and technology students were much more likely to want to go straight into a career; and science students were much more likely to want to undertake further study not leading to a particular career.

Students were also asked about their work preference for sector of work, responding as follows:

- Private sector   33.9%

- Public/voluntary sector   20.4%

- No particular preference   45.7%

There was a very marked gender difference, with women almost three times more likely to prefer to work in the public sector than men. There was a very marked subject effect, with engineering and technology students and to a lesser extent maths students much preferring the private sector and English students overwhelmingly preferring to work in the public sector.

Choice of teaching and other careers

Students were asked to what extent they were considering or had considered a list of eight careers. The proportion of respondents who put 'have chosen/applied/am applying' for school teaching (13.8%) was lower than for industry but higher than for all of the other listed careers (accountancy, civil service, law, retailing, social work and university lecturing). The wide variations amongst different types of students in the extent to which they were considering teaching as a career are shown in Table 1.

Table 1: Extent to which undergraduates were considering school teaching.

Percentages

	Have chosen/ applied/ am applying	Considering applying	May consider as a last resort	Would not consider	Did not reply	All
All	13.8	16.7	32.8	35.6	1.1	100
Male	8.5	14.5	34.3	41.6	1.1	100
Female	20.2	19.4	30.9	28.5	1.0	100
Old university	15.6	16.5	33.5	33.5	0.9	100
New university	7.3	17.1	30.2	43.2	2.2	100
Age: <22	14.9	16.0	32.9	35.3	0.9	100
Age: 22-25	8.1	15.4	32.4	41.9	2.2	100
Age: 26+	8.5	27.7	30.9	29.8	3.1	100
Type of school/college last attended						
Comprehensive school	13.7	17.0	33.7	35.2	0.4	100
Grammar school	21.5	15.2	34.6	28.7	0.0	100
Independent school	8.0	15.6	31.7	43.8	0.9	100
Sixth form college	15.7	15.7	32.3	34.3	2.0	100
F.E. college	11.8	17.6	31.6	36.9	2.1	100
Subject area of degree						
English	24.7	23.3	26.0	22.7	3.3	100
Modern Languages	16.5	21.0	34.9	26.5	1.1	100
Maths	17.9	12.6	30.7	38.5	0.3	100
Science	9.8	20.0	37.7	32.1	0.4	100
Engineering and technology	4.5	12.5	31.5	49.5	2.0	100

Female students were far more likely than male students to have chosen or to be considering teaching. Students from the former polytechnics were less likely than students from the old universities to be intending to go into teaching. Students who had previously attended independent schools were also less likely to have chosen teaching whereas those who had been to grammar schools were more likely to have done so. Older students were less likely than younger students to have chosen teaching but those over the age of 26 were more likely to be keeping their options open and to be at least considering teaching as a career of the last resort. Relatively few Asian students had chosen teaching.

Students taking English degrees were much more likely to have chosen teaching. Very few of those studying engineering and technology had chosen teaching and nearly half of them were not even considering it as an option. Nearly three quarters of the modern languages students were at least considering teaching as a last resort, a larger proportion than in the overall sample. Maths students were more likely to have made a firm decision about teaching, with proportionately more students both having chosen teaching and having ruled it out. This was not the case for science students where a large proportion of students were considering teaching but few had actually chosen it.

There was a fairly strong link between expected degree result of student and extent to which teaching was being considered, as shown in Table 2, with the students expecting higher degrees less likely to have chosen or to be considering teaching.

Table 2: Extent to which undergraduates were considering school teaching, by expected degree class.

Percentages

	Have chosen/ applied/ am applying	Consider- ing applying	May consider as a last resort	Would not consider	Did not apply	All
All	13.8	16.7	32.8	35.6	1.1	100
Expected degree: 1st	9.4	13.1	37.5	39.4	0.6	100
Expected degree: 2:1	11.7	17.4	33.1	36.4	1.4	100
Expected degree: 2:2	18.4	18.1	28.6	34.3	0.6	100
Expected degree: 3rd	27.4	12.9	29.0	29.0	1.7	100

Influences on career choice

Students were asked to indicate and quantify five influences on their consideration of the eight careers. The first row of Table 3 shows the results for school teaching. Numbers greater than zero indicate a positive influence on career choice; numbers less than zero indicate a negative influence and zero indicates no overall effect. Four of the five influences listed in the questionnaire were seen to have a positive influence on consideration of teaching as a career option amongst the students surveyed as a whole. Work experience and people that the students had met were the most significant. Only perceptions of industry benefited more than teaching from these two influences. The negative influence of the media on students' consideration of teaching was marked and higher than for all of the other careers, except social work.

Table 3: Factors influencing consideration of school teaching as a career option.

Indices

	Influences on career consideration				
	Family & friends	Media portrayal	Work experience	People you've met	Careers advice
All respondents (n=1428)	0.20	−0.45	0.37	0.38	0.26
Extent to which undergraduate was considering school teaching					
Have chosen/applied/am applying (n=197)	1.49	−0.04	1.61	1.60	1.13
Considering applying (n=238)	0.86	−0.24	0.77	1.21	0.61
May consider as a last resort (n=468)	0.10	−0.50	0.14	0.32	0.12
Would not consider (n=509)	−0.57	−0.67	−0.11	−0.46	−0.12

Table 3 also indicates the effect of the five influences on students, divided according to the extent of their consideration of school teaching as a career. All five influences exerted a more positive influence on those who were intending to go into teaching, as would be expected. Media portrayal of teaching was a negative influence upon all four subgroups of students, but comparisons of the differentials between the indices shows that it was the least likely of the influences to sway a student's decision about going into teaching or not.

Criteria in choosing careers

Students were asked to rate the importance of a list of criteria for choosing a career. In Table 4, outcomes are presented, with the criteria ordered from most favoured to least favoured.

Table 4: Ratings of job characteristics as they bear on career choice by undergraduates.

Percentages

Importance of job characteristic

Job characteristic	Extremely	Fairly	Slight	Not	No reply	All
Variety of work	54.3	36.8	5.0	0.5	3.4	100
Good working environment	52.5	36.4	6.8	0.8	3.5	100
Intellectual challenge	44.8	42.6	7.6	1.5	3.5	100
Job security	42.2	44.3	9.2	1.1	3.2	100
Opportunity for creative input	41.6	40.8	12.5	1.8	3.3	100
Prospects for promotion	40.3	41.5	12.7	2.2	3.3	100
Respect from others	34.5	43.1	15.1	3.9	3.4	100
Salary and associated benefits	28.4	53.9	12.5	2.0	3.2	100
Working with individuals	25.6	41.4	24.6	4.9	3.5	100
Benefit to society	24.2	42.2	23.1	7.2	3.3	100
Independence in decisions	23.7	53.5	17.9	1.5	3.4	100
Opportunity for travel	22.9	32.4	30.5	10.9	3.3	100
Tangible indications of progress	22.4	50.8	20.8	2.4	3.6	100
Application of degree subject	19.7	34.5	27.5	14.3	4.0	100
Choice of location	19.3	37.7	28.9	10.6	3.5	100

The most highly rated criterion was variety of work, closely followed by good working environment, both of which were felt to be extremely important by more than half of the respondents. Interestingly, job security was rated more highly than prospects for promotion which in turn was rated more highly than salary and associated benefits. This is partly a reflection of the fact that the students were questioned during a period of recession. Three criteria (salary and associated benefits, independence in decisions and tangible indications of progress) were rated as *extremely* important by relatively few respondents but as *fairly* important by more than half of the sample. Comparatively few respondents rated these criteria as being of slight or no importance.

Women tended to rate criteria related to the *quality* of work higher than men (variety of work, good working environment and working with individuals) and also rated benefit to society, respect from others and choice of location higher. Men rated more material criteria higher (prospects for promotion and salary and associated benefits).

There were quite large differences in the ratings of criteria given by students of different subjects. English students attached particular importance to intellectual challenge, opportunity for creative input, respect from others, working with individuals, benefit to society and independence in decisions. They rated the material criteria (job security, prospects for promotion, salary and associated benefits) lower than other students and also attached much less importance to application of degree subject. Students of modern languages gave extremely high ratings to the three most popular criteria (variety of work, good working environment and intellectual challenge) and also to respect from others, working with individuals and, not surprisingly, opportunity for travel. Maths students gave lower ratings for opportunity for creative input, benefit to society and opportunity for travel. Science students gave lower ratings for working with individuals and tangible indications of progress. Students of engineering and technology gave higher ratings for salary and associated benefits and independence in decisions and lower ratings for intellectual challenge and choice of location.

Perception of teaching and other careers

Each student was asked to rate each profession by giving a score between 0 and 3 for each of the job characteristics, where 3 indicated that the profession fulfils the characteristic very well and 0 that the characteristic is not fulfilled at all. The scores given by respondents for school teaching for most characteristics compare fairly well with the seven other careers. Of the 15 characteristics, teaching scored above the average score for all eight professions on 11 of them, and below the average on the remaining four (salary and associated benefits, opportunity for travel, prospects for promotion and good working environment). This was not as high a number of above average scores as law (14), industry and university lecturing (13), but was higher than civil service and social work (5) and accountancy and retailing (3). The average score for teaching was over 2.5 in two criteria (benefit to society and working with individuals), an extremely high level, reached by four other careers but only in one criterion each. The score for benefit to society by teaching was the highest for any career for any job characteristic in the survey. Teaching also scored particularly highly in opportunity for creative input.

Figure 1 on page 538 plots the scores for the 15 job characteristics and the scores given for teaching for each of those characteristics, both as scaled indices, where 1 represents the average score across the eight professions for each characteristic. The characteristics have been ordered, from the highest at the top to the lowest at the bottom. The figure can thus be used to examine several things:

- comparison of how different criteria for choosing a career rate in importance;

- comparison of the extent to which different criteria are fulfilled by teaching;

- comparison of the extent to which teaching fulfils each

criterion with the other seven careers;
- a picture of the extent to which teaching generally fulfils criteria which are seen as important.

In general, teaching was rated highest for those characteristics which were considered relatively unimportant by the undergraduates (opportunity for creative input being the exception).

Women scored teaching significantly higher than men for several characteristics, namely salary and associated benefits, opportunity for travel and application of degree subject, and to a lesser extent variety of work, opportunity for creative input and good working environment. Breaking down the students by subject, for many of the characteristics there tended to be a hierarchy of ratings for teaching, with English students giving the highest scores, followed by modern languages, then science, with engineering and technology and maths students giving the lowest scores.

Finally, it is worth looking at an analysis of the scores given to school teaching by undergraduates according to the extent to which they were considering teaching as a career. Table 5 shows the average scores given to school teaching for each of the criteria (in order of popularity) by undergraduates expressing strong preferences in their consideration of school teaching as a career. The final column shows the difference between these two columns.

The table shows large differences in the perception of teaching between those that had chosen or had not chosen teaching as a career. Discrepancies were particularly wide for good working environment, variety of work and application of degree subject.

Conclusions

There is no crisis in the recruitment of undergraduates into teaching. The survey showed that a reasonable number of students had chosen or were at least considering teaching as a career, although it has to be remembered that the teaching

Table 5: Differing perceptions of school teaching by undergraduates who had chosen or were not considering teaching as a career.

Indices

	Average score given to school teaching		
	Undergraduates who had chosen/ applied/applying for teaching	Undergraduates who would not consider teaching	Difference
Job characteristic			
Variety of work	2.14	1.41	0.73
Good working environment	1.99	1.22	0.77
Intellectual challenge	2.28	1.70	0.58
Job security	2.25	1.89	0.36
Opportunity for creative input	2.54	2.10	0.44
Prospects for promotion	1.73	1.18	0.55
Respect from others	1.90	1.51	0.39
Salary and associated benefits	1.28	0.77	0.51
Working with individuals	2.69	2.43	0.26
Benefit to society	2.90	2.67	0.23
Independence in decisions	1.84	1.41	0.43
Opportunity for travel	1.03	0.55	0.48
Tangible indications of progress	2.14	1.71	0.43
Application of degree subject	2.39	1.72	0.67
Choice of location	1.90	1.51	0.39

profession has the largest graduate workforce. However, those undergraduates intending to go into teaching were not representative of the whole sample. They were much more likely to be female than male and there were substantial differences between undergraduates studying different subjects, with teaching popular amongst those taking English degrees, unpopular for engineering and technology students, and an uncommitted interest from maths and language students. Moreover, those choosing or considering teaching tended to be expecting lower degree results. Teaching is not popular amongst those for whom there is greatest need within the profession.

The sources of the problem are:

- in general, teaching was not seen as fulfilling those criteria in choosing a career which undergraduates consider the most important;

- those characteristics of jobs for which teaching was rated highly were seen as relatively unimportant in determining choice of career;

- wide variations in undergraduate perceptions of teaching;

- wide variations in the way that undergraduates were influenced by different factors in their consideration of teaching as a career.

The main implications for policy from the findings of the survey are as follows:

1 Attention must be paid to the way that teaching as a career is promoted to all undergraduates. Stereotypical images of teachers still seem to put off males and students in the main shortage subjects. The characteristics of teaching that should be more widely projected are opportunity for creative input, variety of work, intellectual challenge and job security.

2 Undergraduates perceive the teaching profession as having a poor working environment, which they see as an extremely important criterion in choosing a career. The poor physical fabric of many schools is not only preventing successful learning by children but is putting off potential entrants to the teaching profession.

3 Undergraduates are more concerned about poor prospects for promotion than low salaries. This would suggest that potential entrants to the teaching profession are more likely to be swayed by opportunities for progression and mid-career pay levels than the starting salary.

4 The way that the media portray teachers is having a negative effect on most undergraduates. It is essential to counteract that; for example, through the way that politicians, teacher unions, careers advisers and

practising teachers project and promote the teaching profession.

5 The survey shows that work experience has a very positive effect on undergraduate choice of teaching as a career. Opportunities for this are far too rare and programmes should be expanded and be ongoing.

Figure 1: Undergraduate rating of career criteria & perceptions of teaching in fulfilling them (scaled ratings with average for all jobs = 1).

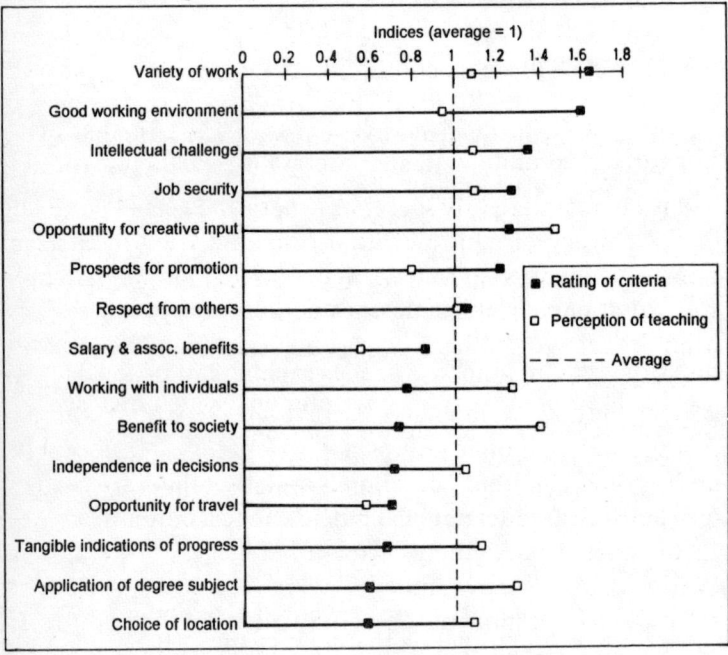

36. Transatlantic Connections: Further Education in the United Kingdom and the United States

Paper by Geoffrey Melling for the National Commission on Education, revised 1993.

Cultural differences

The subject of this paper is the further education (FE) service in the United States, its distinguishing characteristics and their significance for us in Britain as we move towards the turn of the century.

It is often, and rightly said that Americans evince more faith in the efficacy of education than the British. Of course, the inner-city ghettos and some deeply rural localities demonstrate that parts of the American population have withdrawn from the race (or perhaps have never entered it) but communities almost everywhere else give evidence that people are striving for upward mobility. Even in recession, many of those in low socio-economic groups have aspirations for themselves and/or their children. Their hopes and intentions are matched by a belief that education will help them to a better future. Nor is this a new phenomenon: even before the Second World War twice as many students were enrolled in US post-secondary education as anywhere else in the world. The country responded to the pressure by creating a large and highly differentiated post-school education system.

Here in the UK we are only just beginning to see a desire for mass post-16 education. It is likely that, in order to increase participation and satisfy people's requirements, we will have to do as the Americans did and broaden the range of our courses, alter our patterns of attendance, and change our organisational structures. This paper focuses on those characteristics of North American colleges which might help us adapt our institutions for the 21st century.

The structure of American education

The upper rungs of the educational ladder in the US are represented in Figure 1, shown on page 554. The school phase stretches from kindergarten to twelfth grade (K-12) when pupils take their high school diploma; everything beyond school is *post-secondary* or *higher* (the terms are interchangeable). The list of post-secondary institutions includes specialised vocational schools, community colleges, four-year (often private, and usually liberal arts) colleges which award degrees, universities which offer a full range of subjects up to master's level, universities which can award doctorates, and research universities with big post-graduate schools. Those with names which are familiar on this side of the Atlantic are usually four-year colleges (e.g. Amherst, Vassar) or research universities (e.g. Harvard, Princeton, Berkeley), but the community colleges have played a significant part in the provision of education for many people. In the words of a recent book:[1]

> In light of the extraordinary emphasis in the United States on individual economic success and on the role of education as a pathway to it, it is hardly surprising that there has been such a powerful demand from below to expand the educational system . . . The junior college was to play a critical role in this process.

Figure 2 shows the scale of provision in the US.

Community colleges: unity in diversity

Despite the size and heterogeneity of the country, community colleges in America display a surprising amount of similarity. The US has an area of 3.6 million square miles with a population of 250 million. In comparison the UK covers 90,000 square miles and has 56 million people. A physical

Figure 2: Features of Public Community Colleges in the United States

- Over 12m people are enrolled in undergraduate studies in the US, of which about half attend community colleges

- Women form 58% of students

- Enrolment trends
  1945   216,325
  1965 1,152,086
  1985 4,597,838
  1991 6,084,788

- There are over 1,000 public community colleges

- They comprise 40% of higher education institutions

map shows the variety of the terrain but you really need to know the distribution of population and the patterns of settlement and immigration to understand how distant parts of the US are from each other. The variety is compounded in education because it is a sector of responsibility which belongs to the States individually rather than to the federal government.

Yet there are influences which help bind the colleges together so that they have similar purposes and organisational structures. One of the most important is the American Association of Community Colleges (AACC) with 1,222 member colleges across the US which it claims 'form a great network'. This can also be said of institutions in Great Britain, especially as colleges are now funded from central councils in England and Wales and from a government unit in Scotland. In Northern Ireland they are still part of the responsibility of the education and library boards. However, in the UK the institutions have recently formed an organisation of their own, the Association for Colleges (AfC), with the objectives of promoting their image nationally, lobbying central government and its agencies, reminding legislators of the sector's usefulness in fulfilling public policies, and bidding for country-wide projects which can be delivered through its members.

British FE has tended towards fragmentation, either through the ambitions of some establishments to be promoted to a higher league or through the desire of others to demonstrate their subject, organisational or national differences. The North Americans have to date made a better job of shaping a sector while retaining the colleges' variety. AACC does this by creating councils to represent interest groups which want to promote particular aspects of the service such as the views of presidents (i.e. principals), the position of women in the sector and the economy, and education for black Americans. It also gives a voice to international associates. These councils help formulate an annual policy agenda within which the Association and its members work, then AACC promotes the agenda in its lobbying and media activities, keeps in touch with members through newsletters and magazines, and involves itself in major initiatives such as 'Keep America Working' and the 'Futures Commission'. There is something for Britain to learn from programmes such as these. 'Keep America Working' was designed to enhance collaboration between colleges and local employers, and it was financed by a large grant from the Sears Roebuck Foundation. The 'Futures Commission' was the result of a decision by AACC to take stock of the community college movement and develop recommendations to help its members move into the 21st century. Nineteen distinguished Americans were appointed to the Commission under the chairmanship of US Senator Nancy Kassebaum and Professor Ernest Boyer, President of the Carnegie Foundation for the Advancement of Teaching. They undertook 18 months of intensive study, public hearings, campus visits and debate. Their 1988 report, entitled *Building Communities: a Vision for a New Century*, represents a more detailed self-analysis and common prospectus for colleges than anything which has come out of FE in our much smaller nation.[2]

The private sector

Perhaps one reason for British colleges forming AfC rather late in the day is that they are not surrounded by competitors against whom they need to promote themselves as parts of a more important whole.

In America there are 7,500 or so private colleges, 6,500 of which are 'proprietary' (or 'for profit') schools, offering mainly vocational courses. These establishments comprised the fastest growing segment of post-secondary education in the 1980s despite their charging higher fees than the community (or 'non-profit') colleges. They operate in three main areas – business, paramedical and personal care, and technology (including computing) – and they are predominantly monotechnic. In the yellow pages they outnumber community colleges and often have block advertisements which illustrate their specialisms – office work, hairdressing, cosmetics, IT and a whole range of trades. A few of them offer associate degrees (of which more later) but most are content to teach skills for the local labour market in as fast a time as possible. Students at the 'proprietary' schools are eligible for federal loans and grants in the same way as those who enrol at public institutions if their colleges are accredited to offer courses by a federally-recognised agency.

Though private colleges are not a phenomenon to which we pay much attention in the UK at present, we could find them appearing in greater numbers if post-secondary funding were switched to follow the student. They would inevitably compete in those disciplines with high demand and low capital requirements, leaving the FE colleges to deal with less profitable areas. Those who are interested in preserving the public colleges as the main providers into the new century should have an eye to this development across the Atlantic and ensure that their services have a reputation which dominates the market.

Community colleges: their aims and roles

Community colleges are instantaneously recognisable to British visitors as establishments of further education. They are generally bigger (in both size and enrolments), their buildings tend to be more modern, their equipment is better (especially in IT), and their students are older (because they are urged to stay at school to 18 to get their high school diplomas) – but their programmes are similar to ours. If you visit Boston, a city thought by many Americans to be British in outlook, you will be struck by the physical contrast with the UK. Bunker Hill College in the suburbs has its own tube station, and Roxbury Community College, serving a mainly black population deep in the inner city, has brand new buildings. If you venture 60 miles south to Fall River you will be spoiled for choice of parking spaces at the green fields site of Bristol Community College and wonder how long it would take to get around the campus if you were on foot rather than in a car.

Despite this, their work will be familiar. Although American programmes are categorised as *collegiate, career, compensatory* and *community*, you will recognise them as our academic, vocational, special needs and adult non-vocational courses. In the US, collegiate programmes are known as 'transfer' courses, while the other three are sometimes called 'terminal'. This sounds deadly but is merely meant to indicate that they do not count for credit in other forms of higher education. Here in the UK we are still grappling with the issue of a credit base for post-16s. The American model, though limited to academic courses, could help us solve the problem.

Career courses

Career (vocational) courses have come to dominate community college provision since the expansion of the system in the late 1960s and the 1970s. The colleges are now major players on the occupational training field. As early as the 1970s there was a declining market for graduates in the US which added a further stimulus to enrolments in vocational programmes. Similarly, there has been a large increase in compensatory education – not particularly in the special needs areas, though that of course exists, but in helping students make good the deficiencies in their secondary level grades. This work fits with the 'open door' (open access) policies of the colleges and makes good their assertion that they are the institutions which put people in touch with opportunities.

The US is showing great anxiety about the way in which its children fail to attain what the government calls 'world class standards of educational performance' so it has established six national goals (see Figure 3 overleaf) as targets to be met by the year 2000. To that end, the community colleges are helping to bring adults up to the standard of the high school diploma, so that they can progress to more demanding collegiate and career courses. In similar fashion, British colleges are assisting our people to achieve the National Education and Training Targets.[3]

The social role of the colleges, recognised in the term 'community', is similar to that which our institutions have (or have had) in adult education. It is an important concept which helps a college strive to place itself at the centre of its community's learning networks and which encourages it to offer the types of non-vocational and leisure activities which people want, as opposed to the kinds that teachers, government officials or employers think are good for them. The 'Futures Commission' urged colleges to adopt the community concept as their central purpose out of which their other aims would grow. The epigraph at the front of its report reads 'The term *community* should be defined not only as a region to be served, but also as a climate to be created'. That kind of language has not been popular recently in Britain, but the sentiment is something we need to consider seriously if we aim to create a post-school education system capable of attracting all comers.

Figure 3: The Six National Education Goals in the United States

> By the Year 2000:
>
> 1 All children in America will start school ready to learn.
>
> 2 The high school graduation rate will increase to at least 90 per cent.
>
> 3 American students will leave grades, four, eight, and twelve having demonstrated competency in challenging subject matter, including English, mathematics, science, history, and geography; and every school in America will ensure that all students learn to use their minds well, so they may be prepared for responsible citizenship, further learning, and productive employment in our modern economy.
>
> 4 US students will be the first in the world in science and mathematics achievement.
>
> 5 Every adult American will be literate and will possess the knowledge and skills necessary to compete in a global economy and exercise the rights and responsibilities of citizenship.
>
> 6 Every school in America will be free of drugs and violence and will offer a disciplined environment conducive to learning.

Collegiate courses

It is the collegiate courses which give the community colleges the status of institutions of HE. In America they do not constitute a different sector like British FE colleges. Collegiate courses are equal to the first half of a degree at a four-year college or university – a situation which has led to the alternative names for community colleges of 'two-year', 'junior', 'short cycle' or 'lower division' colleges. There is some evidence that William Rainey Harper, the President of the University of Chicago, who stimulated the foundation of the first junior college – at Joliet, Illinois, in 1905 – did so with the intention of 'cooling out' large numbers of students in order to leave an intellectual élite at the higher level or 'upper division' of his institution, but that does not make the transfer function less important. Though it is true that only a minority of those who start collegiate courses today progress immediately to studies at a university, the opportunity is there for them to leave community college with an associate (or two-year) degree (Associate of Arts, Associate of Science, or Associate of Applied Sciences) if they succeed in the required number of subjects. They can then cash the credits at a later time, if they wish. Fully half of first-time degree enrolments in the US occur at community colleges which indicates how common a phenomenon higher education is over there.

The British attempt at creating a two-year higher level course which was both a terminal qualification and a step towards a degree – the Diploma in Higher Education – failed to find a market among students or employers, but it was available only at polytechnics and similar institutions, not in local FE colleges. The new practice of franchising the first year or two of degree courses from polytechnics to colleges will almost certainly grow and give us a major alternative form of entry to HE in the 21st century, which will mark our colleges too as important gatekeepers to higher education. It will probably lead to some tension between the academic and vocational strands of a college, as it has in America where the differences among programmes have not yet been resolved through the credit system. It will be a mark of good management in British colleges of the 21st century to ensure that the programmes can exist and dovetail in the institutions. If interest in the higher replaces commitment to the further, the FE colleges will be accused of 'academic drift', as were the polytechnics in their time.

The distinguishing characteristics of American HE have

been in place since 1900 – the elective system (which allows students to choose from a wide range of subjects), the modular course, credit accumulation, and transfer or progression to other institutions based on attainment (measured by 'grade points'). Thus the US had a structure ready to cope with expansion long before it occurred (though even at the beginning of the century one in four Americans attended college). In the UK we are still not convinced of the virtues of modular courses, and the debate on them is likely to continue for some time yet.

The American system of transfer depends on the acceptable 'distribution' and credit-worthiness of the subject modules which a student takes in years one and two of a degree course. Their acceptability is hallmarked by the recognition accorded to his/her college by one of the regional accrediting associations. Without institutional accreditation, a college has great difficulty in transferring its students because the hallmark is the guarantor of quality. The colleges determine course content and assessment procedures in conjunction with specialist bodies, and they are scrutinised every five years by the accrediting associations to ensure that their standards are suitable and consistent.

The 'distribution requirements' are rules which oblige students to include broadening elements in their courses. There is a stronger tradition of general education in US community colleges than there is in Britain, where the issue is picked up in a different fashion, through a call for core skills for 16–19s on both academic and vocational courses. For example, the National Curriculum Council identify six core skills: communication, problem-solving, personal skills, numeracy, information technology and modern language competence. Americans favour breadth of subject matter whereas the British prefer to embed generic elements in existing courses. As yet, it is impossible to say which stance is better, though something in the American approach develops an admirable self-confidence in their young people. It is something to be evaluated in the next few years.

The service base of college organisation

The American system is very flexible: it allows students to attend the same course on either a full-time or part-time basis; it gives them choice of a wide range of subjects (but around a common core); it permits intermittent rather than end-of-programme assessment; it encourages transfer and progression among institutions. But this flexibility has to be bolstered by a large number of services without which it would not work and the quality of the service would be poor: access and enrolment arrangements; educational advice; personal and financial counselling; vocational guidance and placement; day care for children; learning resource centres for independent and supported study; distance learning; assessment centres and procedures for the assessment of prior learning. If we wish to expand our post-school provision we will have to get heavily involved in activities of this kind. They will all need to be staffed – though not necessarily with teachers. Colleges beyond 2000 are likely to have more cadres of personnel than they have at present. As the Further Education Funding Council suggests, they are also likely to arrange their activities around the three major phases of a student's college experience – entry, learning, and exit – and that will help us develop strong related services.

Community colleges have four levels of organisation: trustees, administration, faculty and staff. The trustees govern the institution; they may be elected or appointed; and they are usually much fewer in number than the governing body of a UK college. The 'administration' is the top management – the president or chief executive officer, the vice president and the deans of faculty. Together with the trustees they negotiate the salaries of other employees, the most powerful body of which are the 'faculty', also known as 'instructors'. This term gives some insight into what the Americans consider to be the prime purpose and methodology of teaching. Faculty, on the whole, just teach

– other functions are undertaken by the 'staff', who may well be professionals in their own right (in for example finance, counselling, vocational guidance etc.). This kind of stratification is beginning to appear in the UK, and is likely to continue up to and beyond the end of the decade. It will lead to our colleges being more flexible and to their working a longer year than many of them cover at the moment. It may also lead to some dissent as teachers lose aspects of their role to other kinds of worker. Our colleges' 'administration' will have to become increasingly more adept at human resource management and development if colleges change in this fashion.

Another consequence of the flexibility of American post-secondary education has been the creation in colleges of sections of 'institutional research' (IR). These sections collect all kinds of data about students, programmes, the college's hinterland, local industry and the like. IR offices were established throughout the system during the 1970s, though, on the whole, they receive a smaller share of a college's budget than equivalent initiatives in universities. Increasingly they are used to demonstrate the effectiveness of an institution, its efficiency and accountability. They are heavily involved in the 'self study' which precedes the five-yearly accreditation visits and which, in the most advanced colleges, is becoming a continuous process. These days IR sections also address important questions related to the quality of provision, institutional priorities and bids for alternative sources of funding. To perform these tasks they employ computerised management information services (CMIS) in a more sophisticated way than we do here, though bodies such as the National Association for Information Technology in Further Education are promoting better use of IT in Britain. There is no doubt that UK colleges will have to use CMIS for student tracking and advice, and for planning and modelling their futures, as well as for collecting data, as the decade wears on.

Four principal goals for community colleges

It is a myth that Americans believe in entrepreneurship rather than state planning; they are happy for the two to co-exist. It is also not true, as is sometimes said in Britain, that community colleges are supported largely by business: their funds come from tax revenue in their localities and States, from fees, and from government contracts in much the same way as ours do here. Thus those who have charge of the public purse have a major say in the provision of college education. The State of California reviewed its master plan for higher education in 1987. The report of the commission which undertook the work recommended that changes be directed to the achievement of four principal goals:

- *unity*, to ensure that all elements of the system worked together in pursuit of common educational goals;

- *equity*, to ensure that all Californians had unrestricted opportunity to fulfil their educational potential and aspirations;

- *quality*, to ensure that excellence characterised every aspect of the system; and

- *efficiency*, to ensure the most productive use of finite financial and human resources.

In the same period, we in the UK were putting the emphasis on the last of the aims – efficiency. We were just beginning to stress the importance of quality; and we were paying little or no attention to equity and unity. Indeed, these latter concepts were brought into sharp focus in England and Wales by the opposition of adult and further education interests to aspects of the FHE Bill which was enacted in 1992. The Californian report recommended that the State's community colleges should continue with all strands of provision; they should offer academic and vocational education at lower division level for the great majority of college-age and older students; they should provide remedial instruction for students who were inadequately prepared for post-secondary education; and they should offer State-supported non-credit courses as deemed appropriate by the Board of Governors as well as fee-supported community-serving instruction. The community colleges should also have the principal but not the exclusive responsibility for vocational education. The commission recommended that the State should guarantee by statute a place in post-secondary education for all qualified California students who wished to attend, and that students who elected to enrol at a community college and succeeded in the lower division should be guaranteed future enrolment as upper division students in the University of California or the California State University. About the community colleges the commission said: 'the success of the whole system depends on them'.

This point is put more forcefully by the 'Futures Commission' of AACC – though we must remember that they are an interested party. Their report says: 'One point emerges with stark clarity from all we have said: community colleges and the nation's future are inextricably interlocked ... Future generations of Americans must be educated for life in an increasingly complex world. Knowledge must be made available to the workforce to keep America an economically vital place'. I believe those statements to be equally true here. If we are to expand education beyond 16 it will have to be done through a range of courses which are relevant to working life because most people have had enough of single subject general education by the time they reach school-leaving age. If we are to raise the skill base of the nation it will have to be done through public agencies because we have witnessed too often the failure of employers (particularly small and medium sized enterprises) to pick up the training burden. If we are to extend education beyond 18 we will have to ensure local access to degree programmes because most adults have commitments which they cannot easily jettison (nor should we encourage them to do so) in order to travel and live away from home. The logical solution to these problems for the 21st century is the local college. It is doing a good job now. It would do an even better one if we adopted some of the characteristics of the North American system.

References

1 Brint, S. and Barabel, J. (1989). *The Diverted Dream.* Oxford University Press, New York.
2 American Association of Community and Junior Colleges (1988). *Building Communities: A Vision for a New Century.* AACC, Washington DC.
3 The National Education and Training Targets specify two sets of goals:

   Foundation Learning:

   1. By 1997, 80% of young people to reach NVQ II (or equivalent)
   2. Training and education to NVQ III (or equivalent) available to all young people who can benefit
   3. By 2000, 50% of young people to reach NVQ III (or equivalent)
   4. Education and training provision to develop self-reliance, flexibility and breadth.

   Lifetime Learning:

   1. By 1996, all employees should take part in training or development activities
   2. By 1996, 50% of the workforce aiming for NVQs or units towards them
   3. By 2000, 50% of the workforce qualified to at least NVQ III (or equivalent)
   4. By 1996, 50% of medium or large organisations to be 'Investors in People'.

554 *Insights into Education and Training*

Figure 1: Levels of education, USA.

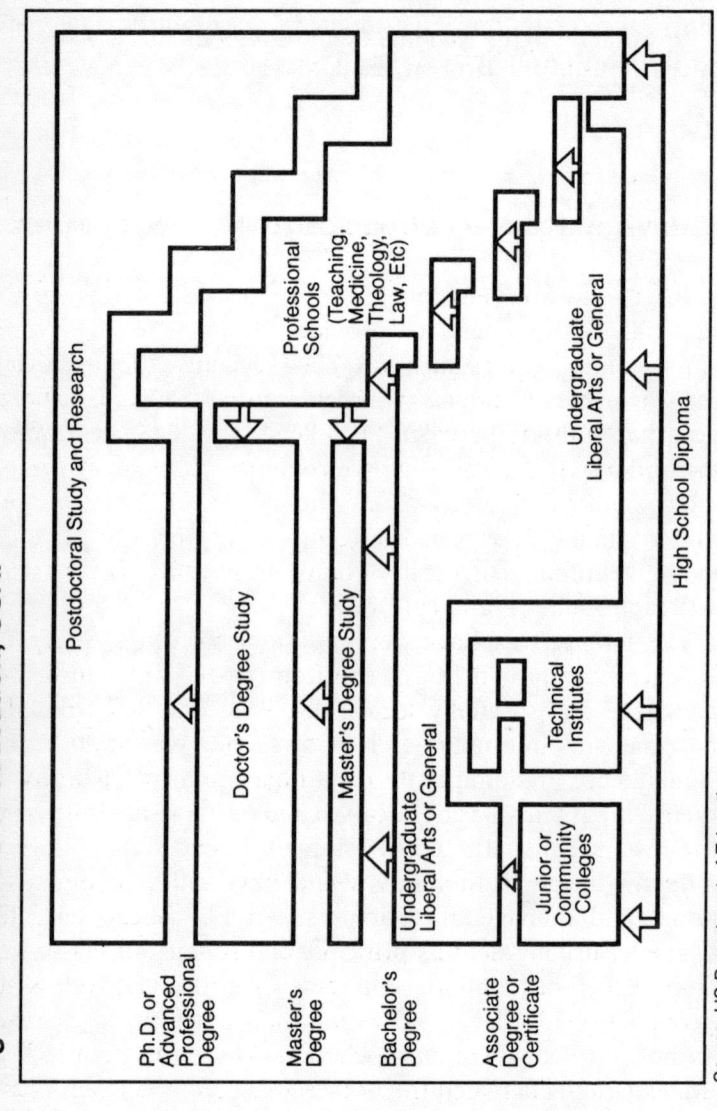

Source: US Department of Education

37. The Interface Between Higher and Further Education

A Presentation to the National Commission on Education by Michael Austin and Dr. Bernard R. MacManus, March 1992.

The view from a college of further education

Further education (FE) colleges are already responding enthusiastically to the challenge provided by plans for significant expansion in higher education. They recognise that achieving the Government's targets will require much greater collaboration than hitherto between FE colleges and higher education institutions (HEIs) and they welcome the new opportunities which will be created within the FE sector. They do not underestimate, however, the complexities involved in creating new working partnerships between institutions with very different traditions and cultures.

The two sectors have very different histories. Many FE colleges have grown out of the former Mechanics Institutes and have an essentially local role, quite different from the national and international role of higher education. Their students are predominantly part-timers, and the majority of their work is fairly basic education and training. Institutions in the two sectors also enjoy quite different status, have a different image of themselves and have different organisational and managerial structures. An FE college will, for example, usually field its principal and senior officers in any cross-sector negotiation, whereas an HEI may well send people at faculty level, who may then need to seek further authority to conclude an agreement. There can be a lack of understanding between the two sectors about their respective approaches to the educational process. The lukewarm reception by university admissions tutors of the vocationally-oriented BTEC qualifications, and their unwillingness, in some cases, to take a look beyond A levels in assessing what is an appropriate preparation for entry to higher education, is just one example.

Where FE colleges are undertaking teaching at higher education level, for example through HND courses, it is a prized part of the portfolio. The sector is now beginning to see the development of a multiplicity of models for institutional collaboration: one plus three degrees, where an 'access' year is provided by the college; two plus two degrees, where students transfer to an HEI after their second year; and franchising arrangements where all three years of a degree course are taught by the FE college. In Accrington and Rossendale College there is now a scheme with Sheffield University whereby youngsters of fourteen are given an early introduction to the idea of higher education.

The nature of institutional links varies considerably. In some places they are geographically determined, with colleges working with their closest higher education neighbour. Other collaborations range over quite a distance. Some HEIs prefer to form exclusive links with a college or consortium of colleges, while some FE colleges are 'promiscuous' in their alliances with higher education. Where institutional interests and objectives have coincided, however, progress has sometimes been remarkably fast. One example is the Open College of the Northwest, which originally linked Nelson and Colne College, Lancaster University and Preston Polytechnic in providing a programme of courses essentially aimed at facilitating access, and has now developed to cover more than two dozen colleges in the North West.

There are distinct advantages for both sides in undertaking collaborative ventures:

- HEIs are supplied with acclimatised students with secure motivation. FE colleges have demonstrated that they have the capability to prepare students to cope with the higher education environment.
- FE colleges benefit in terms of staff and curriculum

development, and in terms of the additional student recruitment.

- The introduction of work at higher education level enhances the status of FE colleges, confirms their role in the locality, and strengthens their claims to be 'one-stop shops'.

There are also impediments:

- The two sectors operate on different timescales. FE colleges are able to respond much faster to new initiatives.

- There are problems about standards. FE colleges have not, as yet, got all the necessary procedures in place to secure standards, not only in terms of the quality of teaching, but also of the supporting environment, i.e. libraries, computer networks, laboratory facilities etc.

- The two sectors have different objectives. FE is very locally oriented. HEIs are sometimes suspected of a 'missionary' attitude in their dealings with FE.

- Financial arrangements can cause friction where franchising deals, under which colleges are paid a per capita fee for students who remain on the books of the higher education partner, can be seen by the FE colleges as unfavourably weighted against them.

- There is a danger of 'academic drift' for the colleges. They have a distinct mission which they do not wish to lose.

There are many opportunities:

- The introduction of new subject disciplines and cognitive areas.

- New modes of study and new interpretations of what constitutes full- and part-time study.

- The greater and more innovative use of new technology, allowing the development of on-line computer links with HEIs.

- The growing interest in the accreditation of prior learning.

- Staff exchanges between HEIs and FE colleges.

- Greater financial flexibility arising from new streams of fee income.

Visitors from community colleges in the US would recognise many of the features of the developing links between the two sectors in the UK, although the context is different. The FE sector in the UK is very willing to work with higher education, but at the same time looks to higher education for guidance, help and support.

The view from a higher education institution

Increasingly, higher education institutions are recognising the value of close working partnerships with FE colleges. There is a growing overlap in the work of the two sectors, particularly in areas such as management studies, nursing and supervisory studies. The development of National Vocational Qualifications (NVQs) and the operations of the Training and Enterprise Councils (TECs) are contributing to this convergence.

The former polytechnics grew up with the idea of ladders of attainment, and were perhaps disappointed that, as the system developed in the sixties, seventies and eighties, A levels established their dominance to the detriment of other more diverse routes. The colleges are, however, becoming recognised as a very good source of engineering and design students. Whereas the school and A level route has difficulty in supplying enough good candidates, the standard and orientation of students coming through the FE route is very encouraging.

Higher education is much more thinly distributed than FE. There is a need to articulate the network of relations between HEIs and FE colleges more efficiently at regional level. The mission of Bournemouth Polytechnic (now Bournemouth University) is strongly oriented towards outreach and aims to use selected FE colleges as the vehicle for taking the facilities and provision of higher education into adjoining territories. Bournemouth has interesting geographical features in that none of the surrounding counties except Hampshire enjoys higher education provision. There is, however, a great deal of interesting industrial activity, and much potential for development and growth, to which higher education could contribute. Technology transfer and the geographical dimension therefore figure significantly in the Polytechnic's institutional strategy.

Bournemouth decided to use franchising as its means of outreach, and identified three colleges, strategically placed within a distance of about thirty to forty miles, in areas of industrial need and opportunity: Yeovil, the Isle of Wight and Bournemouth and Poole. It was decided that if relationships were to work well they must be contractually secured over a number of years. A detailed contract was devised, making provision for an initial five-year relationship, with a three-year rolling format thereafter. The contract gave the Polytechnic a stake in the three colleges' development planning, although it recognised that the major influence on planning would be the new FE Funding Council.

The arrangements provide for the delivery of whole programmes, not just elements of a course. In the first instance HNDs have been franchised. There has been an entry of 90 to the HND course, with the three colleges each taking thirty. Quality has been a key issue in the first year of operation. In particular, the quality of the environment in the colleges as compared to that in the Polytechnic has been a bone of contention with the students. One of the spin-offs of the initiative will be improved access. Students successfully completing the HND will have the opportunity to enter the third year of an appropriate degree course.

The colleges have all been extremely enthusiastic, and there is considerable will to succeed. In one area the local Development Corporation has begun to take an active interest in the project. The extent to which colleges will be able to wrestle with priorities and overcome the undeniable difficulties in delivering remains to be seen, however. The arrangements have only been operating for one year, and there are already differences in the comparative performance of the three participants.

Looking to the future

The development of close collaborative arrangements between higher and further education is a relatively new but fast growing phenomenon. It is clear that there are many different models of interaction, from the opportunistic 'quick fix' to highly structured contractual arrangements such as those at Bournemouth. No one model will necessarily become dominant, as institutions will wish to retain the flexibility to create partnerships and alliances in a form which best supports their individual institutional strategy and mission. There will be a need, however, to ensure that the basic understandings between institutions are clearly articulated from the outset.

Funding arrangements will be particularly important, especially so, perhaps, for the colleges which need to invest in infrastructure if they are to meet the necessary environmental standards. It will be essential to the success of cross-sectoral partnerships that higher education partners concerned to maximise income – as they must in the present funding climate – do not under-fund franchising arrangements, and thereby put quality at risk. Opportunities to acquire top-up finance are available – for example, those provided by the European Community Regional Fund – and, in many areas, it would be possible to mount economic arguments for support.

FE colleges have a strong tradition of providing vocational

and craft training at local level. Grafting a role in higher education on to that well-understood mission has the potential to shift the aspirations of a college, and to lead to its traditional work becoming undervalued. It would be highly undesirable if the distinctive contribution of the colleges were to be overshadowed by a desire to move up in the academic hierarchy, and away from vocational work. The recent establishment of the Further Education Funding Council will strengthen and re-focus the sector, however. It will help to monitor future development and to ensure that relationships between FE colleges and HEIs are grounded in the recognition of complementary strengths and common objectives, rather than imitation or financial opportunism.

The outlook for the future is encouraging, but the successful establishment of collaborative ventures will require the co-operation not just of colleges and universities, but of individual teachers and administrators within them. It will be vitally important that institutions in both sectors recognise the new demands which will be made on staff and that they give sufficient priority to the development and support of those on the front line.

Appendix A. Statistics

A.1 Young people aged 16–18 in the early 1990s.

A.1.1: GCSE attempts and achievements by 16-year-old pupils, 1991-92, England.

Percentages

	No. of pupils on schools' rolls[1] who became 16 years old in the academic year 1991-92 (thousands)	Entered for one or more GCSEs	Achieving one or more GCSEs at grades A-G	Achieving five or more GCSEs at grades A-G	Achieving five or more GCSEs at grades A-E	Achieving five or more GCSEs at grades A-C
Boys 278.9		91.8	90.3	79.4	63.3	34.1
Girls 265.2		94.0	93.0	85.3	72.3	42.7
Total 544.1		92.9	91.6	82.2	67.6	38.3

Source: Department for Education, Statistical Bulletin 15/93, June 1993.

[1] Ninety-eight per cent of the population of 16-year-olds were on school rolls at the start of the academic year.

A1.2: GCSE attempts and achievements by the end of academic year 1991-92 for those reaching the age of 16 during that academic year, England.

Percentages

Subjects	Attempting GCSE	Achieving grades A-C	Achieving grades A-E	Achieving grades A-G
English	88	48	79	87
Mathematics	84	37	64	79
Any science	86	37	67	82
Any modern language	74	34	56	71
English/Mathematics/ Science	80	27	57	75
English/Mathematics/ Science and a modern language	60	20	41	57
Any subject	92	65	86	90

Source: Department for Education, Statistical Bulletin No. 15/93, June 1993, and communication.

A1.3: Participation of 16, 17 and 18-year-olds in education 1988-89 and 1992-93, England.

Percentage of estimated population

	Type of study		
	Full-time	Part-time	All
16-year-olds			
Males			
1988-89	48.5	19.2	67.7
1992-93	67.9	9.5	77.4
Change	+19.4	−9.7	+9.7
Females			
1988-89	55.0	13.8	68.8
1992-93	74.7	7.1	81.8
Change	+19.7	−6.7	+13.0
17-year-olds			
Males			
1988-89	32.9	21.5	54.4
1992-93	51.5	13.7	65.2
Change	+18.6	−7.8	+10.8
Females			
1988-89	38.0	13.8	51.7
1992-93	59.0	8.8	67.8
Change	+21.0	−5.0	+16.1
18-year-olds			
Males			
1988-89	18.8	17.6	36.4
1992-93	33.3	14.9	48.2
Change	+14.5	−2.7	+11.8
Females			
1988-89	18.5	9.8	28.4
1992-93	34.7	8.9	43.6
Change	+16.2	−0.9	+15.2

Source: Department for Education, Statistical Bulletin No. 16/93.

A1.4: Participation of 16, 17 and 18-year-olds in full-time study 1988-89 and 1992-93, England.

Percentage of estimated population

Age and Course of Study	Year 1988-89	Year 1992-93	Change
16-year-olds			
A/AS levels	27.0	35.2	+ 8.2
BTEC National	3.0	6.7	+ 3.7
GCSE	8.9	10.1	+ 1.2
Other courses	12.1	18.6	+ 6.5
All[1]	**51.7**	**71.2**	**+19.5**
17-year-olds			
Higher education	0.2	0.3	+ 0.1
A/AS levels	22.5	32.9	+10.4
BTEC National	4.3	9.7	+ 5.4
GCSE	1.6	2.1	+ 0.5
Other courses	6.4	9.8	+ 3.4
All[1]	**35.4**	**55.2**	**+19.8**
18-year-olds			
Higher education: First degree	7.9	14.0	+ 6.1
Higher education: Sub-degree	1.2	2.3	+ 1.1
A/AS levels	4.0	6.3	+ 2.3
BTEC National	2.2	5.6	+ 3.4
GCSE	0.3	0.5	+ 0.2
Other courses	2.7	5.0	+ 2.3
All[1]	**18.7**	**34.0**	**+15.3**

Source: Department for Education, Statistical Bulletin No. 16/93.

[1] Including those in special schools for whom no course type breakdown is available.

A1.5: Economic activity of 16 and 17-year-olds in autumn 1992, Great Britain.

Thousands and percentages

Whether in full-time education	In employment[1] Thous.	%	ILO unemployed[2] Thous.	%	Economically inactive Thous.	%	Total Thous.	%
Yes	305 [3]	23.3	45	3.4	515	39.4	866	66.3
No	312	23.9	94	7.2	35	2.7	441	33.7
of which with no qualifications [4]	75	5.7	48	3.7	21	1.6	146	11.1
Total	617	47.2	139	10.6	550	42.1	1,307	100.0

Source: Labour Force Survey, Autumn 1992. Employment Department (Crown Copyright).

[1] Including those on government training programmes.
[2] Those looking for employment and available to start work or those waiting to start work.
[3] Employed outside normal school and college hours, including those on government training programmes involving full-time education at the time of the survey.
[4] Including those who did not state whether they had qualifications or not.

A1.6: Education and labour market status of 16 and 17 year olds, autumn 1992, Great Britain.

Thousands

	Labour market status			
	In employment	ILO unemployed	Economically inactive	Total
16 year olds				
In full-time education	143	31	307	481
Not in full-time education	101	44	14	159
Total	243	75	321	640
17 year olds				
In full-time education	163	14	208	385
Not in full-time education	211	51	21	282
Total	374	64	229	667
All 16 and 17 year olds	617	139	550	1,307

Source: Labour Force Survey, Autumn 1992. Employment Department (Crown Copyright).

A1.7: Education and training condition of 16 and 17 year olds, autumn 1992, Great Britain.

Thousands and percentages

	Males Thous.	%	Females Thous.	%	Persons Thous.	%
In full-time education	419	63	447	70	866	66
Not in full-time education						
On government employment and training schemes[1]	78	12	56	9	134	10
In employment						
With job related training	30	4	17	3	48	4
Without job related training	69	10	56	9	125	10
Self employed	5	1	—	—	5	—
ILO unemployed	52	8	42	7	94	7
Economically inactive	15	2	20	3	35	3
Total	249	37	191	30	441	34
Total	668	100	638	100	1,307	100

Source: Labour Force Survey, Autumn 1992. Employment Department (Crown Copyright); NCE estimate for self-employed.

[1] Estimates from the Labour Force Survey of those on government schemes tend to be lower than those based on administrative records.

A.2. Maintained and independent schools compared.

A2.1: GCSE attainments for maintained and independent schools for those aged 16, 1991, England.

Percentages

	Independent schools (46,600 pupils)		Maintained schools (508,600 pupils)	
5+ at grade G or better	92.9		82.1	
of which: 5+ grades A-C		80.1		32.8
1-4 grades A-C		11.4		29.4
no grades A-C		1.4		19.8
4 at grade G or better	0.3		3.5	
1-3 at grade G or better	2.4		7.4	
No graded result	4.4		7.0	
Total	100		100	

Source: Derived from DFE School Examination Survey 1990/1.

A2.2: A level attainments of school leavers for maintained and independent schools, 1991, England.

Percentages

Percentage of school leavers with:	Independent schools (47,700 leavers)	Maintained schools (494,200 leavers)
3+ A level/AS passes	57.2	12.0
2 A level/AS passes	10.0	5.4
1 A level/AS pass	5.6	3.6
Total: 1+ A level/AS pass	72.7	21.1

Source: Derived from DFE School Examination Survey 1990/1. NB: 2 AS passes = 1 A level pass.

A2.3: A level attainments of school leavers for maintained and independent schools, 1961-1991, England.

	% of leavers with 1 or 2 A levels		% of leavers with 3+ A levels		Total number of leavers (000s)	
	Independent	Maintained	Independent	Maintained	Independent	Maintained
1961	18.0	3.0	19.6	3.1	41.6	571.2
1971	24.7	7.2	34.1	6.5	41.4	572.0
1981	17.7	6.4	45.3	7.1	44.1	689.9
1991	15.6	9.0	57.2	12.0	47.7	494.2

Source: Derived from DES Statistics of Education.

A2.4: Chances of attaining 3+ A levels in maintained and independent schools, 1961-1991, England.

	% of leavers with 3 or more A levels						
	1961	1966	1971	1976	1981	1986	1991
Maintained school	3.1	5.4	6.5	6.5	7.1	7.4	12.0
Independent school	19.6	26.2	34.1	38.7	45.3	46.4	57.2
Odds Ratios	7.6	6.2	7.4	9.1	10.8	10.7	9.8

Sources: (i) DFE School Examination Survey. (ii) Halsey, A. and others (1984). The Political Arithmetic of Public Schools. In: Walford, G. (1984). British Public Schools: Policy and Practice. Falmer Press.

A2.5: Independent schools' share of attainments of school leavers, England.

Percentages (and nos.)

	1 or more O level/ GCSE grade A-C	5 or more O level/ GCSE grade A-C	1 or more A levels	3 or more A levels
1961	21.9 (36,700)	27.1 (25,300)	31.0 (15,700)	31.3 (8,100)
1971	16.5 (38,200)	21.9 (29,000)	23.8 (24,400)	27.5 (14,100)
1981	12.4 (41,300)	20.5 (33,000)	23.0 (27,800)	29.1 (20,000)
1991	11.9 (42,600)	18.3 (37,300)	25.0 (34,700)	31.5 (27,300)

Source: DES Statistics of Education.

A2.6: Shares of A level attainments of independent schools, maintained schools and FE colleges.

Percentages (and nos.)

	\multicolumn{3}{c}{1 or more A levels}	\multicolumn{3}{c}{3 or more A levels}
	Independent school	Maintained school	F.E. college	Independent school	Maintained school	F.E. college
1981	19.8 (27,800)	66.3 (93,000)	13.8 (19,400)	26.9 (20,000)	65.3 (48,600)	7.8 (5,800)
1991	20.3 (34,700)	60.8 (104,000)	18.9 (32,400)	27.6 (27,300)	60.2 (59,400)	12.2 (12,000)

Source: Derived from DFE School Examination Survey.

A2.7: Activities of 16 year olds from independent and maintained schools, 1991, England.

Percentages

	Independent school (46,600 pupils)	Maintained school (508,600 pupils)
Staying on at school	83.4	38.6
Going to full-time FE/HE	12.0	22.0
of which: A/AS level	4.2	4.3
GCSE	0.2	1.3
other courses	7.5	16.6
YTS	0.3	9.4
Available for work	1.8	17.1
Other/not known	2.6	12.9
Total	100	100

Source: Derived from DFE School Examination Survey.

A2.8: Participation of 16–18 year old age group in independent and maintained schools and F.E. colleges doing different courses, 1991-92, England.

Percentages

Age	Independent School 16	17	18	Maintained School Inc. 6th Form College 16	17	18	F.E. College Inc. Tertiary College 16	17	18	Total 16	17	18
A/AS	5.8	5.3	0.6	23.9	20.8	2.5	5.1	5.4	3.0	34.9	31.4	6.1
BTEC	—	—	—	—	—	—	8.9	8.1	4.3	8.9	8.1	4.3
GCSE	0.6	0.1	—	8.1	0.9	0.1	2.9	1.1	0.4	11.6	2.1	0.5
Other	0.3	0.2	0.1	2.7	0.4	0.1	8.2	6.1	3.4	11.2	6.7	3.7
All courses	6.6	5.6	0.7	34.6	22.0	2.8	25.2	20.7	11.1	67.1	49.0	28.5

Source: Derived from DFE Statistical Bulletin 14/92.

NB: Total figures for all courses for 17 and 18 year olds include participation in HE.

A2.9: Applicants to universities by A level point score, 1991, England and Wales.

Percentages (and nos.)

	Independent school	Maintained school	F.E. and H.E.
2 + A level passes or equivalent: points scored			
30-26	31.8 *(8,911)*	18.0 *(14,136)*	9.1 *(2,174)*
25-21	17.7 *(5,251)*	14.9 *(11,654)*	11.4 *(2,700)*
20-16	23.6 *(6,621)*	24.7 *(19,174)*	24.6 *(5,846)*
15-11	11.6 *(3,627)*	15.9 *(12,440)*	18.1 *(4,303)*
10-6	9.7 *(2,730)*	16.5 *(12,981)*	21.2 *(5,049)*
5 or fewer	1.0 *(273)*	2.1 *(1,665)*	3.0 *(710)*
Less than 2 A level passes	3.6 *(1,007)*	8.1 *(6,387)*	12.6 *(3,001)*
Total with A levels	100 *(28,060)*	100 *(78,437)*	100 *(23,783)*
Average score	20.7	17.8	15.7

Source: Derived from UCCA Statistical Supplement to 29th Report.

A2.10: Success rates of applicants to universities by A level point score, 1991, England and Wales.

Percentages (numbers of acceptances in brackets)

	Independent school	Maintained school	F.E. and H.E.
2 + A level passes or equivalent: points scored			
30-26	87.7 *(7,812)*	93.2 *(13,174)*	90.1 *(1,959)*
25-21	83.3 *(4,373)*	84.8 *(9,888)*	80.0 *(2,158)*
20-16	59.0 *(3,906)*	58.8 *(11,272)*	53.3 *(3,115)*
15-11	34.6 *(1.131)*	34.7 *(4,316)*	32.3 *(1,389)*
10-6	21.4 *(584)*	22.4 *(2,904)*	19.5 *(987)*
5 or fewer	13.2 *(36)*	15.8 *(263)*	13.7 *(97)*
Total with A levels	63.6 *(17,842)*	53.3 *(41,817)*	40.8 *(9,705)*
Average score of those accepted	23.2	21.2	19.3

Source: Derived from UCCA Statistical Supplement to 29th Report.

A2.11: Senior members of élite occupations educated in HMC schools, 1939-1984, United Kingdom.

Percentages

	1939	1950	1960	1970-1	1984
Ambassadors	95	82	86	87	78 (+5)
Judiciary	90	92	88	84 (+3)	84 (+2)
Bishops	91	84	80	78	66
Bankers	92	90	84	82 (+3)	70 (+2)
Civil servants	91	68	69	68	49 (+4)
Army	84	83	91	90 (+2)	74 (+3)
RAF	85	79	68	70 (+3)	36 (+4)
Navy	42	18	23	39	25 (+8)
All	83	74	74	71 (+1)	60 (+3)
All non-service	89	80	78	77 (+1)	63 (+3)

Sources: (i) Boyd, D. (1973). Elites and their Education. NFER.
(ii) Reid, I and others (1991). The Education of the Elite. In: Walford, G. (ed.) (1991). Private Schooling. Paul Chapman.
NB: Figures in brackets for 1970-1 and 1984 show the percentages from non-HMC independent schools.

A3. Education expenditure

A3.1: Public expenditure on education in the 1980s, United Kingdom.

	1979-80	1980-1	1981-2	1982-3	1983-4	1984-5	1985-6	1986-7	1987-8	1988-9	1989-90
Total in cash terms (£m)	10,539	12,941	14,041	15,037	15,946	16,516	17,288	18,802	20,401	22,137	24,102
Real terms (1990-1 prices using GDP Deflator)	22,911	23,745	23,519	23,495	23,836	23,494	23,299	24,546	25,249	25,562	26,141
Year on year changes in real terms (%)	−1.1	3.6	−1.5	−0.1	1.4	−1.4	−0.8	5.3	2.9	1.2	2.3
Volume terms (1990-1 prices using education deflator)	26,177	25,821	25,053	25,124	25,393	25,165	24,901	25,274	25,398	25,625	26,088
Year on year changes in volume terms (%)	2.2	−1.4	−3.0	0.3	1.1	−0.9	−1.0	1.5	0.5	0.8	1.9
Cash terms as % of GDP	5.1	5.4	5.4	5.3	5.1	5.0	4.8	4.8	4.7	4.6	4.6
Cash terms as % of public expenditure	11.7	11.9	11.6	11.3	11.3	10.8	10.7	11.1	11.4	11.9	11.8

Source: National Commission on Education (1993). Learning to Succeed, p389, notes 5 and 6.

A3.2: Public expenditure on education in countries of the United Kingdom, 1990-1.

	England & Wales	Scotland	Northern Ireland	United Kingdom
Overall expenditure on education (£m)	22,849	2,799	954	26,602
Total population (thousands)	50,904	5,068	1,590	57,562
Population aged 0-24 (thousands)	16,995	1,733	665	19,393
Expenditure per capita (£)	449	552	600	462
Expenditure per person aged 0-24 (£)	1,344	1,615	1,435	1,372

Sources: Communication with DFE and OPCS.

A3.3: Public expenditure per school pupil on specific items in the 1980s, England.

£

	1979-80	1980-1	1981-2	1982-3	1983-4	1984-5	1985-6	1986-7	1987-8	1988-9	1989-90
Repairs and maintenance											
Cash terms	28	35	37	43	48	50	51	59	63	64	75
Real terms (1990-1 prices using specific deflator)	72	79	76	84	85	84	78	86	84	74	79
Books											
Cash terms	2.8	3.1	3.5	4.1	4.3	4.6	4.9	5.9	6.3	6.9	7.8
Real terms (1990-1 prices using specific deflator)	9.6	9.0	8.8	9.0	8.0	7.5	7.2	8.0	7.9	8.1	8.5

Source: National Commission on Education (1993). Learning to Succeed, p391, note 25.

Appendix B. The Commission's Vision and Goals

The Commission's Vision

1. In all countries *knowledge and applied intelligence* have become central to economic success and personal and social well-being.

2. In the United Kingdom much higher achievement in education and training is needed to match world standards.

3. Everyone must want to learn and have ample opportunity and encouragement to do so.

4. All children must achieve a good grasp of literacy and basic skills early on as the foundation for learning throughout life.

5. The full range of people's abilities must be recognised and their development rewarded.

6. High-quality learning depends above all on the knowledge, skill, effort and example of teachers and trainers.

7. It is the role of education *both* to interpret and pass on the values of society *and* to stimulate people to think for themselves and to change the world around them.

The Commission's Goals

Goal No 1: High-quality nursery education must be available for all 3- and 4-year-olds.

Learning starts from birth. Parents are key educators. Nursery education reinforces learning in the home. All children benefit from it, and for many it is essential if they are to learn to succeed. We recommend that it should be made available to all 3- and 4-year-olds.

Goal No 2: There must be courses and qualifications that bring out the best in every pupil.

The framework of curriculum and qualifications for pupils aged 5–18 must offer attractive routes to success. The full range of pupils' abilities must be recognised and their development encouraged and rewarded. There must also be paths forward into further or higher education or into work in accordance with individuals' choices and abilities. We recommend an improved curricular framework and a new General Education Diploma at Ordinary and Advanced level.

Goal No 3: Every pupil in every lesson has the right to good teaching and adequate support facilities.

Every pupil has the right to be taught the curriculum offered by the school or college. That means that every pupil is entitled to be taught every lesson by a highly professional teacher competent to teach that lesson. The supporting facilities – the classroom itself, for example, books and the learning technology – must be at least adequate. We recommend a new deal in the classroom to bring this about.

Goal No 4: Everyone must be entitled to learn throughout life and be encouraged in practice to do so.

Learning does not stop at 16, at 18, at 21 or at any other age. Everyone must have the entitlement to go on learning whether for employment purposes or to fulfil other personal goals. There must be real opportunity to use the entitlement, and incentive and encouragement to do so. We make recommendations in order to bring this about.

Goal No 5: The management of education and training must be integrated, and those with a stake in them must have this recognised.

Within the past few years the power of central government in education and training has grown by leaps and bounds. Management of education and of training must be integrated both at the centre and at local level. All those with a major stake in the system must have a place in its management, and full accountability at each level is essential. We recommend robust and adaptable arrangements for the future.

Goal No 6: There must be greater public and private investment in education and training to achieve a better return.

There must be continuing efforts to cut waste and raise productivity and quality through innovation and the use of technology. Nevertheless, greater public investment will be required as economic circumstances permit. At the same time there is a need to achieve a better balance in resourcing. More of the costs need to be borne by beneficiaries, both employers and students. We make recommendations for better resourcing, better directed.

Goal No 7: Achievement must constantly rise and progress be open for all to examine.

The country is faced by a massive and continuing challenge in a fast-changing world. Targets for achievement are already demanding, but they will go on rising and we must therefore constantly seek higher levels of performance. We recommend measures to enable progress to be checked and made the subject of searching and well-informed debate.